Justice on Trial

JUSTICE
on TRIAL

The Kavanaugh Confirmation and the
Future of the Supreme Court

Mollie Hemingway
Carrie Severino

REGNERY
PUBLISHING
A Division of Salem Media Group

Regnery® is a registered trademark of Salem Communications Holding Corporation

Cataloging-in-Publication data on file with the Library of Congress

ISBN 978-1-62157-983-0
ebook ISBN 978-1-62157-984-7

Published in the United States by
Regnery Publishing
A Division of Salem Media Group
300 New Jersey Ave NW
Washington, DC 20001
www.Regnery.com

Manufactured in the United States of America

10 9 8 7 6 5 4 3 2

Books are available in quantity for promotional or premium use. For information on discounts and terms, please visit our website: www. Regnery.com.

To Our Lady of Victory—CCS

To Mark—MZH

CONTENTS

CHAPTER ONE

The Primary

With a rap of his gavel on June 27, 2018, Chief Justice John Roberts declared another Supreme Court term over, and the nine justices disappeared behind the dark red curtains that hang behind the bench. The assembled journalists politely stood at attention until the last justice was out of view, then rushed to file stories about a non-event—no justice had announced his retirement. Speculation had been running high that Justice Anthony Kennedy, appointed by President Ronald Reagan and nearly eighty-two years old, would be leaving now that a Republican again occupied the White House. Senator Charles Grassley of Iowa had publicly advised the justices in early May that if they were "thinking about quitting this year, do it yesterday." Grassley, and the powerful Senate Judiciary Committee he chaired, would have to manage the intense confirmation process, and with the midterm elections looming, they would need all the lead time they could get.

The members of the Court retired to their private dining room for the traditional end-of-term luncheon before they dispersed for the summer. As they dined, an armored black car, dispatched from the White House Military Office, pulled into the parking garage three floors below them. After his meal, Justice Kennedy got into the car, where Don

McGahn, the White House counsel, was waiting to take him to a meeting with President Trump.

It was a busy day at the White House, the president having held a mid-morning press conference on trade policy and the economy on the South Lawn. After lunch with Secretary of State Mike Pompeo, he would host President Marcelo Rebelo de Sousa of the Republic of Portugal. The press usually lingered around the famous but surprisingly small briefing room at the north side of the mansion, hoping to catch additional stories or details from their White House contacts.

The day before, Steve Engel, the head of the Justice Department's Office of Legal Counsel, had told McGahn's trusted chief of staff, Annie Donaldson, that he had just had a meeting with his old boss and needed to talk to McGahn. It took a minute for the significance of what he'd said to register. Engel's old boss was Anthony Kennedy. He'd clerked for him at the Supreme Court in 2001–2002, and they had remained close.

Engel and Kennedy had met two days before the end of the term at an outdoor café near the National Gallery of Art's Sculpture Garden. Kennedy had slipped away from a tour of the museum with his clerks to meet Engel, hoping the location was discreet enough to avoid wandering members of the press. After the justice's security detail evaluated the café for threats, he sat down with Engel and explained that he expected to announce his retirement in the next few days. He wanted to tell his fellow justices immediately after their final sitting on Wednesday but knew the odds were good that the news would leak shortly thereafter.

Hoping to deliver the message to the president in person before it went public, Kennedy wanted Engel to ask McGahn to arrange a meeting without anyone's noticing. Later that day, Engel called the White House counsel's office and asked about the president's schedule. The two offices spoke frequently, so the question didn't arouse suspicion. He was told the president was leaving for the Midwest on Wednesday evening, so the meeting would need to happen before then.

The next day, Kennedy gave Engel the green light, and the White House counsel's office quietly arranged the meeting through Jeffrey Minear, counsel to Chief Justice Roberts. A White House car with a pre-cleared driver would make the entry into the White House quick and easy. Chief of Staff John Kelly arranged for President Trump to leave his lunch promptly at one o'clock and come to the White House residence, where the justice would be waiting with McGahn.

That morning, none of the other associate justices knew that Kennedy was stepping down. The scholarly Californian, known as a swing vote on the Court, had hired four clerks for the coming year and had discussed cases coming up in the next term. When the term ended with no announcement from the bench, the justices proceeded to their stately, paneled conference room for one final discussion.

While the nine justices often disagree sharply about the issues before the Court, they know they are working together for life, so they go out of their way to be friendly to one another. But the last conference of each term tends to be a bit testier. The most contentious decisions are usually released in the final days of the term, justices sometimes reading their fiery dissents from the bench, and the 2017–2018 term ended with its share of high-profile five-to-four decisions on such hotly debated subjects as abortion and immigration.

When the justices had concluded their business—voting on the disposition of cases related to their recent decisions—Kennedy informed his shocked colleagues that he had decided to retire. He asked them to not tell anyone until two o'clock so he could speak with the president privately.

No one from the press noticed Kennedy's arrival at the Executive Residence, which was chosen for the meeting because of its relative privacy. The Oval Office's large bank of windows makes it a fishbowl for prying eyes. Kennedy and Trump chatted pleasantly for about twenty minutes until, feeling the time was right, the justice handed the president an envelope. Inside was a letter dated June 27, 2018, beginning, "My dear Mr. President," a sign of the genuine "affinity," as one observer put it, that the two men had for each other.[1] The letter was Kennedy's formal announcement of his resignation.

President Trump was surprised by Kennedy's retirement but not unprepared. He had heard rumors the previous year that after more than forty years as a federal judge, Kennedy was thinking about a change. His judicial nominations team wanted to reassure the justice, without applying pressure, that his legacy would be in good hands if he retired. Kennedy was disliked by many conservatives for his opinions redefining marriage[2] and upholding *Roe v. Wade*.[3] But many conservatives simultaneously supported his approach to federalism and the First Amendment, particularly as it concerns free speech. The White House indicated to him that his record would be treated respectfully and that his successor's confirmation battle would not be a referendum on his tenure. When the White House got word that Kennedy was displeased one of its nominees for an obscure federal court had called him a "judicial prostitute," the nomination was allowed to expire.

The stature of a justice is measured not only by the influence of his legal opinions but also by the careers and reputations of the clerks he has handpicked and mentored. The White House had sought Kennedy's opinion about his former clerks who were under consideration for the federal judiciary and had nominated several of them to prestigious appeals courts. Most flattering of all, Trump had chosen one of Kennedy's star former clerks, Neil Gorsuch, to join him on the Supreme Court one year earlier.

In his letter to the president, Kennedy said that on July 31 he would assume "senior status," a semi-retirement that would enable him to continue to serve in a reduced capacity in the lower federal courts, but his days on the high court would be over. Having informed the president privately of his retirement, Kennedy returned to the Supreme Court building, no one the wiser as to what had just taken place. The biggest secret in town had remained a secret until the end. Justice Kennedy was retiring on his terms. The news was then released, and it rocked Washington.

■   ■   ■

Conservatives were elated at the opportunity to replace Kennedy with another Trump appointee. When a group of Republican senators, including the majority leader, Mitch McConnell of Kentucky, heard the news at a lunch, they looked up at each other and smiled. Not only would this be an opportunity to strengthen the Court, but in a midterm election year, a nomination fight could excite conservative voters and remind them of the importance of keeping control of the Senate. Senator Grassley, already miked up for his weekly conference call with Iowa reporters, heard the news while on air. Afterward he told his staff, "I guess we're going to do this."

News of Kennedy's retirement touched off a minor media maelstrom. "Abortion will be illegal in twenty states in 18 months," CNN's chief legal analyst, Jeffrey Toobin, tweeted.[4] Other outlets entertained even crazier possibilities. The *New York Times* noted that Kennedy's son worked for Deutsche Bank, the same bank that had provided the Trump organization more than one billion dollars in real estate loans.[5] There was no reason to think that President Trump's acquaintance with Kennedy's son was nefarious, but the *Times* report launched all manner of conspiracy theories. Neera Tanden, the president of the influential liberal think tank Center for American Progress, tweeted, "Just to state this: Justice Kennedy's son gave a billion dollar loan to Trump when no one would give him a dime, and Justice Kennedy has been ruling in favor of the Trump Administration position for 2 years as the Court decides 5-4 case after 5-4 case."[6] Why a Deutsche Bank loan to Trump would make Kennedy beholden to the president rather than the other way around was never explained, but Tanden's theory was retweeted twenty-one thousand times. Both the *Washington Post* and Politifact eventually ran fact checks that debunked the supposed conspiracy between Kennedy and Trump.[7]

When Kennedy's retirement was announced at a Democratic National Committee meeting, participants gasped and expressed concern. Because of his liberal rulings on abortion and same-sex marriage, Democrats and progressives considered Kennedy the best of the Republican-nominated justices.

But for all of their fawning over him when he reached conclusions they liked, liberals did not respect Kennedy. They turned on him immediately when he gave Trump the opportunity to name his successor, adopting some of the same criticisms conservative critics had leveled in the past. Ian Millhiser of ThinkProgress sneered, "Justice Kennedy was a Cadillac's intellect in a Lamborghini's job," highlighting *Lawrence v. Texas*, the case that overturned anti-sodomy laws, as "an opinion that was constructed largely from discarded Age of Aquarius lyrics." Of his opinion in *Planned Parenthood v. Casey*, in which Kennedy famously changed his vote to uphold *Roe v. Wade*, Millhiser wrote that he agreed with the outcome, but "the problem is that its hippie-dippie, decidedly unlegal language renders its rule vulnerable."[8]

That same night, MSNBC's Chris Matthews told Senate Democrats they had to do what they could to obstruct and delay the nomination past the midterms in the hope that the Democrats, a one-vote minority after winning a valuable seat from Alabama the year before, would take control of the upper house.[9] McConnell had already promised that Trump's nominee would be voted on "this fall."[10] But first there had to be a nominee.

■   ■   ■

A president's appointments to the Supreme Court shape his legacy more than almost any other decision he makes, but each administration handles the selection of nominees in its own way. The death of Justice Antonin Scalia early in the primary season of the 2016 presidential campaign and the Republican-controlled Senate's refusal to consider President Obama's nomination of Judge Merrick Garland as his successor guaranteed a vacancy on the Court for the next president to fill. Hoping to reassure Republican voters who doubted his reliability to appoint a conservative, Donald Trump had released a list of possible nominees to the Supreme Court during the primary elections—an unprecedented but successful political stroke. For that first Supreme Court nomination, the list was whittled down to top contenders, who interviewed before a limited panel of key advisors. A few of those contenders interviewed with President Trump. He chose Judge Neil Gorsuch of the Court of Appeals for the Tenth Circuit, and the relatively smooth confirmation of this conservative originalist from Colorado was seen as one of the key victories of Trump's first year in office.

The list had been expanded with five new names in November 2017 and now included Judge Amy Coney Barrett of the Seventh Circuit and Judge Brett Kavanaugh of the D.C. Circuit, the latter of whom had clerked for Justice Kennedy the same year as Gorsuch. Upon Kennedy's retirement, Trump announced that he would again select his nominee from that list.

A weakness of the judicial selection process in recent Republican administrations has been the involvement of too many people. The inevitable rival factions in the White House and the Department of Justice knocked out one another's top contenders and settled on consensus candidates who often proved disappointing. Trump's Justice Department was led by Attorney General Jeff Sessions, who had recused himself from overseeing the department's far-reaching investigation into whether Trump had colluded with Russia to steal the 2016 election. That conspiracy theory, a major distraction for the Trump administration in its first two years, was eventually debunked with the release of Special Counsel Robert Mueller's report in April 2019. Sessions's self-imposed inability to manage the destructive investigation damaged his relations with the White House and the Justice Department. He had played a limited role in judicial selection, as had the Office of Legislative Affairs and most other executive offices apart from the White House counsel's office. The judicial selection and confirmation process to that point had received extremely positive press coverage and enjoyed the approval of the president's supporters, so when Justice Kennedy retired, it was decided to keep the team that had won last time on the field.

Inside the White House, the counsel's office had handled not only the Gorsuch nomination but dozens of other federal court nominations, and although they had no advance notice of Kennedy's retirement, they were prepared for it. They had refreshed the list months earlier in anticipation of a Supreme Court vacancy. Deputies had constantly updated files of prospective nominees, all of whom had already been vetted.

Within a day of Kennedy's announcement, word leaked that two of his former clerks, Judge Ray Kethledge of the Sixth Circuit and Kavanaugh, were the front-runners for the open seat, while others said the top two were really Kavanaugh and Barrett.

The press soon became a problem for Kavanaugh, staking out his house and following him everywhere. At the suggestion of his colleagues on the court of appeals, including a cordial Merrick Garland, he was eventually assigned a security detail, including a car with federal marshals to drive him around.

■   ■   ■

In his twelve years on the D.C. Circuit, Judge Kavanaugh had authored more than three hundred opinions, always guided by the text and original meaning of the Constitution. He was known as a uniquely effective jurist, and the Supreme Court had adopted his reasoning in at least thirteen decisions.[11]

Despite his illustrious pedigree—Yale College and Law School—he was down to earth and affable. The fit, fifty-three-year-old, Irish-American Catholic with a full head of hair and a quick sense of humor was well liked by his colleagues and friends and always had been.

He was on the president's list of potential nominees by the time rumors of Kennedy's retirement began to circulate, but he had not been given any advance warning by the justice. Nevertheless, he had put off finalizing his family's vacation plans until the end of the Supreme Court term, just in case. When the final session ended with no retirement announcement, he texted his wife, Ashley, to go ahead and make summer plans with their daughters, Margaret and Liza. By the time he returned from lunch, McGahn had called to tell him the news. Vacation planning would have to wait; the White House counsel wanted to interview him in his chambers on Friday.

McGahn already knew Kavanaugh, who had administered his oath of office for the Federal Election Commission in 2008. McGahn was exceedingly familiar with his judicial philosophy, having pored over his opinions. The interview that Friday was not about his opinions but about any potentially embarrassing information the White House needed to know before deciding. Known as an "SDR" review—short for sex, drugs, and rock and roll—this kind of interview became common after the failed Supreme Court nomination in 1987 of Judge Douglas Ginsburg of the D.C. Circuit, who was forced to withdraw after reports emerged that he'd smoked marijuana with some of his students while a professor at Harvard. Before Anthony Kennedy was nominated for the same seat, he was confronted with hundreds of embarrassing questions about when he'd first had sex, with how many different women, and whether any pregnancies had resulted. He was asked about sexually transmitted diseases, aberrant sexual activities, drug use, drunk driving, and even animal abuse.[12]

Kavanaugh's interview with McGahn went well, but he knew it would ultimately be President Trump's decision. He'd had an up-close view of the Supreme Court selection process when he served as White House staff secretary under President George W. Bush, seeing how judicial advisors would narrow down a list of contenders before presenting the finalists to the president so that he could take their measure. He wasn't entirely sure Trump would like him.

A D.C. native who had worked closely with President Bush, Kavanaugh was not what the anti-establishment Trump was looking for. The Bush family had publicly opposed Trump, and the disdain had been mutual. Trump defeated former Florida governor Jeb Bush in the 2016 Republican presidential race by brutally criticizing his brother George's record as president. Kavanaugh's name hadn't even appeared on Trump's initial lists of prospective Supreme Court nominees.

At the same time, Kavanaugh had a broad network of friends and allies—from federal judges to conservative media stars to his family dry cleaner—who could vouch for his ability and character and thought he should not just be *on* the list but at the *top*. His name had been openly discussed in major media as the most likely Republican nominee for the Court since at least 2012.[13] His lengthy record as a conservative appellate judge was well known and widely respected.

■   ■   ■

Kavanaugh had a particularly loyal network of former clerks. He had hired twenty-five women and twenty-three men as law clerks in his dozen years on the D.C. Circuit. An astounding thirty-nine of them went on to clerk at the Supreme Court, securing his coveted spot as the top "feeder judge" on the federal bench. The first time Kavanaugh had really thought about the Supreme Court was when, as a fifteen-year-old, he read *The Brethren*, Bob Woodward's behind-the-scenes account of the Court in the 1970s. The stars of the book were the clerks, and he thought it seemed like a great job—even better than the job of a justice.

Kavanaugh was regularly in touch with his former clerks, hosting them at holiday parties and baseball games. Every five years they would get together with their spouses for a reunion, where the judge would introduce those who were new since the previous reunion, describing in detail where he met each clerk and what he liked about him or her. He offered personal touches, as when he recounted a funny toast given at a clerk's wedding or reminisced about trading belts with a clerk who was underdressed on his way to interview with the chief justice.

As devoted to their mentor as he was to them, Kavanaugh's former clerks took on the task of lobbying for his nomination, talking to anybody who would listen at the White House and in conservative legal circles. Some of them worked inside the White House counsel's office itself. Whether from the inside or the outside, the lobbying helped. Not only was Kavanaugh now on the list, he was widely considered a front-runner.

The president met with Kavanaugh on Monday, July 2, asking him about his background and White House experience. Trump was looking for someone who could sit on the court for thirty to forty years, was exceptionally well qualified, was an originalist, and was not weak. Kavanaugh emphasized that he'd been tested throughout his career and had stood by his principles in moments of difficulty. It was a friendly conversation, not a quiz, and it was over in less than a half-hour. The president felt that Kavanaugh had shown signs of courage and decisiveness in his interview, and that kept him in contention.

Judges are not supposed to be political, but their selection and confirmation, committed by the Constitution to political actors, is unavoidably so. Court watchers knew Kavanaugh was the one to beat from the moment he was added to the list, and online bettors gave him the best odds for securing the nomination as soon as Kennedy retired.[14] But there were other contenders, some of whom had serious bases of support. Other than Kethledge, Kavanaugh, and Barrett, Trump was considering Thomas Hardiman of the Third Circuit and Amul Thapar of the Sixth Circuit. He met with all of them that Monday except Hardiman, whom he'd met during the previous nomination process. He also interviewed other candidates by phone.[15]

■   ■   ■

Demand Justice, a left-wing interest group recently founded by Brian Fallon, the campaign spokesman for Hillary Clinton, the Democratic presidential nominee in 2016, announced plans to spend $1 million in television ads against the eventual nominee, whoever he or she might be, and dropped online ads against three of the contenders within a day of Kennedy's retirement.[16] One of the targets was Amy Coney Barrett, a favorite of conservatives since her deft handling of hostile questions about her Catholic faith from Democratic senators and the media after her nomination to the appellate bench the previous year. The *New York Times* suggested a religious organization to which she belonged was a cult, while Senator Dianne Feinstein, the top Democrat of the Senate Judiciary Committee, criticized the role of faith in her life, sneering that "the dogma lives loudly within you."[17] That tortured phrase became a rallying cry for Christian youth groups and others who were impressed that Barrett held firm under fire for her faith.

Demand Justice's ads signaled that the left was serious. But on the right, nothing was being taken for granted. The Judicial Crisis Network was prepared to spend tens of millions of dollars, as it had already done in the effort to confirm Justice Gorsuch to Justice Scalia's seat. JCN (of which one of the authors is chief counsel and policy director) had served as a hub of outside groups supporting conservative judicial nominees since 2005. And by the time Justice Kennedy retired, it was ready for its greatest test yet. The group would supervise an extensive research operation, organize rapid response, brief journalists and opinion leaders, and activate grassroots leaders across the country while running the most robust paid media campaign in the history of Supreme Court confirmation battles. JCN's first ad, which began running the day the vacancy was announced, built on the success of the Gorsuch confirmation of the year before. "Like Justice Gorsuch, all of the men and women on President Trump's judicial list are the best and brightest in their field." It concluded, "We look forward to President Trump nominating another great justice."[18]

■   ■   ■

In the twelve days between Kennedy's retirement and Trump's announcement of his nominee, the major media were focused on the horse race—which candidate was gaining, which was falling behind. But the conservative media were hosting a vibrant debate over the merits of potential nominees, a debate fed by various interest groups concerned about how each candidate might treat their particular issue and by the advocates of each candidate.

Since all of the judges on Trump's list were highly qualified and had conservative track records, most criticism of particular candidates took place behind the scenes. Everyone was alert to the problem of political primaries, in which the eventual nominee emerges bloodied with another battle ahead of him. All the candidates on the list were at least acceptable, and no one wanted to weaken the eventual nominee's prospects for confirmation, so the most intense debates were kept behind the scenes. Nevertheless, some individuals and organizations were speaking out, and a few were aiming their fire directly at Kavanaugh.

Conservative media praised Kavanaugh for his approach to administrative law, the body of rules that govern the multitude of federal regulatory and administrative agencies. The average citizen hears little about this arcane and rarely glamorous field of law, but in recent decades, as Congress has delegated to the bureaucracy the real work of governing the United States, administrative law has become enormously consequential for Americans' rights and freedoms.

Many worried, however, that Kavanaugh had hidden in the tall grass by avoiding controversial social-policy issues. His recent handling of the question of whether a teenager caught entering the United States illegally had a constitutional right to an abortion had not inspired confidence among pro-lifers. His opponents circulated a summary paper criticizing him for seeking "a compromise that would allow [the girl] to obtain her abortion" and for refusing "to take a stand" with another judge who questioned whether such a person even had a constitutional right to abortion. He was also criticized for a dissent that some argued had presumed a compelling government interest in facilitating access to contraception. His decisions on religious liberty, it was said, were not sufficiently bold at a time of increasing encroachment by the government.[19]

Conservatives worried about more than Kavanaugh's commitments on social issues. They charged that a dissent from 2011, in which he discussed how a mandate to purchase insurance could pass constitutional muster, amounted to a "roadmap for saving Obamacare."[20]

The defining feature of his jurisprudence, critics said, was "avoidance." Principles were less important to him than his "reputation." And "nothing" suggested he would "find the courage to embrace conservative principles" on the Supreme Court. There was "no reason to risk it," an opposition document warned. "There's a difference between a home run and a grand slam," opined one writer in National Review.[21] These conservatives were not fully opposed to Kavanaugh's nomination, but having been burned many times before, they feared that he was another establishment Republican who would swing to the left once he was on the Court.

Even people within the White House were concerned, but as they dug deeper into his record, they believed he viewed his role on the circuit court as writing for Justice Kennedy. Kavanaugh understood how Kennedy thought, and even when he disagreed with him, he admired him.

He always carried a pocket Constitution signed by Kennedy. Kavanaugh tried to craft a solid, constitutionally correct result that Kennedy would adopt rather than being swayed by the liberal bloc on the court.

Others close to the process were swayed by the weight of his judicial record. No conservative appeals court judge—including even then-Judge Gorsuch—had as many opinions on significant and controversial questions as Kavanaugh, from his defense of First Amendment protections for political speech, to his bold Second Amendment dissent that had garnered repeated citations from Thomas and Scalia, to his pathbreaking separation of powers cases, which had pointed out constitutional infirmities in the structure of several administrative agencies.

■   ■   ■

Each time a piece expressing concerns was published, an army of former clerks and other surrogates rose in Kavanaugh's defense, sometimes within minutes. Clerks generally serve a one-year term with a judge after law school, assisting in the research and drafting of judicial opinions. They work closely with their judge, almost as apprentices, and it's not unusual for them to form lifelong bonds. Clerkships are like being adopted into a large extended family with one patriarch or matriarch at the head. Some of Kavanaugh's former clerks took leave from their jobs or did double duty to participate in the effort to secure his nomination. Roman Martinez, a former clerk turned Supreme Court litigator, was abroad on a family vacation and worked remotely and across five time zones. The same day the vacancy was announced, Travis Lenkner, who had also clerked for Justice Kennedy, packed his bags and hopped on a plane from Chicago, texting the judge that he was on his way to help.

Kavanaugh's chambers in the E. Barrett Prettyman U.S. Courthouse on Constitution Avenue, near the Capitol, comprised a few offices for the judge and his staff and a small conference room. This became the cramped headquarters of the Kavanaugh "campaign." Being in Washington was a huge advantage, but with spotty cell phone and internet service and no televisions, the offices themselves made a poor communications nerve center. The air-conditioning was shut off at six p.m., leaving the offices stiflingly hot in the D.C. summer evenings. And because the volunteers were not employees of the court, none of them had badged access to the courthouse. The judge's capable executive assistant, Eva Roney, had to stay there as late as they did. Apart from the difficulty of getting in and out of the building, the neighborhood had few restaurants open in the evening, so even getting dinner was a big production.

Beyond the team of former clerks working in chambers were dozens volunteering as they could from across the country. One collected news clips and tweets from prominent figures, arranging them into what needed to be seen immediately, hourly, and daily and then distributing them to the team, a contribution that was essential for responding to critiques from fellow conservatives.

Some former clerks, hoping that their judge would be added to the White House list and confident that he would be a leading contender, had begun preparing for a Supreme Court vacancy at least a year earlier. That work, which accelerated as the 2017–2018 term drew to an end, included reading through Kavanaugh's hundreds of opinions, sorting them by topic—gun rights, free speech, search and seizure, the administrative state, and so on—and preparing excerpts from significant cases, contextualizing them for their importance. These were invaluable aids for surrogates talking about Kavanaugh in the media.

The Kavanaugh team emphasized his influence on the court, noting his skill at strategically framing an opinion to convince other judges on the same case to take a more conservative position than they might otherwise have done. It was important that his persuasive techniques be appreciated for their effectiveness rather than misunderstood as a sign of weak convictions. They also wanted to make sure people remembered Kavanaugh's long record of public service prior to being a judge. He had taken on a politically risky role in the independent counsel Kenneth Starr's "Whitewater" investigation of Bill and Hillary Clinton's Arkansas land deals. And he had served with distinction in the frequently besieged Bush White House. Unlike some lawyers angling for judicial office, he had not built his career by avoiding conflict and keeping his powder dry. Brett Kavanaugh was not timid.

The former clerks spoke privately with persons of influence and lob-bied publicly as well. Sarah Pitlyk, a litigator on issues of life and religious liberty, responded to criticisms about Kavanaugh's jurisprudence by writing, "On the vital issues of protecting religious liberty and enforcing restrictions on abortion, no court-of-appeals judge in the nation has a stronger, more consistent record than Judge Brett Kavanaugh. On these issues, as on so many others, he has fought for his principles and stood firm against pressure. He would do the same on the Supreme Court."[22]

Sometimes the criticism of Kavanaugh baffled them. The day after Kennedy's retirement, the popular conservative pundit Ben Shapiro, himself a lawyer, had written that he "has the most red flags" of the top five contenders, suggesting that Kavanaugh—who was particularly well known for his critiques of bureaucratic overreach—supported "the notion that administrative agencies ought to be granted deference by the judicial branch."[23] The former clerks found people who could talk to Shapiro and pass along an effective response, and he corrected the error.[24]

As hard as his former clerks and the White House were working, nobody was working harder than Kavanaugh himself, who was famous for his diligence.[25] The round-the-clock news cycle meant late hours. Stories would break late into the evening, requiring a rapid response no matter the time. The judge was in his chambers past midnight most nights, country music playing on the radio, the influence, perhaps, of his Texan wife. Ashley tended to think that what was meant to happen would happen. He, by contrast, believed that if you prepared enough, you could be ready for anything. The decision of whom to nominate to the Supreme Court was not his to make, but he wouldn't be able to live with himself if he were not chosen because he had failed to prepare. The longtime athlete believed in leaving everything on the field. So he reread his opinions and pored over his record, thinking about how to talk about them. He described and evaluated his judicial philosophy, winnowing down volumes of work into talking points he could use in meetings.

■   ■   ■

The Constitution gives the president the power to appoint Supreme Court justices, subject to the advice and consent of the Senate. The advice of senators was solicited early. The list of potential nominees had been public prior to Kennedy's retirement, of course, and the White House sought the views of five moderate senators—the Republicans Susan Collins of Maine and Lisa Murkowski of Alaska and the Democrats Joe Donnelly of Indiana, Heidi Heitkamp of North Dakota, and Joe Manchin of West Virginia—each of whom could have a decisive vote.

Collins was on the floor of the Senate the day after Kennedy's retirement when she got the email inviting her to the White House to discuss the nomination. She told Murkowski, who had also just received an invitation. They decided to combine their appointments, which were back to back. Collins told the president she hoped he would nominate a judge with intelligence, integrity, and experience and noted her concerns about adherence to precedent and the separation of powers. They did not discuss particular candidates as much as the desired judicial philosophy. Collins encouraged the president to not feel limited to his initial list, though she was pleased when she learned he had refreshed it. As the two Republican women were departing, Senator Manchin arrived to discuss his views with the president and McGahn.

Senator Mitch McConnell, who saw judicial appointments as an important part of his legacy, was ecstatic at the opportunity to confirm another Supreme Court appointment. An open supporter of Thapar, a fellow Kentuckian whom he had first brought to Trump's attention, he expressed serious concern about the volume of paperwork a Kavanaugh nomination would produce. Besides the papers from his time on the Whitewater independent counsel's staff and in the White House counsel's office, there was his tenure as the White House staff secretary, when every piece of paper in the White House crossed his desk.

The staff of the Senate Judiciary Committee shared McConnell's concern and discussed it with reporters. An article on the *Daily Caller*, citing Senate aides, reported that the prospect of Kavanaugh's nomination had "some influential conservatives cringing behind the scenes.... 'The White House Counsel's Office is reeling today on Kavanaugh,' says one GOP judicial insider with direct knowledge of the selection process. 'Kavanaugh is crashing and burning today. I cannot figure out how this happened in one day.'" Quoting an unnamed "senior administration official" who called Kavanaugh the "low-energy Jeb Bush pick" and an "influential Hill staffer" who called him "John Roberts incarnate," the article emphasized Kavanaugh's ties to the Bush administration and to McGahn.[26] It also included a leak of confidential information about how many millions of records would have to be processed. Kavanaugh's team had hoped to avoid such "process" stories and to keep the focus on qualifications. They quickly determined that the leaker was a key aide on the Senate Judiciary Committee who supported Kethledge.

■   ■   ■

These were trying days for Ashley Kavanaugh. She had met her husband in 2001, when they both worked in the White House. Having begun her service to George W. Bush as a personal secretary when she was still a student at the University of Texas and he was governor, she came to the White House after working on his presidential campaign. She was from Abilene, a couple of hours from Midland, where Bush had grown up. A warm and welcoming woman with a kind smile and an easy laugh, Ashley Estes was beloved by her colleagues. She was encouraging, optimistic, determined, and, importantly, tough.

Kavanaugh and Ashley had crossed paths early in the Bush presidency, while he was working as an associate counsel in the White House counsel's office. She found him nice, perhaps too nice, and wasn't sure she was interested in him. Friends encouraged her to give him a shot. Finally, on September 10, 2001, she had a late dinner with him at Cafe Deluxe in Georgetown after work. They had a nice time, but the next morning everything changed. They were evacuated from the White House after terrorists attacked the World Trade Center and the Pentagon and it looked like another airliner was headed their way. Kavanaugh distinctly remembers watching her, in a black-and-white-checked shirt and black pants, running down West Executive Avenue, the closed street that borders the West Wing.

Amid the trauma and intense activity in the White House following 9/11, they paused their dating, but Kavanaugh, a baseball fan, eventually took her to Cal Ripken's last game on October 6, the first of many sporting events they'd attend together. It was a busy and stressful period at the White House, but they made time for each other. They were discreet about their relationship, but after a year or so, one of Laura Bush's personal aides let the news slip. The Bushes were immediately supportive, and the president began good-naturedly teasing them. When Kavanaugh became staff secretary in July 2003, Ashley's work and his began to overlap. He also saw more of President Bush, who encouraged the two to get married. They were engaged by Christmas of that year and celebrated a Texas-sized wedding the next July in D.C. President and Mrs. Bush even hosted a party for them in the Rose Garden a couple of days before the wedding.

After Bush's reelection, Ashley decided to leave her position, which required extremely long hours. When she discussed her options with President Bush, he encouraged her to consider a few different paths, including having children, telling her she'd make an excellent mother. That night, spurred on by the conversation, she went home and took a pregnancy test. She was pregnant with her and Brett's first child, Margaret. The Bushes were thrilled by the good news. President Bush always said Ashley was a good soul, and everyone around her found her a source of cheer. She left the White House but stayed in the Bush fold for an additional six years, albeit in a less intense position, helping set up the George W. Bush Presidential Library.

The Kavanaughs genuinely loved the Bushes and admired the president's character and how he treated his wife, friends, and employees. President Bush nominated Kavanaugh to the U.S. Court of Appeals for the D.C. Circuit in 2003, although his confirmation took three years and two separate nomination hearings because of obstruction from Senate

Democrats. They were outraged that someone who had worked on the Whitewater investigation of President Clinton and was so closely associated with President Bush would be elevated to the federal bench, but in 2006 he was finally confirmed.

Perhaps because that earlier confirmation battle had been so brutal, Ashley prayed that God would deliver them from another. They had a wonderful life with their children and with both their jobs—she was now a town manager in Chevy Chase, Maryland. She was proud he was a front-runner for the Supreme Court, but she hoped he would not be nominated.

■   ■   ■

President Trump, relying on the recommendation of his judicial advisors, saw this as Kavanaugh's race to lose. But he sought advice from a wide variety of sources, to the consternation of many who wished he would simply go with Kavanaugh.

Part of the problem was the high quality of those from whom he had to choose. It was hard to disagree that Barrett, for instance, was an attractive pick. But she had been a judge for only a few months, which meant she had few opinions to analyze. Conservative groups usually require a track record before they endorse a nominee. In Barrett's case, they felt the Catholic mother of seven who had defended her faith before the Senate Judiciary Committee could be counted on to stay strong in the face of liberal opposition. Part of her support came from outside groups who worried that any male nominee, in the wake of the #MeToo movement, would be accused of inappropriate sexual behavior, regardless of his merits.

As much as the president and his advisors liked Barrett and trusted that she was an originalist, they knew she would have difficulty getting through a barely Republican Senate. When moderate senators whose votes were necessary had been asked for their advice early in the process, they had discouraged choosing her. The White House concluded that the decision not to nominate Barrett had been made by the people of Alabama when they elected a Democrat to the Senate the previous December. Losing that seat meant that the White House had almost no margin for error.

Kethledge was also strongly considered, but he had not written the range of opinions that Kavanaugh had, and some of his opinions worried groups focused on strong immigration laws. Late in the process Trump became interested in Hardiman again, a judge with a history of good opinions, but perceived as lacking Kavanaugh's depth of reasoning or commitment to originalism. Still, all had excellent opinions. All would be excellent justices.

Vice President Mike Pence interviewed finalists, speaking with Barrett and Kethledge at a family lake house in Indiana and with Hardiman and Kavanaugh at the vice president's residence in Washington. Pence asked Barrett, a fellow Indianan, who she thought should be nominated if not her. She strongly endorsed Kavanaugh.

Kavanaugh's interview with the vice president, on Independence Day, was a cordial chat that lasted more than an hour, in part because of the judge's habit of answering questions thoroughly. In every interview, Kavanaugh wanted to perform well. He did not see himself as a shoo-in, and he knew how many finalists were reported to have stumbled in their meetings with the president and his team. He would not stumble.

Kavanaugh was asked whom he recommended for the seat if not himself, and he praised multiple contenders, including Barrett. The world of federal judges is small, and Kavanaugh knew and respected several of the short-listers. He had become acquainted with Barrett through visits to Notre Dame Law School and discussions about candidates for clerkships. He had even attended her formal installation at the Seventh Circuit earlier that year. Kavanaugh and Kethledge and their wives had sat together at a reunion of Kennedy clerks the previous summer.

President Trump spent the following weekend at his resort in New Jersey, but he continued asking people for advice.[27] It may have been Kavanaugh's race to lose, but losing was a real possibility. In multiple conversations with both formal and informal judicial advisors, the president went back and forth about the decision. McConnell was complaining about documents, and the base was pushing for a more exciting pick. And

Kavanaugh was about as pure a specimen of the "Bush" Republican as one could imagine.

Leonard Leo, the executive vice president of the Federalist Society, who had advised Bush and Trump on past Supreme Court nominations, told the president he had an extraordinary group of judges. He should pick whomever he felt most comfortable with and then own the decision. Leo's advice was carefully considered. The Federalist Society, a power-house organization of lawyers, legal academics, judges, and law students, is the cornerstone of today's conservative legal movement. It champions three core principles: (1) the state exists to preserve freedom; (2) the separation of governmental powers is central to the Constitution; and (3) the judiciary is to say what the law is, not what it should be. Other than that, the Federalist Society takes no policy positions, and robust debate is common and encouraged.

McGahn and Leo had hoped Trump would make his announcement before the weekend, worrying that more time would not improve the decision. Leo found out not only who was golfing with the president that weekend but who was slated to ride in his golf cart each round, and he spoke with two of them—Mike Ferguson, a former congressman from New Jersey, and Sean Hannity of Fox News. He told them that he would not be surprised if they favored a particular candidate but asked them not to speak ill of any of the potential nominees. He also asked them to impress upon the president that he had to own the decision and pick the person with whom he was most comfortable.

Ferguson knew only Barrett, whom he thought the world of, but had a favorable view of the entire list because he respected Leo's judgment. The president discussed the decision over golf and again that night at a dinner with many members of the Trump and Pence families. As he weighed the pluses and minuses of each candidate, Trump came to the conclusion that Kavanaugh would be among the safer choices.

The evening before, the *New York Times* published what amounted to a plea from McConnell to not pick Kavanaugh. "McConnell Tries to Nudge Trump Toward Two Supreme Court Options," was the headline of the article about McConnell's strong preference for Kethledge or

Hardiman, either of whom he thought would have a better chance of getting through the Senate. He'd cited the "millions" of pages of documents the Senate Judiciary Committee would have to sift through if Kavanaugh were the nominee.[28]

White House advisors did not think paperwork was a deal-breaker, but Kavanaugh's team knew that McConnell's concern was not a good sign. His former clerks countered that the paperwork was actually a strength, showing he had a record and had been involved in public service. People should not be penalized for working to advance conservative principles.

But then other articles appeared suggesting his front-runner status was in peril. The *New York Times* was playing up his closeness to the Bushes and reporting that his critics were passing around a photo of Bush's political guru Karl Rove with his arm around Kavanaugh.[29] He had always known that his Bush ties could be a problem, but it was a problem that was out of his control.

Time magazine reported that "Kavanaugh had been considered a frontrunner, but his fortunes may be torpedoed by Trump's grudges," again citing Kavanaugh's closeness to the Bush dynasty. The article ended ominously: "White House Counsel Don McGahn, a Kavanaugh booster, has largely stopped making the case for his friend, sources say."[30]

Saturday night, July 7, was a dark moment for the Kavanaugh team. It appeared that McConnell was opposed, McGahn had lost faith, and Trump was desperate to find another candidate. Gathered in the hot conference room, empty pizza boxes piled high, the team started coming to terms with their likely loss. Roman Martinez told stories about his time working for the U.S. government in postwar Iraq, finding parallels with the high-stakes political fights there. Later that night, Kavanaugh sent them an email encouraging them to act with dignity and remain calm no matter how the process ended, a sure sign that no one thought he would win the nomination.

But they had to keep working. The White House was constantly asking for information, including lists of people who would be invited to a nomination announcement if Kavanaugh were selected. They had to prepare a speech for that event, however unlikely it now seemed, and

Kavanaugh, who had taught a class at Harvard on the Supreme Court, knew it would be important. It would be his only chance to make a first impression on most of the country. And it would be his only public remarks before the confirmation hearings eight weeks later, an interval when the opposition could be counted on to raise a deafening howl. Chris Michel, a former Bush speechwriter who had also clerked for Kavanaugh, was helping with the speech. The judge himself was an experienced wordsmith, having worked on presidential speeches from the State of the Union on down, but his first draft clocked in at thirty-seven minutes, far longer than the five minutes that would be appropriate. "We've got to go long before we can go short," he joked.

Sunday arrived, and Trump called Leo again asking for his thoughts on Kavanaugh. Leo suggested that he meet with Kavanaugh again if he was so uncertain.

Kavanaugh, a regular churchgoer, served as a lector at Blessed Sacrament parish in Chevy Chase every eight weeks. As Providence would have it, his turn was up again, and he was struck by the passage he would read that evening. It was from St. Paul's Second Epistle to the Corinthians:

> Therefore, that I might not become too elated, a thorn in the flesh was given to me, an angel of Satan, to beat me, to keep me from being too elated. Three times I begged the Lord about this, that it might leave me, but he said to me, "My grace is sufficient for you, for power is made perfect in weakness." I will rather boast most gladly of my weaknesses, in order that the power of Christ may dwell with me. Therefore, I am content with weaknesses, insults, hardships, persecutions, and constraints, for the sake of Christ; for when I am weak, then I am strong.[31]

He thought the reading was so comforting that he shared it with his clerks. As affecting as he found the apostle's words at that stressful moment, he could little imagine how apropos they would be in the coming months.

On his way to church for the 5:30 Mass, Kavanaugh got a call asking if he could meet with the president again at seven o'clock that evening. He was wearing a coat and tie but not a suit. Ashley was just getting home from a lacrosse tournament with the girls. He called her to see if she could bring a suit to church and stick it in the car driven by his security detail. She met the car in the parking lot, rolled up the suit so it wasn't obvious what she was carrying, and made the transfer.

The marshals had told Ashley to clear herself and the girls out of the house. Whether or not her husband was chosen, the cameras already set up across the street would be following the family's every movement, looking for clues about the nomination. So they packed their bags and left the home by a hidden passageway connecting their yard and the neighbors', undetected by the press across the street. To hide their escape plans, they stashed their luggage in a neighbor's tree house and asked a neighbor girl to retrieve it for them later. Then they went out to dinner as normally as possible. Afterwards, they made sure they weren't being followed and instead of returning home drove to the house of close friends who were vacationing on Martha's Vineyard.

After Mass, Kavanaugh's security detail switched cars in the Woodley Park neighborhood of Northwest D.C. to lose any potential tails, and he changed clothes as the car made its way to the White House. He met for more than an hour with the president and Melania Trump in the Yellow Oval Room, used for receptions for important guests, on the second floor of the White House residence. They discussed his background, his family, his views on the Court, and his impressions of Justice Kennedy.

At the end of the conversation, President Trump told Kavanaugh he had made his decision. He wanted to nominate him to the Supreme Court. The confirmation, he assured his nominee, would be the quickest and easiest ever because of the judge's impeccable credentials and background. He told him to have fun.

The news, known only to a precious few, was overwhelming. No one suspected what had been set in motion.

CHAPTER TWO

The List

Justice Scalia was dead.

Almost thirty years after his appointment to the Supreme Court, Antonin Scalia was found dead in his bed at Cibolo Creek Ranch, a thirty-thousand-acre hunting resort near Marfa in West Texas. The seventy-nine-year-old jurist was the longest-serving member of the Court at the time of his death, but he kept an active schedule and was not ailing. Appointed by President Ronald Reagan, Scalia was beloved by conservatives for his sparkling wit, incisive intellect, and compelling advocacy of constitutional originalism, a judicial philosophy that pushed back on judge-driven constitutional "evolution" by attempting to interpret the Constitution according to its actual words as they were understood at the time of their ratification.

Senator Mitch McConnell had just landed on St. Thomas in the Virgin Islands when he received the startling news from Leonard Leo. The 2016 presidential primary season was in full swing, and McConnell and his wife, Elaine Chao, who had been the secretary of labor in the George W. Bush administration, had escaped to the Caribbean during the Washington's Birthday holiday. He immediately went to the hotel and turned the television on.

McConnell had first met Scalia at a staff meeting at the Department of Justice during the Ford administration, when McConnell was a lowly deputy assistant secretary for legislative affairs. Robert Bork was the solicitor general; Laurence Silberman, a future D.C. Circuit judge, was deputy attorney general; and Scalia was the assistant attorney general in charge of the Office of Legal Counsel. McConnell, intimidated by their sense of humor and brilliance, was worried he'd say something stupid and barely opened his mouth. He later returned to Kentucky and was elected to the U.S. Senate in 1984, just in time to vote for Scalia's confirmation. Not that his vote was needed. Scalia was unanimously confirmed, becoming the first Italian American on the Court.

After reflecting on the personal loss of a man he'd known for more than four decades, McConnell turned to thinking about how the Senate he led should handle the vacancy. What if the shoe were on the other foot, he wondered, and the Democrats controlled the Senate and a Republican president was in the last year of his term of office? Surely a Republican president would never get a Supreme Court nominee confirmed by the opposing party in an election year. Days later, his staff would tell him that his instincts were correct. There had been only three confirmations in the final year of a presidency when the opposing party controlled the Senate, most recently in 1888, when Grover Cleveland nominated Melville W. Fuller to be chief justice.

President Obama's own vice president, Joseph Biden, had given a floor speech in June 1992 when he was chairman of the Senate Judiciary Committee and George H. W. Bush was running for reelection, arguing that presidents should not try to fill a vacancy on the Supreme Court once campaign season was underway but should follow the example of "a majority of [their] predecessors" and wait until the election is over. Even if such a nomination were made, it should not be considered, as "Senate consideration of a nominee under these circumstances is not fair to the President, to the nominee, or to the Senate itself." Instead he suggested that the Senate Judiciary Committee should wait to schedule nomination hearings "after the political campaign season is over."[1]

Democrats took the same stance during George W. Bush's second term. A full eighteen months before that term ended, Senator Charles Schumer of New York declared that, absent "extraordinary circumstances," no Supreme Court nominee should be confirmed if a vacancy arose while Bush was still president.[2]

Within an hour of the news of Scalia's death, McConnell announced that the vacancy would not be filled until after the election of 2016 and that President Obama should not bother with a nomination. "The American people should have a voice in the selection of their next Supreme Court Justice. Therefore, this vacancy should not be filled until we have a new President," McConnell said.[3]

McConnell's speed in releasing the statement was intentional. He knew Scalia's death was major news, and most of the fifty-four Republican senators, home for a week-long recess, would be peppered with questions about what they thought should be done. Contradictory statements from various Republican senators would breed confusion. He also believed that confirmation hearings would be both politically riskier and less respectful to the nominee. By refusing to consider anyone to fill the vacancy, McConnell would spare a nominee unnecessary criticism of his judicial opinions and philosophy. Despite their earlier position, Democrats were livid with McConnell's stance, and their reactions led news coverage for days.

Notwithstanding McConnell's preemptive statement, the politically vulnerable Republican Mark Kirk of Illinois called for Senate hearings.[4] Senator Jerry Moran of Kansas also briefly supported a hearing on an Obama nomination, but he reversed himself in the face of a furious backlash.[5] When President Obama eventually nominated Judge Merrick Garland for Scalia's seat, Maine's Susan Collins told reporters she was "more convinced than ever that the [confirmation] process should proceed," but she was "not optimistic that I will be changing minds on this issue."[6] Senator Jeff Flake of Arizona at one point encouraged Republicans to consider Garland's nomination after the election and before newly elected senators took their seats.[7] Still, McConnell's statement proved remarkably effective at keeping Republican senators from announcing that they looked forward to a confirmation battle.

Chuck Grassley, the senator in charge of judicial confirmations, was in his home state of Iowa at the time of Scalia's death. It had snowed, and true to his reputation as a self-sufficient farmer, the octogenarian was shoveling his driveway, so he missed the numerous phone calls from his staff trying to alert him to the news. He first heard of Scalia's passing from a *Des Moines Register* reporter who called him for comment. He demurred when asked what the next steps would be, but within hours he released an official statement that noted the futility of making a nomination. Ultimately, the decision whether to hold hearings on a nominee would be Grassley's, and he was typically blunt:

> The fact of the matter is that it's been standard practice over the last nearly 80 years that Supreme Court nominees are not nominated and confirmed during a presidential election year. Given the huge divide in the country, and the fact that this President, above all others, has made no bones about his goal to use the courts to circumvent Congress and push through his own agenda, it only makes sense that we defer to the American people who will elect a new president to select the next Supreme Court Justice.[8]

Grassley's position was politically riskier than McConnell's. He was in a reelection campaign himself, and polls suggested that two-thirds of the country thought his committee should hold hearings on a nominee. The *New York Times* described Grassley as the "face of his party's refusal to hold a hearing on President Obama's nominee to the Supreme Court," and warned that as a result he would face a "strong" and "formidable challenger" named, appropriately enough, Patty Judge, a former lieutenant governor and state agriculture secretary.[9] (Grassley ultimately won reelection by a nearly twenty-five-point margin). Democrats focused their ire on Grassley and Harry Reid of Nevada, the minority leader, berated him on the floor of the Senate day after day. To force hearings,

President Obama even considered nominating his Harvard Law School classmate Jane Kelly, a federal appeals court judge from Iowa, whom Grassley had supported when she was confirmed to the Eighth Circuit.[10] "They did all their tactics, attacking him in town halls, chasing him in the hallway here, and all that kind of stuff," one staffer reported. "It felt like you were in a foxhole, but at no point was he ever going to crack."

Senators were one thing, but candidates vying for the Republican nomination for president were another complication. The crowded primary field had narrowed from seventeen to the six who were to appear in a debate in Greenville, South Carolina, the night of Scalia's death: former Governor Jeb Bush of Florida, the neurosurgeon and author Ben Carson, Senator Ted Cruz of Texas, Governor John Kasich of Ohio, Senator Marco Rubio of Florida, and the businessman Donald Trump.

The Trump campaign's legal counsel, Don McGahn, was driving down Route 50 to play guitar at a gig for his 1980s cover band in Ocean City, Maryland, when his wife texted him about Scalia's death. McGahn pulled over to a gas station and cried. He had no relationship with Scalia, but the admiration and reverence for Scalia among conservatives (and even some on the left) was so strong that his passing was deeply and broadly felt. McGahn quickly pulled himself together. The new Supreme Court vacancy would come up in the debate in just a few hours. He needed to have a plan.

A partner in the Washington office of the law firm Jones Day and a former chairman of the Federal Election Commission, McGahn was an ideal pick for the lean and scrappy anti-establishment Trump campaign, which needed someone who knew the system. He set up the legal structure for the campaign and would go up to New York to check in every few weeks. He'd been in Iowa earlier in the month for the caucuses, where Trump placed second behind Cruz. He'd also fought off an effort to keep Trump off the ballot in New Hampshire, whose primary Trump decisively won.

While Trump had not made judges a focus of his campaign, as Senator Cruz had, his limited comments about them had already caused problems. Social conservatives in Iowa had been telling voters that

Trump would not appoint good judges. He wasn't a real conservative, and he had called his sister, Maryanne Trump Barry, a semi-retired senior judge of the U.S. Court of Appeals for the Third Circuit, "phenomenal."[11] Judge Barry had once issued a ruling finding constitutional protection for partial-birth abortion, in which the living child is partially extracted, feet first, from the womb before his or her skull is pierced and the brains sucked out. "Trump's recent suggestion that he would nominate his sister, Maryanne Trump Barry, [to the Supreme Court] is troubling to some conservatives. Trump has said that Barry, who was a Clinton appointee, would be a 'fantastic' and 'phenomenal' justice," the *Washington Examiner* reported.[12]

The reporting, however, misinterpreted his remarks from an interview on August 26, 2015, with Bloomberg's Mark Halperin and John Heilemann. Trump had defended Justice Clarence Thomas, critiqued Chief Justice Roberts's recent rulings, and said it was "inappropriate" to identify who he thought would be good on the Court. "What about your sister?" Halperin asked. Trump effusively praised his seventy-eight-year-old sister before saying of her nomination that he'd have to "rule that out for now."[13] The carefree comment was obviously not serious, as he clarified later.

Still, however his views had been mischaracterized, Trump did not emphasize judicial appointments as other candidates did. "The next president will have the awesome responsibility to pick up to four Supreme Court justices that will decide issues of life and religious liberty," Carly Fiorina told the crowds gathered at the March for Life in January 2016.[14] Judges were arguably Ted Cruz's main selling point to voters. The first Hispanic to clerk for a chief justice of the United States, Cruz had personally argued eight cases before the Supreme Court as the solicitor general of Texas.[15]

In an early debate on September 16, 2015, Cruz attacked Jeb Bush by pointing to the appointments of David Souter and John Roberts as examples of the Bush family's failure to put "rock-ribbed conservative" jurists on the Court.[16] He told Bloomberg News in December 2015 that every Supreme Court appointment he made would be of a "principled judicial conservative." Lamenting Republicans' record of picking weak justices who drifted to the left, Cruz promised to fight hard to keep conservatives from being disappointed. "The Republicans have an abysmal record. We bat about .500," he said. "About half of the nominees Republicans have put on the court have not just occasionally disappointed but have turned into absolute disasters." He said he would look for judges who had refused to bow to pressure and who had a "long paper trail" of taking principled stands.[17]

Cruz accurately reflected the concern of politically astute Republican voters. The anxiety wasn't new, but it was becoming acute.

■   ■   ■

Supreme Court nominations took on a new importance in Republican politics during the presidency of Dwight D. Eisenhower. Of the five appointments he made to the Supreme Court in his eight years in office, the first was the most consequential: the recess appointment of Governor Earl Warren of California as chief justice.[18] That was followed by the appointments of Associate Justices John Marshall Harlan, William Brennan, Charles Evans Whittaker, and Potter Stewart.

Eisenhower's focus in his Supreme Court appointments was on political, not jurisprudential, considerations. His appointment of Warren was, in part, a reward for withdrawing from the 1952 Republican presidential race, a move that ensured Eisenhower's success. Because Warren was a Republican, as was Harlan, Eisenhower's recess appointment of the Democrat William Brennan was a gesture of bipartisanship, and he hoped that naming a Catholic Democrat to the Court in the closing days of his 1956 reelection campaign would help him with northeastern voters.[19] Eisenhower's legal affairs adviser had heard Brennan give a speech that he interpreted as conservative. Brennan became "probably the most influential justice of the century," according to Scalia, but certainly not as a conservative.[20] Eisenhower was known for saying that the two biggest mistakes of his presidency were sitting on the Supreme Court—Warren and Brennan.

Americans remember the Warren Court as the most liberal in the nation's history. It is true that the *results* of its decisions—desegregation,[21] the banning of prayer in public schools,[22] the expansion of rights for those accused of crimes,[23] and the elimination of laws against birth control[24]—coincided with much of the progressive agenda of the mid-twentieth century. But judicial conservatives' criticism was focused on the anti-democratic *means* by which the Court sought to reshape American society. The proper constitutional means to achieve any societal or legal change is legislation passed by elected representatives, not the fiat of unelected judges. Progressives disagreed. Frustrated by their inability to achieve all they wanted through the political process, they applauded each time the Warren Court intervened in their favor. Justice Brennan described the power of these unelected justices with chilling clarity when he told his incoming clerks that the most important rule in the law was the "Rule of Five." With a majority of five votes, the Court could do anything.

It soon became evident that the Warren Court was willing to rewrite any law to achieve its transformative political desires, regardless of precedent or the Constitution's clear language. For example, in *Griswold v. Connecticut*, the Court determined that the Constitution required states to allow contraceptive use by married couples, locating this new "right to privacy" in "penumbras, formed by emanations" of no fewer than six constitutional amendments.[25] The dissenters argued strongly that a law may be "offensive," "uncommonly silly," "unwise, and even asinine," but still not run afoul of the Constitution.[26] And they expressed concern that allowing judges to overturn laws without a clear constitutional mandate would lead to "a great unconstitutional shift of power" that would "jeopardize the separation of governmental powers" envisioned by the Constitution.[27] *Griswold* became a precedent on which the majority of the Court relied eight years later in *Roe v. Wade* to establish a constitutional right to abortion.[28]

Other decisions, such as *Brown v. Board of Education*, may have been correct in their result but were decided on the basis of sociological studies rather than constitutional and legal principles.[29] The renowned Judge Learned Hand, himself an opponent of segregation, criticized the decision at the time because the Court, instead of concluding that any segregation on the basis of race was unconstitutional per se, framed its decisions as bound up in the state of public education and appeared to be acting as a "third legislative chamber" rather than as a judiciary properly limited to "keeping Congress and the states within their accredited authority."[30]

Some of the Warren Court's decisions, particularly *Engel v. Vitale*, which blocked public schools from opening with a nondenominational prayer even when non-compulsory, activated a grassroots movement of evangelicals. The Court cited not a single precedent for its decision, which conservatives viewed as an exercise of raw political power. Americans inundated both the Supreme Court and Congress with mail. In his doctoral dissertation on the rise of the religious right, Ben Sasse, now a U.S. senator from Nebraska, wrote, "The House of Representatives evaluated an unprecedented 145 proposed constitutional amendments in 1964 to reestablish school prayer by changing the First Amendment, followed up by scores more proposals in 1966 and 1970."[31]

The Court's constitutional improvisation fueled Barry Goldwater's 1964 presidential campaign, an apparently devastating defeat now widely regarded as the genesis of the conservative movement that would eventually carry Ronald Reagan to the White House. Goldwater decried the Court's diktats on reapportionment and prayer in schools, calling them an exercise of "raw and naked power," proof that "of all three branches of Government today's Supreme Court is the least faithful to the constitutional tradition of limited government, and to the principle of legitimacy in the exercise of power."[32] Echoing the *Griswold* dissenters, Goldwater declared that "the job of keeping the law up to date should be in the hands of the legislatures, the Congress and the common law courts, not just in the hands of the nine appointed Justices." If the policy that resulted was not the one favored by conservatives, so be it. "[T]o a constitutionalist, it is at least as important that the use of power be legitimate than that it be beneficial."[33]

Following the decision in *Miranda v. Arizona*, which went beyond constitutional prohibitions on forced self-incrimination to mandate the now-famous formulation of rights recited at every arrest, Richard Nixon made "law and order" the central theme of his presidential campaign in 1968.[34] He promised to nominate "strict constructionists who saw their duty as interpreting and not making law."[35] Nixon thought strategically about his judicial appointments, but his constitutional views were in fact more liberal than those of many of his voters.[36] While he really did care about law and order, he was not noticeably devoted to constitutional originalism, and his appointments to the Supreme Court were not much better than Eisenhower's. Chief Justice Warren had already announced his retirement before Nixon took office, but President Lyndon B. Johnson's attempt to replace him with his friend and political ally Abe Fortas ran into a Senate filibuster. Nixon appointed Warren E. Burger, who, though not the radical that Warren was, oversaw seventeen years of muddled opinions, including the infamous *Roe v. Wade*. Nixon also appointed Associate Justices Harry Blackmun, the author of *Roe*, Lewis F. Powell, and William Rehnquist. Only Rehnquist was consistently a constitutionalist.

President Gerald Ford's only Supreme Court appointment, John Paul Stevens, also turned out to be a disappointment for conservative voters. Stevens's liberalism might have "surprised his appointer," as George Will has written, but it apparently did not displease him.[37] In 2005, Ford reflected, "I am prepared to allow history's judgment of my term in office to rest (if necessary, exclusively) on my nomination 30 years ago of Justice John Paul Stevens to the U.S. Supreme Court."[38] Conservatives, however, certainly were displeased. Among his other affronts to sound constitutional interpretation, Stevens authored the opinion that conferred on government agencies broad discretion in interpreting acts of Congress,[39] and he dissented from the landmark *Heller* decision, which affirmed that the right to bear arms is an individual right.[40]

The records of Eisenhower, Nixon, and Ford showed conservative voters that they could not trust Republican presidents to appoint justices who felt bound by the text of the Constitution as understood by those who ratified it.

■   ■   ■

By the time Ronald Reagan was elected president in 1980, the conservative electorate was actively concerned about judges. The Republican
platform called for judges who respected "traditional family values and
the sanctity of innocent human life,"[41] leading liberal media and special
interest groups to accuse Reagan of imposing an abortion "litmus test" on
potential judges. He denied the charge, but he promised to appoint judges
who opposed the judicial activism of the Warren and Burger Courts. He
also promised that one of the first Supreme Court vacancies of his administration would be "filled by the most qualified woman" he could find.[42]
"It is time for a woman to sit among our highest jurists," he said.[43]

Justice Potter Stewart resigned at the end of the Court's term in 1981,
Reagan's first year in office. Edwin Meese III, one of Reagan's closest
advisers, recalls that the list of possible nominees contained only two
qualified Republican female judges, one of whom was Sandra Day
O'Connor, a state appellate judge in Arizona. When O'Connor met with
President Reagan, they didn't discuss anything of substance but chatted
about cattle ranching.[44] A Republican politician before she became a
judge, she seemed conservative enough in her hearing and was confirmed
easily, but she soon began to drift left.

The elevation of Justice William Rehnquist to chief justice after
Warren Burger's retirement in 1986 was unusually controversial for its
time. With his record as the most conservative member of the Court,
Rehnquist became the target of more than 150 liberal interest groups,
who placed damaging stories with friendly media outlets. They accused
him of having harassed and intimidated black and Latino voters in the
1960s and unearthed a racially restrictive covenant on property he
owned (of which he was unaware and which was probably unenforce-
able). While the effort to defeat him failed, it was a rough road to confirmation, and the thirty-three Senate votes against him were the most
cast against a chief justice up to that time.

Antonin Scalia, on the other hand, was easily confirmed to fill
Rehnquist's seat as an associate justice even though he was one of the

fathers of the conservative legal movement. His hearing, in which he joked with senators while smoking a pipe, was easier in part because he would be the first Italian American on the Court and in part because of disgust with the brutality of Rehnquist's confirmation.[45] And perhaps the Democrats were simply exhausted after that battle.[46]

The Senate had begun taking its constitutional role of "advice and consent" in the appointment of justices much more seriously during Nixon's presidency. Three of Eisenhower's five nominees—Warren, Brennan, and Whittaker—were confirmed by voice vote. Voting for the record by name became a matter of course only under Nixon. This growing self-assertion by the Senate, along with the Court's ever-bolder activism, which raised the political stakes of each appointment, made the confirmation process increasingly contentious. Americans learned just how contentious it could be when Justice Lewis Powell retired in 1987.

■   ■   ■

On July 1, President Reagan nominated Judge Robert Bork of the U.S. Court of Appeals for the D.C. Circuit to replace Powell. The disastrous confirmation battle that followed would galvanize a generation of conservative lawyers and jurists, who viewed the scurrilous attacks on Bork, one of the greatest legal minds of his generation, as unconscionable.

Within an hour of the announcement, Senator Edward M. Kennedy, attempting to strangle the nomination in its cradle, took to the floor of the Senate and delivered a shockingly vicious speech:

> Robert Bork's America is a land in which women would be forced into back-alley abortions, blacks would sit at segregated lunch counters, rogue police could break down citizens' doors in midnight raids, schoolchildren could not be taught about evolution, writers and artists would be censored at the whim of government, and the doors of the federal courts would be shut on the fingers of millions of citizens for whom

the judiciary is often the only protector of the individual rights that are the heart of our democracy. America is a better and freer nation than Robert Bork thinks. Yet in the current delicate balance of the Supreme Court, his rigid ideology will tip the scales of justice against the kind of country America is and ought to be. The damage that President Reagan will do through this nomination, if it is not rejected by the Senate, could live on far beyond the end of his presidential term. President Reagan is still our President. But he should not be able to reach out from the muck of Irangate, reach into the muck of Watergate, and impose his reactionary vision of the Constitution on the Supreme Court and on the next generation of Americans. No justice would be better than this injustice.[47]

The accusations were completely unfair. Bork had never suggested that he opposed the teaching of evolution. The evocation of "rogue police" breaking down doors in midnight raids was a reference to Bork's criticism of the judge-created "exclusionary rule," which forbids the presentation at trial of evidence that was obtained improperly. In general, Senator Kennedy confused Bork's legal arguments with policy positions and then further mischaracterized the outcomes of the cases at issue. Supporting the right of Nazis to march in public, as the Supreme Court did in *National Socialist Party of America v. Village of Skokie*, does not suggest support for Nazi beliefs.[48] It does, however, indicate support for free speech and the right to assemble.

Kennedy's speech was a pivot from evaluating a nominee's qualifications to judging his politics. Liberal activists approved, and they noticed that it worked. As the legal correspondent Jeffrey Toobin observed, "It was crude and exaggerated, but it galvanized the opposition as nothing else, and no one else, could."[49]

Four hundred special interest groups, an unprecedented number, weighed in on Bork's nomination, three hundred of them in opposition. A few groups had campaigned for or against Supreme Court nominations intermittently prior to that, but Bork's hearing was the first time that sophisticated marketing techniques were deployed against a Supreme Court nomination. Arguments were tailored to specific audiences for radio ads and newspaper op-eds.

People for the American Way ran a national television ad, likely the first of its kind, featuring the actor Gregory Peck, whose association in the popular imagination with the fictional lawyer Atticus Finch made him a symbol of integrity. Peck asserted that Bork had "defended poll taxes and literacy tests, which kept many Americans from voting. He opposed the civil rights law that ended 'Whites Only' signs at lunch counters. He doesn't believe the Constitution protects your right to privacy. And he thinks freedom of speech does not apply to literature and art and music." Ending on an ominous note, Peck reminded viewers that "if Robert Bork wins a seat on the Supreme Court, it will be for life—his life and yours."[50]

Bork's Senate testimony dragged on for five days, and the published record stretched to 6,511 pages. The hearings lasted twelve days and included testimony from twenty special interest groups. Reagan made more than thirty public statements on Bork's behalf, and the White House launched a public relations offensive, but it was too little and too late.[51] "We thought it was going to be a coast job, to tell you the truth— that it was going to be easy," recalled Reagan's communications director, Tom Griscom. "[We had] never seen somebody run the type of effort they ran [against Bork], and we let it get away from us."[52]

Yet the Reagan team ought not to have been surprised after the warm-up campaign against Rehnquist a few years earlier, when Senator Kennedy had even given his "Robert Bork's America" speech a dry run:

> Imagine what America would be like if Mr. Rehnquist had been the Chief Justice and his cramped and narrow view of the Constitution had prevailed in the critical years since World War II. The schools of America would still be segregated. Millions of citizens would be denied the right to vote under scandalous malapportionment laws. Women would be

condemned to second class status as second class Americans. Courthouses would be closed to individual challenges against police brutality and executive abuse—closed even to the press. Government would embrace religion, and the walls of separation between church and state would be in ruins. State and local majorities would tell us what we can read, how to lead our private lives, whether to bear children, how to bring them up, what kind of people we may become.[53]

Despite Democrats' efforts, Rehnquist was elevated to chief justice, and held the position for nineteen years. None of Kennedy's apocalyptic predictions came true.

The intellectual leader of the opposition to Bork was Professor Laurence Tribe of Harvard Law School, a prominent proponent of judicial activism whose book *God Save This Honorable Court* influenced many Democrats on the Judiciary Committee and was the "primer used by Judge Bork's opponents to defeat his nomination."[54] Tribe urged senators to break with tradition: a qualified candidate should be rejected if he would change the ideological balance of the court, which conveniently leaned left. Senators should not shrink from evaluating the social, political, and legal views of the nominee. For two hundred years, the judicial ideal had been political impartiality, but Tribe wanted senators to think of judges as political forces. And he was right. Time after time, a liberal Supreme Court majority has shown itself to be the nuclear bomb of political warfare.

The offensive against Bork's nomination was so devastating that it spawned a new word. To "bork" means "to attack or defeat (a nominee or candidate for public office) unfairly through an organized campaign of harsh public criticism or vilification," according to the Merriam-Webster dictionary.[55]

As the confirmation process degenerated into farce, Bork faced pressure to withdraw. His support from Attorney General Edwin Meese and others at the Department of Justice was strong, but in the wake of Iran-Contra and other scandals, Reagan had replaced his conservative circle of White House advisers with moderates who were far less enthusiastic about continuing the politically costly battle. Vice President George Bush's office had encouraged Bork to withdraw as well. His confirmation by the Democrat-controlled Senate seemed impossible.

Bork understood that his nomination was doomed, but he would force the Senate to hold a vote and urged the country not to permit this travesty to be repeated. Using political campaign tactics against a Supreme Court nomination was "not simply disturbing," he said, but "dangerous," for it would "erode public confidence in the impartiality of courts." No good judge, moreover, could effectively respond to such a campaign since his judicial responsibilities were "flatly incompatible" with doing so.[56] Bork's nomination was defeated by a vote of forty-two to fifty-eight.

After a second unsuccessful nomination—Judge Douglas Ginsburg was forced to withdraw after reports of past marijuana use—the president nominated Judge Anthony Kennedy of the Ninth Circuit. Conservatives had argued that nominating a moderate would reward the mob that had taken down Bork. "Even worse, it would be a powerful and haunting statement of acknowledgement that the President's agenda is no longer salable to the American people," warned Gary Bauer, a domestic policy adviser.[57]

Memoranda prepared at the time show that conservatives in the Reagan administration knew Kennedy might be a disappointment.[58] But others in the administration were more optimistic, including Attorney General Meese. He had worked with Kennedy in California on projects for then-Governor Reagan, who had recommended that President Nixon appoint Kennedy to the federal bench. Meese described Kennedy's Ninth Circuit record as "unblemished" and praised his early recognition of the overreach of the Supreme Court's Commerce Clause decisions, decades before those became a national issue in the 2012 Obamacare challenge. Reagan was asked if the nomination of Kennedy meant that he had caved in to liberals. "When the day comes that I cave in to the liberals, I will be long gone from here," he replied.[59]

Liberals in the media were of two minds. Linda Greenhouse, the Supreme Court reporter of the *New York Times*, observed that Laurence

Tribe was a witness in *support* of Kennedy at his confirmation hearings, where he praised his willingness to recognize rights not spelled out in the Constitution and his rejection of originalism.[60] Nonetheless, Greenhouse later described Kennedy's first full term on the Court as "The Year the Court Turned to the Right."[61]

■   ■   ■

When Justice William Brennan retired in 1990, President George H. W. Bush got his first chance to move the Court to the right. His chief of staff, John Sununu, pushed for David Souter, whom he had appointed to the Supreme Court of New Hampshire when he was governor and whose appointment to a federal appeals court he had secured earlier in Bush's presidency. Souter had been introduced to Sununu by Warren Rudman, a liberal Republican senator from New Hampshire, who later bragged about surreptitiously getting the liberal on the Supreme Court.[62] Sununu touted Souter's light judicial record as a benefit, since he would have to win confirmation from a Democratic Senate. Only one person in the Justice Department, George Smith, even tried to vet Souter. While it was difficult to say much given the short paper trail, he was not encouraged.

When Souter was nominated, Sununu personally assured suspicious conservatives that he would be a "home run for conservatives" on the Court.[63] But by the time the hearings opened, it was apparent that Souter's nomination was a horrible mistake. His effusive praise for Brennan and the Warren Court alarmed conservatives. He quickly became one of the Court's most reliably liberal votes. Many conservatives regard the appointment of this unknown jurist with no paper trail as Bush's most consequential blunder.

The retirement of Justice Thurgood Marshall the following year gave Bush an opportunity to make amends for that mistake, and he tacked decisively to the right with the nomination of Judge Clarence Thomas of the D.C. Circuit. Leftist groups pounced immediately. The National Organization for Women held a press conference in New York, where the feminist activist Florynce Kennedy, joined by Patricia Ireland and

Gloria Steinem, threatened, "We're going to bork him. We're going to kill him politically." She added, graciously, "This little creep, where did he come from?"[64]

This was just days after his nomination and months before Thomas's former colleague Anita Hill accused him, without evidence, of sexual harassment. Her allegation turned his confirmation into a horrific ordeal, but Thomas was ultimately confirmed by a vote of fifty-two to forty-eight, the last time a justice was confirmed by a Senate controlled by the opposing party.[65]

The Reagan-Bush years taught judicial conservatives several lessons. First and foremost was the importance of controlling the Senate. Republican control was why Rehnquist won and Bork lost. Second, inadequate vetting can have disastrous results. While Kennedy's record gave White House lawyers enough information to know what to expect from him—and they chose him anyway—the records of O'Connor and Souter did not have enough information to warrant a nomination. O'Connor simply hadn't ruled on the types of cases she would deal with at the federal level. Souter, likewise, had been nominated after only two months on the federal bench. Finally, the Thomas battle taught them that scurrilous allegations could arise at the last minute if all other efforts to derail a nomination failed.

The Supreme Court was a major issue before the 2000 election, with liberal pundits fearing what Bush would do if elected. "Wake up, America," Helen Thomas urged in her November 4 column, headlined: "The Supremes: They're What the Election Is All About." She prophesied that if George W. Bush won, an "ultraconservative majority" would dominate the Court for years. "All I can say is 'cry the beloved country' if Bush-appointed conservatives prevail on the high bench."[66] The Democratic nominee, Al Gore, joined her doomsday chorus, warning that Bush had promised to move the Court "to the extreme right wing."[67]

Bush won, and in his two terms he appointed two justices, but Helen Thomas's apocalyptic predictions proved inaccurate. John Roberts was first nominated to replace Sandra Day O'Connor, but when William Rehnquist died, Roberts was re-nominated for the chief justice's seat.

He was billed as a strong conservative, and his confirmation was relatively easy. But conservatives would later lament his lack of courage on the bench. His two opinions upholding the Affordable Care Act, also known as "Obamacare," looked like desperate efforts to rewrite the law to avoid the political firestorm that overturning it might ignite.[68] In the first constitutional challenge to Obamacare, which forced Americans to purchase health insurance or face a heavy penalty, he initially voted to overturn the law as outside Congress's Commerce Clause authority. Worried that overturning a major piece of legislation would arouse public anger and that the insurance markets might be thrown into chaos, he voted to uphold the law by redefining the penalty as a tax.[69] From a conservative perspective, the problem with Roberts was not that he was a liberal but that the prospect of intense controversy affected his rulings or caused him to avoid taking a strong stand, whether by voting not to hear cases on controversial issues or by going out of his way to decide them on extremely narrow grounds. For conservatives yearning for justices who would be strong under pressure, Roberts's appointment became a cautionary tale.

Bush then nominated his longtime friend and White House counsel Harriet Miers to replace O'Connor, but she immediately drew opposition from senators and others concerned about her lack of judicial experience. Grassroots conservatives also rebelled. Miers's character and talent had won the confidence and loyalty of the president and the admiration of many in the legal community of Texas, where she had been one of the first women to reach the highest levels of private corporate practice. But her career, however impressive, afforded little evidence of the unshakeable commitment to a principled judicial philosophy that conservatives were demanding. She withdrew within a month, and Judge Samuel Alito of the Third Circuit was nominated instead, an appointment that conservatives regard as remarkably successful.

Starting with President Eisenhower, Republicans had filled nineteen Supreme Court seats, compared with eight for Democrats. Yet the reign of liberal activism on the Supreme Court had encountered few challenges.

■   ■   ■

Scalia's death was a crushing blow to GOP voters and the conservative legal movement, frustrated by decades of blown opportunities to secure control of the Court. And it came just as Republicans were seeking to coalesce around a presidential candidate who could beat Hillary Clinton, already the front-runner in the race.

While the stunned Don McGahn sat at a Maryland gas station trying to figure out the Trump campaign's response to Scalia's death, people associated with the influential Federalist Society immediately began to strategize. On law school campuses, the group of conservatives and libertarians is known for hosting debates, which are also a major feature of their national conferences. Leading lights from across the political spectrum have debated, for example, whether district courts have the authority to enter nationwide injunctions, whether the Constitution presumes a moral and religious people, whether the government's collection of phone records violates the Fourth Amendment, and whether courts are too deferential to legislatures.

In early 2016, the Federalist Society had few connections with the Trump campaign, which was a much smaller organization than the other campaigns and was profoundly anti-establishment. McGahn was one of the few Washington insiders associated with it. The political class—the "establishment"—was downright oppositional. But then, the feeling was mutual.

When Jonathan Bunch, the director of external relations for the Federalist Society, finally spoke to McGahn before the Iowa caucuses, the conversation got off to a rocky start. The soft-spoken Bunch wanted to know about Trump's views on judges. McGahn responded dryly that Trump had it all under control—in fact, John Sununu was handling the issue for him. The man who had given America David Souter was working on two lists—one of pragmatists with no paper trails who would be easily confirmed, and the other of people whose conservative records made them too hot to handle.

Bunch was speechless. Finally, he asked McGahn what they were going to do with the two lists. When, after a long pause, McGahn said the list of pragmatists would be thrown in the trash and the second list would be jammed through the Senate, Bunch realized that he had been joking about Sununu. McGahn told Bunch that he had been president of his Federalist Society chapter in law school. Everything would be fine. He was a judicial conservative.

Back on the road and headed to the Eastern Shore of Maryland, McGahn was expecting a call from Trump to discuss Scalia's death. After the loss in Iowa, Trump had soundly defeated all comers in the New Hampshire primary earlier in the week. South Carolina and Nevada were next, and Super Tuesday, when eleven states would select nearly half of the delegates needed to win the Republican nomination, was two weeks away. Many Republican voters' chief concern about Trump was that he wasn't actually conservative. He'd been a registered Democrat a few years earlier and had previously been outspoken in his support of abortion. "I am very pro-choice," he declared on *Meet the Press* in 1999. His views on judicial philosophy were largely unknown, and he hadn't given Republican voters reason to trust him.

When Trump called, McGahn told him that he should move cautiously—extend his condolences to Maureen, Scalia's beloved wife, and get a feel for the situation. As luck would have it, McConnell's statement against confirming an Obama nominee dominated the news, giving the GOP presidential candidates some breathing room.

Trump and McGahn discussed the high probability that the first question of that evening's debate would be about Scalia. As it turned out, not only was that the first question, but Trump was the first candidate asked to respond to it. "Mr. Trump, I want to start with you," began John Dickerson, the even-keeled CBS moderator. "You've said that the president shouldn't nominate anyone in the rest of his term to replace Justice Scalia. If you were president and had a chance with eleven months left to go in your term, wouldn't it be an abdication to conservatives in particular not to name a conservative justice with the rest of your term?" Trump responded that he would certainly nominate someone and was "absolutely sure" that President Obama would try as well, adding that he hoped Mitch McConnell and the Republican Senate would be able to delay until the election.

And then he did something that turned out to be pivotal: He cited Diane Sykes and William Pryor as the kind of judge he would nominate to fill Scalia's seat. Sykes, a former member of the Wisconsin Supreme Court, sits on the U.S. Court of Appeals for the Seventh Circuit. Pryor sits on the Eleventh Circuit. Both are known as bright lights in conservative jurisprudence, and attentive voters took notice.

The decision to name names was a result of the phone call with McGahn. Trump suggested he should name specific persons who would be good replacements for Scalia. McGahn agreed, noting that Ted Cruz might have the same idea and they'd love to beat him to it. But whom should Trump name that evening? He was already familiar with Pryor, who had a large conservative fan base. McGahn suggested Sykes because she had recently authored one of the strongest free-speech opinions since the *Citizens United* decision.

A third judge was also discussed: Brett Kavanaugh. While McGahn emphasized Kavanaugh's stellar credentials and right instincts on separation of powers, he acknowledged he might be viewed as an inside-the-beltway candidate, the kind of judge Jeb Bush might pick. And a Kavanaugh opinion on Obamacare, which some read as the blueprint Chief Justice Roberts used to save the legislation when it came before the Supreme Court, had aroused the suspicions of legal conservatives. Not wanting to overload the candidate in the middle of his debate preparation, McGahn stopped the conversation there.

Later in the debate, Cruz took a shot at Trump. "The next president is going to appoint one, two, three, four Supreme Court Justices. If Donald Trump is president, he will appoint liberals." Trump responded by pointing out that Cruz had supported George W. Bush's pick of John Roberts for chief justice. "They both pushed him, he twice approved Obamacare," Trump said.[70] Cruz had spent months needling Trump about his sister, handing out summaries of her decisions. For the debate, he expected Trump to suggest that Cruz himself would make a good justice. Trump's naming two well-qualified judges took him by surprise.

Republican nominees had long gotten away with merely signaling the type of justice they would nominate. In an interview for the

Weekly Standard in 1999, Fred Barnes asked then-candidate George W. Bush about the kind of judge he would want. "Bush was quite specific. 'I have great respect for Justice Scalia,' Bush said," citing his "strength of mind, the consistency of his convictions, and the judicial philosophy he defends."[71] But Bush was careful not to be any more specific than that. In the October 2004 debate with John Kerry he was asked, "If there were a vacancy in the Supreme Court and you had the opportunity to fill that position today, whom would you choose and why?" Bush's response fit the conventional wisdom of the day: "I'm not telling."[72]

But some were beginning to recognize that disappointment with previous Supreme Court appointments was animating conservative primary voters. Following the September 2015 debate in which Cruz focused on the Court, the *Washington Post* ran an article headlined "How the Bush-Nominated Chief Justice Roberts Became Target in GOP Debates."[73] Scalia's death, then, was not the only reason that Supreme Court appointments were a central issue in the debate that evening.

The next morning Cruz and Trump were interviewed by the former Clinton spokesman George Stephanopoulos. Cruz said, "The one person he has suggested that would make a good justice is his sister, who is a court of appeals judge appointed by Bill Clinton. She is a hardcore pro-abortion liberal judge. And he said she would make a terrific justice."[74] Trump responded that he had "said it jokingly," that she "happens to have a little bit different views than me," and she "obviously would not be the right person." Appointing his own sister, moreover, would involve a "conflict of interest." He reiterated that the Bushes and Cruz had supported Roberts. It "was among the worst appointments I've ever seen. We have Obamacare because of Ted Cruz, Jeb Bush, and George Bush," Trump declared.[75]

Still, the issue of judicial appointments had been troublesome for Trump in Iowa, and the conventional wisdom was that Scalia's death would be a blow to the campaign. "In Death, Scalia May Succeed in Blocking Trump," read the headline to a *Roll Call* article by Melinda Henneberger, arguing that conservatives wouldn't risk a vote for Trump with a Supreme Court seat hanging in the balance.[76] And yet Trump's response to Scalia's death, that evening and in the weeks to come, helped propel him to a victory that nobody thought he could win.

Voters responded so well to Trump's reference to Sykes and Pryor in debates and speeches that he decided to make a longer list of judges who met with conservative approval. To get on the list, a judge (1) had to adhere to an originalist and textualist judicial philosophy,[77] (2) had to have a clear record of following that judicial philosophy, and (3) had to have demonstrated the courage of his convictions— criteria that reflected a determination to avoid the failures of previous Republican presidents.

■   ■   ■

McGahn organized a meet and greet with Trump at his law firm Jones Day in Washington on March 21 for members of congress who had endorsed him. Representative Tom Price of Georgia, a physician whom Trump would eventually tap to run the Department of Health and Human Services, wanted to come, but he wasn't invited. The only invited official who had not yet endorsed Trump was Senator Tom Cotton of Arkansas. Other key players at the reception included former Speaker of the House Newt Gingrich; Jim DeMint, the president of the Heritage Foundation and a former senator; and Leonard Leo. McGahn laid the groundwork for the meeting by explaining to Trump the importance of the Federalist Society in the legal community and by asking Leo to come to the meeting with the names of some judges who would be worthy replacements for Scalia. Leo brought a card with a handful of names, and McGahn put it in his breast pocket.

During the meeting, Trump asked everyone what he thought of his naming names during the debate and whether publishing a longer list was a good idea. The guests were surprised, but they approved, and Trump asked for their help. Afterward, he met privately with McGahn and Leo, and they discussed Souter and Roberts. Trump said he didn't like Roberts's Obamacare decision because the chief justice "made it up."

Then Trump asked Leo for suggestions for his list, and McGahn pulled Leo's card out of his pocket. Trump asked if he could keep it, and he did. (After the election, when Leo met with the president-elect at Trump Tower, Trump pulled the card out for reference. He had written "Paul Clement?" on it with a Sharpie, a reflection of how many people had urged him to consider George W. Bush's solicitor general.)

Immediately after the meeting at Jones Day, Trump went to the construction site of the Trump Hotel on Pennsylvania Avenue for a press conference. The last question was whether he had a litmus test for Supreme Court nominees. He said he'd be looking for smart conservatives. Then he announced he'd be "making up a list" of seven to ten people and "distributing that list in the very near future."[78] There was no going back.

When Jim DeMint returned to the Heritage Foundation, he immediately asked for help from John Malcolm, the head of Heritage's Meese Center for Legal and Judicial Studies. Malcolm was concerned about making sure Heritage didn't appear to be playing favorites with its advice, so he decided to publish the list for everyone, making it equally available to Bernie Sanders and Donald Trump. DeMint gave Malcolm relatively free rein, insisting only that the list be produced quickly. It was. Malcolm published a non-exclusive list of eight potential Supreme Court nominees just nine days later, on March 30.[79]

Trump's team was also working quickly, but it was a daunting task. Determining who had the proper judicial philosophy, a clear record, and the courage of his convictions required combing through a multitude of opinions.

In addition to Leo, McGahn was assisted in finding candidates and reading their opinions mainly by his Jones Day associate James Burnham. People were eager to promote their favorite judge, so the recommendations poured in. One of the more valuable ones was Tom Hardiman, a Third Circuit judge who had gone to law school with McGahn's law partner, Richard Milone. Leo also considered him a good candidate, and Trump's sister, Hardiman's colleague, praised his collegiality and work ethic. Her disagreement with many of his opinions may have been the perfect recommendation.

The team talked to the judges for whom candidates had clerked and to those who had clerked with them. McGahn was particularly interested in what candidates had been like in their mid-twenties, the stage of life when he believed most people's views solidified. Justice Kennedy was eager to help, offering the names of at least six former clerks who were in his "top five." Kavanaugh was one of them. While Kennedy called his other clerks good or excellent, he tended to describe Kavanaugh as "brilliant."

To enable his team to arrive at a thorough and reliable evaluation of each candidate's judicial philosophy, McGahn required that he or she already be a judge. A lawyer can always distance himself from an argument, even an aggressive one, made on behalf of a client. But to sign one's name to a judicial opinion takes courage and conviction. Leo helped confirm that candidates had been committed to conservative legal principles over the long haul and were not just opportunists showing up now that Obama's presidency was ending and a Supreme Court nomination was in the offing.

Political considerations, though not the top concern, were necessarily present. The campaign's strategy of realigning a winning coalition through the Rust Belt and its anti-establishment message militated against candidates from Washington, like Kavanaugh and Janice Rogers Brown of the D.C. Circuit. The latter, a favorite of McGahn's, was at age sixty-seven probably past nomination age anyway.[80]

Candidates needed to understand separation of powers and administrative law. Trump and McGahn shared a skepticism of the deference shown to bureaucracies, though they arrived at that skepticism for different reasons. For Trump, it was an instinctive frustration with the red tape that slows down or even kills construction projects. McGahn, on the other hand, had worked in the sausage factory himself. He learned at the Federal Election Commission about the inordinate control agencies have in shaping the law through the regulatory process.

The team looked at how quick candidates were to defer to agencies. Some judges thought judicial restraint required deference to any governmental decision, including those of unelected bureaucrats. Others believed in deference to the constitutionally established branches of government, whose powers are checked and balanced, but approached the regulations spun out by unelected agencies with considerably more skepticism.

The candidates had to show they understood the ins and outs of statutory interpretation. It was always a good sign to see citations to Justice Scalia's treatise *Reading Law* in their footnotes, but showing they understood how to apply the canons of statutory construction in practice was even more crucial. Justice Tom Lee of the Utah Supreme Court stood out on the list on the strength of his crisp style and cutting-edge textualist research.

Younger judges had an advantage simply because of the expectation that they would serve a long time, but McGahn's team also liked them because they had come of age after the Bork hearings. Bork and Scalia had taught the law students of the 1980s and '90s that they could be aggressive in fighting for their principles while still being engaging and witty. The concurrent rise of the Federalist Society was also of incalculable importance in forming and fortifying the generation of judges now coming into their own.

As research for the list progressed, it became clear that there was a whole generation of people in their forties who hadn't followed the traditional career path of conservative attorneys. It used to be that promising law students came to D.C. for prominent clerkships, worked at the Department of Justice, and continued to rise through the Washington ranks until they were eligible to be judges. But that default career path had changed.

In its last two years, the Bush administration had been beset by foreign and domestic crises, and then came the eight years of the Obama administration. Republican prospects for 2016 and beyond looked dim. With no administration positions on the horizon, conservative lawyers had moved back home and developed careers there. Appellate practices took off at the state level. People who would have been at the Department of Justice in a Republican administration, such as Andy Oldham from Texas and Kyle Duncan from Louisiana (whom Trump would eventually appoint to appellate judgeships), instead went home and worked for state attorneys general. Many ended up on state supreme courts, such as David Stras of Minnesota and Allison Eid of Colorado (also now Trump-appointed circuit court judges). So even though the federal bench had been closed to young conservative talent for nearly a decade, McGahn's team could choose from an abundance of rising stars with state judicial experience.

Trump's opportunities to appoint a Supreme Court justice would be limited, of course—three or four at the most, perhaps only one. But in compiling the Supreme Court list, McGahn's team was identifying candidates for the circuit courts as well. The next president would enter office with a historic number of judicial vacancies—more than awaited four of his five predecessors—and many more judges were ready to take senior status, opening more seats. It would be a tremendous opportunity to influence the federal judiciary starting on day one.

■   ■   ■

The list was done and ready to go for weeks, but Trump didn't release it. A previously released list of unvetted foreign policy advisors had caused the media to accuse him of being a Russian stooge, and now he wondered whether such lists were a good idea. Believing that the Supreme Court list would help Trump defeat Cruz in the primaries, McGahn had wanted it out before the Indiana primary on May 3. When Trump won that contest, securing the Republican nomination without the list, McGahn figured it would never be released.

On May 18, however, Trump called McGahn and told him he wanted to put the list out. He asked McGahn for assurance that each name had been thoroughly vetted. When Trump pressed him about the quality of the candidates, McGahn offered to put the list out under his own name, an offer Trump declined. Within minutes of receiving the final approved list, the campaign posted it:

Steven Colloton of Iowa
Allison Eid of Colorado
Raymond Gruender of Missouri
Thomas Hardiman of Pennsylvania
Raymond Kethledge of Michigan
Joan Larsen of Michigan
Thomas Lee of Utah
William Pryor of Alabama
David Stras of Minnesota
Diane Sykes of Wisconsin
Don Willett of Texas

No one on the list knew that he or she would be on it. Don Willett of the Texas Supreme Court was at a book-signing for Governor Greg Abbott when news broke that he'd been included. Asked to comment on his inclusion, he declined. On the day Trump announced his candidacy, Willett had tweeted:

Donald Trump haiku—
Who would the Donald
Name to #SCOTUS? The mind reels.
weeps—can't finish tweet[81]

It wasn't his only tweet critical of the candidate. Nevertheless, Trump eventually appointed Willett to the Fifth Circuit. The media highlighted the tweets again, to the consternation of the president, but the quality of his opinions was what mattered. The media's reaction focused on tangential issues, such as Willett's tweets or the absence of D.C. insiders such as Kavanaugh and Clement, but most treated the list as largely respectable, if conservative.[82]

The Cruz campaign, still hoping to make a play at the Republican convention, was paralyzed. Chuck Cooper, a topflight litigator, head of Reagan's Office of Legal Counsel, and an adviser to the campaign, said the list was brilliant. Campaign staff contemplated putting out their own list but couldn't find anyone on Trump's list that wouldn't be on theirs. Other conservatives loved the list as well. But because Trump had not promised to take his nominee from the list—he called it a list of "potential" nominees—some said it didn't mean anything. The "NeverTrump" movement within the Republican Party, which would make a last-ditch effort to deprive him of the nomination at the GOP convention in August, argued that he couldn't be trusted to take his nominee from the list.

Leo and McGahn, appreciating the amount of vetting still required before anyone on the list could be nominated to the Court, did not regard it as definitive and did not want to be confined to it. Besides, plenty of other people were under consideration, including Neil Gorsuch. He had written around 175 opinions on the Tenth Circuit, and it would take time to go through them all. They also knew that the conventional wisdom about the dangers of such a list was right about one thing: putting names out opened them to attack. They didn't mind having a few top candidates like Gorsuch spared some of the barrage. For his part, Trump liked putting up the trial balloon.

Steve Bannon, the bombastic head of Breitbart News, became chief executive of the campaign in August. In light of how well the first list of judges had been received and because the NeverTrump faction was capitalizing on the conditional terms in which the first list was presented, he wanted an updated list with additional names and a firm commitment to take the nominee from it. And locking in a solid choice for the Supreme Court now would be an insurance policy in case someone with different judicial priorities became White House counsel or attorney general in a future Trump administration.

On September 23, 2016, three days before the first presidential debate with Hillary Clinton, Trump released an updated list with ten additional names, and he promised, "This list is definitive and I will choose only from it."[83] The new candidates were:

Keith Blackwell of Georgia
Charles Canady of Florida
Neil Gorsuch of Colorado

Mike Lee of Utah
Edward Mansfield of Iowa
Federico Moreno of Florida
Margaret Ryan of Virginia
Amul Thapar of Kentucky
Timothy Tymkovich of Colorado
Robert Young of Michigan

Senator Mike Lee, whose brother Thomas was already on the list, was the only non-judge to be included. He was added at the request of Cruz, who was preparing to endorse Trump after refusing to do so outright at the 2016 Republican convention. The radio and television host Laura Ingraham, a former law clerk for Justice Thomas, brokered the arrangement. Once the list was released, Cruz gave his endorsement, citing the Supreme Court and Lee's inclusion on Trump's list as his primary reason. "For some time, I have been seeking greater specificity on this issue, and today the Trump campaign provided that, releasing a very strong list of potential Supreme Court nominees—including Senator Mike Lee, who would make an extraordinary justice—and making an explicit commitment to nominate only from that list. This commitment matters, and it provides a serious reason for voters to choose to support Trump," he wrote in a Facebook post.[84]

The publication of a list of hard-core conservatives in the middle of a general election campaign spoke to how different Trump was from a traditional Republican. Most GOP candidates run to the right during the primaries, only to tack to the center during the general election campaign. Trump's approach was to stay right where he was but force his opponent farther to the left.

Trump thought his list showed that he was *for* something. If Hillary Clinton provided her own short list, it would make her appear more radical. She was in a difficult situation, for she had to support Obama's nominee, Judge Garland, while also signaling that her own nominees would be much farther to the left.[85] Reflecting the prematurely triumphant mood of the left, Mark Tushnet of Harvard Law School argued that Democrats controlled the courts and should act like it by becoming even more aggressive in their push to enact a liberal agenda.[86]

In the final presidential debate, Clinton offered a list not of names but of political requirements for prospective justices. Specifically, she wanted a justice who would back women's rights and LGBT rights, support *Roe v. Wade*, and reverse the *Citizens United* decision to get "dark money" out of politics.[87] She often railed against the *Citizens United* decision, but she was rarely called to account for criticizing a case that decided whether it was a campaign finance violation to publicly screen a film criticizing...Hillary Clinton. These desiderata did not form a consistent, principled judicial philosophy so much as a wish list for liberal special interest groups.

■   ■   ■

When Trump shocked the world by winning, exit polls showed that the Supreme Court was at the top of the list for many voters. The list had played a huge role.

The ensuing transition was fairly chaotic. The chief of staff and White House counsel are usually named the day after the election, but Trump took several weeks to decide who would run his White House. Warring factions led multiple transition efforts, and McGahn was occupied with three recounts and other legal issues.

A week after Trump's victory, Leo and Bunch were summoned to Trump Tower to winnow the twenty-one names on the updated list to a more manageable list for final vetting. They met with President-Elect Trump, his adviser Kellyanne Conway, and the incoming attorney general, Jeff Sessions. Bannon, Republican National Committee Chairman Reince Priebus, and Ivanka Trump also attended portions of the meeting. McGahn was away on lingering campaign business, including multiple recounts. He was under consideration for White House counsel, and at that meeting Leo, knowing the role would be decisive for the success of Trump's judicial selection process, argued strongly in McGahn's favor.

Trump began the meeting by discussing how consequential the Supreme Court issue was for voters. He knew the polling data, which showed that 26 percent of Trump voters said the Supreme Court was the basis of their decision.[88] Trump joked that Clarence Thomas's name received more applause at rallies than his own.

The president-elect told the group he wanted a nominee who was young enough to serve for decades, exceptionally well qualified, not weak, and would interpret the Constitution as the framers intended.[89] Further discussion revealed that Trump cared a great deal about credentials, seeking someone at the top of the legal profession. He wanted someone who would not be swayed by the political and social fashions of the day, someone who would be courageous in his decisions. The group discussed the courage and independence that had made Scalia special, and at Leo's recommendation, Trump even called Maureen Scalia to discuss her husband.

Leo provided a list of six names who he said matched Trump's criteria well: Colloton, Gorsuch, Hardiman, Pryor, Sykes, and Thapar.

Leo, on leave from the Federalist Society to work on the transition, conducted screening interviews with the short-listers, covering a range of topics. Some of his questions were predictable enough, the kind the judges themselves might ask a potential clerk: Who's the best judge of your lifetime? Who was the best judge before that? What are the strongest arguments for and against textualism and originalism? He probed their judicial philosophy, asking what made their own philosophy attractive and what was the most difficult question they had struggled with on the bench. Finally, he touched on the issue of fortitude, asking them to speculate what caused so many judges to drift from their judicial philosophy and first principles.

Some talked about the "Greenhouse effect," which was Judge Laurence Silberman's term for the influence of the media, personified by the notoriously liberal Linda Greenhouse of the *New York Times*.[90] Others cited the corrupting effects of power. Everyone handled the interviews well. Gorsuch described the importance of courage, recalling how his mother, Anne, had been targeted politically when she worked in Washington as the administrator of the Environmental Protection Agency under Reagan.

"The 'not weak' category became pretty damn clear," Leo said.

Short-listers then met with McGahn one-on-one at Jones Day, where he gave them their "sex, drugs, and rock-and-roll" screening. They also discussed judicial philosophy. This was the first time many of them had met McGahn.

The next interview was conducted by a panel put together by McGahn. It included himself, Vice President Elect Pence, Bannon, and Priebus. He feared Priebus would try to make it a typical Republican process. He also included Pence's counsel, Mark Paoletta, who had worked on nominations going back to Clarence Thomas.

Meanwhile Pence, McGahn, and Marc Short, the White House director of legislative affairs, headed over to Capitol Hill to talk to senators about whom they wanted to see on the Supreme Court. The list of twenty-one names had been public for months, but some Democrats said they hadn't seen it. Senator Murkowski expressed support for Gorsuch. Many senators expressed concern about Pryor. Senator Collins pointed out that she had voted against Pryor when he was confirmed to the court of appeals in 2005 because he had once described *Roe v. Wade* as the "worst abomination in the history of constitutional law." She would be unlikely to change her vote if he were nominated to an even higher court.

While Kethledge, who had become a short-lister, had an extremely successful interview and the enthusiastic support of the vice president elect, he had a shorter and less illuminating paper trail than several of the others. Pryor hit it out of the park in his interview, but there were concerns that he might not pass through the Senate, which still had a filibuster rule enabling the minority party to kill a nomination with only forty votes. Hardiman also had a strong interview and less opposition. Sykes's interview was satisfactory.

Pence showed each candidate a graph from the *New York Times* showing the ideological slide justices took after confirmation—almost always to the left. It's a trend that conservatives regularly bemoan. One conservative justice said newcomers to the court have to be prepared to stand up against the American Bar Association, business groups, and the liberal media. They have to be prepared to be disliked and to accept that nasty and unfair things will be said about them. And they have to be confident in their ability to analyze cases and not be influenced by liberal law clerks.

Pence asked candidates to explain the drift, and he received a range of answers: the influence of liberal media, Washington elites, their peers. Each candidate was asked whom he or she would pick if he or she were not chosen. Everyone picked Gorsuch. Kethledge strongly advocated for him, and Pryor discussed a criminal law decision Gorsuch wrote that helped him understand a key issue. Gorsuch was the only one who didn't name his choice, but he declined for a compelling reason. He praised them all but said he couldn't make a decision until he read each candidate's complete record. His judicial colleagues' answers gave the vetting team further comfort about Gorsuch.

The short-listed candidates next met with the vice president elect. Of those, Pryor, Hardiman, and Gorsuch were interviewed, in that order, by the president-elect in the presence of McGahn at Trump Tower in January. They were the best of show in three categories. Pryor was the best conservative darling, Hardiman was the best representative of the Trump voter, and Gorsuch was the best with the typical elite résumé.

McGahn prepped Trump before the interviews, explaining to the businessman the need to be careful to not say anything that could be construed as a request for a commitment to rule in a certain way on any issue, for senators would ask the nominee if such a commitment had been requested. Trump was impressed by all the candidates, but Gorsuch ended the day as he began it—as the front-runner.

While many people participated in the selection process, Leo and McGahn felt strongly that it needed to be the president's decision. After Trump chose Gorsuch, the confirmation process ran like clockwork, culminating in his confirmation on the target date of April 7, which McGahn had set back in December, before Trump even took office.

Two months later, Leo and McGahn talked to the president about refreshing the list. They mentioned Kavanaugh's name again. Clement, the other popular D.C. figure left off the first lists, was also discussed. But as Clement had never been a judge—and reportedly wasn't interested in a lower-court position—he had no demonstrable record of how he would perform on the bench.

It was a tumultuous summer at the White House. Priebus was fired as chief of staff and there were riots in Charlottesville. Leo and Trump met for dinner in September and talked more about judicial confirmations. An updated list was assembled in October and early November, and released on November 17 in the middle of the Federalist Society's annual lawyers' convention in D.C. The list now included four newly confirmed judges: Amy Coney Barrett of Indiana, Kevin Newsom of Alabama, Britt Grant of Georgia, and Patrick Wyrick of Oklahoma. And—raising the eyebrows of everyone who knew what his inclusion signaled—Brett Kavanaugh.

CHAPTER THREE

Complicit in Evil

66 **T**hese things are won or lost in the first forty-eight hours," Kava-naugh would always tell his students when he taught about judicial confirmations in his Supreme Court and Separation of Powers class. He had learned this from reading the history of confirmation battles, but also from his experience at the White House. President George W. Bush announced his nomination of John Roberts to the Supreme Court in a prime-time televised address, making a compelling case for the judge's qualifications. Democratic senators said they'd keep an open mind. The harshest criticism in the wake of the announcement was an attack in the *Washington Post* on the seersucker suit worn by Roberts's young son, a tasteless jab that simply increased sympathy for the Roberts family.[1] He was confirmed by a vote of seventy-eight to twenty-two.

By contrast, Harriet Miers's nomination was probably lost in the first ten minutes. President Bush asked conservatives to trust him when he nominated his White House counsel, who had no experience as a judge. "I've known Harriet for more than a decade. I know her heart. I know her character," Bush said.[2] Democratic senator Harry Reid praised her, but by sidestepping the conservative legal movement, the president forfeited the confidence of the individuals and organizations whose support he needed, and the ill-considered nomination was quickly withdrawn. And most famously, Judge Bork's nomination was defined by Senator Kennedy's brutally unfair "Robert Bork's America" speech, delivered within minutes of the announcement.

As he had done with the Gorsuch nomination the previous year, President Trump announced his selection of Kavanaugh in a prime-time speech delivered to an audience in the East Room of the White House. Trump thanked Justice Kennedy, who was in Europe, for his "incredible passion and devotion" and "lifetime of distinguished service." He praised Kavanaugh as a "judge's judge," a "brilliant jurist, with a clear and effective writing style, universally regarded as one of the finest and sharpest legal minds of our time."[3]

Trump, always conscious of stagecraft, had been keen to have Ashley Kavanaugh and her daughters, ten-year-old Liza and twelve-year-old Margaret, next to the judge for the announcement. Both girls handled the nationally televised event well. They'd been told to treat it as if they were at the front of the gym on awards night at Blessed Sacrament School. If they got scared at all, they were to look over at MarMar, their grandmother, in the front row. Ashley had spent years in the White House, and she enjoyed the reunion with the permanent staff, including photographers she'd met during the Bush administration.

Liza, giving her father a low five, seemed perfectly at ease. Earlier in the evening, she'd comfortably chatted with President and Mrs. Trump. At his confirmation hearings a few months later, Kavanaugh joked that she called this her "television debut."

Part of the stagecraft was keeping the identity of the nominee a surprise. Kavanaugh knew not to tell anyone that Trump had chosen him, and he didn't. Not even Ashley, though he did tell her it looked "good" following the meeting at the White House the previous evening. The clerks noted that he returned to his chambers several hours late and in his suit and seemed particularly focused on finishing his speech, but he didn't say a word about it to them. He told them to prepare as if he would get the nomination, and if he didn't, they'd all go out to dinner anyway.

The White House had prepared rollouts for each of the finalists, and even people at the highest levels didn't know that Kavanaugh was the choice until the last moment. Claire Murray of the White House counsel's office had to cut her family vacation short to work on the Hardiman rollout, even though Kavanaugh, unbeknownst to her, had already been chosen. McGahn's deputy, Annie Donaldson, knew Kavanaugh had been chosen, but her husband, Brett Talley, who was also working on judicial selections for the White House counsel, was kept in the dark—something he would tease her about, particularly since she'd also been discreet about Kennedy's retirement.

The press was consumed with speculation throughout the day. Kavanaugh arrived at the White House at midday and continued revising his speech from the Lincoln Bedroom, asking assistants to print updated versions. Ashley understood the need for discretion but also worried about making plans. It would take time to get the judge's parents down to D.C., and she and the girls would need to be dressed and ready to go. He agreed to call his parents, confirming that the nomination was on.

Meanwhile his clerks felt optimistic but unsure, particularly given President Trump's flair for drama. While emails went out earlier in the day to people who would be invited to an announcement regardless of the nominee, it wasn't until the five o'clock hour that Kavanaugh-specific guests received their invitations. Even then nobody felt fully confident. As the clerks waited in the East Room, they noticed a large group of empty chairs, set aside for senators who were due to arrive at the last minute. "We think it's us, but that's where all the Kethledge people sit," someone joked. It wasn't until Kavanaugh walked on stage that everyone breathed a sigh of relief.

The standard critique of every male Republican nominated to the Supreme Court is that he is hostile to "women's rights," a euphemism for unregulated abortion. It was the main attack on John Roberts, but it was also levied against those who would turn out to be defenders of abortion, such as David Souter.[4] Everyone knew that Kavanaugh would face the same attack, but he would meet it with a lifelong record of being shaped by and working alongside strong women. He was determined to showcase them in the key first forty-eight hours.

In his speech that evening, Kavanaugh's love for his mother shone through. He praised her work as a teacher at two largely African American public high schools in Washington, D.C. He expressed his pride in her for going to law school when he was ten—an unusual career path for a woman at that time—and becoming a prosecutor and eventually a judge. He recalled his mother's customary advice to a jury: "Use your common sense. What rings true? What rings false?" And he said, "The president introduced me tonight as Judge Kavanaugh. But to me that title will always belong to my mom."[5]

An only child, Kavanaugh was extremely close to his parents. They had both attended law school at American University when he was a boy and used to tease each other about who got better grades. With two parents who were lawyers, he got to see the creative ways working mothers balance all their responsibilities. In eighth grade, Kavanaugh was in a five-person carpool at his Catholic school. On her day to drive, Mrs. Kavanaugh would send a taxi to pick up her son and the other kids, one of whom was a third-grader.

He expressed gratitude to Justice Elena Kagan, who had hired him as an adjunct professor at Harvard Law School when she was its dean. Kagan was known for her efforts to hire conservatives, having included three among her forty-three full-time faculty hires, more than doubling (to 2 percent) the conservative share of the overwhelmingly progressive law faculty. She realized that her students would be disadvantaged as lawyers if they were taught only by liberals, because they would never be forced to defend their views vigorously and because many judges are themselves conservative.

A majority of Kavanaugh's clerks had been women. He talked about his "spirited daughters," Margaret and Liza, whose basketball teams he coached. And he expressed love and respect for his wife.

Kavanaugh was already well known in the legal community as a powerful judge on one of the most important federal courts. But in his speech, he tried to share more about himself. "The girls on the team call me 'Coach K,'" Kavanaugh noted wryly, jokingly comparing himself to the legendary Duke University basketball coach Mike Krzyzewski. Some of his clerks had urged him to remove the jest, but it was one of a few lines that elicited laughter in the otherwise staid ceremony.

Kavanaugh recognized how effective previous Supreme Court nominee speeches had been. Elena Kagan had depicted herself as the child of immigrants who were the first in their families to go to college.[6] Sonia Sotomayor had talked about growing up in a housing project and the importance of taking into account the "real world consequences" of her judicial decisions, echoing President Obama's call for empathetic judges.[7]

NBC's Chuck Todd called Kavanaugh "a very confirmable pick."[8] But his invocations of the women in his life irked the *Washington Post*'s Aaron Blake, who wrote, "The nominee's introductory speech was remarkably political. Over and over again, Kavanaugh returned to the women in his life and the diversity of those around him."[9] The following night, Stephen Colbert made fun of his focus on women, calling him a "cover model for Generic Dads Monthly" and mocking his first name.[10] The abortion advocacy group NARAL ridiculed Kavanaugh on Twitter as a "frat boy named Brett," an ominous preview of his opponents' eventual strategy.[11]

Blake continued to vent his disapproval in another article, lashing out at Kavanaugh's statement that "[n]o president has ever consulted more widely, or talked with more people from more backgrounds, to seek input about a Supreme Court nomination," a claim he dismissed as "thoroughly strange and quite possibly bogus."[12] It is difficult to quantify presidential consultation on Supreme Court appointments, of course, but Kavanaugh knew what he was talking about, and he wasn't exaggerating. He had seen and read how other administrations had kept deliberations internal. After all, he worked in the White House that nominated Harriet Miers. By all accounts, Trump began his Supreme Court search in the middle of the primaries and sought advice from a variety of individuals and organizations. He talked about it in meetings and even at his rallies. He and his team made sure those on "the list" had been thoroughly vetted, talking to the judges they had clerked for and to their co-clerks and reading their opinions and articles. From Kennedy's retirement announcement until Sunday's meeting with Kavanaugh, the president discussed his potential nominees with senators, pundits, friends, and advisers.

Trump closed his introduction of Kavanaugh by saying, "The rule of law is our nation's proud heritage. It is the cornerstone of our freedom. It is what guarantees equal justice. And the Senate now has the chance to protect this glorious heritage by sending Judge Brett Kavanaugh to the United States Supreme Court."[13]

The numbers in the Senate left no room for error. Some Democrats, such as Senator Bob Casey of Pennsylvania, had announced they would vote against anyone the president nominated.[14] The *New York Times* had instructed Democrats and progressives to "take a page from 'The Godfather' and go to the mattresses" on any nomination.[15] Immediately after the announcement, the Senate minority leader, Chuck Schumer of New York, declared he would "oppose Judge Kavanaugh's nomination with everything" he had, adding, "If we can successfully block this nomination, it could lead to a more independent, moderate selection that both parties could support."[16] Schumer knew what Republicans also knew—if Kavanaugh's nomination were scuttled, his replacement would probably be more liberal.

Realistically, very few if any Democrats would consider voting for Kavanaugh. When Trump nominated the eminently qualified Neil Gorsuch, the only Democrats to vote for him were Joe Donnelly of Indiana, Heidi Heitkamp of North Dakota, and Joe Manchin of West Virginia. All three represented states that Trump had carried and were facing tough reelection bids in 2018. The other potential Democratic votes were Missouri's Claire McCaskill, who was also on the ballot in 2018, and Alabama's Doug Jones, who would have to decide between embracing his liberal roots and moderating to preserve his chance for reelection in 2020.

Republicans held a slim majority of fifty-one to forty-nine in the Senate, made even more tenuous because one Republican was not expected for the eventual vote. Senator John McCain had returned to Arizona months earlier, following his diagnosis of glioblastoma, a rare and aggressive brain cancer. Without McCain, Republicans could not afford to lose a single vote. But the Republican caucus was not a monolith. Senator Rand Paul and others from the libertarian side of the party had reservations about Kavanaugh's Fourth Amendment jurisprudence. Senators who support abortion rights sought assurance that the nominee's respect for *stare decisis* (Latin for "to stand by things decided," that is, conformity to legal precedent) meant he would not upset the status quo in abortion law. And some "NeverTrump" senators were in the midst of battles with the president that occasionally spilled over into their work in Congress.

Most of the anxiety on the left concerned abortion and other culture-war issues. The problem was not with Kavanaugh personally as much as the fact that he would replace a pivotal justice. In their haste to respond to the nomination, the organizers of the Women's March accidentally issued a statement opposing "Trump's nomination of XX to the Supreme Court."[17] Democracy for America's press release, apparently drafted with Amy Barrett in mind, referred to Kavanaugh as "she."[18] Protesters at the Supreme Court avoided the embarrassing "Mad Libs" signs—"#Stop _____"—they had used when Gorsuch was nominated.[19] This time they had multiple printed versions ready to go, but the occasional "#StopKethledge" or "#StopHardiman" sign showed up in television shots of the crowd.[20] These lapses confirmed what everyone already knew—to the left, it didn't matter *whom* Trump nominated.

As the announcement of Kavanaugh's nomination was made, a large crowd gathered outside the Supreme Court in a protest organized by the Center for American Progress (CAP), funded by George Soros and founded by John Podesta, a close aide to Barack Obama and the Clintons. As they waited to find out who it was, they chanted "Hey, hey! Ho, ho! The patriarchy has got to go!"[21] As soon as Trump's nominee was announced, CAP's president, the longtime Clinton insider Neera Tanden, shouted to the crowd that Kavanaugh was an "extremist who will damage our country for decades.... We must ensure that we defeat Brett

Kavanaugh. All our rights are at stake. *Roe v. Wade.* Health care. Democracy itself."[22]

Senators Bernie Sanders of Vermont, Elizabeth Warren of Massachusetts, Kirsten Gillibrand of New York, Cory Booker of New Jersey, Richard Blumenthal of Connecticut, Jeff Merkley of Oregon, and Tina Smith of Minnesota also spoke. Their rhetoric was apocalyptic. Kavanaugh would "pave a path to tyranny," proclaimed Merkley. Gillibrand said that to keep Brett Kavanaugh from becoming justice, it would take "all of us fighting as hard and as long as we can." Elizabeth Warren warned, "I'm not going to sugarcoat this. We are in the fight of our lives."

The progressive groups represented at that night's anti-Kavanaugh protest included the Service Employees International Union, Planned Parenthood, People for the American Way, the National Women's Law Center, the National Center for Transgender Equality, the National LGBTQ Task Force, Lambda Legal, the Constitutional Accountability Center, the NAACP, the Leadership Conference on Civil and Human Rights, End Citizens United, Giffords.org, Americans United for Separation of Church and State, Earthjustice, Generation Progress, the League of Conservation Voters, and the Progressive Change Campaign Committee.

"I have some news for you, Mr. President! We are every bit as determined to block Judge Kavanaugh's nomination as you are to realize your anti-woman, anti-civil rights, homophobic agenda," said Debra Ness of the National Partnership for Women and Families. "This will be the fight of our lives and we will win." Ilyse Hogue of NARAL Pro-Choice America announced a fifty-state day of action to oppose Kavanaugh, with eighty organizations participating.

Several speakers, such as Adam Green of the Progressive Change Campaign Committee and Ben Wikler of MoveOn, identified Republicans Susan Collins and Lisa Murkowski, both of whom support abortion rights, as the senators they would press to vote against Kavanaugh. They were off to a rough start with Collins, who felt that some of her colleagues and liberal activists were whipping people into a frenzy. She was determined to fulfill her constitutional duty of "advice and consent" and approach the nomination with an open mind.

The rally was raucous. The crowd grew. Reporters were jostled. For large events, Supreme Court police typically put up barriers to ensure the safety of both protesters and media. They didn't expect the crowds to be as big or as boisterous as they were.

Shannon Bream, a longtime Supreme Court correspondent, had planned to host her eleven o'clock television show *Fox News @ Night* from the Supreme Court, but at 9:31 p.m. she tweeted, "Very few times I've felt threatened while out in the field. The mood here tonight is very volatile. Law enforcement appears to be closing down 1st Street in front of SCOTUS."[23] Minutes later she announced that the production team was forced to move back to the safety of the Fox News studios.

Across the street in the U.S. Capitol, Republican senators' senior staff met that night at ten o'clock to begin preparations for the confirmation fight.

By the end of the night, the battle lines had been drawn. Establishment Republicans were delighted with the nomination of an official from the Bush administration. Grassroots conservatives were accepting if not enthusiastic. In their eyes, Kavanaugh was a standard-issue Bushie, a milquetoast nominee. Most conservative leaders kept their mild disappointment to themselves, understanding the precarious situation of the Senate. In fact, some in the White House had expected far more pushback both for selecting Kavanaugh and for not selecting the conservatives' favorite, Judge Barrett. A few spoke out, but they were discouraged from making too much of it. While Tony Perkins of the Family Research Council did not oppose the nomination, he urged conservatives to "trust but verify" that Kavanaugh would be the justice they wanted.[24] As for the progressive left, they didn't need any more verification. They were enraged and ready to fight.

One of their first attacks was that any nomination by President Trump was illegitimate. As the NAACP's Hilary Shelton put it, "We have a criminal investigation into the presidency itself. That investigation must be completed before the Senate even thinks of evaluating a lifetime appointment of a Supreme Court justice." The actress and activist Alyssa Milano had tweeted out the same argument, in all capitals, right after

Kennedy stepped down: "TRUMP SHOULD NOT BE ABLE TO CHOOSE A LIFETIME APPOINTEE WHILE HE IS UNDER FEDERAL INVESTIGATION. FULL STOP."[25]

Paul Schiff Berman, a professor at George Washington University Law School, wrote in the *New York Times* that no nominee could be confirmed until Robert Mueller had completed his investigation of the Trump campaign's possible "collusion" with Russia: "People under the cloud of investigation do not get to pick the judges who may preside over their cases. By this logic, President Trump should not be permitted to appoint a new Supreme Court justice until after the special counsel investigation is over, and we know for sure whether there is evidence of wrongdoing."[26]

Whatever its intuitive appeal, Berman's proposition had no legal basis and was almost laughable in light of recent history. In fact, a majority of the present Court had been appointed by a president who was then under investigation. Anthony Kennedy himself was appointed just a year after an independent counsel began investigating President Reagan's role in the Iran-Contra affair. President Clinton appointed Stephen Breyer eight months after Attorney General Janet Reno appointed a special prosecutor to investigate the Whitewater scandal. Both Roberts and Alito were appointed while the Bush administration was under investigation by a special counsel in the Valerie Plame affair. And the FBI's investigation of Trump was already underway when Neil Gorsuch was appointed.[27]

Other Democrats attempted to impose a "Garland rule." Still incensed that Senator Grassley had refused to hold hearings on Merrick Garland's nomination in 2016, they demanded that hearings on this nomination be delayed until after the midterm elections. "With so much at stake for the people of our country, the U.S. Senate must be consistent and consider the president's nominee once the new Congress is seated in January," Senator Dick Durbin said.[28]

Of course, while there were numerous precedents for not holding hearings in a presidential election year when the Senate was controlled by a party other than the president's—and even for an oppositional

Senate holding seats open for years to outlast a president—there was no such precedent regarding midterm elections, particularly when both the Senate and the White House were controlled by the same party.

One Supreme Court reporter expected liberals to try to defeat Kavanaugh's nomination as they had defeated Robert Bork's but cautioned, "Pulling off a sequel like that would seem to require all the plot twists, special effects and movie magic that Kavanaugh's antagonists can muster."[29]

That was precisely the model progressive activists had in mind.

■　　■　　■

Conservatives had been blindsided by the well-financed and well-organized political campaign against Robert Bork's nomination in 1987, but by the time of the Kavanaugh confirmation they had learned the techniques pioneered by the left and had invented a few of their own. Now that the Supreme Court seat that had been denied to Bork was open again, they were ready.

The Judicial Crisis Network—originally called the Judicial Confirmation Network—was established in 2005 to rectify the imbalance in confirmation battles that was revealed with Bork's nomination.[30] People for the American Way (PFAW) had dropped a hundred thousand dollars for cable TV spots, far more than the entire budget of the pro-Bork Coalitions for America.[31] While PFAW was buying thirty-thousand-dollar full-page ads in the *New York Times*, Concerned Women for America could afford only two ads in small newspapers at about four hundred dollars apiece. The heavily outgunned pro-Bork forces were limited to grassroots work, on the cheap, their leaders licking their own envelopes for mass mailings. The liberals, by contrast, were able to carpet-bomb the political battlefield through the major media.[32]

The one-sidedness of the fight was the result, in part, of a deliberate decision of the Reagan administration not to engage on the same terms. After Gregory Peck took to the airwaves to defame Judge Bork, both Clint Eastwood and Charlton Heston offered to appear in a counter-ad.

The White House turned them down. Bork's many former clerks working in the Department of Justice, lawyers who knew his record better than anybody, were explicitly forbidden to defend him publicly.[33] Such advocacy was considered unseemly.

Since the Bork disaster, the right had recognized that refusing to fight on the new terms would guarantee defeat, and the attacks on Clarence Thomas's nomination showed how savage those new terms could be. The Marquess of Queensberry Rules were out. A powerful media and surrogate campaign was the only way to combat the inevitable onslaught from the left.

The Judicial Crisis Network, agreeing with Kavanaugh about the importance of the first forty-eight hours, was ready on day one with a twelve-million-dollar war chest.[34] It had prepared videos and websites supporting each of the leading candidates before the nominee was announced. The paid advertising that the Reagan White House eschewed has become an important feature of judicial confirmations. It is a means of communicating with the average American, signaling strength to the politicians who will determine the nomination's fate, and grabbing headlines.

JCN immediately launched the website ConfirmKavanaugh.com and a 1.4-million-dollar ad campaign in the key states of Alabama, Indiana, North Dakota, and West Virginia. Complementing the advertising was a targeted grassroots outreach to key senators. But the most important work of JCN, which was the hub of expertise on judicial issues and the confirmation process, may have been shaping the message of the confirmation campaign by getting its own spokesmen on the air and by coordinating the many other conservative groups that cared deeply about the Court.

Activists from the Tea Party Patriots, the Susan B. Anthony List, Americans for Prosperity, and other groups were already going door to door talking about the importance of the upcoming 2018 elections. Senate elections had been a key part of their strategy since 2014, precisely because of judicial nominations. They wanted their field-workers to be able to add the Kavanaugh confirmation to their list of talking points and were grateful to have allies they could trust to vet the nominee's philosophy.

■   ■   ■

Although the initial effort to defeat Kavanaugh was vigorous, it flailed about in search of a message. On July 11, the *Washington Post* broke the news that he incurred credit card debt when purchasing group tickets for Washington Nationals baseball games.[35] This scandal, if you could call it that, was covered so assiduously that the left-wing news service ProPublica asked the public to help stalk Kavanaugh at sporting events: "Did you see Judge Kavanaugh at a game? Did you attend a game with him? Do you have any photos, and if so, will you send them our way?"[36] The *Yale Daily News* went so far as to report that as a college student, Kavanaugh didn't put toppings on his pizza and occasionally ate pasta with ketchup.[37]

The articles were widely mocked—the law professor and commentator Orin Kerr joked that Kavanaugh's taste in Italian food showed he was "no Scalia clone, clearly"—and Twitter users joked about other silly scandals, using the hashtag #KavanaughScandals: "He neglected to add the plus 4 zip codes on all his Christmas cards," "Didn't rewind a VHS before taking it back to Blockbuster," and "Sources say that Kavanaugh once failed to turn off his brights for an oncoming vehicle." The satirical news site The Onion ran an article headlined "Kavanaugh Nomination Falters after *Washington Post* Publishes Shocking Editorial Claiming He Forgot Daughter's Piano Recital."[38]

The organized opposition included a letter-writing campaign. But that hit a snag when it was revealed that twenty-one identical letters condemning Kavanaugh were published in twenty-one different newspapers, each under a different name without the knowledge of the purported signer. While no one claimed responsibility, the episode suggested that opposition to Kavanaugh was centrally coordinated rather than a popular groundswell.

The problem for the opposition was that Kavanaugh was a remarkably straight arrow in and out of the courtroom. His rulings were based on principle, whether they would help liberals or conservatives, as when he ruled in favor of the pro-abortion group Emily's List in its political speech battle with the Federal Election Commission.[39] Deputy Press Secretary Raj Shah was in charge of White House communications for the confirmation campaign. Within three days of the nomination, a war room was set up in the Eisenhower Executive Office Building staffed by former clerks, including Zina Bash, Claire Murray, and Chris Michel. Kerri Kupec was brought in as a spokeswoman from the Department of Justice. The office had eight computers, a wall of filing cabinets that were quickly filled with reams of court decisions, and a snack counter that was stocked on Monday and completely ransacked by the end of Friday.

The office's early work was mostly responding to spurious allegations—one participant called it playing "whack-a-mole." Geoff Bennett and Leigh Ann Caldwell of NBC tweeted that Justice Kennedy had negotiated his retirement with Trump to secure Kavanaugh's nomination. After calls for a congressional investigation, the reporters backed away from the story, but not before major media outlets were openly discussing it. Conspiracy theories cooked up on the political fringes—like the Center for American Progress's yarn about Kennedy's son and Deutsche Bank—made their way into the mainstream.[40]

The Trump presidency had been profoundly disorienting to the media and the Washington establishment. Many had not thought it possible for someone whose views were so different from theirs to win the presidency. By July 2018, a Supreme Court appointment was hardly necessary to fuel the media hysteria that had become a feature of American life—Trump was a Russian agent, Trump was a threat to NATO, Trump's confrontation with China over its unfair trade practices would plunge the United States into recession.

In such an atmosphere, it became popular to speculate that Kavanaugh was Trump's "get-out-of-jail-free card" because of a law review article in which he had written that presidents should not be encumbered by investigations while they were in office. Kavanaugh had served on the special counsel staff that investigated President Clinton, but in

2009, during the presidency of Barack Obama, he wrote, "This is not something I necessarily thought in the 1980s or 1990s. Like many Americans at that time, I believed that the President should be required to shoulder the same obligations that we all carry. But in retrospect, that seems a mistake."[41]

That month the feminist group UltraViolet attempted to link Kavanaugh to allegations of sexual harassment against Judge Alex Kozinski of the Ninth Circuit, for whom Kavanaugh had clerked more than a quarter-century earlier. Why hadn't the young Kavanaugh reported the sexual predations that had now, so many years later, come to light? UltraViolet's insinuations of complicity in sexual misconduct eventually evaporated when no one who worked in Kozinski's chambers with Kavanaugh—including a female intern—could remember seeing any inappropriate behavior.[42]

If charges of tolerance of sexual crimes would not stick, there was always racism, and an activist group called Demos was ready with a counterintuitive theory to convict Kavanaugh of that ugly offense: "Kavanaugh has also made it clear that he buys into the problematic trope that the Constitution should be 'colorblind'—a shorthand for the view that race-conscious efforts to remedy our long history of slavery, Jim Crow segregation, and state-sanctioned violence against people of color are themselves discriminatory."[43]

The denizens of the left-wing fever swamps took it from there. In a "Rise Up for Roe" speaking tour, which featured Chelsea Clinton, Alyssa Milano, and Planned Parenthood's Cecile Richards, the *Teen Vogue* columnist Lauren Duca fingered Kavanaugh for almost every mortal sin in the progressive catechism, telling an audience in Los Angeles, "This is a man that we know, from the way he has ruled in the past, that he wants to rule over this country with 'textualist originalist' mindset, which is a very safe way of saying, 'white supremacist patriarchy.'" Kavanaugh's nomination, she added, "marks the nativism, the ugliness, the lack of compassion for the marginalized, the authoritarianism, all of that that stains that on American life, like the cum stains that are probably all over my room at the Holiday Inn Express."[44]

The manic search for anything negative related to Kavanaugh included requests by major media organizations for records of 911 calls from his home. The press submitted public information requests to the town of Chevy Chase for any emails of Ashley Kavanaugh's that included, among others, the words "abortion," "gun," "gay," "liberal," and "Brett" and *all* of her email correspondence with her husband. It was a ridiculous request that violated personal privacy and had nothing to do with Kavanaugh's qualifications. It was also costly. The town had to hire lawyers to dig through emails, ultimately turning up nothing more than a few newsletters Ashley had forwarded to her husband for proofreading.

Kavanaugh's team of clerks was quickly disabused of the notion that the confirmation process would be dignified. The special-interest opposition was intense, the press coverage was crazy, and many Democrats would not even meet with him.

■   ■   ■

Laurence Tribe's *God Save This Honorable Court* had helped to change the philosophy of confirmations in the 1980s. In the early years of the George W. Bush administration there was a major change in their procedure, and Tribe had a role in that as well.

It had to do with the filibuster, which is what happens when a vote to end debate, called cloture, does not pass. The Senate cannot hold a final vote on a nomination without either unanimous consent or a vote for cloture. Under Senate rules, a senator does not actually have to keep talking, like Jimmy Stewart in *Mr. Smith Goes to Washington*, to keep a filibuster going. It's enough simply not to pass a cloture vote. Because sixty votes were needed for cloture, the minority party could block a majority-supported action without resorting to reading the phone book.

The filibuster had been part of the Senate's legislative process since the early nineteenth century. But the cloture rule as a means to end debate came about only in 1917 and did not apply to nominations until 1949; in theory, then, debate on a nomination could have gone on forever. The

Senate never took a cloture vote on a nominee until 1968, and no majority-supported nomination was defeated with a filibuster until 2003. Even Clarence Thomas, confirmed with only fifty-two votes and without support of the Senate Judiciary Committee, was not subjected to the sixty-vote threshold of a cloture vote. Filibustering judicial nominations simply wasn't done.

After Bush's election in 2000, the Senate Democratic leader, Tom Daschle, announced that his caucus would use "whatever means necessary" to defeat Bush's nominations.[45] When John Ashcroft, himself a former senator, was nominated to be attorney general, forty-two Democrats voted against him. Senator Chuck Schumer called it a "shot across the bow."[46] Daschle said he wanted to assemble enough votes to signal that a filibuster could have been waged, even though some who voted against Ashcroft nevertheless thought he deserved an up-or-down vote.

In April 2001, the Democrats held a retreat in Pennsylvania to discuss how to change the rules of the confirmation process to defeat Bush's judicial nominations. Tribe spoke at the retreat, along with Professor Cass R. Sunstein of the University of Chicago Law School and Marcia D. Greenberger, the co-president of the National Women's Law Center. They helped the Democrats come up with strategies for blocking qualified candidates who were not liberal, one of which was dramatically to change the use of the filibuster.[47]

The next month Bush made eleven nominations to appeals courts. They were never confirmed in that Congress. After the Democrats lost seats in the 2002 elections, they began forcing cloture votes, a tactic that some members were reluctant to pursue. Ten of Bush's nominees endured twenty-one filibusters in that Congress.

Miguel Estrada, nominated to the D.C. Circuit, was the most prominent victim of the new strategy. A leaked Democratic Senate strategy memorandum revealed that liberal groups had met with Senate Democrats in 2001 and identified Estrada as "especially dangerous because he has a minimal paper trail, he is Latino, and the White House seems to be grooming him for a Supreme Court appointment."[48] Democrats could not allow Republicans to put the first Hispanic on the

Supreme Court, so they filibustered Estrada seven times, eventually forcing him to withdraw.

Frustrated with the weaponization of Senate procedure, Republicans began talking about getting rid of the filibuster. But senatorial inertia took over when a bipartisan "Gang of Fourteen" senators brokered a deal to keep the filibuster option.[49]

They agreed to finally hold a vote on three of the filibustered judges—Janice Rogers Brown (D.C. Circuit), William Pryor (Eleventh Circuit), and Priscilla Owen (Fifth Circuit)—saving the filibuster for the remainder of that Congress for undefined "extraordinary circumstances."[50]

The nomination of Samuel Alito to the Supreme Court in November 2005 tested the strength of the Gang of Fourteen alliance. He was widely considered to be more reliably conservative than the unpredictable Sandra Day O'Connor, whom he would replace, and liberals were worried. The *New York Times* ran a story questioning whether Alito's father really was an immigrant from Italy, and genealogists were hired to investigate the conspiracy theory. (The Italian government eventually presented Alito with a copy of his father's birth certificate.) His nomination sparked a filibuster attempt by Democrats worried that the Court would shift to the right. Although twenty-five senators, including Joe Biden, Barack Obama, Hillary Clinton, and Ted Kennedy, voted against cloture, the Gang of Fourteen held firm in opposing the filibuster. While Alito was eventually confirmed by a vote of fifty-eight to forty-two, fourteen of his opponents nevertheless voted to let the nomination proceed to a floor vote.

A second nomination that tested the Gang of Fourteen's compromise was that of Brett Kavanaugh, President Bush's staff secretary, first nominated to the D.C. Circuit in July 2003. Democrats, incensed that a former Whitewater prosecutor and a close ally of a president they considered illegitimate might sit on the second-most important court in the land, stalled his nomination. After Bush re-nominated him in 2005, he submitted to a second hearing before the Senate Judiciary Committee, and the Gang of Fourteen met to discuss the nomination.

Senator Lindsey Graham reported that they couldn't find "extraordinary circumstances" to oppose him. All but two of the Gang of Fourteen voted for cloture, and Kavanaugh was confirmed by a margin of fifty-seven to thirty-six.

At the beginning of the 113th Congress in 2013, Democrats were eager to fill a number of vacancies on the D.C. Circuit. Republicans negotiated a temporary deal reducing the delays on votes for district court and sub-cabinet positions, and Senator Harry Reid, the majority leader, took full advantage of it, confirming forty-three judges and twenty-seven executive nominees. A few months later, however, to push through Obama's appointments to the D.C. Circuit, the Democratic majority abolished the filibuster altogether for nominations below the Supreme Court level. Pro-abortion activists were afraid that abolishing the filibuster for Supreme Court nominations would come back to haunt them under the next Republican president, so it was left in place.

More importantly, they changed the rules with a bare majority of Senate votes rather than the usual two-thirds majority—the so-called "nuclear option." Reid had maligned this method of changing the rules when Republicans were considering it during the Bush administration. The Gang of Fourteen had worried about opening the floodgates to rule changes with only fifty-one votes, and the Republicans had refrained.

After Reid and the Democrats exercised the "nuclear option," Senator McConnell, the minority leader, warned, "I say to my friends on the other side of the aisle, you'll regret this. And you may regret it a lot sooner than you think."[51] Only a year later, Republicans took back the Senate. Some members wanted to bring back the filibuster, but McConnell persuaded them not to. Limiting their own majority's influence in that way, given the certainty that the Democrats would eliminate the filibuster again when they regained a majority, would be political malpractice. And those who were squeamish about eliminating the filibuster had to acknowledge that the effect of the rule change had been to return the Senate to the way it had operated prior to 2003, when filibusters were generally regarded as off the table for judicial nominations.

It only got worse for the Democrats when Trump shocked Washington by winning the 2016 election. Moving through the classic stages of grief, Democrats hovered between denial and anger. A "resistance" formed, rioting in the streets, pressing electors to change their votes, and concocting conspiracy theories about Trump and the Russians.

The "resistance" spilled over into the Senate, where Democrats delayed every cabinet nomination. Even without a filibuster, the cloture process became a way to use up the currency of the Senate: floor time. In the six administrations before Trump's, the majority leader had to file cloture to advance a nomination in the first two years of a presidency only twenty-four times combined. In Trump's first two years, McConnell had to file cloture 128 times.

■   ■   ■

The nomination of Neil Gorsuch, submitted eleven days after Trump's inauguration, went more smoothly than most Senate Republicans had expected. The new administration was still finding its way, dealing with incessant leaks, strong resistance within its own party, and the delayed confirmation of key staff members. The Democrats attempted to misconstrue Gorsuch's record, most famously seizing on the "frozen trucker" case, in which Gorsuch had ruled that a trucker fired for leaving his disabled trailer to seek shelter from the cold was not entitled to reinstatement. Calling him heartless for asking not whether the employer's decision was wise or kind but whether it was legal, Democrats pilloried him for stating that it was Congress's job to change the law, not the courts'. They also charged that he had plagiarized part of his dissertation and had posed misogynistic questions in a legal ethics course. But when the author he had quoted defended his use of her work and his former students pointed out that his discussion questions were taken from the teachers' manual, those attacks faded away.

His nomination hit only two real snags. First, in a conversation with Senator Richard Blumenthal, he was asked about the president's tweets criticizing a judge who had ruled against him. Gorsuch expressed solidarity with his fellow judge without criticizing the president. Blumenthal mischaracterized his statement as being critical of Trump. The president was deeply concerned, but McGahn had been in the room and knew that Blumenthal's description was inaccurate. He pleaded with the president to withhold judgment for twenty-four hours, and in that time was able to get things back on track.

The second serious challenge Gorsuch faced was the filibuster. Even the left-leaning American Bar Association rated him well qualified; he was well regarded by his peers and he had emerged from his hearings unscathed. Yet he still couldn't get sixty votes for cloture from the bitterly divided Senate. Egged on by a resistance still outraged by Trump's election, the Democrats mustered forty-five votes to filibuster Gorsuch, the first time in history a partisan filibuster had been used to block a Supreme Court nominee with majority support.

The Republicans couldn't believe their luck. By filibustering Gorsuch, the Democrats had overplayed their hand. Republicans knew that they could never confirm the kind of judges on Trump's list with a filibuster in place. McConnell could now tell his members that if a Republican-nominated justice as exceptional as Gorsuch couldn't get sixty votes, nobody could. And it was untenable to leave a Supreme Court seat open indefinitely because of Democratic intransigence. McConnell reminded his colleagues that filibustering a nominee was itself a recent innovation and that removing the filibuster for Supreme Court justices would simply finish the job the Democrats had started in 2013. Besides, if Democrats regained control of the Senate, wouldn't they end the Supreme Court filibuster without a second thought to get their own nominee confirmed? So with the bare majority of fifty-one votes required to change the Senate rules, the filibuster was eliminated.

Getting the votes to eliminate the filibuster wasn't easy. Many moderate senators, including former members of the Gang of Fourteen, wanted to keep it, as did many conservatives led in the Senate by Mike Lee and outside by Heritage alums Ed Corrigan and James Wallner. Even though McConnell suspected early on that the filibuster would have to be eliminated to get Gorsuch on the Court, he never said so. He simply told reporters that he was confident Gorsuch would be confirmed. Had he talked about the filibuster before Democrats had shown themselves to be unwilling to confirm a nominee like Gorsuch, his own moderate senators might have dug in. Waiting to discuss the question also enabled Republicans to see how hard McConnell was fighting to get to sixty votes in the traditional way.

Gorsuch was confirmed on April 7, 2017. Despite the bloodless filibuster mounted by Democrats, the drama had been kept to a minimum— no mean feat, considering the turmoil that engulfed the Trump White House in that first year. The success of the Gorsuch nomination, hailed as one of the administration's most impressive victories, laid the groundwork for the initial success of Kavanaugh's confirmation battle.

Senator Schumer's decision to filibuster Gorsuch is now widely recognized as a serious political miscalculation, as it allowed Republicans to eliminate the filibuster with a minimum of effort. Still, the pressure from the Democratic base to put up a strong show of resistance was overwhelming. Bill Scher made the case for the filibuster in *Politico*: "No matter what Democrats do, Gorsuch is almost sure to get confirmed. But how Democrats lose is important. They need to keep their base energized. They need to protect vulnerable senators. They need [to] maintain party unity."[52]

As later events would show, it would have been wiser to save the move for the second Supreme Court nomination, when it almost certainly would have succeeded. Not having to obtain a filibuster-proof majority was essential if Kavanaugh was to have any hope of confirmation.

CHAPTER FOUR

Mootings, Meetings, and Mobs

Fifty-four votes.

On their way to the first round of meetings with senators, Don McGahn told Kavanaugh that it didn't matter if he was the best person or most beloved judge ever—he probably wasn't going to get more than fifty-four votes. When McGahn administered the same reality check to Gorsuch a year earlier, the nominee was taken aback. He had hoped for the backing of as many as seventy-five senators. (In the end, only fifty-four supported him.) Kavanaugh, on the other hand, had already been through one heavily politicized Senate confirmation, and he was keeping his expectations in check.

Kavanaugh's White House experience made him more realistic about the political process than many other nominees. Partisan votes were part of the ugliness of American politics, but the political environment at the time of his nomination was particularly challenging. Almost any Democrat who voted for him could expect that if a Justice Kavanaugh later angered the Democratic base in an important case, he might well face a primary challenge from the left and lose his Senate seat.

The ceiling for votes may have been fifty-four—all the Republican senators plus three vulnerable moderate Democrats—but the confirmation team also understood that their floor was below fifty. Republicans Lisa Murkowski and Susan Collins were targeted not only by Kavanaugh's team but by progressives.

Getting those votes lined up began right away with one-on-one meetings with as many senators as possible. Kavanaugh's first meetings were with Grassley and McConnell the morning after the White House announcement. He and Ashley had stayed up talking until five in the morning, leaving him slightly punchy. He could easily talk at length under normal circumstances, but the lack of sleep made him especially wordy. When they left the meeting with Grassley, McGahn teased him, saying he could tighten up his answers for subsequent meetings. "They don't need to hear all that," he advised.

Each meeting was different. Senator Lindsey Graham offered advice, explained the process, and tested him on tough questions he might face during his hearings. Senator Ted Cruz acted out the antics he felt Kavanaugh should be prepared for from Democrats, at one point shouting "Treason!" in a booming theatrical voice so loud it echoed down the hallway. A two-hour meeting with Senator Mike Lee about Kavanaugh's approach to originalism provided a preview of Lee's questions in the hearings. These meetings with friendly senators allowed him to address concerns that might be raised in his hearings and to learn about the particular legal interests of the people whose votes he had to earn.

Kavanaugh would have to address Senator Rand Paul's concern that he was too deferential to the government in Fourth Amendment cases, which deal with the question of unreasonable searches and seizures. Concurring in 2015 with an opinion of his court that affirmed the National Security Agency's right to collect telephone metadata without a warrant, Kavanaugh wrote that the collection of such data is a "critical national security need" that is "entirely consistent with the Fourth Amendment" and outweighs privacy concerns. Now he attempted to show Senator Paul that he had not ruled for the government in every Fourth Amendment case. In fact, he had developed the constitutional rationale that Justice Scalia adopted in *United States v. Jones* rejecting the use of GPS tracking by the police.[1] Kavanaugh also emphasized his work on the separation of powers, which dovetailed nicely with Paul's concerns on the overgrowth of a constitutionally suspect regulatory state. Paul was not entirely convinced on the Fourth Amendment question, but he recognized that Kavanaugh was on the whole a good pick. He had his vote.

Early in the process, Kavanaugh's team was not worried about Senator Jeff Flake, but he was one of a few senators, along with his fellow Arizonan John McCain and Robert Corker of Tennessee, whom the White House was worried about because of their antipathy to President Trump. Corker addressed the question head-on, asking why he should reject a good Supreme Court nominee just because he didn't like the president. He viewed Kavanaugh's qualifications and his own feelings about Trump as unconnected.

The meeting with Flake went well and offered Kavanaugh a preview of the questions Flake would ask at the hearings about Trump's use of executive power. But unlike most of his Republican colleagues, Flake declined to meet with the press immediately after their visit. Favorable comments from Republican senators before or after their meetings with the nominee were an important part of the public relations effort, but Flake's office would not play along, to the annoyance of the White House. Jon Kyl, Flake's immediate predecessor in his Senate seat, elegantly solved the problem. Acting as Kavanaugh's guide—the D.C. slang for the role is "sherpa," after the Himalayan natives who help climbers scale Mount Everest—he attended many of the senatorial meetings alongside the prospective justice. As Kavanaugh's team left the meeting with Flake, members of the press were gathered outside. Kyl walked right up to them to tell them what a productive meeting Kavanaugh had had with the senator. Not to be outdone in front of the cameras, Flake came out of his office and joined the gaggle as well.

Senator Rob Portman of Ohio not only met with Kavanaugh but also gave him advice. The two men had worked together when Portman was the U.S. trade representative in the Bush administration. Portman acted as another ear to the ground in the Senate, helping Kavanaugh think about how to handle certain meetings and how to manage the hearings. In a sea of loud-mouth senators, Portman and Kyl were among the most effective, quietly and effectively lobbying their colleagues and addressing their concerns.

The most important meeting would be with Susan Collins. The White House had solicited her opinion about whom to nominate, and both sides had targeted her as soon as Justice Kennedy announced his retirement. Progressive groups started a full-court press on June 29, before Kavanaugh's nomination, sending hangers—supposedly the implement of choice in the days of illegal abortion—to her offices in Washington and Maine as a sign of their vigilance in defense of *Roe v. Wade*. At the rally outside the Supreme Court the night of Kavanaugh's nomination, protesters warned, "Susan Collins, we are watching you!" It was the wrong approach to take with Collins, who bristles at bullying and who is known for her even-tempered, thoughtful, and reasonable approach to contentious issues.

She had prepared meticulously for her meeting with Judge Merrick Garland in 2016, even as her Republican colleagues made sure his nomination went nowhere, and she did the same now. By far the most prepared of all the senators for her meeting with the nominee, Collins posed detailed questions about his opinions, right down to the footnotes.

Not a member of the Judiciary Committee, Collins did not have staff dedicated to judicial nominations. Her able judiciary aide, Katie Brown, also handled civil rights, education, and a host of other issues. Knowing she would need outside assistance, Collins brought in three accomplished attorneys who had previously worked for her and fifteen attorneys from the non-partisan Congressional Research Service to assist her staff in reading through Kavanaugh's hundreds of opinions, law review articles, and speeches. The team prepared summaries organized by topic in binders with supporting documents. Poring over these materials, Collins requested additional analysis, discovering that Kavanaugh and Garland voted the same way in 93 percent of the cases that they heard together.

In fact, Garland dissented only once from a majority opinion authored by Kavanaugh.

In a discussion with a prominent attorney concerned about Kavanaugh's dissent in an abortion rights case, Collins, who had read his footnotes, realized that she understood Kavanaugh's work better than many of his critics. She might not agree with all of his decisions, but she wanted to ensure he had a proper respect for precedent and that he was in the mainstream of legal thought.

Kavanaugh knew that Senator Collins's vote was decisive, and he prepared as if it were the final exam of his life. The meeting had run two hours and fifteen minutes when a bell rang announcing a vote. The longest-serving current member of the Senate never to have missed a roll-call vote, Collins was constrained to end the meeting. The judge offered to meet with her again, to the dismay of his attendants, who were relieved to have that meeting behind them. They arranged a follow-up phone call for after the hearing. Kavanaugh's team sensed he had done well. He had. The senator was coming to the conclusion that he was incredibly intelligent and thoughtful, had been misrepresented by his critics, and would be an extraordinary justice.

After the meeting, she reported that Kavanaugh had told her he agreed with Chief Justice Roberts that *Roe v. Wade* was "settled law." Dismayed social conservatives wondered why he would say that about the controversial decision. Yet the judge had been careful to say nothing in private meetings that would contradict what he said to other senators or that he couldn't say at his public hearings. He had told Senator Collins that he agreed with Chief Justice Roberts's comments in his own confirmation hearings, but the Delphic formulation "settled law" had tipped neither Roberts's hand nor Kavanaugh's. After all, no jurist believes that *stare decisis* requires every prior decision to be left in place. In striking down racial segregation[2] and anti-sodomy laws,[3] the Court overturned precedent, just as it did when it overturned campaign finance regulations[4] and blocked unions from forcing non-members to pay dues.[5] Acknowledging that a case is "settled law" is merely descriptive and doesn't indicate whether a judge would overturn it if given the opportunity.

On the second day of John Roberts's hearings in 2005, the chairman of the Senate Judiciary Committee, Arlen Specter, had grilled him on whether he would overturn *Roe v. Wade*. Roberts responded that he would follow the precedent of previous nominees and not discuss particular cases, adding that previous decisions should be overturned only on the basis of the law, not mere disagreement with the outcome. Still, he showed high deference to prior legal decisions:

> I do think that it is a jolt to the legal system when you overrule a precedent. Precedent plays an important role in promoting stability and evenhandedness. It is not enough—and the Court has emphasized this on several occasions—it is not enough that you may think the prior decision was wrongly decided. That really doesn't answer the question. It just poses the question. And you do look at these other factors, like settled expectations, like the legitimacy of the Court, like whether a particular precedent is workable or not, whether a precedent has been eroded by subsequent developments. All of those factors go into the determination of whether to revisit a precedent under the principles of *stare decisis*.

Roberts also said that a judge must not say whether he will or will not overrule a given decision.

Kavanaugh's meeting with Senator Tim Scott of South Carolina, the only black Republican in the Senate, focused on race. Immediately before they met, Scott had voiced a dramatic last-minute objection to the appointment of Ryan Bounds to a federal appeals court because of racially insensitive writings from college. Knowing the senator's concern, Kavanaugh told Scott about his law review note—a capstone article that each student member of a law review gets to publish on a topic of his choice—on eliminating racial discrimination in jury selections. He explained that his concern about racial inequality stemmed from his mother's work in inner-city schools. Scott was favorably impressed with how much time he had devoted to the issue.

While Kavanaugh met with senators, the Center for Popular Democracy, having brought some six hundred protesters to Washington, staged a demonstration in and around the Capitol. On August 1, following the group's rally, seventy-four protesters were arrested when they tried to block the Senate hallways to prevent the meetings with Kavanaugh from taking place.[6]

■   ■   ■

After weeks of refusing to speak with Kavanaugh, the Democratic leadership relented, agreeing on August 3 to meet with him later in the month, in the last two and a half weeks before the hearings. The minority leader, Chuck Schumer, and the ranking Democrat on the Judiciary Committee, Dianne Feinstein, had imposed the boycott to force the release of not only all the papers Kavanaugh had seen while serving in the Bush administration but every one of the millions of documents produced by the Bush White House while he served as staff secretary. By contrast, Mitch McConnell had met with Elena Kagan on her first day on Capitol Hill, two days after she was nominated, before her paperwork had even been processed.

Senator Joe Manchin, who was running for reelection in Trump-friendly West Virginia, had already broken the Democratic boycott, meeting with Kavanaugh on July 30. After a chat about sports and their shared background in Catholic schools, Manchin wanted to talk about Obamacare. When Kavanaugh, predictably, declined to go into specifics, they instead discussed his approach to "severability," a sometimes-arcane concept that figured in several legal challenges to Obamacare. Kavanaugh was also able to go over his record with Manchin, rebutting the misguided charge that he always favored corporate interests. His rulings in favor of both workers and corporations attested to his fidelity to the principle that the law, not a judge's policy preferences, should determine his decisions. Immediately after their meeting, Manchin went to see Schumer in person, which the White House viewed as an excellent sign that he planned to break with his partisans and vote for Kavanaugh. Good news can be shared over the phone, but bad news has to be shared in person, they surmised.

Claire McCaskill of Missouri, also on the short list of Democrats who were in play, told Kavanaugh that while everybody expressed confidence she'd do the right thing politically, she wished someone would tell her what the right thing was. She was in a difficult reelection battle in a state that Trump had carried by an eighteen-point margin.[7] But she had voted against Gorsuch and was prepared to vote against Kavanaugh, citing her objections to the *Citizens United* decision. Kavanaugh, an equal-opportunity supporter of the First Amendment, had anticipated the Supreme Court's reasoning in *Citizens United* in his own opinion in *Emily's List v. Federal Election Commission*, ruling that the abortion advocacy group had a right to raise and spend money to promote the candidates or policies of its choice.[8] McCaskill was open about her growing unease with the Senate, finding it an unpleasant place to work in part because of the decline of centrists. She attributed this polarization to the flood of special-interest money into campaign coffers. Indeed, her own campaign had received $1.6 million from Emily's List alone, including over half a million dollars in that very cycle.[9]

A meeting with Senator Sheldon Whitehouse of Rhode Island was unproductive, but Feinstein couldn't have been friendlier. Meetings with Cory Booker of New Jersey, Kamala Harris of California, and Amy Klobuchar of Minnesota went well. All allowed the judge to preview some of the issues they would address during the hearings, ranging from race to antitrust law. Still, these meetings were very different from those with Republicans. Cory Booker, appearing at a press conference with other potential presidential candidates, had depicted Kavanaugh's confirmation as a question of good versus evil. There were no bystanders, he said, descending into the most offensive hyperbole: "You are either complicit in the evil, you are either contributing to the wrong, or you are fighting against it."[10]

Kyl was occasionally unable to attend Kavanaugh's meetings with senators, but McGahn was in every one, an irenic presence amid the partisan tension. He knew most senators from campaigns he'd helped them with or from seeking their advice on judicial nominations.

"Of all the White House Counsels going back to 1981, I don't think there's been one that made judicial selection a more central part of his daily business than Don McGahn," observes Leonard Leo. "And there certainly has not been one who engaged in more direct shuttle diplomacy with Capitol Hill on behalf of individual nominees. Don knew the transformation of the federal judiciary was a top priority of President Trump's, and he got right down to business."

McGahn was also savvy about dangerous situations. On a heavily scheduled August day, the team got split up in the underground tunnels of the Senate office buildings on the way to a meeting with Patrick Leahy of Vermont, who had already denounced the nomination in a column in the *New York Times*.[11] Kyl and McGahn arrived at Leahy's office to find Kavanaugh already there with the harrumphing seventy-eight-year-old senator. Leahy announced that he wanted to meet with Kavanaugh alone. Kyl got up to leave despite the team's firm policy of no one-on-one meetings with hostile senators, but McGahn protested. After Senator Blumenthal's twisting of Neil Gorsuch's words from their pre-confirmation meeting, he did not want the same thing to happen to Kavanaugh. He had no option but to leave, but he was thankful nothing bad came out of the private meeting.

■   ■   ■

Arranging personal visits with the men and women who would vote on Kavanaugh was the easy part of the confirmation effort. His background in the Whitewater investigation and his tenure in the White House, especially as staff secretary, however, produced an enormous logistical challenge. Before Kavanaugh's nomination, McConnell had fretted about the staggering amount of paperwork senators would have to sift through to evaluate him. His legal opinions, emails and memos, and the papers that simply crossed his desk in the White House might amount to some seven million pages.

Kavanaugh's paper trail was vastly larger than any previous nominee's, and paperwork had been a point of contention in previous confirmation fights. In fact, William Rehnquist's nomination as chief justice hit a major speed bump when President Reagan refused to release to the Senate just a few sensitive documents Rehnquist had written fifteen years earlier. There were about 70,000 pages relating to John Roberts's time in the Justice Department and the Reagan White House and about 182,000 pages for Gorsuch. Elena Kagan was trailed by 173,000 pages from the Clinton White House. At the time of her hearings in 2010, many observers weren't sure that her documents could be handled in such a short period. In fact, the Obama White House had the same concern and had begun requesting her documents from archivists before she had been officially nominated.

Kagan had no experience as a judge, and her published writings were not extensive. In fact, she had barely any litigation experience before becoming the U.S. solicitor general, so documents from that phase of her career were considered particularly revealing of her thinking. At the same time, since the papers reflected the deliberative discussions between the government and its attorney, they could not be handed over indiscriminately. So while the bipartisan agreement about which documents to request included records from her time at the Clinton White House, the Senate did not even request documents from her time as solicitor general.

White House documents requested by the Judiciary Committee for Kagan's confirmation had to go through two presidential reviews. After they were located and pulled, they were analyzed to determine whether there might be legal restrictions on their publication. They were then subject to claims of executive privilege by former President Clinton as well as by President Obama, since some of the documents might involve ongoing national security or other concerns. The paperwork battle heated up, with some Republicans threatening to boycott the hearings if they didn't get Kagan's papers before they started. In the end, most of the documents were released by the deadline, a few thousand of them marked "committee confidential," which meant only the committee could review them.

This was the same process followed for Kavanaugh. By 2018 the Senate was moving toward greater transparency in its document releases. Chairman Grassley in particular was known as the Senate's "chief transparency officer." While he and his staff had worried about the number of documents Kavanaugh's nomination would produce, once he was chosen, they set about getting the work done.

The documents from Kavanaugh's time on the independent counsel investigation of President Clinton were the first to be produced. Scholars and journalists had already scrutinized them, and they showed Kavanaugh to have been by and large a voice of restraint in the investigation. According to Stephen Bates, the associate independent counsel who helped draft the Starr Report, Kavanaugh had urged the independent counsel "to excise the factual summary from the report, on the ground that it was excessively explicit." Bates also reveals that Kavanaugh drafted a letter for Kenneth Starr's signature urging the House not to release the report to the public, although "after hearing the arguments on both sides, Ken decided against sending the letter."[12]

Grassley's staff sought Senator Feinstein's help in narrowing the scope of the request for documents, especially those from his time as staff secretary. "A review of all the paperwork that circulated through Kavanaugh's office when he was staff secretary would pretty much amount to a review of all the paperwork that circulated through the White House in those years, and yet would also reveal essentially nothing about Kavanaugh. It would mostly amount to a monumental waste of the Senate's time," wrote Yuval Levin, a domestic policy adviser in the Bush White House.[13]

Staff secretary is not a legal position. A law degree is not a requirement, though it is commonly held by lawyers. The documents from that office would involve trivial matters such as whether flags should be flying at half-staff, menus, and Arbor Day speeches, as well as sensitive national security matters.

One reason Kavanaugh had so many more documents to review than everybody else was that his tenure as staff secretary corresponded with the advent of email and the convenience of Blackberry phones.

Water-cooler conversations about where to grab lunch were now handled in texts and emails that became historical records. Documents from the White House counsel's office had to be turned over even though they often included legal advice, since such documents had been submitted for Kagan's confirmation.

In any case, chasing down millions of White House documents was an almost pointless exercise considering that the senators—indeed, anyone with an internet connection—had ready access to the most important evidence of Kavanaugh's thinking: his judicial record. In twelve years on the D.C. Circuit, Kavanaugh had authored 307 opinions and joined hundreds more. And the judicial questionnaire he answered for the Senate Judiciary Committee was the most extensive in history, stretching to 6,168 pages.[14] By contrast, Kagan had no judicial opinions to her name, and John Roberts had fifty-two.[15] Gorsuch, whose tenure on the bench was of a length comparable to Kavanaugh's, had 240.[16]

Grassley spent weeks trying to work with Democrats on the process for handling Kavanaugh's unwieldy paperwork, even though many of them had announced their opposition to the nominee from the beginning. He proposed making use of the electronic nature of the documents to allow keyword searches, but after Democrats refused to discuss reasonable ways to pare down the universe of documents, Republicans abandoned the keyword negotiations, convinced that Democrats were simply on a "government-funded fishing expedition."[17]

Democratic recalcitrance ended up saving the nomination. Had they requested a large but defensible set of documents, the hearings could have been delayed for months. In fact, Feinstein had brokered such an agreement with Grassley, only to have her staff, with whom she was frequently at odds, back away from it. She was both more moderate politically than her staff and less inclined to blow up bridges with senators with whom she had long-standing relationships. Receiving no reasonable proposal from the Democrats, Grassley ended up requesting a manageable set of documents on his own. His obvious efforts to work with Feinstein had impressed Collins and Murkowski, who found Democratic obstruction outrageous.

The Senate Judiciary Committee decided to hire an "e-discovery firm," marking the first time such techniques would be used in a Supreme Court confirmation process. The contractor they had in mind was already handling e-discovery for the Bush Presidential Library as it vetted Kavanaugh-related papers for release, so it could seamlessly share those documents with the Judiciary Committee. After committee Republicans got Senate approval for the contract, they notified the Democrats, and the company suddenly pulled out of the deal. The committee contracted with the e-discovery firm Relativity instead, this time opting not to let Democrats know beforehand.

Bill Burck, a former special counsel and deputy counsel to President George W. Bush, was Bush's designated representative to review his records under the Presidential Records Act. Grassley's team was on the phone with him several times a day. As soon as Burck and his team cleared each tranche of documents, they would be released. Documents were released on a rolling basis, whether they arrived at two a.m. on a Saturday or in the middle of the week.

Grassley put together a team of dozens to go through the documents. Working out of a windowless, rat-infested, cinder-block suite in the basement of the Dirksen Senate Office Building that they called "the dungeon," the team of attorneys and law clerks pored over the paperwork. They looked for anything politically sensitive, and categorized them according to topic areas, such as detention, guns, abortion, executive power, and torture.

The staff were extremely proud of the innovative way they handled the paperwork, rapidly navigating arcane Senate contracting procedures and securing the manpower necessary to get through the many documents. But the Republicans' focus on the mundane topic of document retrieval was also strategic. The goal, says Garrett Ventry, a communications strategist hired by the Judiciary Committee, was to "make it really, really boring, where the public wouldn't care and their base would be deflated because they were fighting us over whether or not they had documents to review." Fighting about documents meant they were not talking about *Roe v. Wade* or Judge Alex Kozinski.

Chuck Schumer unwittingly helped Grassley's office keep the focus on documents when he held a press conference on July 31. Joined by his Senate colleagues Dick Durbin and Dianne Feinstein and by assorted leaders of left-wing activist groups, he posed with a small pile of empty boxes labeled "missing records" and said he'd like to see them filled with Kavanaugh's papers from his time as staff secretary. "I want to make clear, for just a sec, how aggressive the obstruction is," he said.[18]

A few days later, Republicans on the Senate Judiciary Committee posed with a striking backdrop of 167 boxes representing the hundreds of thousands of pages that were being made available to the committee. In fact, they had been provided in digital form, which allowed for even easier searching and review.[19] "If you were to stack up all these pages, it would be taller than the Big Ben, taller than the Statue of Liberty, taller than the Capitol dome, and taller than the Taj Mahal," noted Senator Thom Tillis of North Carolina. "I think it's more than enough for the Democrats to make a rational decision about supporting Judge Kavanaugh."

Grassley reminded the press that Democrats were already on record opposing the judge, suggesting that their document requests were more about delaying the nomination than learning about the nominee.

The media's focus on transparency and the thorough nature of the document review reflected the Judiciary Committee's diligence in dropping a press release every time a new batch of documents was made available. New subject lines continually appeared in reporters' inboxes: "New Batch of Kavanaugh Records Becomes Public," "Committee Releases Third Batch of Kavanaugh Records," "Committee Receives New Production of Kavanaugh Records," "Committee Releases Additional Kavanaugh Records," "Historic Transparency: Volume of Kavanaugh's Public Exec Branch Material Tops Levels of Past SCOTUS Nominees."

Continuing to play into the Republicans' hands, Schumer on August 20 called on Grassley to allow all senators to see the "committee confidential" documents, a label he called "bogus."[20] Grassley responded with a tweet reminding Schumer that even the confidential documents were already available to all senators "any day (& nite) incl wknds" and asking if Schumer's request meant that he was backing away from his "pre-determined" vote against Kavanaugh.[21]

■   ■   ■

By the time the hearings came around, conservatives and other interest groups were fully on board with Kavanaugh. The Office of Public Liaison's Justin Clark had produced sophisticated messaging tailored for farmers, business groups, gun-rights groups, and social conservatives. Kavanaugh's record had something to please every interest group. Even the social conservatives' initial preference for Amy Barrett now served the purpose of making Kavanaugh look more moderate.

To prepare for the hearings, the White House team ran Kavanaugh through several "moots," or mock hearings, similar to a lawyer's preparation for oral arguments. The Department of Justice had given him binders covering various topics, including major Supreme Court cases and his own opinions. His meetings with senators were interspersed with initial preparation sessions, avoiding excessive cramming just before the hearings and contributing to his conversations with the lawmakers. It still made for long days, but when the team asked if he wanted a break to eat, perhaps hoping for a snack themselves, he would generally decline, preferring to push through.

In the full-blown moots that followed, the team, taking on the roles of senators, peppered him with questions about his cases and hot-button issues. Actual senators participated in one moot, but the questioners were usually administration staff, academics, or former Kavanaugh clerks. His more liberal clerks were particularly helpful in anticipating how senators from across the political spectrum—including the all-important Susan Collins—would view his responses. Some non-lawyers were invited to see how his answers would play with the public watching at home. They even prepared for protesters by having younger White House staffers sit in on the moots and spontaneously erupt with rage. Ashley and the girls left for a friend's house on Martha's Vineyard to escape the stress and the stalking press in D.C and to allow Kavanaugh to focus on his preparation.

The hearings were scheduled to begin the day after Labor Day, Tuesday, September 4, and to continue through Friday, a duration that was typical of recent Supreme Court confirmation hearings. But little else about Kavanaugh's hearings would be typical. Apparently worried that his path to confirmation was secure, the Democrats considered staging a mass walkout or not showing up.[22] Fearing that such an action might backfire, however, they came up with a different plan: disruption.

On Tuesday, the hearing room in the Dirksen Senate Office Building was packed as senators arrived. Dozens of photographers positioned themselves in the pit between the dais where the senators sat and the table from which Kavanaugh would face them. All the seats for visitors and the press were filled. The atmosphere was tense. Women in red robes and white bonnets lined the walkways from the elevators to the hearing room, their costumes intended to evoke *The Handmaid's Tale*, the dystopian novel and television series about women being forced to bear children. On the other floors, groups from the NAACP and NARAL wore shirts of various colors and lined the walkways, forming a rainbow of protesters. One man was dressed as a giant condom.

Kavanaugh walked in with his two daughters and wife, greeting each senator individually. Light chatter and the loud shutters of cameras filled the room. Senator Grassley shook hands with Senator Feinstein, seated to his left, and chatted with her briefly. Then he slowly gaveled the room to order: "Good morning, I welcome everyone to this confirmation hearing on the nomination—"[23]

"Mr. Chairman! Mr. Chairman!" interrupted Senator Kamala Harris. "Mr. Chairman, I'd like to be recognized for a question before we proceed!" She said there had not been enough time to review the documents. A large tranche of forty-two thousand new documents had been released just the day before.

"You're out of order. I'll proceed. I extend a very warm welcome to Judge Kavanaugh, to his wife, Ashley, their two daughters—"

Each time Grassley opened his mouth, a new objection was raised.

"Mr. Chairman, I agree with my colleague Senator Harris," said Senator Mazie Hirono of Hawaii, calling for a postponement of the hearing.

"Mr. Chairman, if we cannot be recognized, I move to adjourn," said Senator Blumenthal as protesters erupted in cheers. He called the hearing a charade and mockery, as organized protesters shouted that it was a "travesty of justice."

Protesters shrieked and were arrested, a pattern that would continue throughout the hearings. Several of the seats made available to the public by senators were continually filled with new protesters, who were arrested after outbursts.

Senator Booker also began complaining about documents, as Grassley calmly told him he was out of order. "What is the rush? What are we trying to hide?" Booker asked. More protesters cheered him on. "I appeal to be recognized on your sense of decency and integrity," Booker said, alluding to Grassley's well-known gravitas and fairness. Hirono interrupted Booker's interruption.

"You spoke about my decency and integrity, and I think you're taking advantage of my decency and integrity," replied Grassley.

On and on it went. Senator Tillis cited an NBC News report that the disruptions were a "coordinated effort by Senate Dems on the Judiciary Committee, and that it was discussed during the holiday weekend on a call organized by Schumer," casting suspicion on the spontaneity of the protests.[24] Schumer was unusually involved in the process, not trusting Feinstein to handle the political machinations he felt were needed. Senator Christopher Coons, a Democrat from Delaware, later told *Politico*, "It was important that we lay down a marker that this is not a normal hearing." Senator Durbin said they wanted to "singl[e] out the hearing as something unusual."[25] They succeeded.

Appalled by the spectacle, Senator John Cornyn of Texas decried the "mob rule" that was marring the hearings and added that it was "hard to take [the objections] seriously when every single one of our colleagues in the Senate Judiciary Committee on the Democratic side have announced their opposition to this nominee even before today's hearing."[26] Technically, Coons had not announced his opposition yet, but the point stood.

It took nearly an hour and a half, with dozens of interruptions, for Grassley to get through his ten-minute opening statement. Feinstein followed with hers, declaring that the confirmation battle was about abortion. She went on to list a few other issues, such as gun rights, attributing the anxiety of so many to the "pivotal" character of the seat Kavanaugh would fill. "Behind the noise," she said, "is really a sincere belief that it is so important to keep in this country, which is multi-ethnic, multi-religious, multi-economic, a court that really serves the people and serves this great democracy." Grassley's hard-charging judicial aide Mike Davis leaned over to Feinstein's chief of staff, Jennifer Duck, and asked if her boss approved of the protesters' behavior. He was told she did, but the senator known for her collegiality looked mortified.

The interruptions angered the Republicans, and many Democrats appeared uncomfortable as well. Leahy lashed out after one protester on his own side interrupted him. Durbin acknowledged that such protests must be difficult for Kavanaugh's children to witness, but called them "the noise of democracy."

Senator Mike Lee pointed out that such anxiety over any single nominee reveals what is wrong with the courts and offered a brief lesson on the history of Supreme Court confirmation hearings. Justice Louis Brandeis was the first Supreme Court nominee to have a public hearing, in 1916. While Brandeis was opposed for being Jewish, he was also opposed for his progressive views and his history of basing decisions not on the law but on the social sciences.

Brandeis himself didn't even attend his own hearing. It was not until 1939 that a nominee, Felix Frankfurter, would appear in person at a confirmation hearing. Senators were again concerned about the nominee's politics—specifically, Frankfurter's defense of the violent anarchists Sacco and Vanzetti in Massachusetts.

Lee reviewed various hearings, noting that senators were always trying to get judges to talk about specific cases, while nominees always refused on the grounds that they could not comment on an issue that might come before them on the Court. He brought up Justice Scalia's refusal even to say whether the foundational decision establishing judicial review, *Marbury v. Madison*, was settled law, for which he was roundly derided.[27] Yet, Lee noted, in the previous term the Supreme Court had considered a case involving *Marbury*. He also referred to the "Ginsburg standard," by which the nominee Ruth Bader Ginsburg declined to offer any previews, forecasts, or hints about her views, refusing to answer a remarkable sixty different questions. Lee continued:

> If Senators repeatedly ask nominees about outcomes, then the public will be more entitled—or at least more inclined—to think that judges are supposed to be outcome-minded, that that is supposed to be their whole approach to judging, that that's supposed to be what judging is in fact about. But this, of course, undermines the very legitimacy of the courts themselves, the very legitimacy of the tribunal you have been nominated by the president to serve on. Over time, no free people would accept a judiciary that simply imposes its own policy preferences on the country, absent fidelity to legal principle. There's a better way for the Senate to approach its work. This process, in my opinion, should be about your qualifications, about your character, and, perhaps most importantly, about your approach to judging, your own view about the role of the federal judiciary. It should not be about results in a select number of cases.

Back and forth the senators went until it was time for Kavanaugh to be introduced. Former Secretary of State Condoleezza Rice, Senator Rob Portman, and Lisa Blatt, a high-powered liberal feminist lawyer—all of them longtime friends and colleagues—took turns singing his praises.

In his opening statement, Kavanaugh reflected on his background, his judicial philosophy, and his optimism. "I live on the sunrise side of the mountain, not the sunset side of the mountain," he said. "I see the day that is coming, not the day that is gone. I am optimistic about the future of America. I am optimistic about the future of our independent judiciary." That image was taken from a painting in George W. Bush's Oval Office, *Rio Grande*, a West Texas landscape by Tom Lea, which the president liked to refer to. The idea of the "sunrise side of the mountain" stuck with staffers, particularly in the heavy days following September 11. Kavanaugh's genuine optimism encouraged his clerks and others involved in the confirmation battle. He had worked relentlessly, remembered to thank those assisting him for their good work, and brought pizzas to staffers working long nights and weekends.

Kavanaugh came into the first day of hearings determined to remain positive, but by the end of the day the hearings had turned hostile. Raj Shah counted sixty-three interruptions from Senate Democrats, mostly related to demands for more of Kavanaugh's irrelevant paperwork and other trivial delaying tactics that had nothing to do with evaluating his substantive qualifications.[28] More than seventy protesters were arrested.

Those protesters didn't arrive spontaneously. Planned Parenthood Action Fund flew in "storytellers" from as far away as Alaska and North Dakota. Winnie Wong, a senior advisor to the Women's March, explained their carefully coordinated messages. Members going into the hearing room were given "a script where we suggest certain messaging that may resonate more." The storytellers' travel and accommodations were paid for, as were their legal aid and bail if they were arrested, which was generally the goal. Later in the hearings, the organizers of the protesters—the Women's March and the Center for Popular Democracy—were warning activists that being arrested three times might lead to a night in jail. The group raised sums of more than six figures to finance the protests. "This is well-organized and scripted," said Wong, "This isn't chaos."[29]

Outside the hearing room, one of the stranger social media frenzies was sparked by televised images of Kavanaugh's former clerk Zina Bash sitting behind him as he testified. Her arms were crossed, the thumb and forefinger of her right hand touching to form something like an "okay" gesture. An urban legend, nurtured on the internet, has it that the "okay" gesture signals "white power." Eugene Gu, a prominent anti-Trump activist with 271,000 Twitter followers, tweeted, "Kavanaugh's former law clerk Zina Bash is flashing a white power sign behind him during his Senate confirmation hearing. They literally want to bring white supremacy to the Supreme Court." Some fourteen thousand people retweeted Gu's absurd and baseless accusation.[30]

Bash's husband, a U.S. attorney, took to Twitter himself to defend his wife's honor and point out how ludicrous the charge was, adding that his wife is half-Mexican and half-Jewish and her grandparents were Holocaust survivors.[31] Nonetheless, many major news outlets, including *Time* and the *Washington Post*, reported on the conspiracy theory, fanning the flames on social media.[32] If the first day of the Kavanaugh hearings was a circus, the "white power" Twitter follies proved to be the most appalling sideshow.

■   ■   ■

On Wednesday, Senator Leahy began a line of questioning that would continue over the next two days. He wanted to know about emails Kavanaugh had received when he was at the Bush White House from Manuel Miranda, then a Senate Judiciary Committee staffer. In 2001, Miranda discovered sensitive Democratic memoranda that had been left on a server shared with Republicans. One of them, which was leaked in 2003, revealed that Democrats were blocking Miguel Estrada's confirmation to the D.C. Circuit because he was Hispanic.

Kavanaugh had already been asked in his appellate court confirmation hearings in 2004 and 2006 if he knew about this security lapse. He said he didn't and wanted to make it clear that he had never seen the memoranda. If he received information from those documents, he said, he did not know how it was obtained. Now, on day two of his Supreme Court confirmation hearings, he was asked the same questions.

Leahy began, ominously, by asking if he wanted to change anything from his previous testimony. Kavanaugh said he did not. Leahy noted that in previous hearings he had been asked more than a hundred questions about the memoranda and had denied knowing anything about how Miranda gained the information. "My question is this: Did Mr. Miranda ever provide you with highly specific information regarding what I or other Democratic senators were planning on asking certain judicial nominees?" Leahy asked this question twice. Kavanaugh explained that such exchanges of information were quite common between staff on the Senate Judiciary Committee and the White House during a confirmation process.

Leahy then informed Kavanaugh that among the documents marked "committee confidential" was "evidence that Mr. Miranda provided you with materials that were stolen from me. And that would contradict your prior testimony." He asked Grassley to make the documents public. During the Gorsuch confirmation, Grassley had asked senators to alert him if they wanted any confidential documents released for use in the hearings. For Kavanaugh, Democratic senators were making outlandish requests, such as every document related to executive power or the environment. When Senator Klobuchar asked for four specific and relevant documents to be released for the hearing, Grassley made a show of thanking her for following an appropriate process. The Democratic strategy had been obstruction at all costs, so Klobuchar was annoyed at repeatedly being singled out for being cooperative and reasonable. At one point, Democratic staff accidentally shared with Republican staff their "hot list" of Kavanaugh documents they would eventually publicize through different senators. After sending the email that identified all of the documents they felt were most sensitive, the Democrats told the Republican staff to ignore the email. It was valuable information, even if Republican staff had already flagged most of the same documents. In any case, for Leahy's request, Grassley obtained clearance from both the Bush and Trump White House staffs to make the documents available the next day.

Leahy's smoking gun was nowhere to be found. The emails contained discussions about judicial nominees and required some contextual parsing, but nothing indicated that Kavanaugh had reason to suspect that Miranda had obtained the information improperly.[33]

In response to questions from Senator Graham, Kavanaugh twice mentioned a book that would have more significance in the weeks to come. In the sixth grade he had studied *To Kill a Mockingbird*, Harper Lee's novel about a man wrongly accused of rape. He kept his old copy of the book in his chambers as a reminder of the importance of not judging others and of empathizing with the accused and downtrodden.

The next attempt to paint Kavanaugh as a perjurer was a baffling line of questioning by Senator Kamala Harris, a former prosecutor who was preparing to run for president. She began by asking Kavanaugh if he had ever discussed Robert Mueller, the independent counsel then investigating the Trump presidential campaign, with anyone. He explained that he used to work with Mueller. She asked if he had ever discussed Mueller's investigation. He said he had. Then she asked repeatedly if he had ever had any discussions with employees of Kasowitz, Benson & Torres, the firm of President Trump's personal lawyer, Marc Kasowitz. As though she had him right where she wanted him, Harris warned the judge dramatically, "Be sure about your answer, sir."

Kavanaugh was utterly confused. While he didn't think he even knew anyone at the Kasowitz firm, he was alert to the danger of a perjury trap. "Is there a person you're talking about?" Kavanaugh asked haltingly.

"I'm asking you a very direct question," Harris snapped. "Yes or no?"

"I don't know everyone that works at that firm," Kavanaugh said.

Implying that she had damaging information, the senator said, "I think you're thinking of someone and you don't want to tell us."

A Democratic staffer told reporters that they had reason to believe Kavanaugh had had conversations with people at Kasowitz's firm, and a compliant press ran with the story that the nominee appeared to have committed perjury.[34] "Kavanaugh Stumbles," read the headline in *Politico*.[35] "Harris Lands First Blow on Kavanaugh," announced *Roll Call*.[36] The coverage of Harris herself verged on fawning. The *Washington Post*'s Jennifer Rubin gushed about a "break-out moment" that showed "her prosecutorial skill" and made her "an instant Democratic heroine."

She opined further, "Kavanaugh looked confused, if not nervous. He hadn't seen this coming."[37]

But in fact he *had* seen it coming, which was why he was so cautious. Senator Ted Cruz had warned him that Democrats would try to trick him into inconsistencies. In other lines of questioning, Kavanaugh had responded with marked openness. Being on offense was part of his strategy from the beginning. While he followed the Ginsburg precedent of not giving his views on particular cases, he eagerly engaged even the most hostile questioner. He was happy to talk at length about the Federalist Papers, his own decisions, the doctrine of *stare decisis*—anything but how he would vote in a specific case. He was not a man of one-sentence answers. But he recognized that Harris was trying to lay a perjury trap. It didn't matter that her questions would have been unacceptable and unethical in a courtroom. He had to be careful not to say anything that could be perceived as untrue. Who knew who might have just been hired at Kasowitz, Benson & Torres?

It turned out that Kavanaugh had not talked to anyone at Kasowitz, Benson & Torres, and Harris never offered any evidence of such a conversation. The White House had set up a war room down the hall from the hearing room, manned by Kavanaugh's team, where they quickly determined that Harris must have been fishing for conversations with Edward McNally, a partner in the firm's New York office who had worked in the Bush White House when Kavanaugh did. They tracked him down and confirmed that Kavanaugh had not spoken to him about the Mueller investigation. The law firm itself denied that any of its personnel had spoken to Kavanaugh, and the judge then testified under oath that the answer to Senator Harris's question was a straightforward "no."

■   ■   ■

Senator Whitehouse had an ax to grind against "shadowy dark-money front groups" participating in the judicial appointment process. "Here's how the game works," he said in his opening statement. "Big business and partisan groups fund the Federalist Society, which picked Gorsuch and now you."

He went on:

> Then big business and partisan groups fund the Judicial Crisis Network, which runs dark-money political campaigns to influence senators in confirmation votes, as they've done for Gorsuch and now for you. Who pays millions of dollars for that and what their expectations are is a deep, dark secret. These groups also fund Republican election campaigns with dark money and keep the identity of donors a deep, dark secret. And of course, 90 percent of your documents are, to us, a deep, dark secret.

Behind him his aides hoisted a sign stating that JCN had spent $17 million in connection with the Garland and Gorsuch nominations.[38]

Whitehouse's horror at the Federalist Society had arisen suddenly. Like every sitting justice of the Supreme Court, he himself had spoken at an event hosted by the Federalist Society.[39] His outrage over "dark money"—a pejorative term for donations made according to section 501(c)(4) of the Internal Revenue Code, which does not require an organization to disclose the identity of its donors—was similarly selective. The League of Conservation Voters, a 501(c)(4) organization and "dark money heavyweight," according to the Center for Public Integrity, used its PAC to endorse Whitehouse and was his single largest donor.[40]

Senator Whitehouse told only half the story. In an article in *Politico* in January 2019, "Why There's No Liberal Federalist Society," the law professor Evan Mandery bemoaned how sophisticated the conservative legal network has become. He is correct that the Federalist Society dwarfs its closest liberal counterpart, the American Constitution Society (ACS), in both breadth and effectiveness, but he incorrectly assumes that the right is therefore Goliath to the left's David. Quoting the ACS's president, Caroline Frederickson, on the Supreme Court decision *Bush v. Gore*, which shocked liberals into starting the ACS, Mandery unwittingly acknowledges the left's long-standing dominance in the courts: "'Courts that the left had taken for granted since [Chief Justice Earl] Warren had handed the presidency to Bush.'" He also admits that the American legal education system acts as a "counterweight" to the Federalist Society: "There's no question that law school faculties are overwhelmingly liberal...."[41]

The progressive journal *Mother Jones* has recognized as much, describing the interconnected web of liberal groups from the National Association for the Advancement of Colored People (NAACP) and the American Civil Liberties Union (ACLU) to the Sierra Club and the League of Women Voters[42] as a "vast, well-funded movement that's far older and far more influential than the Federalist Society. Its only problem is that it doesn't have a name."[43]

In the battle over Kavanaugh's confirmation, the most visible liberal organization was Demand Justice, formed only a few months before Kennedy's retirement by veteran Democratic operatives with experience in the Hillary Clinton campaign and the Obama administration. If money given to the Judicial Crisis Network is "dark" because JCN's annual 990 tax filings don't disclose its donors, Demand Justice's bank account is a black hole. "Fiscally sponsored" by the Sixteen Thirty Fund, an under-the-radar liberal intermediary group that passes money from donors to dozens of liberal organizations, Demand Justice doesn't even file the disclosure forms that "dark money" groups do. Senator Whitehouse couldn't put it on one of his pie charts if he tried. Both the donors to Demand Justice and the amount of money they contribute are completely invisible.[44]

The Sixteen Thirty Fund does file an annual Form 990, but it does not reveal the identities of its donors. Although its budget dwarfs that of the Judicial Crisis Network and the Federalist Society combined, it has failed to pique Senator Whitehouse's interest. In 2017 it brought in $79 million and ended the year with $43 million in assets, growing by an astonishing 1,547 percent in only eight years.[45] In pursuit of its cryptically worded mission—"promoting social welfare, including, but not limited to, providing public education on and conducting advocacy regarding key policies"—the fund bankrolls liberal groups focused on everything from judicial appointments, organized labor, and abortion to Senator Whitehouse's own favorite dark-money heavyweight, the League of Conservation Voters. They also fund Majority Forward, a 501(c)(4) group closely tied to Senator Chuck Schumer's Senate Majority PAC. Majority Forward alone accounted for one-third of all the dark-money spending in the 2018 election, giving liberals a comfortable dark-money lead over conservatives.[46]

The Sixteen Thirty Fund is managed by Arabella Advisors, a philanthropy consulting firm in Washington, D.C., that works with high-dollar liberal donors and nonprofits. Arabella manages four nonprofits, including the Sixteen Thirty Fund, reporting total revenues of $1.6 billion and expenditures of a whopping $1.1 billion since 2013.[47] Arabella was founded and is still run by Eric Kessler, who worked on conservation issues in the Clinton White House and was, coincidentally, the national field director for the League of Conservation Voters.

If Senator Whitehouse had been interested in teasing out the many interconnected threads of that dark-money web, he would have learned that Kessler is also the president of the Sixteen Thirty Fund and the chairman of the board of the New Venture Fund, its sister group in the Arabella orbit, which has sponsored more than two hundred projects and reports an annual revenue of $358 million. These entities are linked to a dizzying array of anti-Kavanaugh organizations, including the Sierra Club, the Leadership Conference on Civil and Human Rights, the Center for American Progress, Color of Change, Health Care for America Now, Health Care Voter, and the NAACP.[48] The Center for Popular Democracy, one of the groups promoting the protests in the Dirksen halls during the hearings, received substantial funding from the New Venture Fund.[49]

Political and special interest groups have every right to protect the anonymity of their donors, of course. Indeed, there are strong arguments—some of them made by those sitting on the Supreme Court in recent years—that the First Amendment limits the ability of the government to force their disclosure. But Senator Whitehouse's pursuit of a vendetta against conservative nonprofits while ignoring the considerably more opaque funding streams of organizations on his side reveals his true interest. He did not advance the cause of transparency per se, but used the disclosure of donors as a weapon against his political opponents.[50]

■   ■   ■

On Thursday, September 6, Cory Booker stunned the committee by announcing even before questioning began that he would violate Senate rules by releasing emails that had been marked "committee confidential." He tweeted a link to documents that he said revealed troubling racial messages but that actually consisted of discussions about security screening procedures in the immediate aftermath of 9/11 and whether they should include race and national origin.[51] In fact, Kavanaugh opposed racial profiling. In an email to a colleague in the White House counsel's office in 2002, Kavanaugh had written:

> The people who favor some use of race/natl origin obviously do not need to grapple with the interim question. But the people (such as you and I) who generally favor effective security measures that are race-neutral in fact DO need to grapple—and grapple now—with the interim question of what to do before a truly effective and comprehensive race-neutral system is developed and implemented.

The year after Kavanaugh wrote that email, the Bush administration issued guidance prohibiting law enforcement agencies from using racial profiling.[52]

The emails were a dud, but Booker—also preparing to announce his run for the presidency—tried to call attention to his breaking of Senate rules. "I knowingly violated the rules put forward," he said, adding that he realized he was engaged in civil disobedience and would accept the consequences. He practically begged the Republicans to try to expel him from the Senate and remarked that this was the closest he would come to an "I am Spartacus" moment. Since there was nothing to connect Booker's situation with the famous scene from the 1960 Kirk Douglas movie, in which a group of slaves all claim to be the outlaw Spartacus to help the real Spartacus avoid being crucified, the remark came across as silly, exposing the senator to no small amount of mockery. He was in no danger of expulsion, in any case, because, despite his self-accusation, he had not violated any rules. He had requested the day before that the documents in question be cleared for release, and staff worked through the night to clear them. Bill Burck had informed him at four o'clock that morning that he was free to release them, as Grassley had noted at the hearing just before Booker's Spartacus moment.[53]

Booker was intent on violating the rules, however, and he released what he believed to be confidential emails throughout the day. The grandstanding was unnecessary. "Had we been consulted on these universally released documents, we would have consented to their public disclosure," Burck wrote in a letter.[54] The White House and Senate staffs worried that Booker's theatrics would make future nominees and administrations less willing to share information about nominees, which is the property of the administration. After the experiment with modern e-discovery procedures and providing digital documents that are easily searchable, the confirmation process might return to the closely guarded rooms of filing boxes of previous decades.

Senator Blumenthal tried to embroil Kavanaugh in a controversy over President Trump's harsh rhetoric. Reading tweets that criticized Justice Ruth Bader Ginsburg for her critique of him, Blumenthal asked if Kavanaugh agreed with the president that she was an embarrassment for making political statements about him. Kavanaugh said he wouldn't get "within three zip codes" of a political controversy. It was Blumenthal's questioning of Gorsuch about a different set of Trump tweets that caused the president to briefly waver in his support of the nominee. Kavanaugh navigated the minefield more nimbly, and it would pay off.

After a long day of questioning that kept Senator Grassley up past his normally firm nine-o'clock bedtime, the public portion of Kavanaugh's testimony closed after ten p.m. The nominee had testified for thirty hours across three days. The protesters and supporters went home, but the judge and the senators stayed for the closed portion of the hearing. The spirited debate about "committee confidential" documents obscured the fact that senators would have this opportunity to question the nominee on all manner of confidential topics, including work product, sensitive personal financial information, and other ethical or legal questions uncovered by the FBI background investigation. The group remained in closed session for about an hour. It is customary to continue the closed session for that long even if there are no concerns about a nominee's record, so as not to call attention to nominees for whom there are confidential vetting concerns. The senators spent much of the time sparring with one another over things that had nothing to do with Kavanaugh. Senator Grassley, particularly disappointed with some members' behavior, was in rare form. The closed session would be the occasion to ask about confidential allegations against a nominee or to raise concerns about his ethical behavior. No such allegations were mentioned during the closed session. Senator Feinstein did not even attend.

■   ■   ■

The fourth day's testimony was comparatively uneventful. Paul Moxley and John Tarpley, two members of the American Bar Association's Standing Committee on the Federal Judiciary, explained their method for awarding Kavanaugh the ABA's "well qualified" rating (unanimously). Then came a seemingly interminable parade of witnesses for and against Kavanaugh's confirmation. Law professors, noted Supreme Court advocates, and former clerks spoke on his behalf, and the testimony of a few friends was intended to put a human face on the judge.

Then it was the opposition's turn: young people, union members, a Methodist minister who wanted the government to force her church-employer's insurance to pay for her IUD, and even Congressman Cedric Richmond, a civil rights leader who warned that Kavanaugh's textualist approach to the law would threaten voting rights, education, and his favored criminal law policies. There was a woman with cerebral palsy who had been led to believe that Kavanaugh would take away her right to make her own medical decisions. (He had decided a case addressing how to manage care for wards of the state who were incapable of giving consent, a group to which this woman clearly did not belong.) The day ended with the Watergate figure John Dean testifying for the Democrats about Kavanaugh's excessive deference to presidential authority. The hearings ended with a whimper, not a bang.

"This week's hearing lacked the sordidness of the Thomas hearing," reported the *Washington Times*, "but made up for it in vitriol—both on the dais and in the viewing gallery. One Republican senator said he counted more than 200 protesters ousted over three days."[55] A major source of the hearings' drama was political ambition. Ever since Joe Biden's grandstanding during the Bork hearings, senators have been powerfully tempted to exploit a perch on the Senate Judiciary Committee for public attention. Senators Booker and Harris attracted the most attention with their antics, but Senator Klobuchar would do her share of aggressive self-marketing when the Judiciary Committee resumed its hearings after the nominee was accused of sexual assault. The presence of those three presidential hopefuls on the committee encouraged other candidates to sound off about the nomination as vociferously as possible, lest their competitors on the committee steal the limelight. Senator Elizabeth Warren, for example, conspicuously stopped by the lobby in Dirksen to express her support for the protesters.[56]

Senator Jeff Merkley, who was considering a run for president but later decided against it, contributed to the partisan atmosphere with a litigious gesture. He filed a nuisance lawsuit against the president, the Senate majority leader, the chairman of the Senate Judiciary Committee, the Senate sergeant at arms and secretary, and Bill Burck. The Senate's constitutional "advice and consent" responsibility was at risk, he alleged, because of a failure to supply senators with enough documents to assess the nominee thoroughly. The judge, an Obama appointee, let the frivolous suit die a procedural death.

Even Justice Ruth Bader Ginsburg, the most celebrated liberal on the Supreme Court, lamented that Kavanaugh's hearing was a "highly partisan show." "The vote on my confirmation was ninety-six to three, even though I had spent about ten years of my life litigating cases under the auspices of the ACLU," she told an audience at the George Washington University Law School on September 13. She reminded the audience that Antonin Scalia's confirmation was unanimous, adding, "That's the way it should be.... I wish I could wave a magic wand and have it go back to the way it was."[57]

Despite the circus-like atmosphere, Kavanaugh performed well enough that his confirmation was widely expected. "Brett Kavanaugh coasts toward Supreme Court confirmation despite document dispute, public protests" was *USA Today*'s assessment.[58] Senator John Kennedy of Louisiana was so pleased, he declared, "I want to marry Brett Kavanaugh."

Senator Grassley announced that the committee would vote on the nomination one week later, on September 20. A handful of Democrats, however, knew that there was more to come. What followed would make the contentious hearings that Kavanaugh had already endured pale in comparison.

CHAPTER FIVE

All Hell
Breaks Loose

After the hearings, there was one more step before the Judiciary Committee could take its important next vote on the nomination. Kavanaugh had to respond to written "questions for the record" from members of the committee. Senators began posing written questions to Supreme Court nominees only in the 1970s. Scalia received three questions. Gorsuch received 324.

And on the afternoon of Monday, September 10, Kavanaugh was asked to respond to a record-shattering 1,287 questions—more than all previous nominees combined. To keep the nomination on track, he would have to return his answers by Wednesday evening, a nearly impossible task.

It was obvious the unheard-of number of questions was not submitted in good faith. Four of the ten Democrats on the committee had already announced they would vote against Kavanaugh, another four had indicated they were likely to vote against him, and the ranking member, Dianne Feinstein, had assured supporters in mid-July that she was ready to lead the opposition against the nominee, yet Democrats accounted for all but four of the questions. Kavanaugh's supporters were convinced this was yet another delaying tactic by Democrats hoping that the nominee would be unable to respond by the deadline or would stumble into a perjury trap.

Answering the questions began in the Department of Justice, where a team sorted questions by topic and distributed them to clerks in charge of each issue. Each clerk drafted answers based first and foremost on what had already been said at the hearing. Any new material would have to come from the judge himself and would have to be carefully expressed to avoid contradicting anything that had been said at the hearing or privately to a senator. They knew the senators would seize on any opportunity, fair or unfair, to allege perjury.

The questions revisited all the topics that had been brought up in the hearings, from Kavanaugh's views on abortion jurisprudence to his personal credit card debt, as well as tough new questions arising out of the hearings.

For example, Kavanaugh was asked about an incident in which the father of a victim of the school shooting in Parkland, Florida, had approached him after his testimony in the hearing room. The judge had turned away and continued out of the room, an apparent snub that became a major news story. Kavanaugh responded that he did not recognize the man and had assumed he was one of the many protesters at the hearing. Ordinarily, Kerri Kupec accompanied him to identify the people who approached him and to keep him from getting mobbed, but she had not received a pass that day. In the commotion of the hearing room, most members of the White House team couldn't hear what the man was saying. Everyone's nerves were on edge, and the marshals hustled Kavanaugh toward the exit as the man approached. "If I had known who he was, I would have shaken his hand, talked to him, and expressed my sympathy. And I would have listened to him," Kavanaugh wrote.[1] It was true. Claire Murray was the aide who informed Kavanaugh who the man was, and he was mortified.

Little new information emerged from the myriad questions and answers. One exception was confirmation that he had spoken to Attorney General Jeff Sessions about the position of solicitor general. He had decided to remain a judge, and the position went to Noel Francisco, his former colleague in the Bush White House.

Despite the lack of good faith behind most of the questions, Kavanaugh's answers were still important, and not merely because his opponents would exploit any error. Senator Hirono, for instance, asked him about *Rice v. Cayetano*, in which the Supreme Court struck down as racially discriminatory a law restricting a certain state office to "Native Hawaiians."[2] Hirono, who had already announced her "no" vote, was trying to persuade Senator Lisa Murkowski to vote against Kavanaugh on the grounds that his views on race-based voting would be detrimental to Native Alaskans. In his answer, Kavanaugh carefully clarified that the "Supreme Court's 7-2 opinion 18 years ago in *Rice v. Cayetano* had no effect on the rights and privileges of American Indians and Alaska natives that the Court had long recognized" and that the case had "nothing to do with the sovereign rights of Alaska Natives and American Indians to run their own government affairs, including administering Tribal elections."

Senator Jeff Flake was the only Republican to submit a question with potential pitfalls for the nominee. His staff told Kavanaugh's team before the hearings that he was bothered by the politicization of the Department of Justice. Kavanaugh's team had encouraged the senator to be more specific—the department is part of the executive branch, after all, and so accountable to the president—and ask about particular decisions, but he did not want to narrow the scope of his question. Unsatisfied with Kavanaugh's response at the hearing, Flake submitted a similar question in writing: "Should a president be able to use his authority to pressure executive or independent agencies to carry out his directives for purely political purposes?"

Kavanaugh's response carefully threaded the needle. He began by noting that no one, including the president, is above the law. While he acknowledged that political leadership of agencies is expected and appropriate, good political leaders should follow the "principle that everything the Government does must be based on sound legal principles and a legitimate factual basis." It is the courts that must remain independent of political considerations, he wrote, citing his opinion in *Hamdan v. United States*, which contradicted a strongly held view of his previous boss, George W. Bush.[3]

A first draft of Kavanaugh's answers to all the questions was completed in twelve hours and sent to Brett Talley, who was working with Michel and Murray at the White House. A former deputy assistant attorney general (and prolific author of Lovecraftian horror novels), Talley had accumulated invaluable institutional knowledge working on Supreme Court appointments in the Bush administration and, more recently, on Gorsuch's nomination. Getting Kavanaugh confirmed was personal for him. He had been nominated for a district court judgeship in September 2017, but his confirmation went down in a storm of partisan attacks. Throughout the confirmation process, Talley had managed to dodge the press, lest some reporter recognize him and stir up controversy. The indispensable bridge between the legal minds and the communications people, he was also valued for what one colleague called his "buoyant spirit."

The White House team began reviewing and tweaking the answers, sending them in batches to Kavanaugh when they were ready for him to review with his signature black Sharpie, sending edits to the clerks for incorporation into the final document. The last questions were on his desk by noon on Tuesday. That night, the White House group, including Talley, Murray, and Michel, returned to chambers, where they found Kavanaugh going over each answer in detail. To keep him from getting bogged down, Talley told the judge that if he divided the time left by the number of questions, he had only about two minutes per response, and that wasn't allowing time for sleep or even a bathroom break. It was a grueling pace.

Kavanaugh had run marathons before and knew the kind of focus that was needed. He reviewed the answer to every single question, ensuring not only its accuracy—the smallest slip might expose him to a perjury charge—but that it met his high standards. The task of responding to nearly 1,300 questions in two days was abusive, but there was no option but to complete it. The group ordered pizzas and settled in for yet another all-night work session.

■   ■   ■

When Wednesday arrived, Kavanaugh was still working, and Talley was nervous about getting the final answers. They were starting to roll in late in the day when Raj Shah turned to Talley and said, "Hey, have you ever heard of *The Intercept*?" He hadn't.

The online news publication, which describes itself as "adversarial," is owned by Pierre Omidyar, the billionaire founder of eBay, and edited by Glenn Greenwald. It gained notoriety in 2013 by publishing documents released by the National Security Agency whistle-blower Edward Snowden.

On the evening of Wednesday, September 12, *The Intercept* published a report by Ryan Grim that Senator Feinstein possessed a letter from a California constituent that described "an incident involving Kavanaugh and a woman while they were in high school." Committee Democrats wanted to view the letter, but Feinstein declined. The letter writer was a client of Debra Katz, a lawyer known for representing women who accused powerful men of sexual harassment.[4]

The Kavanaugh team were so focused on answering the committee's written questions that they first assumed this was a Democratic ploy to get them off track. And in any case, unsubstantiated allegations were a regular part of the confirmation process. Some members of the team recalled a rumor they had heard from a source close to liberal activists about a three-part plan to prevent Kavanaugh's confirmation. First, someone would accuse him of sexual misconduct. Second, someone would accuse him of knowing something specific about Judge Kozinski's sexual misdeeds. Third, someone would accuse him of improprieties with students at Georgetown Law School, where he had taught constitutional interpretation in 2007.

No one wanted to bother Kavanaugh with the *Intercept* story because of the importance of finishing the questions. Besides, the screening process had already included sensitive questions about any episodes that needed to be addressed. With nothing more to go on than "incident," "high school," and "California woman," there wasn't anything to ask about.

Still, McGahn called to check in. Kavanaugh was confident it was nothing to worry about.

At eight o'clock, the team emailed the answers to the 1,287 questions to the committee and headed to the Justice Department to celebrate. It felt as if they had cleared the last major hurdle.

At ten o'clock the next morning, September 13, the Judiciary Committee held an executive business meeting. Rumors had been circulating that Democrats might try again to delay the procedure, and Republican staff members were preparing for the possibility that Democrats would try to prevent a quorum by simply not showing up.

They did show up, and Chairman Grassley immediately held over the nomination of Kavanaugh. Any member of the committee can issue a "hold" on a nomination for a week. It happens so regularly that it is built into the schedule. So as he gaveled the meeting to order and noted a quorum, Grassley announced that he himself was holding the nomination over, a procedure known as "burning the hold." He was interrupted by Senator Blumenthal, who moved to adjourn on the grounds that they needed more time, documents, and—curiously—witnesses before Kavanaugh could be confirmed.

Even though all the Democrats planned to vote against confirmation, they spent much of the meeting in parliamentary maneuvers to prevent the committee from setting a time to vote on sending the nomination to the full Senate. Their efforts failed, and a vote was scheduled for September 20.[5]

As soon as the meeting adjourned, Feinstein and a staff member pulled Grassley and one of his staffers into the small lavatory off the committee's anteroom and closed the door. In that awkward setting she told him for the first time about the letter that had been in her possession since July 30. She wouldn't show it to him.

News about the letter spread rapidly. *BuzzFeed*, confirming the *Intercept* story, reported that the Democrats on the Senate Judiciary Committee had huddled in a room off of the Senate floor the previous night to press Feinstein to do something with the letter.[6] She had briefed them on its contents but had kept it hidden from the Republicans. Debra

Katz, conveniently enough, had been on the Hill on Wednesday to testify before the Bipartisan Women's Caucus on workplace sexual harassment.[7] Reporters spotted her leaving the Hill Wednesday night.

Feinstein confirmed the reports on Thursday afternoon, saying, "I have received information from an individual concerning the nomination of Brett Kavanaugh to the Supreme Court. That individual strongly requested confidentiality, declined to come forward or press the matter further, and I have honored that decision. I have, however, referred the matter to federal investigative authorities."[8]

Some members of the committee had learned about the letter many days earlier. Senator Dick Durbin later said that he had heard about it from a third senator on the Judiciary Committee around September 8.

Reporters gathered for the hearings peppered the Democrats with questions about the *Intercept* story, but oddly enough, none of the senators responded. Not even Richard Blumenthal, who was known to deliberately walk past reporters two or three times hoping to attract an interview. After all his bluster during the meeting, he didn't even offer a perfunctory comment about the need for a delay.

A special division of the FBI, separate from the criminal investigation branch, conducts background checks on presidential nominees, looking for anything that suggests they are unsuitable for a position of trust. Acquaintances of the nominee are interviewed about whether he has used drugs, is susceptible to blackmail, or has sought to overthrow the U.S. government, and they are asked to suggest other persons whom agents might interview. The Trump White House followed the same procedure for FBI background checks that the Obama administration followed, in which the reports are given directly to the president, not the FBI or the Department of Justice.

Senator Feinstein had given the letter to the FBI on Wednesday night, redacting the name of the writer, who had requested anonymity.[9] Following the normal procedure, agents placed it in Kavanaugh's background file without evaluating it. The White House received the redacted letter by noon on Thursday and sent it back to the Judiciary Committee, where only the senators on the committee and a total of six staffers were permitted to read it. This was the first time most Republicans on the committee learned about the allegations. All information in nominees' background files is strictly protected, as if it were classified information. The White House, therefore, was gagged from talking about the letter.

The White House and the Senate Republicans were puzzled that Feinstein had not followed this procedure, which was well defined and commonly used, to handle the allegations before the hearing. Doing so would have ensured that the relevant parties were informed and the matter investigated while protecting the anonymity of the accuser.

The Trump administration had worked with Judiciary Committee Democrats on close to one hundred nominees by that point, and the background investigations of several of them had raised questions. They could be minor, such as a claimed residence for which no records could be found, or they could be important, such as allegations of inappropriate behavior. But whether the matter was big or small, the Democratic and Republican staff members would hold a confidential call with the nominee in which both sides could ask questions. If the matter was resolved, the nominee would be cleared for his hearing. If it was not resolved, the senators would meet with the nominee in a confidential session in which any question could be asked. At that point senators who still had concerns could simply vote against the nominee. If the chairman decided on his own that the question was serious enough, he could choose not to hold hearings. This process routinely protected confidential information.

Yet Feinstein had not shared the letter with Republicans or the FBI when she received it, and it had not been mentioned prior to the confidential call with staff before the hearing. Most of Kavanaugh's confidential session with senators after the hearing was spent discussing committee business. Feinstein hadn't even attended. Now the White House team, unable to discuss the letter and not knowing the name of the accuser, was at a serious disadvantage.

On Thursday afternoon, the first details of the story emerged when *The Guardian* reported, erroneously, that a seventeen-year-old Kavanaugh and a friend were alleged to have locked a high school girl in a room at a party, but that she had been able to get out of the room.[10] In fact, the letter alleged much more than that, but conservatives immediately made fun of the allegation as unworthy of so much concern.[11] The White House press shop knew that if the real allegation came out, the conservative press's dismissiveness would look bad. But there was nothing they could do if they were to respect the limits placed on information in a candidate's background file.

Waiting for details was the most stressful part of this ordeal for the Kavanaugh team. How could they respond to a charge about which they had no information? The unavailability of details did not discourage the media from speculating about what had happened, and the story was getting legs. Kavanaugh, having no idea where the allegation came from, skipped back-to-school night at his daughters' school to keep his head down and prepare.

On Thursday, a reporter found Scott McCaleb on Nantucket, where he was attending a conference with his wife, Meghan, and asked him about the *Intercept* and *BuzzFeed* reports. The McCalebs were high school friends of Kavanaugh, and Scott had already spoken publicly on his behalf. Kavanaugh had dated Meghan's sister in high school. Meghan knew him well and wanted to support him against what she considered ridiculous smears. "I could count on one hand how many guys I would have come out for and defended against such allegations. In fact, maybe not even five," she said. Kavanaugh was one of them.

She came up with a plan to send a letter to the Senate Judiciary Committee from women who had been Kavanaugh's friends in high school. She and Scott skipped dinner to compose it, and by 7:49 p.m. the letter was being sent around by text and email for review. Friends sent it to friends, and the distribution list kept growing.

"For the entire time we have known Brett Kavanaugh, he has behaved honorably and treated women with respect," the letter said. "Through the more than 35 years we have known him, Brett has stood out for his friendship, character, and integrity. In particular, he has always treated women with decency and respect. That was true when he was in high school, and it has remained true to this day."[12]

Some sixty-five women, with a broad range of political views, signed the letter that night, but they didn't want to go public with it if doing so would fuel the interest in a story they thought should be dismissed as ridiculous. So they waited to send it.

■   ■   ■

On Friday morning, the *New Yorker* published a story by Ronan Farrow and Jane Mayer providing more information about the allegation. Farrow, who had received a Pulitzer Prize for his reporting on the sexual assault allegations against the Hollywood producer Harvey Weinstein, had written about several other clients of Debra Katz, who had served as a source for him.[13] Farrow and Mayer reported:

> In the letter, the woman alleged that, during an encounter at a party, Kavanaugh held her down, and that he attempted to force himself on her. She claimed in the letter that Kavanaugh and a classmate of his, both of whom had been drinking, turned up music that was playing in the room to conceal the sound of her protests, and that Kavanaugh covered her mouth with his hand. She was able to free herself. Although the alleged incident took place decades ago and the three individuals involved were minors, the woman said that the memory had been a source of ongoing distress for her, and that she had sought psychological treatment as a result.[14]

Now that there were some specifics to respond to, Kavanaugh announced: "I categorically and unequivocally deny this allegation. I did not do this back in high school or at any time."

The follow-up phone call that Kavanaugh and Senator Collins had agreed to have after their meeting at her office was scheduled for this day. At the end of the call, Collins dismissed her staff from her office so she could discuss the matter with him privately. He categorically denied the charge. The first thing Collins noticed was that the letter to Senator

Feinstein was dated July 30. She was flabbergasted that such serious allegations had been held until the last moment.

The *New Yorker*'s new details about the allegation provoked rampant speculation among Kavanaugh's classmates and friends. Who might have a grudge against Kavanaugh? Who might have interpreted an interaction in such a way? Nobody in his set of friends believed that Kavanaugh had done what was alleged. An erroneous report that the accuser was a professor at Stanford University caused speculation briefly to focus on the wrong woman. But even with the meager details provided, reporters and investigators narrowed their search for the accuser to three women in the Bay Area who fit the profile of having graduated from a Washington-area high school.

Once it became clear the story wasn't being dismissed, the letter from women who knew Kavanaugh in high school was sent to the Judiciary Committee, which released it on Friday afternoon. The women were immediately bombarded with phone calls from reporters and harassed on social media platforms.

John Bresnahan, the Capitol bureau chief for *Politico*, tweeted that the letter showed that Republicans "knew about this high-school rape allegation." A half-hour later, he noted that committee Republicans denied knowing the substance of the Feinstein letter or the nature of the allegations. "But clearly it took some effort," he insisted, to find "65 women who attended high school at same time as Kavanaugh 30-odd years ago. This took some time to round up signatures."[15] In fact, Meghan McCaleb had responded to public news reports, confirming that it had taken her only a few hours to compose the letter and collect the signatures.

Kavanaugh's friends and colleagues of both sexes had been appearing on television throughout the confirmation process, but now it was time for women to take the lead. On Friday evening, McCaleb appeared on Laura Ingraham's television show with Helgi Walker, a colleague of Kavanaugh's in the White House counsel's office, and Porter Wilkinson, who had clerked for him. All four women vouched for his character and integrity.

Walker and Ingraham, who had clerked for Justice Thomas on the Supreme Court, noted that his name had already come up in the coverage of the allegations against Kavanaugh. After the *New Yorker* story was published, Thomas's accuser, Anita Hill, called for a "fair and neutral process."[16] Memories of Thomas's contentious confirmation battle shaped many people's reactions to the allegations against Kavanaugh.

■   ■   ■

Clarence Thomas was nominated on July 1, 1991, by President George H. W. Bush to fill the seat vacated by Thurgood Marshall, one of the Court's most prominent liberals. Because the appointment promised to shift the ideological balance of the Court, liberal activists prepared a reprise of the campaign that had prevented Robert Bork's confirmation four years earlier. The Judiciary Committee hearings in September were brutal and prolonged. Thomas testified for more than twenty-four hours over five days, longer than any Supreme Court nominee to that point save Bork himself. The committee's vote on his nomination was seven to seven, all Republicans and one Democrat voting in his favor. The nomination was sent to the full Senate for consideration on September 27.

Two days before his expected confirmation, Nina Totenberg of National Public Radio and Timothy Phelps of *Newsday* both disclosed allegations of sexual harassment against Thomas by a young law professor named Anita Hill, who had worked under him at two federal agencies. The accusation had been leaked from the FBI's background investigation, probably by a Democratic staff member.[17] (In fact, the confidential closed-door session with senators that Feinstein intentionally sidestepped was instituted in 1992 by then-chairman Joe Biden in response to the debacle, in which Thomas's reputation was damaged by an unsupported allegation.) The confirmation vote was suspended, and the hearings were reopened. From October 11 through 13, the nation's attention was riveted on the dramatic, often wrenching, testimony of the nominee and his accuser.[18] Thomas was confirmed by a vote of fifty-two to forty-eight, the closest for a Supreme Court appointment since the nineteenth century. Opinion polls found that the American public, by a two-to-one margin, had not found Hill's allegations credible. The balance of opinion was similar among both men and women and among both blacks and whites.

■   ■   ■

Early Sunday morning, Emma Brown of the *Washington Post* left a voicemail for Kavanaugh. She was about to publish a lengthy story that would detail an allegation of sexual assault against him. This was the first time Kavanaugh heard the name of his accuser: Christine Blasey Ford.

He was shocked to hear his name used in the same sentence as the term "sexual assault," and when he heard the woman's name, he realized that her accusation was not about something misinterpreted on a date. He did not remember who she was or what high school she had attended, so he called a high school friend to ask if the accuser's name rang a bell. Kavanaugh went to Georgetown Preparatory School, an all-boys school in North Bethesda, Maryland, and he and his schoolmates had socialized with students from several other single-sex schools in the Washington area. His friend remembered Blasey, who had attended the all-girls Holton-Arms School, also in Bethesda, and immediately shared some of his unfavorable impressions of her from her high school days.

Kavanaugh went downstairs to tell Ashley about the phone call from the reporter. It was possible that he had met his accuser when they were in high school, he said, but he never went out with her and had never been in an intimate situation with her. It went without saying that he had never attempted to rape her. Ashley responded calmly and expressed her support. Believing that everything happens for a reason, she assured him that they'd get through it.

Kavanaugh also called McGahn and Shah to tell them about the *Post* story. Shah, who was in Connecticut, where his mother was recovering from a brain aneurysm, spoke with Emma Brown from the hospital. She shared a few details, such as the names of Ford and others she said were present at the incident.

Brown had been working on the story with Ford since early July, when Kavanaugh's name was still on the short list of potential nominees.[19] Just a few hours after Brown's call to Kavanaugh, the story was published. It was explosive.

The angle chosen by the reporter was that Ford did not want to go public, but that the *Intercept* and *New Yorker* stories had exposed her allegation without her consent. Amid the intense speculation about the identity of Kavanaugh's accuser, she preferred to tell the story herself.

That story was a remarkable combination of vagueness and specificity:

> [O]ne summer in the early 1980s, Kavanaugh and a friend—both "stumbling drunk," Ford alleges—corralled her into a bedroom during a gathering of teenagers at a house in Montgomery County. While his friend watched, she said, Kavanaugh pinned her to a bed on her back and groped her over her clothes, grinding his body against hers and clumsily attempting to pull off her one-piece bathing suit and the clothing she wore over it. When she tried to scream, she said, he put his hand over her mouth. "I thought he might inadvertently kill me," said Ford, now a 51-year-old research psychologist in northern California. "He was trying to attack me and remove my clothing."[20]

She said she had not told anyone about the incident until 2012, during couples therapy with her husband. She provided excerpts from what she said were her therapist's notes, which recorded that four boys at an "elitist boys' school" attacked her. The discrepancy in the number of boys involved was the fault of her therapist, she said.

Brown described Ford, "a registered Democrat who has made small contributions to political organizations," as "a professor at Palo Alto University who teaches in a consortium with Stanford University, training graduate students in clinical psychology. Her work has been widely published in academic journals." The article included but downplayed evidence that contradicted Ford's insistence that she wanted to keep quiet, noting for example that Ford had "engaged Debra Katz" more than a month previously and that she had taken a polygraph test in early August to buttress her credibility.

Ford's memory was foggy, Brown reported. She thought the incident might have happened in 1982. She wasn't sure whose house they were in, how she got there, or where exactly it was. She had drunk only one beer, she said, but Kavanaugh and his friend, Mark Judge, were heavily intoxicated. Brown mentioned that Kavanaugh's yearbooks made references to drinking and that Judge was public about his own heavy drinking in high school.

Ford managed to flee from the house where she was assaulted, Brown reported, but she wasn't sure how she got home. The attack deeply affected her for the next four to five years and later induced anxiety and post-traumatic stress. The story could not have been more sympathetic to Ford.

The worst part of the day for Kavanaugh was calling his mother. He knew she would be devastated. The hearings and follow-up questions had been abusive, but a public accusation of sexual assault showed how much worse it could get.

■   ■   ■

McGahn reassured Kavanaugh, reminding him that they had always known something like this might happen. Was it a case of something "going south" with someone he'd dated? Kavanaugh flatly denied he had ever sexually assaulted anyone, much less this woman, whom he didn't even remember meeting. McGahn had already talked to President Trump, who showed no interest in abandoning Kavanaugh. That show of support was an important first step, but in the wake of the *Post* story, it would be difficult to convince others.

Then, pondering the newly revealed details of the accusation, Kavanaugh realized that crucial evidence of his innocence might be sitting in his basement. His father had started keeping detailed daily calendars in 1978. Kavanaugh followed suit in 1980, continuing the practice with more or less diligence ever since. These detailed daily records, almost like a diary, provided contemporary evidence of where he had been and what he had done almost every day of his life since high school. He went to the basement and pulled out his calendars for the summer of 1982 to see what they showed.

Reviewing those calendars was like traveling back in time to high school. He was preoccupied with colleges, basketball camp, going to the beach with his friends, and visiting his "Gramy" in Connecticut. Above all, he was focused on sports, which had been an obsession since he started playing basketball in the fourth grade and football and baseball in the fifth grade.

He would continue with basketball and football throughout high school. When he wasn't playing or practicing sports, he was thinking about them or watching games on television. He went with his father to Redskins football games, Washington Bullets basketball games, Baltimore Orioles baseball games, and Washington Capitals hockey games. They'd also attend University of Maryland basketball games.

Sports focused his competitive instincts, taught him how take a hit and get back up, and provided camaraderie. He broke his collarbone in the ninth grade in football practice. The pain was brutal, but even worse was missing the last two games of the season and half the basketball season. Being sidelined so long drove him crazy, but it taught him patience.

His own coaches taught him lessons he'd later impart to the athletes he coached—keeping things in perspective and being sure you could say you gave it your all even if you lost. He learned about the importance of practices, workouts, and summer preparation. And he learned about the bonding that comes from being on a team with a great work ethic.

Usually he took more from the losses than the wins, but some of the wins were unforgettable. In seventh grade, his football team crushed a rival, twenty-six to nothing. On the bus ride home, the boys were screaming with excitement. Their coach, who was driving the bus, pulled over and put the flashers on. They prepared to get yelled at. Instead, he stood up and shouted, "I'm so proud of you guys!"

Besides the endless practices and games, Kavanaugh's calendars noted social activities and parties. After an event, he would return to its entry to add the score of a game or note who was at a party. Neither Christine Blasey nor a party like the one she described was mentioned. In fact, the calendars showed that he had been out of town almost every weekend that summer. By 1982, girls were on his radar, but he was known among his female friends as the opposite of what Ford described. He would talk on the phone with his many female friends, help them with their homework, and lightly discuss the girl he was interested in at the time. One woman said he was like a gay friend you'd feel comfortable having your daughter hang out with, except he was not actually gay. His girlfriends from high school reported that he was fun to go out with and had demonstrated nothing remotely close to the aggressive behavior Ford had asserted. He was confident that he could convince any fair-minded observer that he was innocent.

CHAPTER SIX

Delay, Delay, Delay

Within hours of the publication of Emma Brown's story in the *Post*, senators called for the vote on Kavanaugh's nomination to be delayed. Calls for delay were nothing new, but this time it wasn't only the Democrats or members of the Judiciary Committee. Jeff Flake told a reporter that he didn't want to vote until the committee heard more from Ford, and his Republican colleagues Bob Corker of Tennessee and Lisa Murkowski of Alaska also pushed for a delay.[1] Flake's undisguised dislike for Donald Trump was so unpopular with Arizona Republicans that he had decided not to run for reelection in 2018. Journalists now speculated that Flake's support for a delay was an act of revenge against the president.[2]

Mitch McConnell was opposed to reopening the hearings, and he initially thought he could keep the committee from doing so. Grassley also opposed reopening the hearings. Both felt that giving Kavanaugh's opponents a televised platform would be a mistake. Nobody wanted a reenactment of the melodramatic Clarence Thomas–Anita Hill hearings. And nobody wanted to establish the precedent of an uncorroborated allegation against a nominee triggering a full Senate hearing. Reopening the hearings would also invite additional unverified accusations. McConnell and Grassley preferred to conduct a responsible investigation—as they would have done had the information been properly disclosed to the committee and the FBI—and leave it at that. But now other Republican members on the committee were calling for more hearings, and with a one-vote majority there was no room for error.

Leonard Leo, still on leave from the Federalist Society to help with the confirmation, began collecting intelligence on how seriously senators were taking the matter and what they would require to move on. As a way of gauging their sentiments, he asked them if they thought the administration needed a "Plan B"—that is, an alternative nominee. As soon as the *Intercept* story had hit, some people thought it would fade away. By the time Ford's name was public, it was clear to Leo that they faced a replay of the attack on Clarence Thomas and an aggressive battle plan was needed. He began raising money for the ads that would be run between the anti-Kavanaugh "news" segments dominating the airwaves.

The reaction to Ford's accusation was intensified by the ongoing #MeToo movement, which encouraged women to disclose their experiences of sexual harassment or assault. In the past year, powerful men in the entertainment industry, government, academia, and business had been brought down by such accusations.

One dogma of the #MeToo movement, which by now commanded the allegiance of the press, progressive activists, and most Democratic politicians, was that every woman who makes an allegation must be believed.[3] Supporters of due process rejected the slogan "Believe Women" and the presumption that no accusation of sexual harassment is ever malicious or mistaken, arguing that accusers should be treated with respect but that charges must be investigated.

Soon after Ford's allegations were made public, Senator Susan Collins was asked if she believed her. "I don't know enough to create the judgment at this point," Collins replied.[4] But other prominent women were less modest about their grasp of the facts. An article in *The Atlantic* by Caitlin Flanagan was headlined, "I Believe Her: When I Was in High

School, I Faced My Own Brett Kavanaugh." Flanagan believed Ford's accusation because a different boy had tried to rape her when she was in high school.[5]

Within hours of the publication of Brown's story in the *Post*, journalists began speculating that the nomination might be withdrawn. *Roll Call*, citing concerns for the judge's young daughters, said, "Kavanaugh might decide to spare his family what inevitably will be a few weeks of scrutiny and discussion about Ford's charges." And if he didn't, the story added, the White House might pull his nomination anyway.[6]

Reporters were hounding those who had spoken on behalf of Kavanaugh, particularly the women who had known him in high school. Many had to turn off their social media accounts to avoid the deluge of phone calls and emails. But not responding to reporters was treated as a tacit admission that one no longer believed in Kavanaugh's innocence. The *HuffPost* tried to ask scores of friends and students who had expressed support for Kavanaugh's appointment if they still supported him. The "vast majority" did not reply, and the *HuffPost* acknowledged that it did not know how many had even noticed its request for a comment. Almost all who did reply said they continued to support him. (Such support was becoming costly; nearly a third of the former students who still voiced their support did not want their names published.) Nonetheless, the story's headline ran, "Brett Kavanaugh's Supporters Now Far More Reluctant to Speak Up Publicly."[7] In fact, people working on the nomination cited Kavanaugh's incredible base of support among friends as one of the reasons they were willing to fight for him. Raj Shah had worked on other confirmation battles that had heated up and noticed that some nominees' friends would back out. But Kavanaugh's friends and colleagues were unflinching.

One former clerk who wrote and spoke publicly on Kavanaugh's behalf said she felt she had a moral imperative to do so: "You couldn't not say anything. What if everyone who knew and cared about him decided that this is just too controversial or too contentious, or I have too much to lose, and didn't speak up? It would have been a real tragedy."

Despite the revelations, Grassley pushed for the committee to follow the ordinary procedure for an update to a nominee's background
file, which would have meant staff calls with Ford and Kavanaugh.
But by Sunday evening, the ranking member, Senator Feinstein, had
rejected the standard procedure, saying, "The FBI should have the
time it needs to investigate this new material. Staff calls aren't the
appropriate way to handle this."[8]

■   ■   ■

On Monday morning, the White House team gathered to prepare a
response to the allegations. Most assumed that something had happened
between Kavanaugh and Ford but that the details were in dispute. This
would be their first chance to find out exactly what had happened so
they could figure out how to craft a message in response. Their early
assumptions evaporated after talking to Kavanaugh.

McGahn had already talked to Kavanaugh on Sunday, but now he
joined Annie Donaldson and her husband, Brett Talley, in questioning
Kavanaugh, who showed them the calendars. They were astonished that
he had preserved that kind of documentation. From the beginning,
Kavanaugh had been punctilious about avoiding even a whiff of perjury.
He had responded to Kamala Harris's questions with caution despite her
contemptuous accusations of evasion. He had just pulled multiple all-
nighters to make sure none of the 1,287 written answers he submitted
to the Judiciary Committee was marred by the slightest inaccuracy. After
weeks of such lawyerly precision and attention to detail, Kavanaugh's
unequivocal statement that the story was not true made a deep impression on his team. They believed him.

Everyone, including the president, wanted to fight back on every
front, including in the media, in the committee, and with a hearing.
Nobody considered withdrawing the nomination. They knew they might
not win in the midst of a #MeToo media frenzy, but they would go down
fighting. President Trump's eagerness to fight had previously irritated

Republican leaders, but now even they were thankful for it. Other Republican presidents might not have shown the same fortitude.

The battle ahead would be ferocious. Normally, the burden of proof is on the accuser, but the media were not even paying lip service to that principle. "Kavanaugh Bears the Burden of Proof," wrote the legal journalist Ben Wittes, a former defender of Kavanaugh.[9] The team also understood that any criticism of Ford would be treated as a smear. It wasn't that they didn't have damaging information about her. Reports had poured in as soon as her name was known. The Blaseys were well known in their community, and people who knew her in high school and afterwards remembered her or had kept in touch with her. The details they were sharing about Christine's behavior in high school and college were dramatically at odds with her presentation in the media. Some of the reports dealt with her consumption of alcohol, others with her interactions with boys and men.

While the *Post* had suggested that Ford was politically moderate, acquaintances reported that her social media profile, which was completely scrubbed in July, had been notable for its extreme antipathy to President Trump. It also became clear that she had previously gone by her maiden name, but the press was now careful to use her title, "Dr.," and her married name. Some suggested that she was following sophisticated public relations advice to emphasize her relationship with her husband.

The confirmation team knew that mentioning any of this information in public would be depicted as "victim shaming," however relevant it might be to the question of her veracity. Instead of focusing on her, the team would focus on Kavanaugh's lifelong good reputation and the harm his opponents were inflicting on him and the country. Their instincts were right. Even though Kavanaugh's supporters scrupulously declined to go after Ford, the media treated any skepticism about her allegations as a personal attack. "The right-wing smear machine has been lying about Christine Blasey Ford for the past two days," wrote CNN's chief media correspondent, Brian Stelter, after the *Wall Street Journal* and Fox News's Tucker Carlson observed that memory is notoriously fallible.[10]

Kavanaugh's stand-and-fight strategy was nearly stopped before it could start. On Monday morning, September 17, Kellyanne Conway, the counselor to the president, told Fox News that Ford "should not be insulted, she should not be ignored. She should testify under oath and she should do it on Capitol Hill."[11] That's exactly what Kavanaugh and his advisors had decided to ask for, but they were frustrated when Conway got ahead of them, fearing that their statement now would look less like a display of confidence than a concession to a skeptical White House. Still, everyone had to adapt. Even President Trump's comments for most of the week were restrained, essentially echoing what Conway said.

Also on Monday morning, Debra Katz gave interviews to a number of television networks. She told NBC that Ford was willing to testify.[12] On CNN, she revealed that Ford had spoken with Senator Feinstein soon after July 30 and retained counsel. "We were in touch" with Feinstein's office throughout the following weeks, Katz said.[13] On CBS she added that Ford was "willing to do whatever is necessary" to make sure the committee had the "full story" and, ominously, the "full set of allegations."[14]

Prior to the allegations, the judicial nomination process had been handled through the White House counsel's office, with additional help detailed from other offices in the White House and Department of Justice. When the Ford news broke, other parties in the White House tried to intervene, and squabbles were soon breaking out. Some White House surrogates were telling the media that McGahn and his team were botching the response and that President Trump was losing confidence. That wasn't true, but there was intense pressure to allow others to help. Shah and Kerri Kupec had handled communications prior to the allegations, but the broader White House communications team now began to be more involved.

Only one large official moot was held after the Ford allegations broke, even before a hearing was officially scheduled. The White House director of communications, Bill Shine, and the press secretary, Sarah Sanders, along with a number of others, played the parts of various senators. It was important for those supporting Kavanaugh in the media to be convinced of his credibility if they were to do their jobs well. But the involvement of more persons made leaks more likely. The Kavanaugh team had been tight-lipped, priding itself on its discretion in a notoriously leaky administration. But those leading the confirmation effort thought that the advantages of broadening the team were worth the risk. To be safe, they warned Kavanaugh that he shouldn't say anything that he didn't want to be made public. He kept quiet about the existence of his calendars, therefore, so he could reveal them on his own timing. Shah had drafted intrusive questions for Sanders to ask, but she was too uncomfortable to do so. Another participant asked them instead.

At the end of a moot, Kavanaugh ordinarily left so the participants could discuss his performance and decide on a single strategy. After he left the room, someone interrupted the discussion to announce that the media were already reporting that Kavanaugh was mooting with the press team. Later the *Washington Post* cited three sources who reported that "Kavanaugh grew frustrated when it came to questions that dug into his private life, particularly his drinking habits and his sexual proclivities."[15] They added that he declined to answer some questions altogether, which made it sound like he had something to hide. In fact, one of the goals of the moot had been to determine the right place to draw a line on invasive questions, and the only question he had ultimately declined to answer was when he had first slept with his wife.

Their suspicions about the discretion of the broader group confirmed, the core Kavanaugh team resolved to get rid of any nonessential aides. Contrary to the press reports, they felt he had handled the moot so well that another moot could be counterproductive. They didn't want him to go into the hearing sounding scripted.

Kavanaugh also spoke by telephone to the Judiciary Committee staff under penalty of felony on Monday. He "unequivocally denied" the allegations. Democratic staff members could have asked any question they wanted, but they declined to participate in the interview. Kavanaugh requested a hearing right away, the next day if possible. He knew that with each passing day the media would elaborate on their portrait of a sexual predator and activists would redouble their search for dirt.

■　　■　　■

The Judiciary Committee staff tried to talk to Ford on Sunday after her name was revealed and again on Monday when her attorney said she wanted to share her story with them. Ford's attorneys refused the requests, according to a Senate report.[16]

Grassley preferred a private information-gathering process to a public hearing, which was likely to become a circus. He had spent decades protecting whistle-blowers who made serious allegations, and in June he had held a full committee hearing on sexual harassment in the federal judiciary. He wanted to provide Ford a safe, comfortable, and dignified way to tell her story, even if he didn't want the entire judicial confirmation process held hostage.

But by late afternoon on Monday, nearly all the Republicans on the committee wanted to offer Ford a hearing. Kavanaugh also wanted a public hearing to clear his name. The White House had heard from Senator Ben Sasse, who advised them to take the allegations as seriously as possible, citing his experience as a college president.

A committee business meeting had been scheduled for Thursday, September 20, the date they had expected to vote Kavanaugh out of committee, and some White House staff members hoped a second hearing could be held then. But because notice of the witnesses appearing had to be given a week in advance, Grassley could not schedule it earlier than Monday, the twenty-fourth. Katz had now repeatedly said on television that Ford wished to testify, so Grassley went ahead and scheduled hearings. Senator John Kennedy spilled the beans as he exited the meeting with Republican colleagues where the decision was made.

Perhaps unknowingly, Republicans had called Katz's bluff. She immediately shifted to a different strategy, demanding that the FBI investigate the allegation before Ford testified.[17] Democrats, while boycotting the committee's own investigative efforts, joined her in insisting that the FBI should be given time to do a full investigation. The Department of Justice explained on Monday that the FBI had not been called on because the allegation did not involve any federal crime and the letter had already been added to his background information file according to the usual procedure.[18]

The Kavanaugh team's worries about the dangers of delay were soon borne out. In contrast to the skepticism with which the press treated the supportive letter from Kavanaugh's female friends and colleagues the previous week, it lavished favorable coverage on a letter signed by alumnae of Holton-Arms, described as a "response" to the first letter.[19] The signatures had been collected quickly, as had the signatures to the letter in support of Kavanaugh, but this time there was no suggestion that such speed was suspicious. Unlike the pro-Kavanaugh letter, it was signed overwhelmingly by people who didn't actually know the person they were vouching for, but their support was treated as relevant to her credibility nonetheless.[20] The *Washington Post*'s report, under the headline "As Conservatives Attack, Hundreds Sign Letters Supporting Kavanaugh Accuser Christine Blasey Ford," remarked that one of the letters of support "directly challenges the narratives being thrown at Ford—alleged political bias; the decades-long delay in making the allegations—to impugn her character."

The media, however, were not even reporting the "challenges to the narrative," to the exasperation of many of Ford's contemporaries in Washington. Nor were they reporting the dismay of Holton-Arms alumnae at the school's public support of Ford. Sara Hayes, an alumna, said she had never "been more disappointed nor felt more detached from a school" she loved, decrying the "rush to judgment" and the "presumption of guilt" that the school was espousing.

■   ■   ■

The next day, Tuesday, September 18, Ford's lawyers finally responded to the many attempts by the staff of the Judiciary Committee to schedule an interview and prepare for a hearing. The attorneys complained that Ford had been forced out of her home by violent messages targeting her and her family, that her email had been hacked, and that she had been impersonated online.[21] Kavanaugh, of course, was enduring similar problems but cooperated by telephone.

Despite having called for a Senate hearing the day before, Ford's attorneys angrily denounced Grassley for expecting her "to testify at the same table as Judge Kavanaugh in front of two dozen U.S. Senators on national television to relive this traumatic and harrowing incident."[22] Allowing Republican senators who had approached Ford's account with skepticism to question her, they suggested, would be an outrage. "[N]o sexual assault survivor should be subjected to such an ordeal," they declared, as though the allegations should be believed without respectful investigation.[23]

Democrats continued to demand an FBI investigation despite the lack of federal jurisdiction and Ford's vagueness about the location and date of the alleged attack. The media joined in the call, raising no questions about the practicality of asking the FBI to investigate an allegation with so few verifiable details. A Democratic state senator in Maryland even asked the governor to have the state police investigate the attack. He declined, but the local police later said they would investigate if Ford filed a complaint.[24] She never did.[25]

In response to condemnations of the Republican men on the Senate Judiciary Committee for not accepting Ford's allegations at face value, Grassley said on Wednesday the committee was "doing everything" it could to make Ford feel comfortable, and he offered her four different ways to deliver her testimony: an open session or a closed session, as well as public or private interviews.[26] They even offered to send female Senate investigators to California to talk to her. The committee's efforts met with no response from Ford and her lawyers and were ignored by the media and other senators.

Grassley's assertion that Republican committee staffers had done everything they could to reach Ford, said Senator Mazie Hirono, was "bulls—t."[27] By that point, the committee had sent nine emails and left two voicemail messages. The same senator would later tell the press, "And I just want to say to the men in this country: Just shut up and step up. Do the right thing for a change."[28] But Ford's refusal to answer the committee finally began to hurt her case. Some conservatives were encouraging the Senate to proceed to a vote if Ford did not show up at the hearing.[29] Even ABC News's Cokie Roberts said Ford needed to stop delaying and testify.[30]

Kavanaugh's opponents still felt they held a strong hand. Democratic strategists began planning the campaign that would follow their sinking of the nomination, promising to "turn the midterms into a referendum not just on President Trump but also women's rights, abortion and the future of the Supreme Court."[31]

A *HuffPost*–YouGov poll showed that only 28 percent of males and 25 percent of females found Ford's allegations credible and that the allegations had not changed their positions on Kavanaugh's confirmation.[32] But other polls showed a decline in support for Kavanaugh.[33] *Vanity Fair* reported that Ivanka Trump had advised her father to "cut bait" and drop the nomination.[34]

The media continued to report that Ford's allegation was bad for Republicans and good for Democrats, but there were reasons to believe that this message was at the very least overhyped. Democrats in high-profile Senate races were keeping their distance from the Ford story. Phil Bredesen, running for the open seat in Tennessee, even said that the Judiciary Committee should vote if Ford did not show up to testify.[35]

Senator John Cornyn of Texas explained on Tuesday why Republicans were eager to have a hearing where questions could be posed: "The problem is, Dr. Ford can't remember when it was, where it was, or how it came to be. There are some gaps there that need to be filled."[36] Cornyn had simply stated the facts. Those were enormous gaps in an accusation of sexual assault that was intended to keep one of the nation's most distinguished judges off the Supreme Court. But the media responded as if Cornyn were maliciously sowing doubt about an account that anyone of sound mind must regard as unimpeachable. Referring to Cornyn's statement, CNN's Chris Cillizza tweeted: "Walking a VERY dangerous line here."[37]

By contrast, it was not considered a dangerous line to misconstrue jokes made by Kavanaugh. On Tuesday, liberal media outlets and Democrats began sharing an edited clip from a speech Kavanaugh had given at Catholic University's law school in 2015. He had said:

By coincidence, three classmates of mine at Georgetown Prep were graduates of this law school in 1990 and are really, really good friends of mine. Mike Bidwill, Don Urgo, and Phil Merkle, and they were good friends of mine then and are still good friends of mine, as recently as this weekend when we were all on email together. But fortunately, we had a good saying that we've held firm to this day as the Dean was reminding me before the talk, which is "What happens at Georgetown Prep, stays at Georgetown Prep." That's been a good thing for all of us, I think.[38]

The audience laughed. MSNBC aired just the portion after the word "fortunately," giving the impression that the prep school buddies covered up sexual assault with a code of *omertà*. Elizabeth Warren tweeted the truncated video with the comment, "I can't imagine any parent accepting this view. Is this really what America wants in its next Supreme Court Justice?"[39] When CNN aired the clip, its White House reporter Jim Acosta added, "There are portions of his childhood he'd rather not come to light."[40] *Politico*, *USA Today*, and the *Washington Post* all reported the remarks as if they were newsworthy rather than acknowledging an obvious jest based on Las Vegas's familiar tagline.[41]

■　　■　　■

By Wednesday, social media swirled with reports that a witness had finally emerged who could corroborate Ford's account. "The incident DID happen, many of us heard about it in school," wrote Christina King Miranda on Facebook. She repeated her story on Twitter: "The incident was spoken about for days afterward in school. Kavanaugh should stop lying, own up to it, and apologize."[42] It was a curious assertion, since Ford herself said she hadn't told anyone about the assault for decades. The Senate Judiciary Committee's Republican staff immediately asked Miranda for more information. She deleted her note within hours, admitting she had posted it because she had felt "empowered" and was sure the assault had happened, despite having no knowledge of it. "I had no idea that I would now have to go to the specifics and defend it before 50 cable channels and have my face spread all over MSNBC news and Twitter," she told National Public Radio.[43] She tweeted that the post had "served its purpose," which apparently was to use a deliberate lie to make Kavanaugh "stop lying."[44]

Hours after Miranda had deleted her post and admitted that she had no knowledge of the attack, NBC published a story about her headlined, "Accuser's Schoolmate Says She Recalls Hearing of Alleged Kavanaugh Incident." It was modestly edited the next day, although the discredited headline remained the same.[45]

Miranda's wasn't the only story that day to take off in the media but be quickly disproved. The *HuffPost* published an anonymous report that Amy Chua and her husband, Jed Rubenfeld, both professors at Yale Law School, had advised a female law student who was applying for a clerkship with Kavanaugh that the judge liked the women in his chambers to have a "certain look."[46] NBC News and *The Guardian* also picked up the story.[47] Chua was said to have recommended that the woman, whose friends described her as "awkward," work on professional dress. This tale of helpful woman-to-woman mentoring was presented as evidence of Kavanaugh's inappropriate treatment of women.

The dean of Yale Law School, wringing her hands, declared the allegation to be "of enormous concern," and the school promised a full investigation.[48] One of Chua's former students, the writer Abigail Shrier, asked, "What McCarthyist hell are we living [in]?"[49] Chua called the story "outrageous and 100% false."[50] "Yale law professor denies reports she groomed Kavanaugh's prospective clerks," wrote NBC.[51]

As the media chased ephemera, the Judiciary Committee was slowly gathering testimony relating to Ford's allegations. She had said that four persons were at the party with her. Kavanaugh had already categorically denied that he was there. Mark Judge had also submitted a statement to the committee saying he didn't remember any such party and that Kavanaugh never behaved as described. On Wednesday a third person, Patrick "P.J." Smyth, identified as having been at the party, submitted his own statement: "I have no knowledge of the party in question; nor do I have any knowledge of the allegations of improper conduct [Ford] has leveled against Brett Kavanaugh." He added, "Personally speaking, I have known Brett Kavanaugh since high school and I know him to be a person of great integrity, a great friend, and I have never witnessed any improper conduct by Brett Kavanaugh towards women."[52]

Grassley was determined to keep things moving. He announced that Ford had until Friday morning to provide prepared testimony for Monday's hearing.[53]

■   ■   ■

Late on Thursday, a prominent conservative judicial scholar posted a series of tweets that suggested a possible case of mistaken identity. Rumors had been circulating that Ed Whelan, the respected head of the Ethics and Public Policy Center (EPPC) and a friend of Kavanaugh's, had exonerating information. Curiosity was high. In the tweets, he noted that none of the persons identified as being at the party lived close to the Columbia Country Club, which Ford said the party was near. None of them had homes that matched the description she had provided to the *Post*. And it was unlikely, he suggested, that no one at the party lived in the house where the party took place. He then posted a photograph of one of Kavanaugh's high school classmates and the floor plan of the boy's house, which was compatible with Ford's description of the house where the party was. That house was within walking distance of the Columbia Country Club. Finally, the boy bore a resemblance to Kavanaugh.

Even though Whelan had said he wasn't accusing the other man, now a middle school teacher, of any wrongdoing, reporters and observers felt he had done just that. Supporters of Kavanaugh immediately distanced themselves from the tweets. The media pounced. Whelan offered his resignation from the EPPC, which was declined by the board of directors. He deleted the tweets within hours and apologized for "an appalling and inexcusable mistake of judgment in posting the tweet thread in a way that identified

Kavanaugh's Georgetown Prep classmate."[54] Reporters speculated that he had hatched the plan with Kavanaugh or the Federalist Society, but Whelan said he bore full responsibility.

The commotion over Whelan's imprudent decision to publicize the name and face of another classmate prevented many people from considering the other arguments that he made in the series of tweets. In fact, none of the persons who allegedly attended the party lived near Columbia Country Club. Since they had a common friend who lived only a half-mile from the club, it is implausible that someone two miles away would have been considered "near" the club. And it is also logical to assume that a small house party would have taken place at the home of one of the attendees.

The theory—perhaps born of wishful thinking—that Ford could have confused Kavanaugh with this other young man was implausible, particularly since it turned out that Ford had dated the other boy at one point. But it was more reasonable to imagine that if Ford had been drinking heavily, as she was known for doing, her memory could have been clouded. And the one possibility the media refused to consider was plain: if Ford were fabricating a story, she could well have used details of locations she knew or parties she had attended. Whelan's tweets were not the silver bullet they were advertised to be, but he did raise legitimate questions about Ford's story, questions that were overlooked in the ensuing furor.

■   ■   ■

That same Thursday evening, Katz said that Ford might testify if certain conditions were met. She told the committee staff that Ford needed time to secure her family and travel to Washington. She ruled out a Monday hearing and began pushing for Thursday. She also stipulated the following conditions:

- Kavanaugh was not to appear in the same room as Ford.
- Kavanaugh must testify first.
- Only senators could ask the questions.

- Mark Judge must be required to testify.
- Ford must have unlimited time for her opening statement.
- The number of cameras in the hearing room must be limited.[55]

Ricki Seidman, a longtime Democratic operative and Clinton White House insider, was revealed to be part of Ford's legal team as well.[56] The *Weekly Standard* had reported in 1996, "Seidman's resume reads like a fantasy of liberal and Democratic activism." She had been the legal director for Norman Lear's People for the American Way, where she was responsible for the vicious attack ad on Robert Bork. While at Ted Kennedy's office, she was credited with persuading the reluctant Anita Hill to come out with her harassment story. When the Judiciary Committee failed to listen, according to contemporary sources, Seidman helped leak the story to the press. She figures prominently in HBO's pro-Hill drama *Confirmation.*[57] When Kavanaugh was nominated, she was bragging of having worked on one side or the other of every Supreme Court nomination since the elevation of Rehnquist to chief justice, the sole exception being the Gorsuch confirmation.[58]

While they decided how to respond to Ford's various demands, Republicans had one problem that required an unorthodox solution. Democratic senators had earlier complained that it was inappropriate for the Republican men of the Judiciary Committee to question Ford, so the Republicans were arranging for an outside lawyer to handle their questioning.

That Friday, President Trump's uncharacteristic Twitter restraint finally ended when he tweeted, "I have no doubt that, if the attack on Dr. Ford was as bad as she says, charges would have been immediately filed with local Law Enforcement Authorities by either her or her loving parents. I ask that she bring those filings forward so that we can learn date, time, and place!"[59]

Senator Susan Collins, whose support was indispensable, was appalled: "I thought that the president's tweet was completely inappropriate and wrong."[60] Trump's comments also dismayed his critics from the right who had grudgingly approved of his judicial appoint-ments. Jonathan Last argued in the *Weekly Standard* that the nomina-tion should be withdrawn and Kavanaugh replaced with someone who could be "portrayed" as more conservative. The Court's rulings, he wrote, "would have more legitimacy in the eyes of the public if the deciding vote is cast by someone other than Brett Kavanaugh."[61]

Whatever its rough edges, Trump's statement did signal the admin-istration's willingness to stand behind Kavanaugh. A more productive, if no less fervent, show of support came from the Senate majority leader the same day. McConnell told an audience at the Values Voters Summit: "You've watched the fight. You've watched the tactics. But here's what I want to tell you. In the very near future, Judge Kavanaugh will be on the United States Supreme Court." Senate Republicans, he promised, were going to "plow right through it and do our job."[62] The crowd went wild.

Kavanaugh's closest supporters were divided over how to proceed. The White House team wanted to fight, but his many friends from the Bush era encouraged an appeal to decency, rebutting the accusations but emphasizing his strong relationships with women. Such an appeal would be insufficient, the White House team thought, but it couldn't do any harm, so they encouraged Kavanaugh's friends to try it. On Friday, eighty-seven women who knew Kavanaugh throughout his life held a press conference. It received almost no media coverage.

Kavanaugh supporters were facing the reality that most of the media were not merely biased against him but were full participants in the opposition. The conservative group Concerned Women for America (CWA) brought its Iowa state director to Grassley's office. CNN's Sunlen Serfaty said there was no time to talk to her, even as the cable outlet pulled protester after protester out of the crowd to interview. Another CNN reporter pretended to be on a phone call when hundreds of female Kavanaugh supporters came to visit Flake. One CBS reporter flat out told CWA that he wasn't there to cover pro-Kavanaugh forces.

One female Kavanaugh clerk who was doing extensive media in support of the nomination said she eventually realized that prere-corded interviews weren't worth the time, since her statements in support of Kavanaugh would be edited out. The only way to break through was to do live interviews where producers couldn't hide support for Kavanaugh.

Conservative and alternative media became a lifeline for the nomination. Outside groups began streaming their own rallies and advocacy efforts on Facebook Live. With the *New York Times* and *Washington Post* serving as the public relations arm of the anti-Kavanaugh movement, conservative media began breaking stories and debunking false story lines. Later, Christopher Scalia, a son of the late justice, tweeted, "Imagine what these past few weeks would have been like without a strong conservative media presence to fight the bias and credulity of so many other outlets." Robert Bork Jr. pointedly responded, "Yes. Yes, I can."[63]

■   ■   ■

Grassley kept extending the deadline for Ford to accept the offer to testify. He had initially set it for Friday morning, then Friday afternoon, then Friday night.[64] Late Friday, after Ford's attorney called the deadline "arbitrary" and an attempt to "bully" her, he moved it to 2:30 p.m. on Saturday. Unappeased, Katz told the committee in an email, "The imposition of aggressive and artificial deadlines regarding the date and conditions of any hearing has created tremendous and unwarranted anxiety and stress on Dr. Ford. Your cavalier treatment of a sexual assault survivor who has been doing her best to cooperate with the Committee is completely inappropriate."[65]

Senator Grassley, who believed he had been more than fair, grew exasperated. He tweeted, "With all the extensions we give Dr. Ford to decide if she still wants to testify to the Senate I feel like I'm playing 2nd trombone in the judiciary orchestra and Schumer is the conductor."[66] In reality, the people calling the shots were Republican senators who insisted they needed a public hearing to feel comfortable voting for Kavanaugh. Collins joined Judiciary Committee Republicans in insisting on accommodating Ford. She thought it silly to fight over which day of the week

Ford would testify. If the Senate needed to send a plane or a private car to get her, that was fine as well.

On Friday, the Judiciary Committee offered to move the hearing from Monday to Wednesday, one day sooner than she had requested. Some of Kavanaugh's defenders saw the further delay as more time to dredge up outrageous charges, and they worried that Katz wanted to wait until Thursday so she could coordinate other allegations or witnesses.

The committee staff felt they had bent over backwards to meet most of Ford's conditions, but as they wrote to her attorneys, "Some of your other demands, however, are unreasonable and we are unable to accommodate them. You demanded that Judge Kavanaugh be the first person to testify. Accommodating this demand would be an affront to fundamental notions of due process. In the United States, an individual accused of a crime is entitled to a presumption of innocence."[67] They also insisted that the committee would designate its own lawyer to conduct the questioning.[68]

Just before midnight on Friday, Grassley tweeted that after five extensions, Ford needed to let him know if she would testify or not.[69] In another tweet a few minutes later, he told Kavanaugh that he had granted yet another extension and that he hoped the judge would understand.[70]

The media reported unquestioningly Ford's assertion that she was so scarred by the attempted rape in 1982 that she required multiple doors and exit routes in rooms and was unable to travel by airplane, "the ultimate closed space where you cannot get away."[71] The *Washington Post*'s Jennifer Rubin lambasted the Republican senators: "They tell a woman who needs to drive cross country she can't have one extra day. None of these people should be in office."[72]

That night, the Judiciary Committee's communications advisor, Garrett Ventry, resigned after NBC published an anonymous report that he had been fired from a job in the North Carolina legislature after an allegation of sexual harassment, an allegation he denied. NBC reported that Republicans felt he "could not lead an effective communications response," implying that Ventry's colleagues did not support him. In fact, the "Republicans" referred to were not members of the U.S. Senate or of the judiciary staff but a source in North Carolina, as the reporter, Heidi Przybyla, confirmed to Grassley's staff.[73] Nevertheless, NBC refused to correct the story unless Grassley would agree to provide comment for the story.

The environment in which the Judiciary Committee staff had to work was verging on the intolerable. "It was no longer like drinking out of a fire hose. It was learning how to grow gills at that point," said Taylor Foy, the communications director for Grassley. When he had scheduled his wedding for October 4, he hadn't dreamed how stressful the closing weeks of his engagement would be. His bride would wear a "Confirm Kavanaugh" button for her "something blue."

■   ■   ■

Thirteen minutes before Grassley's final deadline on Saturday, Ford's lawyers sent a harshly worded email in which they finally agreed to have her testify. On Monday of that week, Katz had declared that Ford was "willing to do whatever is necessary" for the committee to receive the "full story." By Saturday her position was that although many of Grassley's offers were "fundamentally inconsistent with the Committee's promise of a fair, impartial investigation into her allegations, and we are disappointed with the leaks and the bullying that have tainted the process, we are hopeful that we can reach agreement on details."[74] Later that night they agreed to a hearing on Thursday, September 27, at ten o'clock.

It was also announced on Saturday that Michael Bromwich had joined Ford's legal team. An inspector general under President Clinton, he had recently represented Andrew McCabe, a former deputy director of the FBI and a harsh critic of President Trump who was fired for lying about leaking to reporters.[75]

On Saturday night, the name of the fourth and final witness surfaced. Surprisingly, it was a female. All previous media reports had been based on Ford's changing assertions regarding four boys. Ford had told the *Washington Post*'s Emma Brown that her close and lifelong friend

Leland Keyser was one of the four other persons at the party. Though Brown had concealed this from readers, the Judiciary Committee had found it out. Keyser's attorney, Howard Walsh, responded to an inquiry from the Judiciary Committee: "Simply put, Ms. Keyser does not know Mr. Kavanaugh and she has no recollection of ever being at a party or gathering where he was present, with, or without, Dr. Ford."[76]

Later that same evening, Kimberley Strassel, a columnist for the *Wall Street Journal*, obtained a copy of the email that Emma Brown had sent to Mark Judge hours before her explosive story was published in the *Washington Post*. In that email, Brown had referred to Keyser, using her maiden name, Ingham, as one of four persons Ford said was at the party. Yet Brown's story in the *Post* reported that Ford said there were *four boys* at the party, an apparent attempt to reconcile Ford's account with her therapist's notes: "The notes say four boys were involved, a discrepancy Blasey Ford says was an error on the therapist's part. Blasey Ford said there were four boys at the party but only two in the room."[77] Were there three boys and one girl at the party or four boys? It was apparent that Ford's story had changed and that the *Post* was concealing that change, which would have weakened Ford's credibility.

The *Post* scrambled to update its narrative, explaining, "Before her name became public, Ford told The Post she did not think Keyser would remember the party because nothing remarkable had happened there, as far as Keyser was aware."[78]

Strassel noted on Twitter, "That is WaPo admitting that it had the name, and had Ford's response to what would clearly be a Keyser denial, but NEVER PUT IT OUT THERE."[79] It was evident that the newspaper purposely declined to publish Keyser's name, despite publishing the names of the other alleged witnesses. In fact, Brown had been inside Keyser's house earlier that week, failing to get confirmation of Ford's account. Readers were not even told her name or that Ford's story about four boys was now about three boys and one girl.

Katz rushed to dismiss Keyser's statement: "It's not surprising that Ms. Keyser has no recollection of the evening as they did not discuss it. It's also unremarkable that Ms. Keyser does not remember attending a specific gathering 30 years ago at which nothing of consequence happened to her."[80] Whether a sixteen-year-old girl would forget being abandoned by her friend at a small party with three senior boys, including two varsity football players and the captain of the football team, was in dispute.

It had been quite a week for Christine Blasey Ford. On Sunday, she had exploded onto the scene, identifying four specific persons as having attended that long-ago party. By the following Saturday, all four had denied knowledge of any such gathering.

For Ashley Kavanaugh, life had become surreal. Though she had prayed that her husband not be chosen for the Supreme Court, she had supported him when he was attacked by conservatives who feared that he would be. After he was nominated, she had taken care of the children while he prepared for his hearings. She had quietly endured the indignities of those hearings and tried to protect her children from the ugliness and vulgarity of the protests. (The girls were not impressed by what they heard. Liza mocked one of the chants on the grounds that it didn't rhyme.)

Before the details of Ford's allegation came out, the rumors had been so difficult on the family that Kavanaugh had wondered if a seat on the Supreme Court was worth it. Knowing that the story was about to break, Ashley went to stock up on groceries. The press had already been camped out in front of their house, and she knew it was about to get worse. The story broke while she was in the supermarket, and she read it on her phone sitting in the parking lot. It was a relief of sorts finally to have the allegation in front of them. Justice Thomas said the same thing about finding out the specifics of the allegations made against him.

She told the girls what they needed to know, not wanting them to hear it from anyone else, and reassured them that they could ask her and their father anything, and they would be as honest as possible.

Friends hurried to help, offering to bring meals and take care of the girls and making sure everyone was okay. They would take the girls for extended playdates to keep them entertained. One set of friends had taken Liza to the Columbia Country Club for lunch when news about the allegations came on the television in the restaurant. Someone rushed over to turn it off.

Ashley prayed regularly and studied the Bible. After the attacks of 9/11, she had come across a verse in the scriptures about not being afraid. She wrote it on a sticky note and put it on her desk outside the Oval Office where she would see it frequently. It gave her the courage to support President Bush and others who had much more on their minds. Nearly seventeen years later, the day after her husband was nominated, she had come across a passage from Psalm 37: "Commit your way to the Lord, trust also in Him, and He shall bring it to pass." Now, in very different but no less difficult circumstances, she wrote the verse on a sticky note and placed it on her bulletin board at home where it would give her encouragement.

The Monday after the Ford allegations broke, Ashley was incredibly tired. One of the verses for the day in *Jesus Calling*, a popular daily devotional, was Psalm 37:5.[81] Coming across that familiar verse was profoundly comforting. She felt confident that her husband's nomination was meant to be because she had prayed so hard that he wouldn't get it, but the attacks on this good and decent man made no sense. They were hard to take.

Leland Keyser's announcement that she did not know Kavanaugh was gravely damaging to Ford's already improbable account. This life-long friend, a woman who had every incentive to blur the lines, was unable to corroborate the allegation. Hugely relieved, the Kavanaughs expected the story to be big news. When instead it was barely reported, they knew they were in trouble.

CHAPTER SEVEN

Too Big To Fail

"ANOTHER WOMAN?" blared the headline, in all caps and all red for emphasis.[1] It was 5:30 on Sunday evening, September 23, and the Drudge Report, which had famously broken the news about President Bill Clinton's sexual relationship with Monica Lewinsky in 1998, teased the idea that an explosive new allegation against Kavanaugh was coming. The story would be told by Ronan Farrow and Jane Mayer of the *New Yorker*, the website said. Because Farrow helped kick off the #MeToo movement by breaking the Harvey Weinstein sexual harassment scandal a year before, his name gave the headline an air of credibility.

That evening the story was published.[2] Senate Democrats were investigating "a new allegation of sexual misconduct" that had been conveyed to them by an unnamed "civil-rights lawyer."

A Yale classmate of Kavanaugh's named Deborah Ramirez alleged that during their freshman year, "Kavanaugh had exposed himself at a drunken dormitory party, thrust his penis in her face, and caused her to touch it without her consent as she pushed him away."

After contacting "several dozen" classmates, the *New Yorker* was unable to find a witness to corroborate the story. One anonymous classmate said he had heard about the incident from another student at the time: "I've known this all along. It's been on my mind all these years when his name came up. It was a big deal." He said Kavanaugh was "aggressive and even belligerent" when drinking. Kavanaugh's roommate at the time, James Roche, said that although he never witnessed any sexual misconduct, Kavanaugh was "frequently, incoherently drunk."

Senator Mazie Hirono, whose staff had aroused the suspicion of Republican staffers by arriving at work uncharacteristically early that Sunday morning, pounced: "This is another serious, credible, and disturbing allegation against Brett Kavanaugh [that] should be fully investigated." An unnamed Senate aide was quoted as saying, "If established, they're clearly disqualifying." Ramirez herself "is now calling for the F.B.I. to investigate Kavanaugh's role in the incident," Farrow and Mayer reported.

Ramirez acknowledged that she didn't remember much except "laughter at her expense from Kavanaugh and the other students," a detail curiously similar to one in Ford's story. The *New Yorker* noted that Kavanaugh would have been eighteen years old, a legal adult, at the time, and that if the allegation were true, he would have perjured himself, having sworn that he had never "committed any verbal or physical harassment or assault of a sexual nature."

The article was written in a breathless style that gave it a sense of significance, even though it betrayed more than a whiff of desperation. Mayer even admitted that she and Farrow had pursued the story precisely to show a "pattern of misconduct," since "that helps establish who is telling the truth when there is a standoff, and whether there were credible corroborators on either side."[3]

The writers included lurid stories about Kavanaugh's friends and milieu without establishing any connection to Kavanaugh himself. Elizabeth Rasor, who had dated Kavanaugh's friend Mark Judge, reported that Judge had "told her ashamedly of an incident that involved him and other boys taking turns having sex with a drunk woman." Judge "categorically" denied the report. Another woman had told Ford's lawyers that when she was in high school in the 1980s, "she had witnessed boys at parties that included Georgetown Prep students" get girls drunk with "jungle juice"—a mix of grain alcohol and Hawaiian Punch—and then try to take advantage of them. The four-thousand-word story ended with lawyers for both Ford and Ramirez calling for an FBI investigation, the same thing the Democrats were demanding.

When the *New Yorker* article was published, the stories of group sex and spiked punch seemed irrelevant. They shed no light on Ramirez's allegations and were only faintly relevant to statements in support of Kavanaugh in connection with an unrelated allegation. Mark Judge had previously been asked by the *Weekly Standard* whether he recalled any "sort of rough-housing with a female student back in high school" that could be "interpreted differently by parties involved," and the *New Yorker* had noted his flat denial.[4] Rasor's story certainly did nothing to burnish Judge's image, but it didn't contradict his statement about roughhousing. Her story supposedly "undercut Judge's protestations about the sexual innocence of Georgetown Prep," but Judge, who years earlier had written frankly of his substance abuse struggles, never claimed such innocence.

The "jungle juice" story was even weaker. There was no connection between what other Georgetown Prep students may have done at unspecified parties sometime in the 1980s and what Kavanaugh was alleged to have done at one particular party, let alone at Yale. But those stories would be cited again soon enough.

■   ■   ■

At 7:33 p.m., shortly after the *New Yorker* story was published, a lawyer named Michael Avenatti tweeted: "I represent a woman with credible information regarding Judge Kavanaugh and Mark Judge. We will be demanding the opportunity to present testimony to the committee and will likewise be demanding that Judge and others be subpoenaed to testify. The nomination must be withdrawn."[5] His client was not Ramirez, he said.

Avenatti, who had become an anti-Trump hero for his hardball representation of the porn star Stormy Daniels in her legal tangles with the president, promised "significant evidence of multiple house parties" in the 1980s at which Kavanaugh would "participate in the targeting of women with alcohol/drugs in order to allow a 'train' of men to subsequently gang rape them." Multiple witnesses would corroborate the allegation, he said, and they must be called to testify.[6]

As far as the chattering classes of D.C. were concerned, if Kavanaugh's confirmation had any life left in it before Sunday evening, it was indisputably dead now.

For Kavanaugh, the moment was brutal. This was precisely why he had feared delaying a vote on his confirmation. Delays allowed his opponents to troll for people who'd be willing to say something—*anything*—to discredit him. Time was not his friend.

He wasn't worried that the White House would pull his nomination. There may have been no White House in history more temperamentally suited to this fight. But that was only half the battle. He knew enough about U.S. senators to worry about their commitment throughout a long and unrelenting smear campaign. In fact, Senator Rob Portman, who had served as a de facto adviser as Kavanaugh met with other senators, let him know that some senators were taking the Swetnick allegations seriously. It was one of the only times that Kavanaugh reacted loudly, incredulous that anyone could believe such ridiculous claims.

He wasn't reading the stories, not even the initial story in the *Washington Post*. Senator Orrin Hatch had advised him early in the process to turn off the news. But from the accounts he was given, he wondered who this person they were describing was. He had his flaws, but the media's portrayals of him were simply unrecognizable.[7]

Kavanaugh had to act, so he issued a response to Ramirez's allegations: "This alleged event from 35 years ago did not happen. The people who knew me then know that this did not happen, and have said so. This is a smear, plain and simple. I look forward to testifying on Thursday about the truth, and defending my good name—and the reputation for character and integrity I have spent a lifetime building—against these last-minute allegations."[8]

■   ■   ■

"The principle that there is a presumption of innocence in favor of the accused is the undoubted law, axiomatic and elementary," wrote Justice Edward White in *Coffin v. United States*, tracing it from Deuteronomy through Roman Law, Canon Law, and the Common Law and illustrating it with an anecdote about a fourth-century provincial governor on trial before the Roman Emperor Julian for embezzlement:

> Numerius contented himself with denying his guilt, and there was not sufficient proof against him. His adversary, Delphidius, "a passionate man," seeing that the failure of the accusation was inevitable, could not restrain himself, and exclaimed, "Oh, illustrious Caesar! if it is sufficient to deny, what hereafter will become of the guilty?" to which Julian replied, "If it suffices to accuse, what will become of the innocent?"[9]

The presumption of innocence survives in America's criminal courts, but it seemed to have vanished from the court of public opinion by the time of Brett Kavanaugh's nomination. The #MeToo movement had drawn attention to the serious difficulties women had experienced in reporting sexual assault and harassment, but activists were now demanding complete credulity in response to any accusation, despite the prominent and recent cases of fabricated sexual assault charges against the Duke lacrosse team and a fraternity at the University of Virginia. A small but significant portion of sexual assault allegations—between 2 and 10 percent, according to empirical studies—are eventually deemed false.[10]

When asked, Senator Hirono refused to say that Kavanaugh enjoyed a presumption of innocence, suggesting, remarkably enough, that his judicial philosophy made him somehow less credible. "I put his denial in the context of everything that I know about him in terms of how he approaches his cases," she said.[11] Senator Coons was even more direct, stating the next day that Judge Kavanaugh "bears the burden of disproving these allegations."[12] Senate Minority Leader Chuck Schumer of New York said, "There is no presumption of innocence or guilt when you have a nominee before you."[13]

Senator McConnell pushed back against this abandonment of due process, citing as an authority a former senator who, as chairman of the Judiciary Committee, had presided over the confirmation hearings of Clarence Thomas. As the committee prepared to hear from both Anita Hill and Judge Thomas, Senator Joe Biden had told the nominee, "The presumption is with you. With me, the presumption is with you, and in my opinion, it should be with you until all the evidence is in and people make a judgment."[14] In fact, Hill's testimony came nowhere near the standard necessary to credibly accuse, much less convict, Thomas of sexual harassment. She had no contemporaneous witnesses, was contradicted by contemporaneous witnesses, was caught in several lies under questioning, had a dramatically shifting story, and was generally viewed by the American public as lacking credibility. Almost three decades later, Biden, now a former vice president contemplating a run for president in 2020, reversed himself as soon as Ford's allegations were made public: "For a woman to come forward in the glaring lights of focus, nationally, you've got to start off with the presumption that at least the essence of what she's talking about is real, whether or not she forgets facts, whether or not it's been made worse or better over time."[15]

It wasn't just senators. Faculty, students, and alumni of Yale, obviously unmoved by the collegiate connection, supported Ramirez's call for an FBI investigation of Kavanaugh. Four dozen faculty members issued a letter demanding an immediate halt to the confirmation process.[16] Professors in the law school canceled thirty-one classes to accommodate students busy with a sit-in.[17] And more than one thousand female Yale Law School graduates signed a letter supporting Kavanaugh's accusers.[18] Corroboration of the accusations could wait; signatures were being collected even before the *New Yorker* published its article about Ramirez. Alumni reported furious efforts to assemble mass denunciations of Kavanaugh and to ferret out unflattering stories about him from college. Some were uncomfortable with the rush to judgment but felt it was too dangerous to speak up on Kavanaugh's behalf.

At the same time, it began to appear that Ramirez's story might not hold up under scrutiny. The *New Yorker* article itself contained details that undercut its credibility. It acknowledged that Ramirez had "significant gaps" in her memories, that she was reluctant to speak with certainty about Kavanaugh's role in the incident, that it took her six days of "assessing her memories" and consulting with an attorney provided by Democrats to name Kavanaugh, and that a robust effort to find eyewitnesses failed to turn up anyone who could confirm that Kavanaugh was even present at the party.

Four other classmates, two of whom were allegedly involved in the incident and a third whose husband was allegedly involved, all said the story was ridiculous. "The behavior she describes would be completely out of character for Brett. In addition, some of us knew Debbie long after Yale, and she never described this incident until Brett's Supreme Court nomination was pending," said her classmate Dan Murphy.

Karen Yarasavage said she was best friends with Ramirez at the time and had never heard of the incident. "We shared intimate details of our lives. And I was never told this story by her, or by anyone else. It never came up. I didn't see it; I never heard of it happening," she said. Perhaps most damaging to the credibility of the story is the effect heavy drinking may have had on Ramirez's recollection of what took place in 1983 or 1984. Ramirez admitted she "quickly became inebriated" at the party, ending up "on the floor, foggy and slurring her words."

Acknowledging Ramirez's extremely impaired mental state and never quoting her directly and plainly saying that Brett Kavanaugh exposed himself, Farrow and Mayer nevertheless draw surprisingly strong conclusions about Kavanaugh's guilt. The facts that they actually present are that "a male student pointed a gag plastic penis in her direction" and that

Ramirez remembered being on the floor flanked by that student and another male student. They go on to report that a "third male then exposed himself to her" and quote Ramirez as saying, "I remember a penis being in front of my face." Kavanaugh was standing to her side, they write, and they quote Ramirez as saying, "Brett was laughing," "I can still see his face, and his hips coming forward, like when you pull up your pants."

Anticipating that Ramirez "will inevitably be pressed on her motivation for coming forward after so many years, and questioned about her memory, given her drinking at the party," the authors offer a preemptive rebuttal: "And yet, after several days of considering the matter carefully, she said, 'I'm confident about the pants coming up, and I'm confident about Brett being there.'" Readers are again oddly left to connect the dots themselves about the defining event of the entire story.

National Review's Charles Cooke wrote that he was "struggling to remember reading a less responsible piece of 'journalism' in a major media outlet."[19] Even the *New York Times* admitted the story's failures. Noting that the *New Yorker* had not been able to confirm with other witnesses that Kavanaugh was even at the party, the paper conducted its own interviews with "several dozen people" but "could find no one with firsthand knowledge" of the allegations. The *Times* learned that "Ms. Ramirez herself contacted former Yale classmates asking if they recalled the incident and told some of them that she could not be certain Mr. Kavanaugh was the one who exposed himself."[20]

It was at this moment that a number of people on Kavanaugh's White House team suspected the anti-Kavanaugh forces had finally overplayed their hand. The tide was turning.

Farrow, who had become something of a folk hero for exposing other powerful male sexual predators, now had to defend his story. On CNN he said Ramirez's story "exceeds the evidentiary basis we've used in the past in several cases that were found to be very credible," bringing his previous stories into question as well.[21]

"By discarding the basic standards of evidence and journalism, Ronan Farrow has set the Me Too Movement back," wrote David Marcus in *The*

Federalist (where one of this book's authors is a senior editor).[22] It did not help Farrow's credibility that his co-author was Mayer, whose partisan record gave Republicans good reason to believe that her reporting on Kavanaugh was driven by her political agenda. By Monday evening, Drudge's headline "ANOTHER WOMAN?" had given way to "RONAN MISFIRES?"[23]

But the major media were less skeptical, flooding the airwaves and internet with stories of the drunken sexual predator about to become an arbiter of women's rights on the Supreme Court. Although the *New York Times* poked holes in Ramirez's account, two days later it published a lengthy report about an obscure anti-Trump Mormon women's group that was joining the Democrats' call for an investigation.[24]

As if the *Washington Post's* initial effort on behalf of Ford weren't enough, it ran a 2,500-word hagiographical profile of her[25] while publishing stories such as "How in the World Is Mark Judge Not Testifying?"[26] That week, the *Post* also published a ten-thousand-word, multi-part investigative essay about a woman traumatized by rape in high school that acknowledged that she had misidentified one of her schoolmate rapists.[27] The paper failed to acknowledge that Kavanaugh's accusers might commit such errors.

Kavanaugh, as he had done from the beginning, stayed on offense, sending a letter to Senators Grassley and Feinstein that made it clear he would fight back as a matter of principle to clear his name:

> These are smears, pure and simple. And they debase our public discourse. But they are also a threat to any man or woman who wishes to serve our country. Such grotesque and obvious character assassination—if allowed to succeed—will dissuade competent and good people of all political persuasions from service. As I told the Committee during my hearing, a federal judge must be independent, not swayed by public or political pressure. That is the kind of judge I will always be. I will not be intimidated into withdrawing from this process. The coordinated effort to destroy my good name will not drive me out. The vile threats of violence against my

family will not drive me out. The last-minute character assassination will not succeed.

Kavanaugh's defiant statement called to mind what Clarence Thomas said to Senator Orrin Hatch at his confirmation hearing: "I'd rather die than withdraw from the process. Not for the purpose of serving on the Supreme Court, but for the purpose of not being driven out of this process. I will not be scared. I don't like bullies. I've never run from bullies. I never cry uncle, and I'm not going to cry uncle today, whether I want to be on the Supreme Court or not."[28]

Kavanaugh wasn't going to cry "uncle" either, but would he make it to the Thursday hearings? The media, which had sided overwhelmingly with his accusers, were defaming him around the clock. Something had to be done, the confirmation team thought. He needed to be presented to the public as more than a judicial star with a twenty-four-karat résumé. For the first time in history, a Supreme Court nominee would sit for an interview on television, and his wife would join him.

■   ■   ■

Supreme Court nominees used to stay silent and stay away during their confirmation process. Not only did they not testify before the Senate, they rarely spoke to the press.

Even during Louis Brandeis's contentious hearings, which attracted considerable attention from the press, much of it motivated by antisemitism, he said nothing on the record. When the *New York Sun* pestered him, the nominee said, "I have nothing to say about anything, and that goes for all time and to all newspapers, including both the *Sun* and the moon."[29] When Robert Bork Jr., a journalist at the time, went on television to defend his father during his confirmation fight, the elder Bork insisted that he stop: "It's undignified, I don't want you doing this, I don't want my family doing this." Official surrogates were one thing, but the nominee himself, and even his family, must remain aloof.

A television interview with the nominee would be such a break with tradition that the White House wanted to clear it with the Senate. McConnell said to go ahead.

Several interviewers were considered, the leading contenders being Jan Crawford at CBS and Martha MacCallum at Fox News (a cable channel for which one of this book's authors is a contributor). They wanted someone who would conduct a serious interview but who would be fair and let Kavanaugh speak—neither a series of softball questions nor a game of "gotcha."

MacCallum won out, in part because, as much as the team respected Crawford's integrity, some worried that CBS's editors would slice and dice the interview to make Kavanaugh look bad. Also, the Fox News audience included conservatives whose support needed to be shored up. The interview would be broadcast in the seven p.m. hour, but clips would air throughout the day, and it would be discussed throughout Fox's prime-time lineup. As soon as the interview was announced, the major media tried to write it off as a joke. The caustic reaction of Margaret Sullivan, a media columnist for the *Washington Post*, was typical: "Female interviewer, check. Fox News, check. Bill Shine approved, check. When an 'exclusive interview' promises to be a challenge-free infomercial."[30] Dismissing Ashley's presence, she wrote, "Wife at your side, check,"[31] and "Unquestioning adoration would probably be the right look."[32]

In fact, MacCallum asked tough and probing questions—eliciting, for instance, the revelation that Kavanaugh "did not have sexual intercourse or anything close to sexual intercourse in high school or for many years thereafter"—and she won praise for her interview.

Kavanaugh's own performance was hotly debated. He did not seem comfortable, and his answers came off as over-rehearsed. Shortly before the interview, a few members of the White House team met with him at the house where he was staying. At the moot the previous week, he had seemed natural and righteously indignant, but now, they noticed, he seemed cautious and over-prepared. "The Bushies had gotten to him," said one of the White House advisers.

When the White House team stopped holding moots with Kavanaugh, a kitchen cabinet of sorts—including friends who ran communications efforts for President Bush—took its place, providing advice and guidance as he prepared for the next round of hearings. The White House team found Kavanaugh's forceful denials convincing, but many in this group favored a softer, more sympathetic—even hand-wringing—approach, one that emphasized his relationships with women and affirmed that accusers have to be taken seriously. Kavanaugh himself was memorizing lines that were perfectly reasonable sentiments but would come across as verbal tics during the interview. More than ten times he returned to some variation of the phrase, "I'm just asking for a fair process where I can be heard and defend my integrity."[33] The scripting from advisors extended to encouraging Ashley to wear a necklace with a cross, a suggestion she bristled at and declined.

The White House team realized what was happening and tried to encourage more of what they had seen the previous week, but the interview was looming. It was filmed in a Washington hotel, which was supposed to provide a warm, personal atmosphere without invading the privacy of the Kavanaughs' own living room. But the room was a disappointment. It was so unattractive, in fact, that someone ran to buy plants so the setting wouldn't be completely lifeless. The interview was awkward for the typically private Kavanaughs, forced to discuss intimate issues on national television in a room full of cameramen and producers.

Whatever its shortcomings, the interview served its purpose, even if key senators found Kavanaugh a bit robotic. It put him back in the news on his own terms, reminded the media that the man they were accusing of rape was a human being instead of a caricature, and taught him how to respond more effectively. The kinder, gentler Kavanaugh could take him only so far. McGahn would remind him that while he may have worked for Bush, he was a Trump nominee. And Trump fights. For his part, Trump tweeted out his support of Kavanaugh before, during, and after the interview.

Kavanaugh was vexed by the image of him as a crazy drunk. In his mind, he had been a top athlete and a top student who liked to drink on the weekend. He also resented his friends' being dragged into the controversy. People who wanted to score points on Kavanaugh were painting a caricature of privileged and out-of-control prep school boys with no regard for the collateral damage to innocent people.

It was painful for him to see Georgetown Prep's reputation unfairly tarnished by ideological zealots in the media, who demanded to know everything from the school's current enrollment to the details of its sex education curriculum. The Jesuit school took the religious and moral instruction of its students extremely seriously, knowing that adolescent boys would occasionally disappoint, sometimes grievously. And such problems as Georgetown Prep had with sex, drinking, and other teenage failings were hardly unique.

Throughout the ordeal, school officials remained tight-lipped, but their terse and carefully worded statements seemed only to inflame the media's passion for dirt-digging. *New York Times* reporters were showing up at football games and peppering alumni with questions. Eventually, the school's director of marketing and communications, Patrick Coyle, denounced the smear campaign in a letter to the *Washington Post*'s metro reporter, Joe Heim: "The *Washington Post*'s coverage of Georgetown Prep in recent weeks has been marred by shoddy reporting and slanted, agenda-driven framing within those stories. Numerous articles were composed and published, for example, without the *Post* ever offering us the opportunity for reaction or comment."

Coyle wasn't exaggerating. A few days later, the paper ran a gossipy report about Georgetown Prep's search for a new director of alumni relations, playing up the Kavanaugh controversy and asserting that the "listing went up after Georgetown alumni were very much in the news." Coyle had previously informed the newspaper that the job had been posted since July, long before the Kavanaugh controversy. In response to a correction from Coyle, the *Post* altered the article as subtly as possible without acknowledging the error.[34]

Kavanaugh saw that more was at stake than his own career. For the sake of the people at Georgetown Prep and everyone else in his community, he wanted to fight the charges against him.

While the nominee waited to have his say before the Senate and the nation, the president traveled to New York for the annual session of the United Nations General Assembly, where he expressed his opinion of the allegations with characteristic bluntness: "She thinks maybe it could have been him, maybe not. Admits she was drunk. She admits time lapses. This is a person, and this is a series of statements that is going to take one of the most talented intellects from a judicial standpoint in our country, keep him off the U.S. Supreme Court?" He added, "I think it's horrible what the Democrats have done. It is a con game; they really are con artists."[35]

The media were fixated on Kavanaugh's revelation about his sex life. While it helped explain why he was so confident in his denials of the claims against him, it also exposed him to brutal attacks and ridicule. The news that he was a virgin for "many years" after high school "makes sense since the alleged behavior was disgusted, juvenile, emotionally stunted," wrote the *Washington Post*'s Jennifer Rubin.[36]

Jimmy Kimmel relentlessly mocked him, playing the clip about his high school and college virginity to audience jeers. After rehearsing all the unsubstantiated allegations against him, Kimmel said, "I think there's a compromise here; hear me out on this. So, Kavanaugh gets confirmed to the Supreme Court, okay. Well, in return we get to cut that pesky penis of his off in front of everyone."[37]

The *Washington Post* declared, "The virginity defense is a reminder of our ignorance about sexual violence."[38] "Kavanaugh's 'choir boy' image on Fox interview rankles former Yale classmates," read the headline of yet another *Post* piece.[39] The *New Republic* argued that by his defiance in the face of the allegations against him, Kavanaugh had "already disqualified himself" and could no longer be a judge.[40]

The media had not forgotten Michael Avenatti, doing their best to keep his still unspecified charges before the public eye. His client had been fully vetted, he said, and he had spoken to multiple witnesses.[41] In a lengthy interview on CNN, Avenatti said Kavanaugh was "lying" about being a virgin.[42] *Politico* called him an "avenging angel,"[43] while *USA Today* reported his assertion that the as yet unrevealed accuser was "100 percent credible."[44] Not everyone was impressed by Avenatti, however. Grassley's staffer Mike Davis thought the absurdity of his charges emphasized the injustice of what Kavanaugh was having to endure. He called Avenatti "manna from heaven."

■   ■   ■

Conservatives also began explaining the seriousness of the battle to senators. They had a simple choice, wrote Sean Davis of *The Federalist*: stand up to the smear campaign or lose their majority in the Senate. "The mood among GOP voters right now is unmistakable: they are out for blood," he wrote. "If Kavanaugh is confirmed, they'll eagerly turn out in November to defeat Democrats and their lies. But if Kavanaugh is jettisoned, they'll gleefully sit back and let the GOP get destroyed in November," he wrote.[45] As one of Grassley's aides put it, Kavanaugh had become "too big to fail."

The media were lined up against Kavanaugh; left-wing activists, having drawn blood, were newly energized; and Republican senators were wobbling—Kavanaugh needed help. Some of that came from outside organizations.

On the day Justice Kennedy announced his retirement, Penny Nance, the president of Concerned Women for America (CWA), announced, "We plan to devote considerable resources to this effort, and we expect to win. Our happy warrior/activist ladies relish the fight and shine in these historic moments."[46]

Since the nomination of Robert Bork, CWA, with its half-million members, thirty-five state directors, four hundred chapters, and forty-two college chapters, had made the confirmation of Supreme Court justices a priority in its grassroots political work. The group's core issues were "sanctity of life, defense of family, education, religious liberty, national sovereignty, sexual exploitation, and support for Israel," and the Supreme Court played a role in almost all of them.

The conservative CWA was not a rubber stamp for Republican nominees, however, having come out against Harriet Miers. But Trump's list of potential Supreme Court nominees had enabled the group to vet the names and be prepared to step up immediately when one of them was chosen. CWA's prompt endorsement was enormously helpful for Kavanaugh's cause. The American Family Association and other conservative organizations had raised objections. CWA made plans for a "Women for Kavanaugh" bus tour in August in Iowa, Missouri, Indiana, North Dakota, Alabama, Florida, and West Virginia. Trump had carried all these states in 2016 and most of them had competitive Senate races in 2018.

The midterms loomed large for both sides in the Kavanaugh confirmation battle. Republicans held a razor-thin majority in the Senate. Donald Trump's improbable victory had roiled the political classes. Democrats had picked up two Senate seats in 2016 and another one in a special election the following year. The numbers in 2018 were favorable for the Republicans—of the thirty-five seats in the election, twenty-six were held by Democrats—but this would be Americans' first chance to register their opposition to Trump at the polls, and surveys showed many Democrats and disenchanted Republicans were eager to do so. The Republican base, by contrast, wasn't eager to vote in the midterms, particularly for members of Congress, who had accomplished little while in power and weren't seen as supportive enough of Trump.

CWA had shown up for the first round of hearings and for every business meeting held by the Judiciary Committee. Their women had been praying for senators, as they had done in previous confirmation battles. While the media focused on the often-colorful liberal activists, the polite and modest women of CWA sat quietly in the hearing rooms or gathered in small groups to pray in Senate buildings. The Kavanaugh team, afraid of unduly politicizing the confirmation process, had discouraged CWA from busing in women from out of town for the initial hearings, and it was too late to make such plans for the second set of hearings.

CWA was not surprised when the allegation against Kavanaugh came out. The day of Kennedy's retirement, Nance had told colleagues in a staff meeting as well as contacts at the White House that the nominee, whoever he was, would face an allegation of sexual assault, probably from his distant past, such as high school. Nance didn't take sexual assault lightly. She had spoken publicly about the sexual assault and attempted rape she endured when pregnant with her daughter. But she knew that the political incentives were aligned to weaponize #MeToo allegations. One of the reasons she preferred Amy Coney Barrett for the nomination was that it would be more difficult to make a #MeToo accusation against her.

The women of CWA analyzed the allegation and Kavanaugh's response and concluded that there was no reason to drop their support of the nominee. It was a risky move for a women's group, and they worried about their credibility if they were found to have made the wrong decision. They meditated on the biblical story of Jeremiah, who was falsely accused of treason yet trusted in God. When they decided to stick with Kavanaugh, they found that their members rushed to support him. And they added new prayer intentions: the protesters who were testifying to their own pain and brokenness and the women around the world who are victims of abuse and sex trafficking.

Like CWA, Tea Party Patriots (TPP) had been working to change the Senate, with judicial appointments in mind, well before the current vacancy. Though they were not shy about promoting outsiders and rebels in the primaries, they often endorsed and assisted Republicans they had opposed in the primaries because of the overriding importance of judges. They may not have agreed with those candidates on every issue, but they knew that a Democratic senator was a guaranteed vote for Obama's judges or, later, against Trump's.

That decision originated among the membership, not the leaders. As much as they hated "establishment" politicians, these Tea Partiers demonstrated more sophistication than they ordinarily get credit for. They appreciate the importance of the courts because they know their other goals all depend on having judges committed to the rule of law.

TPP had been active during Neil Gorsuch's confirmation process, engaging in its signature brand of person-to-person outreach to build support. They hosted hundreds of house parties, to which activists could invite their friends to learn about Gorsuch and then take some form of action—from writing or calling their senators and writing letters to the editor to collecting signatures on petitions and hand-delivering them to a local senator's office. For Kavanaugh's nomination there wasn't time to organize house parties, but they distributed "how-to" guides to their members, tapping into people's excitement about having specific tasks they could carry out.

When the allegations against Kavanaugh broke, TPP evaluated the evidence and the statements on both sides before proceeding. They had painful experience of unfounded allegations' being deployed as political weapons, as when TPP was blamed for a mass shooting perpetrated by someone completely unaffiliated with the group. "I know how it feels to be accused of something that I did not do and could imagine what Brett Kavanaugh would be thinking and feeling," remarked Jenny Beth Martin, the group's co-founder. Beyond the "he said–she said," all the evidence supported Kavanaugh, and that was enough for their decision.

Susan B. Anthony List (SBA), an organization that supports pro-life politicians, was another group that took a pause after the allegations broke. Senate races were important to them because of the decisive role of judges in abortion policy. They had also switched from opposing Trump to enthusiastically supporting him when he signed—and even added to—their pro-life pledge. That support meant engaging with nearly 1.5 million people in the 2016 campaign, a number that went up to 2.7 million for the 2018 campaign. After evaluating the evidence, SBA resumed its efforts on behalf of Kavanaugh in states with Senate seats in play, sending more than one thousand people to knock on doors by mid-September. The middle-aged women who account for most of SBA's local directors were outraged at the presumption of Kavanaugh's guilt, and they saw that in key states such as Missouri there was actually an increase in support for Kavanaugh following the allegations.

The Koch network, particularly its flagship organization Americans for Prosperity, saw that its activists were fired up by the unfair attacks on Kavanaugh. Volunteers put their families and work on hold to man the call centers late into night. Americans for Prosperity had not seen such engagement since the groundswell of opposition to Obamacare.

■   ■   ■

Media coverage continued to be brutal. The *New York Times*, scrutinizing inside jokes in Kavanaugh's 1983 Georgetown Prep yearbook, declared, "Kavanaugh's Yearbook Page Is 'Horrible, Hurtful' to a Woman It Named."[47] To interpret Kavanaugh's cryptic description of himself as a "Renate alumnius" (sic), the *Times* relied on his classmates Richard S. Madaleno Jr., a Maryland state senator and unsuccessful candidate for governor, whose campaign ads featured him kissing his male spouse and telling voters that he would "deliver progressive results and stand up to Donald Trump," and William Fishburne, a political associate of Madaleno's.[48] The article strongly suggested that "Renate alumnius" was a boastful—and highly disrespectful—claim to have had sex with a girl who was in Kavanaugh's circle of friends.

The classmates implicated by the *New York Times* strenuously insisted that the reference was not sexual and that none of them had had sexual relations with Renate. They said that they attended each other's dances and prep school functions and had maintained the friendship through the ensuing decades. The men the *Times* relied on to decode the yearbook references, they said, would have had no idea what they meant.

The media also succeeded in tracking down Mark Judge, who was lying low on the Eastern Shore of Maryland. He had long been open about the serious alcohol problems of his youth, even writing a book about his experiences.[49] Later, after a political conversion, he had become a conservative writer.[50] The media were eager to publicize rumors of his wild youth. They showed much less interest in examining Ford's background.[51]

While the media's excavation of early-eighties Georgetown Prep could not have been more thorough, the culture of Holton-Arms, the toney girls' school Ford attended (motto: "I will find a way or make one"), was scrupulously unexplored. Yearbooks from Ford's era were filled with discussions of "Beer and Boys" and how they made parties better. Descriptions of drinking games such as quarters and beer pong, photos of teenagers drinking beer, and jokes about skirting drinking laws were a feature of every volume.

A two-page spread in the 1982 yearbook under the headline "Celebrate Good Times" was devoted to partying and drinking: "The party experience is definitely not to be missed. Few have experienced the joy of waking up to find their house creatively redecorated with bottles, cans, and kids. The bottles and cans even manage to find their way to the front yard and street. Your neighbors will love the additions as more and more are discovered by the spring thaw...then comes the infamous BEACH WEEK, where the supreme challenge is how much partying you can fit into 7 days. Who is going to win this year?"

The pages that follow contain references to "Playboy Bunnies" and things that are "X-rated" as well as pictures of beer and rum. The same volume boasts a cavalcade of off-color jokes about "furburgers vs. Cheeseballs," "6 Caucasian females, one Caucasian male," and "Halloween-whores," as well as a lewd riff on the "tube snake boogie."

The following year's edition contained this description of a party: "As you descend into a family's treasured basement, the muffle of parents locked in a closet can be heard from upstairs. A few shoves and one big push, and you find yourself in the center of things: things such as elbows, cigarettes, beers and noise. Unsticking your feet from marshy floor, you make your way towards the keg where one or two senior boys huff and puff but the tap only trickles."

Among the memories enshrined in the 1983 yearbook (when Ford was a junior) are hanging out at a sex shop called the Pleasure Chest and drinking daiquiris. One student was said to have enjoyed "Peppermint Schnapps night at E.J.'s" when a group of juniors drove into D.C. Reflecting on a year of youthful high spirits, Ford's classmates recorded for posterity: "Lastly, one cannot fail to mention the climax of the junior social scene, the party. Striving to extend our educational experience beyond the confines of the classroom, we played such intellectually stimulating games as Quarters, Mexican Dice, and everyone's favorite, Pass-Out, which usually resulted from the afore-mentioned two."

This depiction of Holton-Arms as Studio 54 on the Potomac may be nothing more than adolescent posturing, and only the alumnae can judge how accurately it reflects their social life in the early 1980s. But it is clear that a lack of vigilance by the yearbook's faculty adviser and bacchanalian extracurricular activities were by no means unique to Georgetown Prep.

■   ■   ■

The media frenzy produced an almost violently partisan atmosphere. An anti-Kavanaugh mob chased Senator Ted Cruz and his wife out of Fiola, a D.C. restaurant. Claiming responsibility, a group called Smash Racism DC warned: "This is a message to Ted Cruz, Bret Kavanaugh, Donald Trump, and the rest of the racist, sexist, transphobic, and homophobic right-wing scum. You are not safe. We will find you. We will expose you. We will take from you the peace you have taken from so many others."[52]

To spare the Kavanaughs that kind of abuse, friends brought them casseroles and other food. They couldn't be in public without attracting protesters, or worse. One day, finding herself with more cupcakes from generous friends than her family could eat, Ashley took some to the marshals who were protecting the house. The marshals couldn't eat them all, so she offered the extras to the press who were camped outside the house. News quickly spread on social media that she had handed out cupcakes from the posh bakery Sprinkles, a rare moment of friendly coverage. Ashley hadn't put much thought into it, but she knew from her many years with President Bush that the cameramen and photographers don't usually have a political ax to grind; they are just nice people doing their jobs. No one expected the two dozen flower arrangements that arrived from complete strangers expressing concern for the family or the mountains of supportive letters that Ashley would reread when she needed encouragement.

As the scrutiny escalated, the Kavanaughs looked forward to their chance to tell their side of the story. But it was not clear that Ford even planned to show up at the hearing on Thursday. Even Senator Feinstein said she had "no way of knowing" if Ford would appear, reluctant as she was to be questioned by the Republicans' outside counsel.[53]

The Republicans said they were willing to keep the Senate in session all weekend to confirm Kavanaugh as quickly as possible, and the Judiciary Committee announced that it would vote on Kavanaugh's nomination at 9:30 on Friday morning, just over a week after the vote was originally to have been taken.[54] Republicans hoped that the aggressive schedule could put Kavanaugh on the Court in time for the first oral arguments of the 2018 term the following Monday.

Democrats and their media allies continued to call for an FBI investigation. Republicans got a public relations break when researchers found footage of then–Judiciary Committee chairman Joe Biden downplaying the significance of FBI investigations during the Thomas-Hill hearings. Anita Hill's allegations, unlike Ford's, had been duly submitted to the White House before being shopped to the media, allowing the FBI to investigate before sources were influenced by news reports. The FBI had conducted several interviews and within three days given its results to the White House, which shared them with the Senate. Both the White House and the Senate had concluded from the FBI's report that the allegations were not worth pursuing, but then they were leaked to the media.

When Republicans cited the FBI report as a reason not to delay Thomas's confirmation, Biden fired back, "The next person that refers to an FBI report as being worth anything, obviously doesn't understand anything. FBI explicitly does not, in this or any other case, reach a conclusion. Period. Period.... So when people wave an FBI report before you, understand they do not, they do not, they do not reach conclusions."[55]

He was correct, of course. As both Senator Grassley and the Department of Justice had already pointed out, the task of the FBI background checkers was not to identify crimes or other wrongdoing but to collect statements from acquaintances, colleagues, neighbors—anyone who might know something about the allegation.[56] It was for the White House and the Senate to weigh the testimony collected by the FBI and decide what to do with it. And a Senate investigation carried the same assurances of confidentiality and criminal penalties for lying as an FBI investigation did.

But the powerful rhetorical value of appealing to the FBI was not lost on the Democrats, so as annoyed as they were for Joe Biden to be deployed again as the Republicans' spokesman on judicial issues, they kept the FBI drumbeat going.

■   ■   ■

On Wednesday morning, September 26, the day before Ford and Kavanaugh were to appear before the Senate Judiciary Committee, Michael Avenatti released what he said was a sworn affidavit from his client Julie Swetnick.[57] After stating her current and former security clearances, she detailed allegations against Kavanaugh and Mark Judge that were far worse than anything that had been alleged before.

She said she attended "well over 10" house parties in the early 1980s at which Kavanaugh and the ubiquitous Judge drank heavily and sexually assaulted women. Echoing Kavanaugh's college roommate, she said she personally witnessed him behave as a "mean drunk" and sexually demean women. She said she also saw him behave this way in Ocean City, Maryland. Kavanaugh's claims of sexual innocence in high school were "absolutely false and a lie."

The affidavit seemed designed as an excuse to question Mark Judge. "There is no question in my mind that Mark Judge has significant information concerning the conduct of Brett Kavanaugh during the 1980s, especially as it related to his actions toward women." Echoing other allegations in Farrow and Mayer's New Yorker article, Swetnick said Kavanaugh and Judge attempted to spike punch with drugs and alcohol and that she witnessed them target vulnerable girls at these parties.

It kept getting worse: "I also witnessed efforts by Mark Judge, Brett Kavanaugh, and others to cause girls to become inebriated and disoriented so they could be "gang raped" in a side room or bedroom by a 'train' of numerous boys. I have a firm recollection of seeing boys lined up outside rooms at many of these parties waiting for their 'turn' with a girl inside the room. These boys included Mark Judge and Brett Kavanaugh." Swetnick said she was a victim of one of these rapes in 1982 and had told at least two other people at the time it happened. Witnesses, she attested, would support each of her allegations.[58]

Ashley heard the news while she was getting her hair done. Her hairdresser had suggested, after seeing her Fox television interview, that she needed an update, and he and his partner immediately went into overdrive to finish her appointment when they sensed that she needed to get back home and out of the public eye.

Ashley and her friends continued to share scripture with each other. Two verses from the readings at Mass the day before the hearing seemed particularly apposite: "Put falsehood and lying far from me" (Proverbs 30:8) and "Falsehood I hate and abhor" (Psalm 119:163). While Ashley and her friends drew comfort from the music of the Christian artists Lauren Daigle and Julianna Zobrist, her husband found his mind returning to a song frequently sung in chapel at Georgetown Prep: "Be Not Afraid." He and his friends used to make fun of the way their beloved music teacher Gary Daum sang the hymn. But the joke was on them, as the frequent repetition had the intended effect—Kavanaugh remembered the words and took them to heart. And when he needed them, those three words came back to him: "Be not afraid, be not afraid."

Swetnick's accusations were obviously ridiculous. No one could have hidden such crimes for decades, much less a man who went on to hold high-profile positions in the White House and then became a judge on the second-most prominent federal court. Her presence at any parties with Kavanaugh was implausible, because she attended the relatively distant Gaithersburg High School and then Montgomery County Community College, neither of which was represented among Kavanaugh's circle of friends.

Swetnick, who graduated from high school in 1980, would have been a legal adult throughout Kavanaugh's alleged career as a gang rapist. Her story, if true, was an admission that as an adult she had attended ten or more parties hosted by minors where other minors were raped yet did nothing to stop these child rapes and did not alert the authorities.

The accusations, though incredible, were horrifying, and Democrats seized on them. "In light of shocking new allegations detailed by Julie Swetnick in a sworn affidavit, we write to request that the committee vote on Brett Kavanaugh be immediately canceled and that you support the re-opening of the FBI investigation," the Judiciary Committee's Democrats wrote to Grassley.[59]

Journalists, more interested in publicizing the accusations than in probing their obvious holes, showed no restraint either. Just as Ramirez's allegations shared details with Ford's, Swetnick's shared details with both of them. The inclusion of Mark Judge fit the pattern that Kavanaugh critics were looking for.

The charges were not only implausible but conveniently vague. Swetnick did not name any of the persons whom Kavanaugh supposedly abused, making the allegations impossible to disprove. Many of the alleged misdeeds she said she had heard about but had not witnessed. She mentioned that she had attended "Beach Week," as if she were part of the same social group as Kavanaugh, but she did not bring it up until after the publication of Kavanaugh's high school–era calendars, in which "BEACH WEEK" is written across one of the weeks. The media, nevertheless, dutifully reported the news with all the gravity they could muster: yet another woman had accused Kavanaugh of sexually abusive behavior. That was enough for Chuck Schumer, who called for Kavanaugh to withdraw on account of "another serious allegation of sexual misconduct."[60]

The *Washington Post* liked this new accuser's credentials: "Julie Swetnick, who Wednesday became the third woman to accuse Supreme Court nominee Brett M. Kavanaugh of sexual misconduct, is an experienced web developer in the Washington area who has held multiple security clearances for her work on government-related networks."[61] This was no psychologically fragile academic who was afraid to fly. This was a woman with "multiple security clearances."

MSNBC promptly interviewed Avenatti, and CNN's John King introduced the story by touting Swetnick's security clearances, failing to mention that Kavanaugh himself had been repeatedly cleared at the highest levels. King talked to a sex crimes prosecutor named Julie Grohovsky, who said the allegations reflected on Kavanaugh's ethical behavior and credibility. They needed to be fully investigated, she said.

Citing anonymous sources, CNN reported that Senator Susan Collins "appeared unnerved" by the Swetnick allegations.[62] In fact, Collins had not found the accusations of serial underage gang rape particularly plausible.

Kavanaugh himself soon issued a terse statement: "This is ridiculous and from the Twilight Zone. I don't know who this is and this never happened."[63]

CNN's Wolf Blitzer interviewed Kavanaugh's attorney Beth Wilkinson and treated the Swetnick charges as a game-changer. He played a video clip of Kellyanne Conway from days earlier saying that there was no pattern of behavior that matched Ford's allegation. Acknowledging that Conway had a "significant point," Blitzer added, "But since then Deborah Ramirez has come forward and Julie Swetnick has come forward, and her allegations are very, very brutal in this sworn affidavit." *New York* magazine's Jonathan Chait warned, "As the number of accusations rises...the odds that a charge will be one of the rare hoaxes diminishes," and he confidently concluded that Kavanaugh was finished.[64]

Democrats and the media had gone all-in on Swetnick before vetting her wild accusations, but by Wednesday evening it began to appear that they had made a serious mistake. She had unpaid debts and had been fired for lying on an employment application and for inappropriate sexual conduct toward coworkers. A frequent litigant, Swetnick had made false claims in a personal injury lawsuit against the Washington Metro system, claiming more than $420,000 in lost earnings and naming as her employer a friend for whom she had never worked.

Her ex-boyfriend Richard Vinneccy said that Swetnick threatened him after they broke up—even after he was engaged to someone else and had a baby. She had "harassed and stalked" him, threatening to kill him,

To Leader McConnell, + his legendary foresight. With appreciation, the Scalia Family, Nov. 2018

To my good friend Nino Scalia with fond memories of our days together at the Justice Dept. + high expectations for an outstanding tenure on the U.S. Supreme Court. Mitch McConnell U.S. Senator Ky. 9/17/86

Senator Mitch McConnell (R-Ky.) during Antonin Scalia's 1986 confirmation process. As majority leader during the Trump presidency, McConnell made the confirmation of judges a priority. Scalia, who died in 2016, was beloved by conservatives for his wit, intellect, and compelling advocacy of constitutional originalism.

Photo courtesy of Mitch McConnell

Robert Bork announcing in October 1987 that he would not withdraw from his confirmation battle lest he encourage future "public campaigns of distortion" against nominees. He had been viciously smeared by Senator Edward Kennedy (D-Mass.) and was rejected by the Senate 42-58.

Photo by Bettmann/Getty Images

Clarence Thomas addresses unsubstantiated allegations of sexual harassment during his reopened confirmation hearings in October 1991. His memorable "high-tech lynching" speech was a turning point in his confirmation process.

Photo by Michael Jenkins/Congressional Quarterly/Getty Images

Justice Antonin Scalia and then-Judge Neil Gorsuch after a day of fishing on the Upper Colorado River in October 2014. Gorsuch would replace Scalia and claim his mantle as an outspoken originalist on the Supreme Court. The choice vindicated Republican voters' support of Trump.

The list of Supreme Court candidates that judicial advisor Leonard Leo brought to a meeting at Trump Tower after the 2016 election. Judges Gorsuch, Hardiman, and Pryor would become the top three contenders. President Trump announced his nomination of Gorsuch on January 31, 2017.

Photo courtesy of Leonard Leo

Leonard Leo chats with White House Counsel Don McGahn during the Kavanaugh confirmation. The two worked closely on Trump's list of potential Supreme Court nominees, as well as in the selection and confirmation of justices to fill the Scalia and Kennedy vacancies.

Photo by Annie Donaldson Talley

Kavanaugh (back row, second from left) clerked for Justice Anthony Kennedy (front row, second from left) in 1993–1994. Future Justice Gorsuch (back row, left) also clerked for Kennedy that year. Kavanaugh had previously clerked for Judge Alex Kozinski of the Ninth Circuit.

Kavanaugh (right) would later serve as associate independent counsel for Ken Starr's (center) investigation of various scandals related to President Bill Clinton and his wife, Hillary. Clinton associates would figure prominently among opponents of Kavanaugh's confirmation.

Tom Lea's painting *Rio Grande* hung in George W. Bush's Oval Office. The president often referred to its depiction of the "sunrise side of the mountain," an optimistic phrase that resonated with Brett Kavanaugh and which he invoked during his confirmation process.

Photo courtesy of Tom Lea Institute, El Paso, TX © James D. Lea

After working in the White House counsel's office, Kavanaugh spent three years as staff secretary to President George W. Bush. The position meant regular interaction with the president and key advisors, such as Chief of Staff Andrew Card and National Security Advisor (later Secretary of State) Condoleezza Rice. Fights over the millions of documents that passed through his hands would figure prominently in Kavanaugh's confirmation battle.

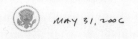

MAY 31, 2006

THE WHITE HOUSE
WASHINGTON

Dear Brett,

I have mixed emotions as I write this letter. One, I'm thrilled that you were confirmed to the court. You will be an excellent judge in all respects. Who knows? Some future President may be wise enough to name you to the Supreme Court. Secondly, I will miss your advice, your leadership, and your presence. You have been a valuable member of the team and have been a close friend. I care for you and Ashley a lot. I thank you for your service. I wish you all the best. Geo.

Kavanaugh was confirmed as a federal judge in 2006 despite opposition from Democrats because of his ties to the Whitewater probe and the Bush administration. President Bush offered his congratulations in this letter: "You will be an excellent judge in all respects. Who knows? Some future President may be wise enough to name you to the Supreme Court."

Justice Anthony Kennedy administers the oath of office as a circuit court judge to Kavanaugh as Ashley holds the Bible. Chief Justice John Roberts looks on. Following his clerkship, Kavanaugh helped Kennedy select law clerks, and the two admired each other.

When Kennedy retired, former Kavanaugh clerks Chris Michel, Travis Lenkner, and Roman Martinez promoted Kavanaugh's nomination. They worked out of his chambers at the D.C. Circuit, heading a team of former clerks who shared their knowledge of Kavanaugh's record and offered strategic advice throughout the confirmation process.

The selection of Kavanaugh was a secret until President Trump announced his nomination in a prime-time address.

Photo by Bonnie Jo Mount/The Washington Post via Getty Images

Supreme Court nominees are confirmed with the advice and consent of the U.S. Senate. Kavanaugh met with most senators individually before his hearings began in September. The vote of moderate Republican Susan Collins of Maine was crucial, and she was targeted by liberal activists as soon as Kennedy retired.

Photo by Zach Gibson/ Getty Images

White House Counsel Don McGahn attended all of Kavanaugh's meetings with senators. His long-standing relationships with senators of both parties proved useful, especially during the more contentious phases of the confirmation. Here they meet with Senator Orrin Hatch of Utah, the longest-serving Republican senator in history and three-time chairman of the Senate Judiciary Committee.

Photo by Chip Somodevilla/Getty Images

Capitol Police removed several hundred protesters during the Senate Judiciary Committee's first set of hearings for Kavanaugh. Activist groups coached protesters on how to get arrested and paid for their bail and other expenses.

Photo by Sarah Silbiger/CQ Roll Call

Penny Nance, the president of Concerned Women for America, prays in the Hart Senate Office Building during the Kavanaugh confirmation. She prayed for Kavanaugh as well as for the protesters and for women around the world who are victims of abuse and sex trafficking.

Photo by Valeria Tkacik

One of the stranger social media frenzies was sparked by televised images of Kavanaugh's former clerk Zina Bash during his testimony. An urban legend, nurtured on the internet, had it that the "okay" gesture was racist, sparking furor in social media.

Courtesy of C-SPAN

On September 16, 2018, days before Kavanaugh was expected to be confirmed, the Washington Post reported that Christine Blasey Ford, pictured here in her 1982 high school yearbook, had accused Kavanaugh of trying to rape her when they were both in high school.

Holton Arms Scribe, 1982

Kavanaugh playing basketball for Georgetown Prep, the suburban-Washington boys' school both he and Justice Neil Gorsuch attended. Kavanaugh's high school activities, including his love of sports, would receive intense scrutiny by the media following Ford's allegations.

Kavanaugh immediately and unequivocally denied the sexual assault accusations against him. He produced calendars from 1982 that recorded his thoughts and activities in detail.

Christine Blasey Ford testified before the Senate Judiciary Committee on September 27, 2018, flanked by her lawyers Debra Katz and Michael Bromwich. The four witnesses she cited as being at the party at the time of the assault were unable to corroborate her account.

Photo by Melina Mara-Pool/Getty Images

Rachel Mitchell, the sex crimes prosecutor from Arizona who questioned Christine Blasey Ford on behalf of the Republican senators, pointed out important discrepancies in her story. Mitchell told Republican senators that Ford's story did not have enough corroboration to obtain a search warrant, much less to prosecute.

Photo by Michael Reynolds/Pool via Bloomberg

The administration's "war room" for the first round of confirmation hearings, located in the vice president's suite in the Dirksen Building. The war room staff handled rapid-response to questions being asked by members of the Judiciary Committee. For example, they confirmed that, contrary to Senator Kamala Harris's suggestion, Kavanaugh had never discussed the Mueller investigation with anyone at the firm Kasowitz, Benson & Torres.

The Senate Judiciary Committee's Charles Grassley (R-Iowa, chairman) and Dianne Feinstein (D-Calif., ranking member) confer with aides Mike Davis and Heather Sawyer during the second round of hearings on the Kavanaugh nomination. Feinstein's relationship with her staff became a point of contention for Republicans worried that her staff were skirting committee rules.

Photo by Gabriella Demzuk/AFP/Getty Images

Senator Lindsey Graham (R-S.C.) condemns the unsubstantiated attacks on Judge Brett Kavanaugh's character: "This is the most unethical sham since I've been in politics. And if you really wanted to know the truth, you sure as hell wouldn't have done what you've done to this guy."

Photo by Tom Williams/AFP/Getty Images

Senate Judiciary Committee members (L–R) Amy Klobuchar (D-Minn.), Cory Booker (D-N.J.), Kamala Harris (D-Calif.), Chris Coons (D-Del.) and Richard Blumenthal (D-Conn.) stand in front of the mirrored door to the anteroom before walking out of the September 28, 2018, committee meeting in protest. After participating in a press conference and then a rowdy debate in the anteroom over a proposed FBI investigation, they returned to vote against reporting Kavanaugh's nomination out of committee.

Photo by Chip Somodevilla/Getty Images

Senator Jeff Flake (R-Ariz.) (C) speaks with colleagues including Senator Lindsey Graham (R-S.C.) (R) after voting on whether to send Kavanaugh's nomination to the whole Senate. After announcing his support, Flake then spent hours negotiating with Democrats and Republicans and eventually requested a supplemental background investigation to be performed by the FBI.

Photo by Brendan Smialowski/AFP/Getty Images

Senator Susan Collins announced that she would vote to confirm Kavanaugh in a dramatic and closely watched speech from the Senate floor on October 5, 2018. Her support meant that Kavanaugh would be confirmed the next day in a vote of the Senate.

Courtesy of C-SPAN

White House Counsel Don McGahn waits in the vice president's Capitol office for the cloture vote on October 5, 2018. Key lawyers from his office were joined by White House Deputy Press Secretary Raj Shah and White House spokeswoman Kerri Kupec.

Upon Kavanaugh's confirmation on October 6, 2018, hundreds of protesters, some of whom had spent weeks fighting the nomination, rushed the stairs of the Supreme Court building, banging on doors and scaling statues.

Photo by Emily Molli/NurPhoto via Getty Images

Justice Kavanaugh at his ceremonial swearing-in at the White House. Justice Kennedy administered the oath of office, as he had for Kavanaugh's appellate judgeship. All eight of his Supreme Court colleagues were in attendance. President Trump opened the ceremony by apologizing for the pain inflicted by the confirmation process.

Photo by Carrie Severino

Senator Richard Blumenthal questioned Kavanaugh about a baseball game he had attended while at Yale, suggesting he had memory lapses because of drinking. Kavanaugh recounted numerous details about the game, including that Hall of Fame third-baseman George Brett had played left field, which he did only twenty-two times in his career. Brett sent him a signed baseball, now displayed in his chambers at the Supreme Court.

Senator Susan Collins and her husband and staff received death threats and harassment from people opposed to Kavanaugh's nomination. Weeks after her vote, her husband opened up a piece of mail that purported to contain ricin. Hazmat professionals quarantined the senator, her husband, and dog and secured the home. Hours later, they pronounced an all-clear.

Photo Courtesy of Senator Susan Collins and her husband, Tom Daffron.

Justice Kavanaugh's clerks for the 2018–2019 term, provisionally hired before his first hearing—the first ever all-female clerk class. Four of his former clerks were working for other justices that term, a testament to Kavanaugh's influence on the Court even before his confirmation. Left to right: Sara Nommensen, Shannon Grammel, Kavanaugh, Megan Lacy, Kimberly Jackson.

Photograph by Fred Schilling, Collection of the Supreme Court of the United States.

The official photo of the Court following Kavanaugh's confirmation. (They are seated by seniority, with the most senior justices in front and toward the center.) Front row: Justice Stephen Breyer, Justice Clarence Thomas, Chief Justice John Roberts, Justice Ruth Bader Ginsburg, Justice Samuel Alito. Back row: Justice Neil Gorsuch, Justice Sonia Sotomayor, Justice Elena Kagan, Justice Brett Kavanaugh.

Photograph by Fred Schilling, Collection of the Supreme Court of the United States.

his girlfriend, and their unborn child. She threatened to file a rape charge against Vinneccy and to have him, a U.S. citizen, deported. She made other bizarre and false statements, telling him that she wouldn't grant him a divorce (they had never been married) and that she was pregnant with twins. He had filed for a restraining order against her but never completed the process for fear of having to see her in person and disclose his whereabouts to her. "I know a lot about her.... She's not credible at all," he told *Politico*. "Not at all."[65] In a statement to the Judiciary Committee he speculated that "[h]er motives may be for financial gain or notoriety but they are certainly not to expose the truth."[66]

It became even clearer that Swetnick was unreliable, to put it mildly, when Dennis Ketterer, a former meteorologist in the Washington area, disclosed that he had had an extramarital affair with her in 1993. Their relationship had become physical but never led to intercourse, in part because she told him that she enjoyed group sex. When she said that she "first tried sex with multiple guys while in high school and still liked it from time to time," Ketterer broke the relationship off, worried about contracting a sexually transmitted disease.

Years later Ketterer tried to get back in touch with Swetnick when he was running for Congress as a Democrat, but her father steered him away, warning that she had "psychological and other problems at the time." Ketterer had gone public with his story after consultation with a church leader, deciding to reveal the affair to prevent Swetnick from misleading others. Taking "eternal considerations" into account and saying that "[m]y heart still feels heavy," he concluded that "based on my direct experience with Julie, I do not believe her allegations against Kavanaugh."

Now his high school friends moved quickly to defend Kavanaugh. Forty of them sent a letter to the Senate Judiciary Committee saying they had never met or heard of a Julie Swetnick, nor had they witnessed any activity that matched her description.

Swetnick's allegations did far more damage to Michael Avenatti's reputation (and to his short-lived presidential aspirations) than to Kavanaugh's. The impression of a pattern of sexual aggression in Kavanaugh's life was undone by a pattern of increasingly implausible false accusations.

Ford could not back up her allegation, but at least it sounded plausible. Each subsequent allegation against Kavanaugh sounded more desperate and ridiculous.

Kavanaugh's supporters warned that the country must not tolerate the political tactic of destroying people's lives and reputations with unsubstantiated allegations and outlandish claims. Swetnick's accusation, which people like Jonathan Chait took at face value but which proved to be absurd, reminded Americans why it is important to treat the accused as innocent until they are proved guilty. Ramirez, Swetnick, and Avenatti changed the course of the nomination. Kavanaugh was no longer on his heels.

■   ■   ■

Grassley's experience investigating whistle-blower claims made him well-suited to pilot Kavanaugh's nomination through his committee. The nominations unit handled it first. When the initial allegations were made public, the powerful oversight and investigations unit joined the work. Forty attorneys and law clerks were now deposing witnesses and investigating alleged crimes.

Federal law enforcement officials with years of experience conducting government investigations had been detailed to the committee, where they worked with the committee's attorneys and investigators to interview witnesses. A court reporter transcribed interviews. Witnesses were also warned that making false statements to Congress is a crime, carrying the same penalties as perjury and lying to the FBI—five years in federal prison.

Working with whistle-blowers requires a high degree of concern for confidentiality, but the committee's investigators had to warn those they talked to that confidentiality could not be assured. Some members of the committee might not have the same policy on confidentiality, as Senator Booker's "Spartacus" outburst made clear.

The committee staff interviewed people who knew Kavanaugh and people who knew his accusers, weighing their credibility. All told, they spoke to forty-five persons and collected twenty-five witness statements. Many of those providing testimony in support of Kavanaugh "asked that their names be redacted out of fear that their statements might result in personal or professional retribution or personal physical harm—or even risk the safety and well-being of their families and friends," according to a Judiciary Committee report on the Kavanaugh confirmation.[67]

As difficult as Ford's attorneys had been to work with, Ramirez's attorneys were even less responsive, rejecting seven attempts by the committee to obtain evidence or statements regarding the allegation. Despite his own lack of cooperation with the committee, Ramirez's attorney John Clune complained to CNN's Anderson Cooper that Senate Republicans were "game-playing" with his client's testimony.[68]

In a previous confirmation process, a statement like Clune's might have stood unchallenged. But Mike Davis, Grassley's chief counsel for nominations, had been unusually open with the media about his correspondence with the accusers' counsel, so Clune's own game-playing was also on display.

Within minutes of the publication of Ramirez's story in the *New Yorker*, Davis had asked her attorneys for any and all evidence she had to support her allegations. Over the next forty-eight hours, he repeated the committee's requests for testimony and evidence six times. He also asked Ramirez to speak to investigators or provide a written statement, but she refused to do so.

Even though the attorneys refused to provide evidence, Grassley's staff still investigated. They interviewed seven witnesses, including James Roche, Ramirez's friend and Kavanaugh's freshman roommate at Yale, and other friends and classmates of Ramirez. They also interviewed Kavanaugh in a phone call, during which he denied that the alleged incident ever took place. In later testimony it was revealed that Roche's relations with Kavanaugh and their third roommate were strained, and sources have suggested that Roche's drug use was an irritant.

A similar process unfolded with the Swetnick allegations. The committee contacted Avenatti ten minutes after he publicized Swetnick's declaration. He responded via Twitter with a list of questions for

Kavanaugh. While he claimed to have evidence to back up his client's accusations, he refused to provide any to the committee despite repeated requests. He submitted a sworn declaration by Swetnick a few days later and posted a declaration from a purported witness whom he refused to identify. He refused an interview with the committee.

Avenatti's refusal to cooperate with the Senate backfired. On September 24—the day after he released Swetnick's sworn affidavit—the Daily Beast ran an article headlined "Democrats to Michael Avenatti: You're Not Helping in the Kavanaugh Fight," which observed, "Democratic senators appeared to be low on patience with [Avenatti's] tactic of dribbling out information before a dramatic big reveal." Senator Coons, the article reported, urged Avenatti not to delay providing the information and witnesses he asserted would validate Swetnick's affidavit.

Still, as John McCormack reported later, "Much of the media let Avenatti run wild, and every Democrat on the Senate Judiciary Committee signed a letter urging Kavanaugh to withdraw following the release of Swetnick's allegations."[69]

In two interviews with committee staffers, Kavanaugh denied knowing Swetnick, whose credibility was dealt a further blow when it was reported that she had been sued for defamation, had lied about her educational background, and had engaged in "unwelcome, sexually offensive conduct" at work.

The allegations against Kavanaugh were getting stranger and stranger. Senator Sheldon Whitehouse of Rhode Island hand-delivered to the committee staff notes from a phone message from a constituent stating that two men named "Brett and Mark" sexually assaulted a woman on a boat in Newport in 1985; based on a yearbook photo, the caller thought one of the men was Kavanaugh. Whitehouse refused to provide the committee investigators with any contact information for the caller, but did refer the man to a reporter.[70] NBC News and other outlets reported the allegation, leading many reporters to tweet about a "4th Kavanaugh accuser."[71] Kavanaugh strenuously denied the accusation, stating that he had never even been on a boat in or around Newport, Rhode Island, let alone assaulted anyone on one.

Eventually, the committee was able to track down the caller, identified as Jeffrey Catalan. He had a Twitter account where he had also
called for a military coup against Trump. He implored the Pentagon to
get rid of the "parasite" Trump and accused the president of "manslaugh-
ter." He later recanted his accusations against Kavanaugh on Twitter:
"[T]o everyone who is going crazy about what I had said I have recanted
because I have made a mistake and apologize for such mistake."[72] A few
days later, the committee referred him to the Justice Department for
perhaps making false statements to Congress and obstructing a congressional investigation—a warning to Democrats about recklessly slinging
allegations to destroy Kavanaugh's reputation.

An anonymous report submitted to Senator Cory Gardner of Colorado charged that Kavanaugh had pushed a woman he was dating against
a wall "very aggressively and sexually." The anonymous woman said
that her daughter was a friend of the victim. The committee determined
that Kavanaugh was dating Dabney Friedrich at the time of the alleged
push. Now a U.S. district court judge, Friedrich signed a statement calling the accusations "offensive and absurd" and saying Kavanaugh had
always treated her with the "utmost respect."[73]

An anonymous letter sent to Senator Kamala Harris's San Diego
office recounted that Kavanaugh, with the help of a friend, sexually
assaulted a woman while driving her home from a party. The same
accuser also sent an email to the Judiciary Committee staff. She alleged
that he physically assaulted her and forced her to perform sexual acts.
Both men raped her repeatedly, she wrote, and Kavanaugh warned her
that nobody would believe her. The letter stipulated neither a date nor a
location for the alleged attack. Kavanaugh denied the allegations.

A woman named Judy Munro-Leighton said she was the victim. She
turned out to be a liberal activist who lived not in California but in
Kentucky. In a phone call, she admitted that her accusation was "just a
ploy," made "because I was angry." Asked if she'd ever met Kavanaugh,
she said, "Oh Lord, no."[74]

As these other allegations came out, some Senate Democrats and
their staff worried that the Republicans on the Judiciary Committee were

releasing all the allegations they were getting to make Ford's allegations look frivolous. And indeed, the allegations were being released strategically by Grassley's aide Davis. While clerking for Justice Gorsuch, he had heard Justice Thomas tell a story from his youth in Georgia. When a dog killed a chicken, they would tie the dead chicken around the dog's neck and let it rot there. The dog would lose its taste for chicken. Davis wanted Democrats to lose their taste for destroying people's lives with unsubstantiated allegations. He would tie every reckless smear and false allegation around their necks so that they would face at least some of the consequences for what they were doing.

Still, the committee was being discreet, even with an allegation made against Avenatti himself. For example, according to a public records request, on September 24, the committee's whistle-blower hotline received an email with the subject line "Michael Avenatti Assaulted Me." The text of the email asserted that Avenatti had sexually assaulted the sender of the email in 2012 at a private party in Seattle: "I'm nervous about what to do with this, as my family doesn't know that I am bisexual. I would like it to be known but don't know if I'm ready for my name and information to be public." The sender added that "this isn't a ploy and I would really like some advicement [sic]." The committee forwarded the email to a sergeant in the Seattle police force as "the appropriate local law enforcement agency." The whistle-blower tip line, the committee noted, "receives a range of claims, ranging from legitimate issues to fabrications to statements from people who seem to be mentally ill."

The sergeant in Seattle wrote that she discussed the allegation and next steps with a lieutenant: "We both discussed the lack of information given for the alleged victim. The only information provided was the possible name of the victim, an email address, and an alleged sexual assault with no details of location aside from 'a private party in Seattle.' The allegation also stated that the alleged sexual assault was unreported and had occurred in 2012. I discussed…that if this crime had occurred, the statute of limitations for this incident would have expired." She tried to reach the alleged victim by email but received no response and closed the investigation.

The Senate Republicans had handled the allegation discreetly, sending it to the appropriate law enforcement authority upon receipt, and not contacting public relations teams or attorneys—in notable contrast to the way Senator Feinstein had handled Ford's allegation. By the eve of the hearing, the conversation among senators and their staff had shifted from the possibility that Kavanaugh had attempted to rape multiple women to Kavanaugh's having drunk more beer than people realized.

Because newsrooms were structurally biased against conservatives, they didn't realize the anger that their one-sided coverage was provoking. William Bennett noted that the "perfect storm of controversy" had turned the Kavanaugh hearing into "the culture war on steroids."[75]

CHAPTER EIGHT

Fear of Flying

After all the delaying tactics, Senate staffers still weren't entirely sure that Ford was going to show up for the hearing on Thursday, September 27. Many assumed that she would be a no-show or that some new allegation would derail the proceedings again.

Grassley had assured Ford's attorneys that he would do everything in his power to "provide a safe, comfortable, and dignified forum." The hearing would be held in the Dirksen building, with its smaller committee room. The large size of the room in Hart had contributed to the "circus atmosphere" of the first set of hearings.

Grassley's staff tried to accommodate the requests of Ford's legal and public relations teams, acquiescing to the request for breaks during her testimony, allowing only one video camera at the hearing, excluding Kavanaugh from the room during her testimony, and providing security. They declined her demands that Kavanaugh testify first, that Mark Judge be subpoenaed, and that only senators ask questions.

There were no female Republican senators on the Judiciary Committee, and the Republicans worried that the spectacle of Ford facing an all-male bank of GOP senators would be a public relations nightmare.

The media would interpret questions that were in any way pointed as further harassment of a victim of a brutal sexual assault.

The Republicans on the committee therefore pushed to hire a female attorney with expertise in such sensitive questioning. They did not need a hearing that scored political points but one that elicited facts to shore up the confidence of Republican senators. It wasn't that they could not trust the senators to ask appropriate questions so much as that they knew the media would spin whatever happened as badgering of Ford, as they had done in Justice Thomas's hearing.

After interviewing candidates on the previous Saturday, before the hearing date was even set, they selected Rachel Mitchell, a respected sex crimes prosecutor from Maricopa County, Arizona. With her long and distinguished background working with victims, even teaching courses in how to interview victims compassionately to get to the truth, she was the perfect choice. She was a government attorney, so she had no law partners who had to approve her appearance. For political reasons, several attorneys had already been forbidden by their firms to participate. And it didn't hurt that Mitchell was from Senator Flake's state, since he was known to be uneasy about how to balance concern for Ford and fairness to Kavanaugh. When the committee staff interviewed Mitchell, they told her that a previous interviewee had described herself as a bulldog. She laughed and told them if that was what they wanted, she was not the right person. She had built up a career of dealing with sex crime victims and would be returning to that job. She had to be true to herself.

Despite their previous outrage that male senators might ask Ford questions, Democrats and the media were outraged by the plan. "Handing off the questioning of Dr. Blasey to female staff members would be a gross departure from Senate practice and based on the risible idea that the questioning of sexual assault survivors is 'women's work,'" declared Lara Bazelon in a *New York Times* op-ed titled "A Sexist, Cowardly Ploy."[1] In fact, the Senate had hired outside counsel for important hearings on a number of occasions, including for the Watergate and Whitewater investigations.[2]

Before the hearing began at ten o'clock, a half-dozen photographers sat in the well between the senators and the witness table. At an ordinary hearing, dozens of photographers might crowd into the well, approaching the witness table and moving around for better angles. Today the small group had been instructed to keep their backs against the dais, as far away as possible from Ford.

PR for Ford was handled by Kendra Barkoff Lamy, who had been Joe Biden's spokesman when he was vice president. She had moved on to the Democratic powerhouse public relations firm SKDKnickerbocker— the same firm used by the Sixteen Thirty Fund. The dark-money group had paid SKDK $7 million in 2017.

Ford's team tried to stipulate which media outlets could cover the hearings, including Getty, Bloomberg, and the Associated Press. Grassley's staff had to explain that media passes were handled by the Senate press galleries, the nonpartisan liaisons between the Senate and the press. The most Grassley's office could do was say how many press positions were allotted. Photographers went in the well, and there were daily, periodical, and radio-television galleries, which had forty-eight seats among them. C-SPAN was the only television outlet, and there were far fewer reporters than the two hundred who had covered the first set of hearings.

The Judiciary Committee closed the hallway outside the hearing room. For the first set of hearings, there had been three stakeout positions for cameras and microphones. There was no press stakeout for the reopened hearings. In fact, the whole floor was closed when the witnesses were moving through the building. One of the accommodations for Ford was that she and Kavanaugh would never cross paths. When not testifying, Ford would wait in the Democratic offices on the second floor of Dirksen. Kavanaugh would wait in an office around the corner. After the hallway was cleared, she would be brought in, and when she had finished, the hallway would be cleared again so that she could be sent back to the Democrats' holding room.

There were only six seats for the public, controlled by Grassley and Feinstein. Since a guest's disruptive behavior would reflect poorly on the sponsoring senator, protests were unlikely. Republicans had tolerated the protests in the first set of hearings because they made Democrats look unhinged. This hearing would be different.

Anticipation for Ford's appearance was high. Despite all the media interest in her story, pictures of her had been thoroughly scrubbed from the internet with the exception of one blurry surfing photo in which she was wearing sunglasses. Her story had been developed and carefully edited by friendly reporters. Tens of millions of Americans were watching as she walked in and took her seat, followed by her attorneys Bromwich and Katz. Viewers saw a middle-aged woman in a navy blue blazer gazing out from behind large glasses, her blonde hair freshly blow-dried and styled. She was accompanied by many attorneys, but her immediate and extended family were noticeably absent. Some of her friends sat in the front row.

The room was more intimate than it appeared on television, giving the audience the sense of observing a private conversation rather than a hearing. Though emotions ran high, everyone was respectful. They shared cell phone chargers, and the actress Alyssa Milano handed out tissues to everyone around her before the hearing started.

Grassley, who had stopped by Ford's waiting room moments earlier to assure her he didn't have horns, opened the hearing with his trademark expression of concern for witnesses, apologizing to both Ford and Kavanaugh for the "vile threats" they and their families had been subjected to during the weeks leading to the hearing.[3] He reminded the audience that the last-minute revelation of a serious allegation that had been received months earlier had derailed the process. It was a sticking point for Republicans on the committee, who were appalled at how the allegations had been handled. Grassley noted that the letter had been kept "secret from July 30...until September 13," preventing the committee from investigating privately, which would have allowed senators to weigh the charges while maintaining the confidentiality that Ford said she desired.

The moment he learned of Ford's allegations, Grassley said, he began investigating them, just as he had investigated all the allegations that had come before the committee, noting that the Democrats declined to participate. When Ford's name became public, the staff interviewed or took statements from all the witnesses she identified, as well as Kavanaugh. They tried repeatedly to interview Ford, offering every accommodation, even proposing to take her testimony in California, but her attorneys declined, insisting on a public hearing.

The chairman then explained the limitations of FBI investigations, which would simply take witness statements in the same manner the committee had done, with the same legal penalty for making false statements. He noted that the attorneys for those making the other high-profile accusations against Kavanaugh had not cooperated either, nor had they made any attempt to substantiate their claims.

The ranking member, Senator Feinstein, followed with her own opening statement, admitting that she had kept Ford's letter a secret for six weeks but then complaining about the speed with which the committee moved once the allegation was public: "What I find most inexcusable is this rush to judgment."

Noting Ford's blue suit, Feinstein said, "Twenty-seven years ago, I was walking through an airport when I saw a large group of people gathered around a TV to listen to Anita Hill tell her story. What I saw was an attractive woman in a blue suit before an all-male Judiciary Committee speaking of her experience of sexual harassment." The media began discussing the "symbolic meaning" of Ford's blue suit, comparing it to the teal suit that Hill had worn.[4]

With that, Ford began her opening statement: "I am here today not because I want to be. I am terrified. I am here because I believe it is my civic duty to tell you what happened to me while Brett Kavanaugh and I were in high school." She spoke in the high-pitched, almost childlike voice that friends remembered from high school—the voice that earned her the nickname "Baby Love" from some of her classmates.

Ford talked about her childhood in suburban Washington and how she came to know Kavanaugh, "the boy who sexually assaulted me." One evening in the summer of 1982, she said, after a day spent swimming at the Columbia Country Club in Chevy Chase, Maryland, she attended a "small gathering at a house in the Bethesda area." There were "four boys I remember specifically being at the house," along with her friend Leland. She did not remember how the group came together, though she surmised it was, like many other such gatherings, spontaneous. She did not remember where they were, whose house it was, or how she got there, but she would never forget the details of the assault. "They have been seared into my memory and have haunted me episodically as an adult."

She had consumed only one beer, she said, while Kavanaugh was "visibly drunk." She was on her way to the bathroom when she was attacked from behind and pushed into a bedroom. Kavanaugh and Mark Judge "came into the bedroom and locked the door behind them." Kavanaugh got on top of her on a bed and manhandled her, she said. "I yelled, hoping that someone downstairs might hear me, and I tried to get away from him, but his weight was heavy." Kavanaugh put his hand over her mouth, she testified, and she feared he was going to kill her.

Kavanaugh was laughing and having a good time, she said, while Judge was alternatively urging him on and telling him to stop. Judge jumped on the bed, causing Kavanaugh and her to tumble off. That was when she ran out of the room and locked herself in the bathroom. The two boys left the room, loudly "pinballing off the walls on the way down" the stairs. She left the house, she said, relieved that they didn't follow her.

Ford said she told no one about the incident at the time. Before sharing the story with the *Washington Post* and her congresswoman, Anna Eshoo, in July, she had given only a vague account to a few persons in recent years. She told her husband she had experienced a sexual assault before they were married and discussed it more fully in marital counseling in 2012. More recently, she had mentioned the attack in other therapy sessions and to friends.

"My hope was that providing the information confidentially would be sufficient to allow the Senate to consider Mr. Kavanaugh's serious misconduct without having to make myself, my family, or anyone's family vulnerable to the personal attacks and invasions of privacy that we have faced since my name became public," she said.

She struggled with whether to come forward, eventually deciding not to. But "once the press started reporting on the existence of the letter I had sent to Senator Feinstein," reporters started showing up at her home and leaving messages. That was when she decided to continue conversations with Emma Brown, the *Washington Post* reporter who wrote her story.

While thousands of people had thanked her for coming forward, Ford said, she had also received death threats and had been "called the most vile and hateful names imaginable."

"It is not my responsibility to determine whether Mr. Kavanaugh deserves to sit on the Supreme Court," Ford told the committee. "My responsibility is to tell you the truth." Then she asked that committee members address her directly and not only through a "professional prosecutor."

At this point, Ford reiterated a request for caffeine she had made before she began reading her testimony. Bromwich, seated next to her, added, "a Coke or something." As they walked out of the hearing room during a later break in Ford's testimony, multiple staffers heard Senator Hirono tell Senator Harris that it was a great idea to have Ford wear a blue suit and ask for a Coke as a throwback to the Thomas-Hill hearings. One of the unsubstantiated claims Hill had made against Thomas involved a Coke can. Senator Hirono had also mentioned Hill repeatedly in her media appearances as soon as the initial *Post* report was published.

Rachel Mitchell was not brought in because she was a professional prosecutor, but because she was one of the nation's foremost forensic interviewers of sex crime victims. She designed and taught a course to detectives, child protection workers, and other dedicated forensic interviewers on how to interview victims of trauma, including victims of sexual abuse and child abuse.[5] An attorney who had defended cases against her for decades told Arizona journalists that she was "extremely meticulous" and "not a zealot in any way." In fact, he said, "I'm surprised they'd pick her. She's not the junkyard-dog type at all."[6]

Mitchell did not hear that Republicans were interested in hiring a sex crimes prosecutor until the Friday before the hearing; they interviewed her twice the next day. She proposed making the questioning of Ford as close to a forensic interview as possible. It would be nothing like a cross-examination of a hostile witness. In a forensic interview, the key is to ask open-ended questions that will elicit the most information. Peppering a victim with questions might elicit responses, but at the expense of the larger narrative. She said she would not criticize Ford for waiting decades to tell her story of sexual assault, as most victims delay disclosure. When Ford finally made her allegation and under what circumstances was relevant, but the delay in and of itself was not. The committee was in complete agreement.

Mitchell flew to Washington on Sunday morning and began work on Monday. Because the committee had already obtained information from all the alleged witnesses, she was able to review their statements as well as the sworn interview with Kavanaugh. She reviewed all the information the committee had put together about the alleged assault. She even read through academic articles in which Ford was named as an author. While the media and other opponents of Kavanaugh insisted that law enforcement interview witnesses immediately, a typical investigation begins with an interview of the victim. Because Ford was so vague on details, the committee had also put together a map showing where every witness lived and the Columbia Country Club.

Mitchell did not know when she accepted the assignment of questioning Ford that she would have to conduct the questioning in five-minute increments on behalf of each Republican senator. She learned of that limitation only the day before the hearing. A standard forensic interview consists of open-ended questions. Under the rules imposed by the Judiciary Committee, Mitchell's questions would have to be more direct. Ford's public relations team tried unsuccessfully to get C-SPAN to turn its camera on the senator on whose behalf Mitchell was asking questions instead of on Mitchell herself, hoping to give the impression of a line of old men attacking a woman.

Mitchell's approach was not what anybody in the media was expecting.

She began by offering words of comfort to Ford. "The first thing that struck me from your statement this morning is that you are terrified, and I just wanted to let you know I'm very sorry. That's not right." She offered some guidelines to alleviate the stress, encouraging her to ask for clarification and to let her know if she got any details wrong.

The questions could not have been milder. Mitchell asked Ford to make her best estimates regarding dates of the alleged attack, and to confirm details she had provided about the attack. As soon as she got going, though, her time was up.

Mitchell's five-minute increments were separated by the Democrats' questioning, which consisted in the main of offering Ford praise and making political speeches about the importance of the #MeToo movement.

The media immediately declared the format of the questioning a disaster for Kavanaugh. MSNBC's Garrett Haake said, "Stopping and starting between emotional testimony, and piece by piece going back through" her allegations "is having a similar effect to what they were worried about—making it look like they're trying to pick apart Dr. Ford's credibility." Mitchell had not "laid a glove on Ford," in the opinion of NBC's Megyn Kelly. Her colleague Chuck Todd said, "They didn't think the five-minute thing through. This is not working for them." These commentators did not realize that this format was an unwelcome condition demanded by Ford and the Democrats. It seemed to be working in their favor.

■   ■   ■

By the time the committee took its first break at 11:30 a.m., Kavanaugh's situation was considered dire. Republican senators were described as "stone-faced" as they filed out of the hearing room, while the Democrats were already raising money off the hearing.[7] Senator Hirono sent out an appeal within a half-hour of the opening of the hearing, for which she later apologized.[8] Senator Kamala Harris's campaign had dropped 3,600 different ads about Kavanaugh on Facebook by the time the hearing began.[9]

The media had already reached their verdict. ABC's George Stephanopoulos, a former Clinton spokesman, praised Ford's "emotional" testimony and relatability. Cokie Roberts agreed. "We know women just like her. She certainly doesn't seem to be somebody with an agenda as she is putting herself in this very difficult position." Ford was "highly credible."[10]

Her credibility, if anything, was viewed as stronger because of her lapses in memory and because of the odder parts to the story, such as her description of how she came to tell her husband about the assault. One of the reasons they were in couple's therapy in 2012, she said, was a disagreement over a home remodeling project. She insisted on a second front door, even though it was not "aesthetically pleasing from the curb." The purpose of the door, which was not readily visible from the street, was purportedly to assuage her claustrophobia, although others pointed out that her home had been used as a therapist's office, for which a side door would be helpful, and she acknowledged that it now made it easier to "host Google interns."[11] Despite the holes in her story, the media clung to these details. "You can't make that stuff up. It is so unusual," said ABC's legal analyst Sunny Hostin. "I found her to be one of the most credible witnesses I think I've seen."[12]

NBC's Kasie Hunt noted that Jeff Flake looked "pained" during Ford's testimony. The Republicans, she said, knew that Ford's perceived credibility was so high that it did not "bode well for Judge Kavanaugh ultimately sitting on the Supreme Court."[13]

Outside of newsrooms, the view was much different. "You know that woman is lying, don't you?" Melania Trump said to her husband, echoing a perspective held by millions of other women and men who were silenced in media discussions that day.

As much as the media loved Ford, they hated Mitchell, often faulting her for the procedure, over which she had no control. After the fifteen-minute break, Mitchell resumed her questioning along the same lines as earlier. Kind and deferential, Mitchell asked where she lived, how she had obtained therapy records, and about her reported fear of flying. Someone close to Ford had tipped off a government attorney that she flew "all the time," including on single-propeller airplanes over the ocean. This person had flown with Ford for years and never heard about her fear of flying. That information was passed along to the Senate Judiciary Committee before the hearing.

"May I ask, Dr. Ford, how did you get to Washington?" Mitchell said gently. "In an airplane," Ford replied, smiling.

Mitchell explained she was asking because of reports that she was afraid to fly. Ford responded that she was "hoping that they would come to me, but I realized that was an unrealistic request." She said she was "hoping to avoid having to get on an airplane, but I eventually was able to get up the gumption with the help of some friends." It would seem, then, that her fear of flying was a legitimate reason to delay the hearing, as the press, relying on anonymous reports from the Ford camp, had reported. It also highlighted her fragility.

Mitchell asked how Ford came to the East Coast in the summer. "In an airplane," she answered. "In fact, you fly fairly frequently for your hobbies, and you've had to fly for your work. Is that true?" Mitchell pushed. "Correct, unfortunately," Ford replied.

Then, citing a consulting position Ford had with a company in Australia, Mitchell asked about travel there. Ford was quick to say she had never been there, suggesting it was too long a journey for her to endure in an airplane. "I don't think I'll make it to Australia!"

Mitchell kept going, noting that Ford had indicated an interest in "surf travel," specifically identifying Hawaii, Costa Rica, the South Pacific Islands, and French Polynesia as places where she had pursued this hobby.[14] Asked if she had ever been to those places, Ford said "correct." Mitchell also asked if Ford had traveled by air in pursuit of her interests in oceanography and in Hawaiian and Tahitian culture. Ford admitted she had. The more than four-thousand-mile flight from Palo Alto to French Polynesia is completely over the Pacific Ocean.

Mitchell also inquired about Ford's seeming not to know about the repeated offers to interview her in California: "Was it communicated to you by your counsel or someone else that the committee had asked to interview you and that they offered to come out to California to do so?"

At that point, Ford's attorneys jumped. "We're going to object, Mr. Chairman, to any call for privileged conversations between counsel and Dr. Ford."

Grassley asked if the counsel could confirm that the offer had been made. Ford interjected that she "wasn't clear on what the offer was" and would have been happy to have them come out.

Mitchell then turned to the polygraph test that Ford had taken on August 7, asking how she had decided to take it. Her attorneys again objected, "You're seeming to call for communications between counsel and client." But Ford answered that she'd done so on the advice of attorneys, that she had no idea who paid for it, and that she had taken the polygraph on the day of her grandmother's funeral or maybe the day after, just before a flight to New Hampshire. She could not remember many details from the August 7 polygraph.

Continuing with that subject, Mitchell asked, "Have you ever had discussions with anyone, beside your attorneys, on how to take a polygraph?" Ford: "Never."

"Have you ever given tips or advice to somebody who was looking to take a polygraph test?" Ford replied, "Never."

As the Judiciary Committee recessed for lunch, the media continued in the same tenor as earlier. On CNN, Jeffrey Toobin reminded viewers that Mark Judge had written a book about his notoriously drunken youth and surmised that Republicans didn't want him to testify because he would be such a bad witness. "It just underlines how badly this has all gone for the Kavanaugh side in this hearing so far," he said, inviting viewers to "dwell for a moment" on how "ineffective this cross-examination has been."[15] Gloria Borger noted that the procedure allowed for no defense of Kavanaugh; it would be "all on" him to repair the damage that was being done.

NBC's Savannah Guthrie acknowledged that Mitchell had "scored some points here and there," including the shocking admission that the woman the media had depicted as afraid to fly actually flew regularly.[16] Megyn Kelly, repeating the maxim that prosecutors should never ask a question to which they do not already know the answer, was critical of Mitchell, who had "gone fishing a couple of times and come up with nothing."[17]

Kelly was mistaken. Mitchell knew more than outsiders realized, and the committee staff could see what she had caught. The question about polygraph coaching might have looked like a fishing expedition, but investigators had already talked to a witness—a former boyfriend of Ford's—who said she had coached a friend preparing to submit to a polygraph test. If that witness was telling the truth, Ford had just lied under oath. Interestingly enough, the woman he had identified as the recipient of the coaching—Monica McLean—was not only in the hearing room but had walked in from the holding area with Ford and her attorneys.

Still, Kelly said, "There has been no Perry Mason moment."[18]

Outside observers were convinced that the day was already a disaster for Kavanaugh. Steve Schmidt, an advisor to Republicans such as George W. Bush and John McCain, said, "Every GOP campaign strategist and Hill staffer wishes they had the button to open the trap door under Rachel Mitchell's chair. What a total and complete political disaster for Republicans."[19]

Media analysts were dazzled by Ford's professional explanations of how memory works. When Senator Feinstein asked her how she could be so sure it was Kavanaugh who attacked her, she answered, "The same way that I'm sure that I'm talking to you right now. Just basic memory functions and also just the level of norepinephrine and the epinephrine in the brain that, as you know, encodes that neurotransmitter that codes memories into the hippocampus, and so the trauma-related experience is locked there, whereas other details kind of drift." When Senator Leahy asked what her strongest memory was, she replied, "Indelible in the hippocampus is the laughter, the uproarious laughter between the two, and they're having fun at my expense."

Ford's displays of professional expertise alternated with expressions of childlike ignorance. In her opening statement, she professed that she had not known how to reach her senator, so she had called her representative's office and the *Washington Post* instead. In response to a question from Senator Whitehouse, she said she didn't know what "exculpatory" meant. He explained it referred to evidence helpful to the accused.

No matter what Ford said, the media lapped it up. Mimi Rocah, a legal analyst for MSNBC, observed that trial lawyers usually supplement the victim's testimony with that of experts who can expand on the victim's statements and explain any gaps in memory. But Ford, she said, was "everything bottled up in one. She's really good at both [roles]." Rocah hoped that Mark Judge, who had previously said, under penalty of felony, that he had no memory of Kavanaugh's acting the way Ford described, would "have a moment of conscience where he needs to tell the truth."[20]

A former U.S. attorney, Joyce Vance, confident of Kavanaugh's guilt, agreed. Judge needed to testify under oath—presumably because his previous statement, which was subject to the same penalty as perjury, was somehow less reliable. If he were to testify, she wondered, "Does he go ahead and confirm his friend's version of events? Or does he finally complete the outreach that Dr. Ford tried to make with him during this event, where she says she locked eyes with him and thought he might help her. You know, will he finally, from across the years, come forth and tell the story and achieve some kind of redemption for what he did?"[21]

The Republican consultant Schmidt seemed to be in agony, tweeting: "The GOP members are putting on a clinic for political cowardice. Will not one of them, while watching a hectoring and minimally prepared Rachel Mitchell harass Dr. Ford, step up and take back their time and denounce this kangaroo court?"[22] The absurdity of this characterization of Mitchell's questioning was best demonstrated, fittingly enough, by a *Saturday Night Live* parody two nights later, in which a mild-mannered Mitchell is repeatedly cut off in the middle of a lengthy and methodically worded sentence by the expiration of her five minutes.[23] The predominant criticism of Mitchell, especially from the right, was that she was too deferential to Ford and that her questioning was meandering and unfocused.

■   ■   ■

In the next round of questions, Ford's lawyers admitted that they had paid for the polygraph. When Ford was asked who helped her work with Senate offices, she seemed confused. She did admit that Feinstein had recommended that she work with Debra Katz's law firm.

It was no surprise that Feinstein's office would recommend Katz. She had been considered one of the best litigators of sexual harassment claims for decades. But they also knew that Katz, a longtime Democratic donor and fundraiser, would be on their team politically. She represented the Feminist Majority Foundation—another beneficiary of the Arabella dark-money empire.[24] And her feelings about the Trump administration were less than sympathetic: "These people are all miscreants," she fumed on Facebook in March 2017. "The term 'basket of deplorables' is far too generous a description for these people who are now Senior Trump advisors."[25] Katz was the perfect person for the job.

Mitchell asked whether Leland Keyser had ever asked Ford why she had left the party so suddenly. She said she had not. Keyser, of course, had already said that she had no recollection of the party Ford described. Ford now suggested that Keyser's denial was tied to "significant health challenges," adding that she was "happy that she's focusing on herself and getting the health treatment that she needs." It was true that Keyser had health problems, but the remark was widely interpreted, including by some close to Keyser, as disparaging.[26]

Mitchell ended her questioning with an expression of admiration at how well-educated Ford was about the neurological effects of trauma, and she wondered if she knew the best way to plumb the memory and get to the truth when interviewing trauma victims. It was not, Mitchell noted, an interview cut up into five-minute increments, but a sustained interview with a trained questioner in a private setting—a technique called a "cognitive interview." "This is not a cognitive interview. Did anybody ever advise you from Senator Feinstein's office, or from Representative Eshoo's office to go get a forensic interview?" Mitchell asked. No one had, said Ford. "Instead, you were advised to get an attorney and take a polygraph, is that right?" Mitchell asked. "And instead of submitting to an interview in California, we're having a hearing here today in five-minute increments. Is that right?"

Mitchell referred to an article about the use of the cognitive interview, a technique that is considered effective at eliciting accurate statements. It is also useful for questioning subjects whose veracity is in question. Studies have shown that, properly conducted, cognitive interviews can distinguish between honest and deceptive witnesses with more than 80 percent accuracy.[27] If the senators on the Judiciary Committee had truly been interested in determining whether Christine Blasey Ford was telling the truth, they could have done so more reliably in a private interview that also would have satisfied her professed concerns about privacy and convenience.

Instead, Mitchell was unable to ask Ford to give an uninterrupted narrative, to repeat it chronologically and in reverse, or to make a drawing of the scene. But she did employ several important features of the cognitive interview. For instance, she established rapport at the beginning by allowing the witness to offer an extended version of her story, only later going back to clarify inconsistencies. She presented her questions in collaborative terms, asking the subject to help her understand. She confronted Ford about inconsistencies in a piecemeal fashion, avoiding an opportunity for her to come up with a single comprehensive explanation for all her inconsistencies, as witnesses often do when they are lying. Mitchell had uncovered a number of problems with Ford's testimony, but she had done so in such a gentle way that it was not clear that Ford had recognized what was happening.

The media certainly didn't pick up on what Mitchell had revealed. The incomprehension that Cynthia Alksne of MSNBC revealed was typical: "You build a cross-exam to a crescendo and you spend hours planning it and you've had this witness for a lot of time. I've never seen a worse crescendo in my whole life. I mean, that was awful. To end on that. I mean, it was mind boggling that's the way it ended about 'this is five minutes' or 'you should have been in L.A.' or 'why weren't you here?' It didn't even go out with a whimper. It went out with a simmer. I mean,

I don't even know what that was. That's the worst cross-exam I've ever seen. Am I wrong?"[28]

■   ■   ■

The Republicans on the Senate Judiciary Committee, however, were not cross-examining Ford, nor were they playing to the cable news peanut gallery. Their only concern was a very small audience—the Republican senators whose votes were in question and which they could not afford to lose—in particular, Senators Flake and Murkowski.

These senators also cared deeply about the protocols of the Senate and suspected that the Democrats were simply using Ford as a weapon against Kavanaugh. They were dismayed by the revelation that Feinstein was responsible for Ford's being represented by the political animal Debra Katz. In fact, the performance of Ford's attorneys during the morning's questioning was, for these senators, the most interesting part of the morning's hearings. Katz and Bromwich had interrupted when Ford was asked about her legal representation and tried to keep her from talking about whether she knew about repeated offers of the Senate interviewers to come to her. Grassley had made that offer to her lawyers and even repeated it on television. If Ford was to be believed, they had kept this information from her, forcing their timid client into the spotlight of a Washington hearing. Republican senators, including some who were key votes, were appalled by Ford's attorneys. They felt that people who cared for her should have told her about the repeated offers to travel to her. And the way they flanked her and interrupted her to keep from answering questions struck them as overly controlling.

The investigators on the staff of the Judiciary Committee were shocked to learn that a polygraph test, which is generally not admissible in court and is of questionable value to begin with, had been administered while Ford was mourning her grandmother's death and preparing for a supposedly terrifying flight. Because the polygraph measures anxiety in response to questions, polygraphers usually avoid administering it against a background of psychological distress. She seemed not to know if she had been recorded, although the state of Maryland requires consent of all parties for recording and American Polygraph Association standards require polygraphs to be recorded from beginning to end. It is typical to release the audio and video of a polygraph for second opinions, but Ford and her attorneys declined to do so.

The anti-Kavanaugh forces, then, had taken some serious blows that morning, but the damage was below the surface. The running commentary in the media coalesced around the theme of Kavanaugh's now-inevitable defeat. The White House reporter Ashley Parker, appearing on MSNBC, declared that "by the end of the day [Trump] might be willing to cut Judge Kavanaugh loose. They don't know. This is a moving situation but the outlook now is fairly grim." The anchor-man Brian Williams responded that Trump's own instincts were damaging Kavanaugh's prospects. In his "inability to read the room," the president had reportedly encouraged the judge to be "'hotter' on camera—to ad lib more, get off his talking points." But for Kavanaugh to come in "hotter," after Ford's "emotional" and "very organic" testimony, Williams warned, would be "off-balance." "That's such a smart point," Parker told him. If Kavanaugh appeared "indignant, more outraged, and more defiant," he might please the president but would not "win over the room" or the general public.[29]

The White House was enthralled by the testimony. Everyone was watching the proceedings on the Hill, leaving the normally bustling corridors of the West Wing oddly silent. The Kavanaugh team thought that Ford had done extremely well, and they were no longer confident that the Republican senators, a handful of whom were not conservative or were consumed by antipathy to Trump, would stick together. They were less worried about Collins than Murkowski and Flake, but they knew it would be hard for Republicans to vote for Kavanaugh unless he hit a home run that afternoon.

The situation at midday revealed the risk of their strategy of not attacking Ford's character, even though they had information that was at odds with her testimony. The ex-boyfriend had told them about her frequent flying and her history with polygraphs. Fearing a backlash against himself, he had been reluctant to speak against Ford but had relented under the weight of an official Senate investigation.

The White House had expected Ford to perform well as a witness. While they believed Kavanaugh was innocent, many of them also believed that Ford had probably suffered an assault like the one she described and had, for whatever reason, come to believe what she was saying about Kavanaugh.

■   ■   ■

False memory has been an important field of research in psychology since the 1990s, when psychologists started turning up "recovered memories," particularly of child sexual assault and ritual satanic abuse. The theory of recovered memory is that certain events may be so traumatic that they are blocked from one's memory and can be recovered only with certain psychological techniques, including hypnosis.

When certain "recovered" memories were proved to be impossible, Elizabeth Loftus, now a professor at the University of California at Irvine, began to study the malleability of memory and whether certain techniques were more likely to produce false memories.[30] She has since become the leading researcher in the field, receiving the American Psychological Foundation's Gold Medal for Lifetime Achievement, and is one of the most frequently cited psychologists in the world.[31] Loftus and others demonstrated the ease with which false memories could be suggested to research subjects who felt them to be true, and the reliability of "recovered" memories came under serious question.

While the number of therapists treating recovered memories as credible dramatically diminished in the wake of the research into the malleability of memory, at least into the 2000s there was a divergence of opinion between clinical psychologists, who were more likely to give weight to recovered memories, and researchers, who were skeptical of such memories' reliability. The majority of research psychologists now believe that memory is malleable—that is, it can be contaminated, distorted, or transformed by external suggestions and even by a person's own internal thoughts about what might have happened. Clinicians, however, along with the public, are more likely to believe that repressed memories can be accurately retrieved in therapy.[32] One researcher firmly in the pro–recovered memory camp is David Spiegel, who collaborated on at least three different papers with Ford. They introduced one joint experiment by emphasizing the usefulness of hypnosis in therapy, including to "assist in the retrieval of important memories."[33]

Loftus, herself a Democrat who professed to be frightened of the prospect of Kavanaugh's joining the Supreme Court, nonetheless found Ford's testimony problematic, particularly her use of scientific terminology: "We got a laugh out of that." She added that "no memory person would say 'indelible in the hippocampus,'" because "things aren't indelible, period, and they aren't indelible in just one part of the brain." One would have to know more about the nature of the marital therapy sessions, she said, to determine how much weight to give those memories, because some techniques are known to produce images and ideas in the mind of a patient that sometimes solidify into false memories. "In this case the question is, when did the accuser attach Brett Kavanaugh's name to the incident?" she said. "Was it right away or did it come much later, say, in therapy?"

Not only memories, but confidence about one's memories can be malleable. Some witnesses may have low confidence when they initially identify someone—for example, picking a suspect out of a lineup—but when their choice is reinforced by police officers or others, they appear highly confident months or years later at trial. This confidence makes them compelling witnesses, even though they may have been initially unsure of their memory. Studies have shown that one's ability to tell whether a witness is making an accurate identification is fairly good if one is judging the witness's confidence of his *initial* identification.[34] But if the judgment of a witness's reliability is based on the witness's confidence *at trial*, after he has been subject to the influence of others, then that judgment is less likely to be accurate.[35] Ford's testimony, of course, was given decades after the event, and there had been abundant occasions for her memory to be influenced by any number of people—her therapist, husband, "beach friends," and lawyers.

Empirical studies suggest that Ford's testimony could have been inaccurate even if she was fully convinced that the events occurred as she described them. In other words, she could have been telling the truth and nevertheless have accused Kavanaugh falsely. Polygraph experts have also identified this problem, pointing out that polygraphs can assess only a person's subjective belief.[36] If the subject of a polygraph test believes what he is saying to be true, the polygraph will rate him non-deceptive. This was illustrated by Blasey Ford's own testimony in the hearing, when she stated that details in the statement she read at the polygraph exam were in fact inaccurate. Because she apparently believed them to be true at the time, the test showed no deception.

■   ■   ■

The Kavanaugh team stuck to its policy of not attacking Ford personally even though damaging information about Ford was being openly discussed by people who knew her, some who knew her quite well. Classmates were surprised by the media's portrayal of her as an ingénue, which was very different from how they remembered her in junior high and high school. Female classmates and friends at area schools recalled a heavy drinker who was much more aggressive with boys than they were. "If she only had one beer" on the night of the alleged assault, a high school friend said, "then it must have been early in the evening." Her contemporaries all reported the same nickname for Ford, a riff on her maiden name and a sexual act. They also debated whether her behavior in high school could be attributed to the trauma of a sexual assault. If it could, one of them said, then the assault must have happened in seventh grade.

Although discussions along these lines were pervasive in the still-close Montgomery County community, none of these details was reported by the media, which were preoccupied with every emerging scrap of information about Kavanaugh's youth.

Investigators on the Senate Judiciary Committee received communications from two men who claimed to have had (consensual) romantic encounters with the teenaged Christine Blasey. Each claimed consensual encounters with her that sounded similar to the assault she described. For instance, one man said that when he was a "19-year-old college student, he visited D.C. over spring break and kissed a girl he believes was Dr. Ford. He said that kiss happened in the bedroom of a house which was a 15- to 20-minute walk from the Van Ness Metro. Ford was wearing a swimsuit under her clothing, and the kissing ended when a friend jumped on them as a joke. [He] said that the woman initiated the kissing and that he did not force himself on her."

Another person, claiming to be a college acquaintance of Ford's, said that Ford used to purchase drugs from another student and regularly attended his fraternity parties. According to this witness, she enjoyed a robust social life in college. Other friends from college reported similar experiences and said Ford had never demonstrated fear of rooms with single entrances.

Contemporaries of Ford's at Holton-Arms said the least believable part of her story was how she left the party. It was inconceivable to them that she would have left Leland Keyser behind and that Keyser would not have found her abandonment to be highly noteworthy. She had always filled a protective role for Ford, so it seemed quite unlikely that she would not have become worried and made sure her friend was well. The story of a fifteen-year-old tenth-grader leaving behind the only other female at a party and then finding her way home, miles away, in pre-cell-phone 1982, with no car, no metro, and no cabs readily available is difficult to believe.

Ford's partying and interactions with boys and young men and the attention they drew had dismayed her family. Some journalists noticed that a letter from "members of Christine Blasey Ford's family" did not include the signatures of any blood relatives. In a story headlined "Christine Blasey Ford's Family Has Been Nearly Silent Amid Outpouring of Support," the *Washington Post* took her parents and brothers to task for failing to sign her in-laws' letter. Her father, Ralph Blasey, responded, "I think all of the Blasey family would support her. I think her record stands for itself. Her schooling, her jobs and so on." Later he added, "I think any father would have love for his daughter."[37]

The media tended to skim over Ford's political views, which ran decidedly to the left and were at variance with most of her family's. Facebook friends reported that she had regularly expressed her hostility to the Trump administration before she deleted her profile around the time of Kavanaugh's nomination. After her retreat from social media, only a few references to her political opinions remained, one mentioning a hat she wore in homage to the anti-Trump "pussy hat" protesters, another protesting Trump's policy on border security.[38]

In one of the *Washington Post*'s deferential profiles of Ford, her husband had suggested that any strain in the family was due to those "differing political views" and misogyny: "It was a very male-dominated environment. Everyone was interested in what's going on with the men, and the women are sidelined, and she didn't get the attention or respect she felt she deserved." The same article emphasized that Ford's father and Kavanaugh's father belonged to the same all-male golf club, Burning Tree.

The *Post* suggested that Ford's family was afraid to defend her, quoting her sister-in-law as saying that supporters of sexual assault victims have trouble coming forward. Hale Boggs III, the scion of a prominent Democratic family and a friend of the Blaseys, remarked, "It's got to be such a difficult situation for that family. It's a very close-knit community where a lot of families know each other."[39] Still, a number of persons close to the family reported that staying silent was actually the family's way of supporting Christine.

It was not fear of showing support for Ford that kept others in the community quiet but the opposite. While many high school acquaintances of Ford's revealed unflattering details about her behavior in high school—some of them truly salacious—the media's hostility to Kavanaugh made them fear for their livelihood if their names were attached to the stories. Some worried that their children's college applications would be affected. And some were reluctant to expose Ford to the kind of ferocious public criticism to which Kavanaugh had been subjected, even if what they said was true.

A person claiming to be an acquaintance of the Blasey family told the Judiciary Committee that several persons who knew Christine in high school had information regarding her drinking and partying, but none was willing to come forward. "I wish I could say all of the things I know," the witness said, "but I don't want to put myself out there."

■   ■   ■

The president and the Senate majority leader chatted by phone after Ford's testimony to assess each other's reaction. Neither was wavering.

No Republican senator thought Ford had performed poorly in her testimony, but the reactions varied strongly. Some thought her attorneys had done her no favors. Others felt the gaps in her recent memory were disconcerting. And one staffer, early on, thought she was doing so well that he joked about calling in a bomb threat to stop the hearing.

But some Republican senators were more fickle. One member of the Judiciary Committee went to Senator Collins with a plan. In light of Ford's testimony, they should go to the White House and make an offer to confirm a different nominee if Kavanaugh's nomination were pulled. Collins, whose diligence and regard for rule of law had remained intact throughout the process, declined. She never would have recommended withdrawing the nomination based on Ford's testimony alone. She was determined to hear Kavanaugh out.

CHAPTER NINE

Miracle

The unwillingness of nearly everyone to question Ford's credibility publicly made the pressure on Kavanaugh before his testimony nearly unbearable. After the Fox News interview, Don McGahn encouraged Kavanaugh by reminding him there was a reason he had been nominated to the Supreme Court. His professional performance over three decades gave people confidence in him. Figure out what you want to do in Thursday's hearing and execute it, he said. Too many people telling him too many things, McGahn thought, was making him come across as too rehearsed. Kavanaugh should just be himself.

McGahn's advice was a huge relief and exactly what Kavanaugh needed to hear. He was being pulled in two directions, which reflected the influence of two very different Republican presidents. His temperament was a perfect match with President George W. Bush, a man adored by those who worked closely with him. But Bush's willingness to brush off slights and to discard conservative principles for the sake of political expediency made many Americans feel he had let them down. At the other end of the spectrum was the brash outsider President Donald Trump. Reviled by the Washington establishment, he had been brought to power by an American people worried about the direction of the courts, the rise of "social justice warriors," and the corrosive influence of the media. Voters were seeking someone willing to stand strong against these forces.

McGahn liked to remind Kavanaugh that he was a Trump nominee, but as Thursday approached, he didn't need reminding.

Kavanaugh and Ford were supposed to submit their written statements to the Judiciary Committee on Wednesday morning, twenty-four hours before the hearings opened, but Kavanaugh's wasn't finished. He had been thinking about his statement for a while, but because of the uncertainty of Ford's appearance, he had not gotten down to writing in earnest until Tuesday. The Kavanaugh team realized that his statement would not be ready by the ten o'clock deadline, but they were not worried about that. Strategically, it did not make sense to submit his full statement in advance, for much of its power would be in the delivery. And given Ford's cavalier attitude toward deadlines, they doubted she would submit her statement in time. They also knew that delivering a statement in a congressional hearing that differed from the written form previously submitted was common. So shortly before noon on Wednesday, the team submitted to the committee an early draft that they knew would need more work. It consisted of seven fairly dry, biographical paragraphs but ended with the promise of more: "Additional testimony to follow."[1] Ford submitted her testimony, a close approximation of the statement she would deliver the following day, at around five o'clock p.m.

Less than two hours later, the Avenatti allegations of gang rape broke. A White House aide suggested to Chris Michel, the former clerk and Bush speechwriter helping Kavanaugh prepare his remarks, that he tear up what he had and start over. The campaign to keep him from being seated had just escalated to accusations of serial gang rape. It was time to get angry.

Kavanaugh had already taken that advice. Michel had presented him earlier in the day with his rough draft of the speech, timed to last about ten minutes. The judge retreated into his office and spent the next several hours rewriting and dramatically expanding the draft. The White House kept asking to see it and he kept declining. Finally, he told them they weren't going to see a draft. McGahn never insisted that he share it, choosing to trust him.

Ford may have been the one who insisted on unlimited time for opening statements, but it was Kavanaugh who took advantage of that opportunity, with a statement that stretched for nearly forty-five minutes. He knew that it would be his one opportunity to make his case directly to the American people, and he would take all the time he needed.

By late Wednesday evening he had a draft he could practice delivering. Perhaps counterintuitively, rehearsal can be more important for an emotional speech than for a dry one. The first few times he practiced, it was almost impossible to get through it without breaking down. But for all its emotion, his remarks were essentially a presentation of the evidence for and against the allegations. This was a lawyer's speech. By eleven o'clock, he had it where he wanted it, and he went home to rest.

He spent the next morning making edits and practicing before going to Capitol Hill with Ashley shortly before noon. They waited for two hours in a holding room in Dirksen furnished with a table, a couch, a few chairs, and a TV tuned to the Golf Channel coverage of the Ryder Cup. They were not watching Ford's testimony and had little to do while they waited, so Kavanaugh read his opening remarks to his wife. She told him they were good.

The one change they made that day was adding a story about their daughter Liza's saying that they should pray for the accuser, which Ashley had told him that morning. He added a note with a black Sharpie permanent marker, his editing tool of choice. Having learned from practice that some parts of the speech would be hard to make it through, he had indicated with his Sharpie where to stop to breathe.

Kavanaugh had been deluged with advice until the end. His Bush friends, by and large, told him to not to show too much emotion. But he received calls from a few senators encouraging him to show his righteous indignation. They intimated that they found him too passive in the interview with MacCallum. There he had followed the advice of some friends to emphasize that he was a father and husband—as a "guilty politician would do," one of his aides said dismissively.

The news Kavanaugh received was mostly filtered through McGahn, who kept him positive but realistic, and Ashley. He knew from them that Avenatti's accusations were striking most people as ridiculous. Though the allegations angered him, they gave him confidence going into the hearing. He had felt the attacks were crazy since the first allegation, but now he knew that the public was starting to see it that way as well.

There were very few people who could understand what Kavanaugh was going through, and they were sitting on the Court. For some of the justices, watching the day's proceedings, or even the first set of hearings, was too painful, even if their own confirmations had been easier.

The drama of this day reminded everyone of Clarence Thomas's reopened hearings in 1991.[2] His nomination had barely made it out of the Democrat-controlled Judiciary Committee on a tie vote. Before it could come to a vote on the floor, Anita Hill's allegations, which had been turned over to the FBI and were supposed to be evaluated by the committee confidentially, were disclosed to the press, putting Thomas in the position of having to prove a negative. A man who had played by the rules was now sabotaged by people who were trafficking in lies, leaks, and rumors. Thomas meditated on the words of the apostle Paul—the same words, it turned out, that Kavanaugh had read at Mass the day before his nomination: "Therefore I take pleasure in infirmities, in reproaches, in needs, in persecutions, in distresses for Christ's sake. For when I am weak, then I am strong."[3]

As Ashley Kavanaugh would do two and a half decades later, Thomas offered a prayer of surrender to the will of God: "If it is possible, let this cup pass from me; nevertheless, not as I will, but as You will."[4] He focused on the second part of that prayer, knowing it was the most difficult.

As in Kavanaugh's case, Thomas's hearings were reopened because it had become clear that the votes were not there without a public airing of the accusation. He had spent years reviewing precisely the type of employment discrimination and harassment allegations that Hill was making, and he knew that her unsubstantiated and contradicted charges would have been thrown out of court immediately. But the court of public opinion was another matter. "The mob was howling, and it wouldn't be satisfied until it had tasted my blood," Thomas would later reflect.[5]

Choosing to testify before Hill, Thomas delivered a statement—seen beforehand only by his wife and his longtime friend and ally Senator John Danforth—in which he denied Hill's allegations and spoke about the pain that the ordeal of intentionally burdensome document production, intrusive reporters digging for dirt in his own garage, and rumor-mongering had caused him and his family. "This is not American; this is Kafkaesque. It has got to stop. It must stop for the benefit of future nominees and our country. Enough is enough." He didn't intend to testify further after this. "There is nothing this committee, this body, or this country can do to give me my good name back. Nothing. I will not provide the rope for my own lynching or for further humiliation."[6]

The powerful statement appeared to have taken the room by surprise, and Thomas left to allow Hill to testify. After his wife, Virginia, relayed to him the specific charges Hill was making against him before the committee, Thomas felt relieved. He had been racking his brain for days to figure out what offhand comment she had misunderstood, but now he knew her charges were unrelated to anything he had actually done.

Although Thomas had not planned on returning to the committee to respond to Hill's charges, Danforth and Senator Orrin Hatch convinced him that the media would have a field day with her story if it was left uncontested. In Danforth's office he lay down to think, settling on one phrase he felt crystallized his thoughts about the process. He wrote "HIGH-TECH LYNCHING" on the legal pad on which Danforth had listed suggested talking points. Thomas reflected on the parallels between his situation and the storyline of *To Kill a Mockingbird*, which dealt with both racial prejudices and a mob bent on short-circuiting the due process of law. That was the same book Kavanaugh had cited in his first round of hearings as teaching him not to prejudge others.

Thomas returned to the hearing room and delivered a speech that would change the momentum of the confirmation process. He began by again "unequivocally" denying "each and every single allegation against me today."[7] Then he turned to the process, which he called a travesty. "This is a case in which this sleaze, this dirt, was searched for by staffers of members of this committee. It was then leaked to the media, and this committee and this body validated it and displayed it at prime time over our entire nation....This is not a closed room. There was an FBI investigation. This is not an opportunity to talk about difficult matters privately or in a closed environment." He continued, "This is a circus. It is a national disgrace. And from my standpoint, as a black American, as far as I am concerned, it is a high-tech lynching for uppity blacks who in any way deign to think for themselves, to do for themselves, to have different ideas, and it is a message that, unless you kowtow to an old order, this is what will happen to you, you will be lynched, destroyed, caricatured by a committee of the U.S. Senate rather than hung from a tree."[8]

Justice Thomas described the moment in his autobiography, *My Grandfather's Son*: "When I was done, my words seemed to hang in the air of the Caucus Room like the smoke from a bomb that had just exploded."[9] And their effect was truly explosive. By the end of his testimony, polls showed that more than twice as many Americans believed Thomas as believed Hill. And an overwhelming majority thought Thomas should be confirmed.[10]

Now it was Kavanaugh's turn. The war room was set up in the vice president's suite in the Dirksen Building as it had been in the first set of hearings, but there was nothing much for people to do. Clever tweets and talking points were not going to save this nomination. A smaller number of aides and officials watched Ford's testimony in the offices of Senator Thom Tillis of North Carolina and relayed necessary information to Kavanaugh. When Ford had finished her testimony, a few aides came and offered advice to the judge, one suggesting that he meekly talk about Ford's courage in telling her story. Don McGahn told them to leave—"Everyone!" he shouted. Even Ashley got up to leave the room, but she was told she could say.

Kavanaugh and McGahn had strategized using sports analogies throughout the process. They shared a love of the 2004 film *Miracle*, which is about the U.S. hockey team's improbable victory over the Soviet team in the 1980 Olympics. Kavanaugh was fond of quoting the line shouted by an exhausted team captain, "I play for the United States of America!" McGahn, wanting to reset the table after Ford's testimony, thought of another scene from the movie. The U.S. coach comes into the locker room after the first period of a game against Sweden. His team is losing and dejected. The coach accuses an injured player of being a quitter, mocks a teammate who comes to his defense, and flips over a table to get everyone fired up. On his way out the door, he says under his breath to the assistant coach, "That'll get 'em goin'."[11] McGahn had watched Ford's testimony. He knew people believed her, but he knew Kavanaugh had it in him to fight for his honor.

They had practiced for a moment like this. Over the previous week, in sessions with just Kavanaugh and a few others, they had tried to prepare the nominee for what he would face. The Gorsuch confirmation process had taught the White House that they could not fully script interactions with senators. Federal judges know what they're doing and should be allowed to trust their instincts. Kavanaugh, a respected judge with a sterling reputation, was seeing his character and life's work demolished. People were already saying he should not return to the court of appeals, let alone take a seat on the Supreme Court. He was being turned into a pariah. It was time for his own "miracle on ice." He was down, he was injured, and he had to win.

■   ■   ■

Kavanaugh entered the hearing room and sat down. He wore a dark suit and a blue tie. His brow was furrowed as he adjusted his microphone and papers. Ashley sat behind him next to her friend, Laura Kaplan.

He began by noting that he had denied the allegations against him "immediately, categorically, and unequivocally."[12] He quoted from the witness statements saying that they had no recollection of anything like the episode Ford had described. He reminded the committee he'd asked for an immediate hearing to clear his name, demanding a hearing the next day. Their ten-day delay had allowed his family and his name to be "totally and permanently destroyed by vicious and false additional accusations."

Kavanaugh said he had welcomed an investigation into the charges and had cooperated fully, knowing that any investigation would clear him. He reminded the committee of the myriad witnesses who all testified to his character.

"This confirmation process has become a national disgrace," he said. "The Constitution gives the Senate an important role in the confirmation process, but you have replaced 'advice and consent' with 'search and destroy.'" He reminded the senators that the moment his nomination was announced, left-wing activists had launched a frenzied search to "come up with something, anything," to block his confirmation. He threw statements of Democratic senators back at them, reminding everyone that the minority leader, Chuck Schumer, had said he would oppose him with everything he had. He reminded the Democrats on the Senate Judiciary Committee that one of them—it was Senator Booker—had publicly referred to him as evil. "*Evil.* Think about that word. It's said that those who supported me were, quote, complicit in evil," he continued, driving his point home. He rehearsed a few more of the reckless and extreme statements by Democratic senators and political leaders.

"I understand the passions of the moment," he said, but he reminded them that people took their words seriously, issuing vile threats against his wife and friends. "You sowed the wind. For decades to come, I fear the whole country will reap the whirlwind."

The behavior of the Democrats on the Judiciary Committee was an "embarrassment" when it was still at the level of a "good old-fashioned attempt at Borking." But when it began to look like he would be confirmed, "a new tactic was needed." He noted that a Democratic member and her staff had kept Ford's allegation a secret for weeks, waiting to unveil it when it was needed and making it public against Ford's wishes.

There followed a "long series of false, last-minute smears" designed, he said, to drive him off the stage:

Crazy stuff. Gangs, illegitimate children, fights on boats in Rhode Island. All nonsense reported breathlessly and often uncritically by the media. This has destroyed my family and my good name—a good name built up through decades of very hard work and public service at the highest levels of the American government. This whole two-week effort has been a calculated and orchestrated political hit, fueled with apparent pent-up anger about President Trump and the 2016 election, fear that has been unfairly stoked about my judicial record, revenge on behalf of the Clintons, and millions of dollars in money from outside left-wing opposition groups. This is a circus.

He lamented the effect the confirmation process would have on others who might seek to serve the country. But though he feared for the future, he would not be intimidated into withdrawing from the confirmation process. "You've tried hard. You've given it your all. No one can question your effort, but your coordinated and well-funded effort to destroy my good name and destroy my family will not drive me out. The vile threats of violence against my family will not drive me out. You may defeat me in the final vote, but you will never get me to quit. Never."

Then he turned to the allegations against him. He said he had never sexually assaulted anyone, emphasizing how seriously he took sexual assault. He reminded the senators that due process requires hearing from those who make allegations and from those who are the subject of allegations.

He repeated something he had said in the East Room at the announcement of his nomination—that his mother's trademark line was, "Use your common sense. What rings true, what rings false?" A good reminder, he said, for the decision before the senators. The last-minute accusations, flung at him by a campaign that had promised to do everything in its power to stop his nomination, was utterly inconsistent with the reputation he had built over decades and did not ring true.

Christine Blasey may have been sexually assaulted, he said, but not by him, adding that he intended no ill will to her or her family. "The other night Ashley and my daughter Liza said their prayers, and little Liza—all of ten years old—said to Ashley, 'We should pray for the woman.' That's a lot of wisdom from a ten-year-old. We mean no ill will," he said, choking up. The hearing room was full of people crying. Kavanaugh's parents were there to support him and could barely maintain their composure. Watching their anguish over their only son's ordeal was brutal for the other members of Kavanaugh's team.

He cited the six FBI background investigations he had undergone in the previous twenty-six years and cited the positions of responsibility he had held that put him under public scrutiny. He noted that he and other members of Kenneth Starr's Whitewater independent prosecutor's office were researched "from head to toe, from birth through the present day," and that while others had been exposed as having engaged in sexual wrongdoing, nothing was alleged about him. He reminded senators that he had served three years in the West Wing and traveled around the world with the president, having been thoroughly vetted. He had sat through two confirmation hearings, in 2004 and 2006, before being confirmed to the second-most important court in the country.

"Throughout my fifty-three years and seven months on this earth until last week, no one ever accused me of any kind of sexual misconduct. No one ever. A lifetime," he said.

More specifically, he said, he had never had any sexual or physical encounter of any kind with Ford and never attended a gathering like the one she described. He said that if he socialized with girls, they tended to be at the Catholic schools, not Holton-Arms. All of the persons named as witnesses said they did not recall anything that matched Ford's account.

"Dr. Ford's allegation is not merely uncorroborated, it is refuted by the very people she says were there, including by a longtime friend of hers," he said, noting that none of the witnesses lived near Columbia Country Club.

Then he pointed to his calendars. He explained why he kept them, choking up as he talked about his father keeping detailed calendars. Ashley, crying, kept supportive eyes on Brett from behind. Noting that while the calendars had "some goofy parts, some embarrassing parts," they documented the summer of 1982 well. He said the only weekend nights he was in Maryland and not grounded were Friday, June 4, and Saturday, August 7. He noted how he listed the names of people with whom he attended parties. His calendars were full of sports camps, summer trips, and hanging out with friends. He talked about his summer business of cutting lawns.

"And as my calendars show, I was very precise," said Kavanaugh, noting that they included the precise list of whom he gathered with. They weren't dispositive on their own, he acknowledged, "but they are another piece of evidence in the mix for you to consider."

Finally, he noted that the charges were inconsistent with his record and character from youth to the present day. He referred to his many women friends. "I remember talking almost every night it seemed to my friends Amy or Julie or Kristin or Karen or Suzanne or Maura or Meghan or Nikki, the list goes on. Friends for a lifetime built on a foundation of talking through school and life starting at age fourteen. Several of those great women are in the seats right behind me today," he said.

He acknowledged that he drank beer in high school, noting that the drinking age in Maryland was then eighteen. And he acknowledged that his yearbook was "a disaster." Students had taken their cues from popular movies of the time, such as *Animal House*, *Caddyshack*, and *Fast Times at Ridgemont High*. He said what he saw in his yearbook made him cringe, particularly the reference to Renate.

"One of our good female friends who we would admire and went to dances with had her name used on the yearbook page with the term 'alumnus.' That yearbook reference was clumsily intended to show affection and that she was one of us, but in this circus, the media's interpreted the term as related to sex. It was not related to sex," he said. He apologized to her and said that one thing he wanted to make sure of in the future was his friendship with her. "She was and is a great person," he said.

He also went through the women who had sent letters on his behalf. After quoting three text messages he had received in the past two days from female college friends, he recalled that in his opening statement at the first hearing, he had said, "Cherish your friends, look out for your friend, lift up your friends, love your friends. I felt that love more over the last two weeks than I ever have in my life. I thank all my friends. I love all my friends."

Turning to his record with women in the professional sphere, Kavanaugh said, "Throughout my life, I've devoted huge efforts to encouraging and promoting the careers of women. I will put my record up against anyone's, male or female." Then he turned closer to home: "I love coaching more than anything I've ever done in my whole life, but thanks to what some of you on this side of the committee have unleashed, I may never be able to coach again."

Finally, he thanked God for Ashley and his family and concluded:

> We live in a country devoted to due process and the rule of law. That means taking allegations seriously, but if the mere allegation, the mere assertion of an allegation, a refuted allegation from thirty-six years ago, is enough to destroy a person's life and career, we will have abandoned the basic principles of fairness and due process that define our legal system and our country. I ask you to judge me by the standard that you would want applied to your father, your husband, your brother, or your son. My family and I intend no ill will toward Dr. Ford or her family. But I swear today under oath before the Senate and the nation, before my family and God, I am innocent of this charge.

After his emotionally powerful opening statement, Kavanaugh first answered some perfunctory questions from Rachel Mitchell about how he knew the people whom Ford had identified as witnesses. But soon enough he had to respond to pointed questions from his accusers on the committee. When Senator Feinstein asked him why he didn't want the FBI to investigate the accusations against him by Ford, Ramirez, and Swetnick, Kavanaugh reminded her forcefully that he had wanted a hearing immediately, instead of waiting ten days while allegations were "printed and run breathlessly by cable news."

She said the committee needed an outside authority to interview witnesses. Kavanaugh replied that it wasn't for him to tell her how to do her job, but that the committee had the same authority to interview witnesses as the FBI, and the FBI would simply turn over its interviews without offering a conclusion. Feinstein, boldly, then brought up Avenatti's rape allegations, saying she understood Kavanaugh was denying them. "That is emphatically what I'm saying. Emphatically," he said, calling the gang rape claim a joke and a farce. "Would you like to say more about it?" Feinstein asked. "No," he responded immediately, eliciting laughter from the room. Some of Feinstein's colleagues, including some whose votes were in play, were surprised and appalled that she gave the outlandish allegations credence.

Mitchell then asked him some more factual questions about his drinking, sexual behavior, and his calendars. Just three questioners in, the team from the White House counsel's office realized that Kavanaugh needed time for his emotions to cool.

■   ■   ■

Everything had changed in the previous hour. And everyone involved in the confirmation effort, whether at the White House or on the Hill, knew it. All of them were surprised at the tearful reaction they had to his emotional testimony.

After so many years of seeing conservatives give in, Kavanaugh's supporters were moved by his bold defense of his life, his reputation, and the of rule of law. The display of courage and righteous indignation moved nearly everyone to tears. Men and women in the war room, in the hearing room, and at the White House were crying. And social media reflected the dismay of people throughout the country at the climate of mob justice that could tear down their honorable husbands and sons. Kavanaugh was fighting not only for himself but for everybody who had been unfairly attacked.

Media personalities, on the other hand, were struggling to accept what they had just witnessed. NBC's Lester Holt said Kavanaugh "still seemed to be trying to find his composure and his footing as he once again continues to deny all the accusations made by Christine Blasey Ford."[13]

"I mean, where do you even begin?" asked NBC's Andrea Mitchell, criticizing Kavanaugh's reference to the 2016 campaign and President Trump. Chuck Todd said that the speech might have played well with the president but might not play well in the rest of America. Because Rachel Mitchell was asking tough questions of Kavanaugh after her apparent gentleness with Ford, Todd concluded that Republican senators had "made that decision to protect themselves, not the nomination, which tells you what they're really probably most concerned about, which is election day. Because this is not how you help *him*, this is how you help the Republicans."[14]

Savannah Guthrie said, "He put it all out there, made a political argument, local argument, personal argument. How could you as a human not watch that and feel gut-wrenched."[15]

Jeffrey Toobin of CNN reacted emotionally to Kavanaugh's assertion that the smears against him were, among other things, "revenge on behalf of the Clintons." Toobin interpreted that remark as a comment on Bill and Hillary Clinton. "This was a deeply political statement designed to appeal to Republicans," he said.[16]

A reliable defender of the Clintons who had written a defensive book on President Clinton's impeachment, Toobin misinterpreted Kavanaugh's remark. He was talking about the Clinton supporters behind the groups that were fueling the attacks on him. Many of these people were clearly motivated in part by his participation in the independent counsel's investigation of the 1990s. Kavanaugh did not say, or even suggest, that the Clintons were themselves orchestrating the campaign against him, even if Hillary Clinton had spoken publicly against his nomination. But the main movers in the campaign against him included Clinton aides Ricki Seidman and Brian Fallon, who were ringmasters in the anti-Kavanaugh circus. And there were Clinton aides and campaign staff at all levels of the effort. That night Fallon would ominously tweet, "Kavanaugh will not serve for life." In the months to come, he would organize efforts to impeach Kavanaugh, harass him with ethics complaints, and get him kicked off campuses.[17]

The hearing reconvened with Senator Leahy's asking Kavanaugh if he wanted Mark Judge as a witness. Kavanaugh responded by criticizing how Ford's allegation was sprung on him at the last minute. As the senator and the judge talked over each other, Leahy's staff hoisted pictures from Kavanaugh's yearbook onto an easel and started confronting him with its entries and interrupting his answers. The hostile exchange was going nowhere, and eventually Grassley cut Leahy off, reminding the Democrat how polite Republicans had been to Ford.

Mitchell then asked Kavanaugh about the summer of 1982 as well as his treatment of women during his professional life and whether he had given sworn statements in response to various allegations.

When it was Senator Dick Durbin's turn, he urged Kavanaugh to "turn to Don McGahn and tell him it's time to get this done. An FBI investigation is the only way to answer some of these questions." He hectored Kavanaugh, "If there is no truth to her charges, the FBI investigation will show that. Are you afraid that they might not?" Kavanaugh stopped responding, just looking at the senator as if he were disappointed in him.

Ordinarily, nominees are deferential to senators, as Kavanaugh had been in his first hearing, politely telling them he understands their concern and respects their wisdom. He wasn't going to do that now. Kavanaugh was not going to take their belittling, mocking, and mischaracterizations without going right back at them. This time his career was on the line, his family was on the line, and his reputation was on the line. He did not know if he was going to make it through to confirmation, and he did not want to destroy his chances needlessly, but he was intentionally firm and forceful. He thought of Miguel Estrada, a qualified nominee whose confirmation was derailed by Democrats who didn't want Republicans to place a Hispanic on a high-profile federal court. After Estrada lost his brutal confirmation fight, his wife died prematurely.

Kavanaugh was fighting not only to vindicate his judicial philosophy and the reasoning of his opinions, but also to vindicate his reputation as a man. He had endured the indignity of having to respond to the most sensitive and embarrassing questions he could imagine. He was not going to let his opponents destroy his life.

After Durbin's questioning, Senator Lindsey Graham asked for the floor.[18] No one was expecting what followed. As he began to speak, Graham's tone was matter-of-fact. "Are you aware," he asked the nominee, "that at 9:23 the night of July the ninth, the day you were nominated to the Supreme Court by President Trump, Senator Schumer said—twenty-three minutes after your nomination—'I will oppose Judge Kavanaugh's nomination with everything I have. I hope a bipartisan majority will do the same. The stakes are simply too high for anything less'? Well, if you weren't aware of it, you are now.

"Did you meet with Senator Dianne Feinstein on August 20?"

"I did meet with Senator Feinstein," Kavanaugh answered.

"Did you know her staff had already recommended a lawyer to Dr. Ford?" Here the senator shifted in his chair, hunched his shoulders slightly, and pursed his lips, the first indication of his rising anger.

"I did not know that."

"Did you know that her and her staff had this allegation for over twenty days?"

"I did not know that at the time."

And then, turning to the Democrats arrayed to his left, Graham snarled, "If you wanted an FBI investigation, you could have come to *us*. What you want to do is destroy this guy's life"—pointing at Kavanaugh—"hold this seat open, and hope you win in 2020. You've *said* that!"

For the next three and a half minutes, Lindsey Graham was a volcano of indignation. With unconcealed contempt, he declared, "If you really wanted to know the truth, you sure as hell wouldn't have done what you've done to this guy," denouncing the proceedings as the "most unethical *sham* since I've been in politics." He reminded everyone that he had voted to confirm Democratic nominees Sotomayor and Kagan.

Pointing out that Christine Blasey Ford was as much a victim of the Democrats' machinations as Kavanaugh was, Graham exposed their true aim with stunning clarity: "Boy, y'all want power. God, I hope you never get it."

To Kavanaugh he said, "Would you say you've been through hell?"

"I've been through hell and then some," Kavanaugh replied.

"This is not a job interview. This is hell," Graham said. He ended with a warning to his fellow Republicans that if they voted against Kavanaugh, they would be "legitimizing the most despicable thing I have seen in my time in politics."

The moment was electric. Kavanaugh was overwhelmed and grateful. Senator Graham had changed the entire dynamic of the day. It was powerful because he was saying what everybody outside of newsrooms and other liberal institutions was thinking but couldn't say. The catharsis was palpable.

Noting that Kavanaugh had interacted with professional women all his life without one accusation, Graham had ridiculed the Democrats for their relentless focus on his high school yearbook. As if to prove the point, Senator Sheldon Whitehouse, who followed Graham, devoted his entire five minutes to parsing the adolescent text on Kavanaugh's high school yearbook page. Obviously intending to humiliate the nominee, the senator explored the meaning of the word "boofed"—"That refers to flatulence. We were sixteen," Kavanaugh explained—revisited the references to "Renate alumnius," which Kavanaugh had addressed fully in his opening statement, and inquired about "devil's triangle," a drinking game that Kavanaugh's opponents had hoped was a reference to some sort of ménage à trois. (In response to Whitehouse's questions, Senate Republicans would later release the sworn statement of four of Kavanaugh's high school friends confirming that it was a drinking game and did not "refer to any kind of sexual activity.")[19]

Senator John Cornyn of Texas, following Whitehouse, stated, "I can't think of a more embarrassing scandal for the United States Senate since the McCarthy hearings."

Senator Amy Klobuchar of Minnesota stood out among Democrats for her respectful treatment of the nominee in the previous hearings and in her meeting with him, as he noted with gratitude at the start of her questioning. After pressing him to ask the president to launch an FBI investigation, she turned to the subject of drinking, asking if he had ever had so much to drink that he could not remember the previous evening. He said no. She asked again. Obviously annoyed, he rudely responded, "Have you?" Taken aback, she said, "Could you answer the question, judge? I just—so you—that's not happened? Is that your answer?" In circumstances that, admittedly, would have strained anyone's patience, Kavanaugh's good judgment seemed to abandon him momentarily, and he doubled down: "Yeah, and I'm curious if you have." Klobuchar responded briskly, "I have no drinking problem," and Kavanaugh added, "Nor do I." They smiled at each other, and the questioning paused for a recess.

■   ■   ■

The media had by now figured out how well things were going for Kavanaugh. It wasn't just his testimony, but his confidence in handling hostile questions. Lindsey Graham's surprising defense—the first defense of Kavanaugh since Senator Grassley's at ten o'clock that morning—was cathartic for those Americans whose views had been sidelined by the media in the previous two weeks.

Kavanaugh's one misstep was his cheeky response to Senator Klobuchar. As soon as they returned to the holding room, McGahn told Kavanaugh it was time to reel it in. Ashley told Kavanaugh to calm down and encouraged him to find a way to address what he had said. Kavanaugh had not intended to be disrespectful; of all the Democrats on the committee, she was the one he would least want to offend.

As soon as the break ended, he apologized to Senator Klobuchar publicly.

The team also realized that the hearing was going as well as could be expected. McGahn told Kavanaugh that he had befuddled the Democrats. His powerful punches were the last thing they expected and made them look foolish for asking about high school antics. It was a good time to cool things down, as he did when questioned by Senators Coons, Harris, Hirono, and Booker.

He did punch back when Senator Blumenthal brought up the "Renate alumnius" again. The senator had begun by condescending to Kavanaugh about jury instructions, stumbling over the common law principle *Falsus in uno, falsus in omnibus* ("False in one thing, false in everything.") Blumenthal, trying to impeach Kavanaugh's credibility, was the last senator who should have pursued this line of argument. He had previously misled the voters of Connecticut about his service in Vietnam.

Many Supreme Court nominees have referred to the galling indignity of having their character questioned by senators whose own characters are seriously besmirched. Joe Biden led the Senate Judiciary Committee's Bork hearings at the same time his presidential ambitions were sinking because of his plagiarism. Ted Kennedy's lengthy list of sexual improprieties never inhibited the "Lion of the Senate" from smearing nominees of exemplary character. Robert Packwood of Oregon, one of only two Republican senators to vote against Clarence Thomas, citing his concern for women's rights, was forced to resign from the Senate four years later under threat of expulsion for a "habitual pattern of aggressive, blatantly sexual advances, mostly directed at members of his own staff or others whose livelihoods were connected in some way to his power and authority as a Senator."

The rest of Kavanaugh's hearing was relatively quiet. The Republicans put the Democrats on the defensive for playing games with Ford's allegation. Pressed by Senator Cornyn, Dianne Feinstein found herself insisting that she was not responsible for leaking Ford's letter, even though her office was the only one that had it. "I don't believe my staff would leak it," she said but admitted, "I have not asked [them] that question directly."[20] It was far from a convincing denial.

By the time the senators spoke to reporters afterward, it was the Democrats who were utterly deflated, while the Republicans spoke with optimism about the committee vote the next day.

The Kavanaughs left immediately. Both Presidents Trump and Bush called the judge to commend him for his testimony. The couple attended a gathering that evening at the McCalebs' house. It would take time for Kavanaugh to appreciate the extent of his support, but that night he began to see how much his hearing had meant to people in his life. Text messages and emails poured in from people he knew in high school, college, law school, the independent counsel's office, and the White House. He heard from people he knew during his clerkships and parents of children he had coached. It was a survey of his life's work, and it was reassuring and encouraging.

CHAPTER TEN

The Anteroom Where It Happened

It had been a rough couple of years in the Senate for Jeff Flake. A conservative from the small-government and free-trade wing of the GOP, he couldn't get over Donald Trump's brash political style, even as the president remained popular with Republican voters. His anti-Trump manifesto, *Conscience of a Conservative*, sealed his electoral fate. Shortly after it was published in the summer of 2017, he announced that he would not run for reelection. John McCain, the senior senator from Arizona, died August 25, and the country had gone through weeks of remembrances of the former prisoner of war who had played a major role in politics for thirty-five years. McCain was particularly well regarded in Washington for his opposition to Trump, and Flake thought of him as a father figure and mentor.

Despite his conservative voting record, Flake could be contemptuous of Republican voters, and his visceral aversion to President Trump sometimes caused him, like McCain, to break from the Republican caucus. Nevertheless, he was considered a likely vote for Kavanaugh.

As the allegations piled up, however, Flake agonized about his vote, bristling at the pressure from his party's leadership. Democrats recognized early on that he might waver. Senator Chris Coons, who was friendly with Flake and worked with him frequently, was a key to the effort to turn him. In the first hearing, Coons questioned Kavanaugh closely about executive power, which he knew to be a concern of Flake's. Kavanaugh, for his part, seemed to reassure Flake by clarifying that he did not view executive authority as unlimited. After the accusations of sexual assault emerged, Coons shifted to emphasizing the need for a thorough investigation.

Republicans trying to secure Flake's vote recognized his sympathy with Ford and other victims of sexual assault, so they did not rely solely on the lack of any evidence for the accusation. They reminded him that Brett Kavanaugh was a human being, a man with a wife and children. If Flake voted against him, he would not only keep a justice of sound constitutional principles off the Court but also destroy a man's reputation. Senator Mike Lee, a former federal prosecutor, felt he could walk Flake, not a lawyer, through the legal analysis. In the United States, the accused is considered innocent until proved guilty. To be convicted of a crime, his guilt must be "beyond a reasonable doubt," while in civil trials, the burden of proof is lighter—a "preponderance of the evidence," that is, it is more likely than not that the defendant is liable. Kavanaugh was not on trial, of course, but the presumption of innocence—an essential part of what Americans mean by "due process"—ought to guide the senators as they evaluated Ford's accusation.

On Friday morning, the day after the second hearing, Flake announced that he would vote to confirm Kavanaugh, assuring that the nomination would be voted out of committee and onto the floor of the Senate.[1] He praised Kavanaugh, noting that in another era he would have been nearly unanimously confirmed, while acknowledging that after such persuasive testimony from both Kavanaugh and Ford he couldn't be sure what had happened. Former President George W. Bush had quietly lobbied Flake and other undecided senators. Senator Lee's emphasis on the burden of proof seemed to have been the decisive point.[2] When CNN's congressional correspondent Sunlen Serfaty broke the news to Senator Coons, he responded, "Oh f—k," and began to choke up: "I deeply respect... We each make choices for our own reason. I'm struggling, sorry."[3]

A group of reporters camped outside of Flake's office met some female protesters who were there to lobby him against Kavanaugh. They all learned about his decision at the same time and gasped. The protesters cried. A few minutes later, when the senator left his office for the Judiciary Committee meeting, they ran after him. Ana Maria Archila, a professional activist with the Center for Popular Democracy (funded by the Arabella Advisors Network), and Maria Gallagher, a member of the liberal feminist group UltraViolet who was in Washington to protest against Kavanaugh, trapped Flake and an aide in an elevator.[4] CNN's cameras were rolling.

"I was sexually assaulted, and nobody believed me. I didn't tell anyone, and you're telling all women that they don't matter," cried Gallagher. "Look at me when I'm talking to you. You're telling me that my assault doesn't matter."[5] Archila shrieked, "You're allowing someone who is unwilling to take responsibility for his own actions, and willing to hurl the harm that he has done to one woman—actually, three women," indicating that even Ramirez and Swetnick must be believed.[6] The exchange lasted for five long minutes, after which emotional CNN correspondents praised the activists uncritically.[7]

Following Thursday's hearing, Senator Collins told the Senate Judiciary Committee that she would find it difficult to vote for Kavanaugh without a sworn statement directly from Mark Judge, not just the attestation of his lawyer. Just before midnight, the committee had released just that, and Grassley read it at the Friday morning committee meeting. Judge said he had no memory of what Ford alleged and added, "I am knowingly submitting this letter under penalty of felony."[8]

Democratic senators and the media were now asserting that the American Bar Association had backed away from its earlier endorsement of Kavanaugh as "well qualified." The truth was rather more complicated. On Thursday, Robert Carlson, the president of the ABA and a donor to Hillary Clinton's political campaigns, had sent the committee a letter asking it to postpone the vote on Kavanaugh until an FBI investigation was completed. The ABA's Standing Committee on the Federal Judiciary, which evaluates judicial nominees, sent its own letter to the Judiciary Committee the next day, clarifying that (1) it had not seen Carlson's letter before it was sent, (2) the standing committee "acts independently of ABA leadership," and (3) it "conducts non-partisan, non-ideological, and confidential peer review of federal judicial nominees." The letter concluded, "The ABA's rating for Judge Kavanaugh is not affected by Mr. Carlson's letter."[9] By the time the clarification was received, however, the narrative was set. A story by CNN's Manu Raju, for example, published five days later, presented Carlson's letter as an act of the ABA itself and made no mention of the standing committee's letter of correction, leaving the impression that Kavanaugh's original "well qualified" rating was now in question.[10]

The American Civil Liberties Union also took part in the campaign against Kavanaugh, despite its ostensible policy against weighing in on Supreme Court nominations—a policy it had also broken to oppose Rehnquist, Bork, and Alito. Having strayed in recent years under the influence of progressive donors from its formerly zealous advocacy of free speech and religious freedom, the organization now abandoned two of its other core principles: the presumption of innocence and opposition to guilt by association.

At the Friday morning Judiciary Committee meeting, the motion to vote later that day was carried, but Senators Booker and Harris refused to respond to the roll call. Without explaining their objection, they walked out in protest, joined by Blumenthal, as Feinstein began complaining about Kavanaugh's temperament. While the ranking member took issue with the nominee's "belligerent" response to her invocation of the serial gang rape charge, her fugitive colleagues conducted a thirty-minute press conference with a group of reporters who had been waiting for them outside. As the trio left the hearing room for the press conference, Senator Harris was heard lamenting that the Republicans were beating the Democrats, liberally punctuating her complaint with f-bombs.

Grassley, meanwhile, informed the committee about various efforts to contact the last-minute accusers and noted that the attorneys for Deborah Ramirez were still refusing to communicate with the committee. He then reminded his colleagues that Ford, oddly enough, had testified that she had been unaware that the committee was willing to interview her in California, suggesting that her attorneys were not on the up-and-up. "This has never been about the truth," Lindsey Graham observed. "This has been about delay and destruction. And if we reward this, it is the end of good people wanting to be judges. It is the end of any concept of the rule of law. It's the beginning of a process that will tear this country apart."[11]

Two hours into the committee meeting, Senator Coons delivered his prepared statement.[12] He addressed all the members of the committee, but he had a specific target in mind—Jeff Flake. Before the hearings the day before, he said, he had prayed for Christine Blasey Ford, for Brett Kavanaugh, and for everyone involved in the process. After the committee's failure to handle the difficult situation creditably, he said, he was now praying for the nation. Coons insisted that the release of Ford's allegation to the press—for which he offered no explanation except to say that it was not the work of Senator Feinstein or her staff—was free of partisan taint, and he argued that an additional FBI investigation, limited to one week, would not occasion undue delay but would get to the bottom of the remaining questions about Ford's allegations and perhaps others—even those of "varying credibility." He closed by reminding Senator Flake of his continued concerns about the scope of executive power, and he warned that, after the previous day's "testimony full of rage and partisanship and vitriol," confirming Kavanaugh without a bipartisan investigation of the allegations would undermine the legitimacy of the Court, placing "an asterisk" after Kavanaugh's name.

When Coons completed his speech, Jeff Flake left the room, motioning for Coons to follow him. White House observers watching on C-SPAN were texting frantically to figure out what was going on.

Over the next two hours, most of the dais cleared as senators vying for Flake's ear began collecting in the anteroom, an L-shaped space off of the Democrats' side of the hearing room with a small conference table and a lavatory. In the narrow corridor sloping down from the anteroom to the hallway is a booth for making private telephone calls.

The anteroom and corridor were so crowded with dozens of senators and staff members that the door from the hallway could not be opened, and the room became unbearably hot. A few noted with amusement that the senators were crammed into the corridor while the staff sat around the conference table, but the senators kept pairing off and retreating to the corridor for private conversations, displacing the staff who were there. Hatch and his counsel were in the lavatory on the phone with the American Bar Association, trying to sort out the confusion caused by its president's anti-Kavanaugh letter. Coons had cornered Flake, trying to convince him to demand a supplemental investigation in exchange for voting the nomination out of committee.

In the epic, hours-long fight outside the meeting room, fistfights nearly broke out. One senator told another that he wanted to wring his neck. A staffer who was bringing lunch to her hungry boss found herself in the middle of the scrum, with Ted Cruz inadvertently standing on her foot and Sheldon Whitehouse spraying her with saliva as he debated a colleague. More staffers were huddled in the hallway outside as savvy reporters started to realize where the action was. Every few minutes a senator would suggest clearing the area of staffers, since the fighting between senators was getting so personal, but the configuration of the anteroom and the large number of senators and staff made that impossible. Veteran staffers had never seen anything so chaotic in the Senate.

Republican senators felt that Democratic senators had not been honest, and they were livid that Feinstein had not followed the rules for dealing with anonymous allegations. Nobody admitted leaking to the press, but clearly someone had. According to Ford's own testimony, only her lawyers and Democratic members of Congress had seen the letter, but her friends also would have known the nature of the allegations. Whoever the leaker was, he or she had ensured that Ford's claims would be addressed in the most public and sensationalized manner possible, despite Ford's own stated wishes for privacy and confidentiality.

Even though Feinstein was a staunch liberal, her Republican colleagues trusted her to play by the rules, in contrast to some of the other Democrats on the committee. Some senators and aides believed that the eighty-five-year-old Feinstein's lucidity declined as the day progressed, an observation others strongly disputed. Either way, the consensus was that her staff took advantage of the situation and used her as a shield while they skirted the rules. The failure to handle the allegation in a timely manner through proper channels had disappointed some undecided senators and made them less likely to take it seriously.

At that moment, Kavanaugh's future was in the hands of Flake, not Collins or Murkowski. Even so, Flake had called Collins and asked for her support for reopening the background investigation. She agreed it was a good idea. If another investigation was necessary to get the nomination out of committee, Grassley would make it happen. It helped that they were confident that any investigation would go well for Kavanaugh. In fact, the White House had strongly considered ordering an FBI investigation when the first allegation broke, but after consulting with top brass at the Department of Justice, they worried that it would take more time than they could afford. The FBI, moreover, had a history of leaking against the Trump White House, engaging in bureaucratic delays, and generally resisting political accountability.

If the price of Flake's vote to send the nomination to the full Senate was going to be an FBI investigation, they would have to accept that. But Republicans wanted it limited in time, not open-ended. Democrats wanted Flake to hold his vote until the investigation came back, regardless of how long it took. In any case, senators had no authority to order a supplementary FBI background investigation, much less to define its precise contours. The request for an additional investigation would have to come from the White House counsel.

Mitch McConnell's chief counsel and "right hand man for every step of this process" was John Abegg.[13] Summoned to the anteroom, he called Don McGahn to see if the supplemental investigation, building on the work the committee had already performed, could be limited to stipulated witnesses and completed quickly. Flake and Coons tried to talk to

Christopher Wray, the director of the FBI, but he wasn't available, so they called Deputy Attorney General Rod Rosenstein. Coons had followed Flake into the phone booth, which was so small that they couldn't close its door. They made an absurd picture huddled around a cell phone, their limbs intertwined, trying to find out how long a thorough supplemental investigation would take. Flake understood the need for a reasonable limit to the investigation because of the Democrats' propensity to keep moving the goalposts. President Bush tried to get through to Flake on the phone but was unable. Senator Cornyn, the Republican whip, was also leaning into the phone booth. He and Tillis kept making the point that nothing, including the FBI investigation, would be sufficient for recalcitrant Democrats.

Grassley kept the committee meeting in suspension while the plan was hatched. Few senators were back in their seats by the time the vote was to take place, so Senator Whitehouse said, "Mr. Chairman, given what's happening in the anteroom, I think if some more time is needed, I think you'd get a unanimous consent to push the vote back pretty easily if you needed a few more minutes." Whitehouse was referring to the "two-hour rule," which prohibits committees from meeting for more than two hours after the Senate floor opens or after two o'clock in the afternoon. The rule is routinely waived, but the Democrats in the anteroom were threatening to invoke it now. Lee and Cornyn were telling Flake that he could take as much time as he needed, even until Monday, but aides impressed on him the need to reach a decision quickly. As soon as he did, the Republicans ran to their seats. Democrats had decided to allow the rule to be waived at the last minute, but word didn't get to Grassley in time. The Democrats, confused, were slower to reach their seats. "You just witnessed history," one top Republican aide said to another staffer.

Explaining the situation to the committee, Flake said that he had been talking with Democrats about the need for due diligence. It would be proper, he said, "to delay the floor vote for up to but not more than one week in order to let the FBI do an investigation limited in time and scope." While he would vote Kavanaugh out of committee that day, his final floor vote would be conditional on what the FBI found. And he clarified that he would not cooperate with further delays.[14] Grassley had the roll called, and Kavanaugh was voted out of committee.

The call for an additional investigation, Flake said, was "an effort to bring this country together." He still expected to vote for Kavanaugh but only after a proper investigation, and he encouraged Democrats to accept his gesture in good faith.

Flake's detractors accused him of pandering to the liberal media. He would be leaving the Senate in January and was looking for a television contract. But Flake loyalists said he was genuinely moved by the distress of women like those who trapped him in the elevator that morning. The additional delay frustrated Kavanaugh's supporters, but the investigation turned out to be a godsend.

■   ■   ■

By the time Kavanaugh learned about the delay from McGahn, he had developed the habit of expecting the worst. A delay was disappointing, of course, but he told a few people that the investigation would be good for him. He knew that anyone digging deeply into the facts would be even more clearly on his side. He was comfortable. Senator Portman shared that confidence with a few others.

Mitch McConnell promptly summoned the Republicans on the Judiciary Committee to his elegantly appointed office in the Capitol to discuss the contours of the investigation. He also invited Susan Collins and Lisa Murkowski, since their votes were still up for grabs. The only non–committee members present, they felt a bit like they had been called to the principal's office.

In his intimate red-walled conference room, the majority leader asked the senators what they needed to feel comfortable that the allegations were being properly investigated. They discussed the key witnesses they wanted the FBI to interview and when they could expect to receive the findings. The senators agreed that there was no need to waste time on Swetnick's charges, but they wanted Ford's and Ramirez's allegations included. Later that day the Senate Judiciary Committee announced, "The supplemental FBI background investigation would be limited to current credible allegations against the nominee," a generous description of Ramirez's story and a subtle dig at Avenatti and his client, "and must be completed no later than one week from today."[15]

Don McGahn, who planned to step down as White House counsel after Kavanaugh was confirmed, had to request the investigation, so the liberal media tried to discredit it by association with him. Eugene Robinson, a columnist for the *Washington Post*, said, "If it turns out, as we suspect, that on his way out, Don McGahn squashed the FBI investigation of his good friend Brett Kavanaugh so it wouldn't find out anything bad, that will be another part of Don McGahn's legacy and also a rallying point for Democrats in the midterms."[16]

The view that McGahn was limiting the investigation was spread by an NBC report about the exclusion of Michael Avenatti's gang rape allegations, which was depicted as a "significant constraint" that would "make it difficult to pursue additional leads" and was "at odds with what some members of the Senate judiciary [sic] seemed to expect."[17]

In fact, McGahn had broadened the scope of the investigation beyond what the Senate requested. McConnell wanted it kept within narrow limits, but McGahn had heard that Flake and Coons thought the proposed investigation was too narrow. They wanted to make sure that the FBI would run down any leads that arose from the initial interviews. Coons had already announced his opposition to Kavanaugh's confirmation, so his views carried little weight, and he had exaggerated what Flake had agreed to. But McGahn and Flake, who had known each other since Flake was in the House, wanted to be straight with each other. McGahn assured senators that the White House would not get in the way of any follow-up.

By demanding a one-week investigation, Flake had hoped to keep the confirmation on track, but some senators were not interested in abandoning their delay tactics. Bernie Sanders now demanded that the FBI also investigate Kavanaugh for perjury, charging that the judge had made numerous untruthful statements. Grassley responded sarcastically, reminding the once and future presidential candidate that he had called for a mobilization against Kavanaugh less than twenty-four hours after his nomination was announced. "Am I to take from your letter that you are now undecided and willing to seriously engage with the Senate's advice-and-consent constitutional duties related to the nomination of Judge Kavanaugh to serve as an associate justice on the Supreme Court of the United States?" Grassley asked. "If so, we should have a conversation about what information you need to assist you in making your decision, and I look forward to that conversation."[18]

■   ■   ■

As the senators waited for the results of the supplemental background investigation, the media began picking up Democratic talking points. Kavanaugh's indignation at being accused of sexual assault and gang rape betrayed, said Senator Feinstein, a belligerent and intolerant temperament unsuited to the work of a judge. Nancy Pelosi, the House minority leader, pronounced him "hysterical" and temperamentally unfit to serve on the Supreme Court.[19]

The Associated Press took it from there, reporting the next day that "Brett Kavanaugh's angry denunciation of Senate Democrats at his confirmation hearing could reinforce views of the Supreme Court as a political institution at a time of stark partisan division and when the court already is sharply split between liberals and conservatives."[20]

Senator Collins thought it was completely understandable that a nominee would be emotional when accused of serial gang rape and other crimes, though she wished he had handled Senator Klobuchar's questioning better. In contrast to some of her peers, Collins had paid attention to the first hearings and remembered that a representative from the American Bar Association had testified that a committee had evaluated Kavanaugh for "compassion, decisiveness, open-mindedness, courteousness, patience and freedom from bias." They found that "lawyers and judges overwhelmingly praised Judge Kavanaugh's judicial temperament," attesting that he "is very straightforward," "maintains an open mind about all things," "is an affable, nice person," "is easy to get along with and even has a good sense of humor," "is really a decent person," "is thoughtful, fair-minded—always fair-minded in his questions to counsel." In fact, Kavanaugh had received the highest rating in the category. Still, temperament became such an issue that Kavanaugh was forced to respond with an op-ed column in the *Wall Street Journal* defending his temperament.

Kavanaugh's opposition shifted its attention to "temperament" in large part because each of the three main allegations against him was crumbling. Ford had made her case publicly to a friendly press. From a prosecutor's perspective, that was an outrageous way to handle allegations. When presented with information about a high-profile person, for example, allegations of corruption, it would be absurd to publicize the allegations without first going through extensive investigation to determine the credibility of the accuser, whether there was corroborating evidence, and whether there was contrary evidence. Rachel Mitchell had begun what typically would have been the first step in the process— determining whether Ford had a case. Even Mitchell's mild-mannered inquiries were much tougher than anything that had been posed by a journalist to that point.

Mitchell spoke in a private meeting of all the Republican senators after Thursday's hearing finished, announcing that she would have not been able even to obtain a search warrant, much less to have prosecuted a crime, with the minimal evidence offered at the hearing.[21] Her by-the-book approach and analysis of the evidence prompted a round of applause. She was so well received, particularly by undecided senators, that she was asked to elaborate in a written report submitted to Republican senators on Sunday: "A 'he said, she said' case is incredibly difficult to prove. But this case is even weaker than that. Dr. Ford identified other witnesses to the event, and those witnesses either refuted her allegations or failed to corroborate them."[22]

Mitchell noted that Ford's account of when the assault occurred was inconsistent, ranging from the early to the mid-1980s. She told a therapist she had been in her late teens but later told the committee that she was fifteen. While it is common for victims to be uncertain about dates, Mitchell said, Ford never explained why "she was suddenly able to narrow the timeframe" to a particular year, as memories would not typically become more precise over time.

Ford had never mentioned Kavanaugh before 2012, when his name was widely reported as a potential Supreme Court nominee, Mitchell noted. Ford had also described the attacks in varying ways when speaking to her husband, according to news reports. She told him before they were married that she had suffered a sexual assault, but after they were married she told him she had been a victim of "physical abuse." Both comments referred to the same incident she described with Kavanaugh, she testified. But she never explained why she would have downgraded her description of an attempted rape to physical assault.

Ford also had no memory of details that could corroborate her account, such as who invited her to the party, how she got there, whose house it took place in, or how she got from the party back to her house, a distance that would have taken twenty minutes by car but would have required a nearly three-hour walk in the dark if she did not have a ride. "Given that this all took place before cell phones, arranging a ride home would not have been easy," Mitchell noted. The difficulty of finding such a ride would have likely made it a salient part of the evening in and of itself.

Ford's account had never been corroborated by anyone, including her lifelong friend and supporter Leland Keyser. All alleged eyewitnesses denied having any memory of the event.

Ford had also not offered a consistent account of the alleged assault, Mitchell wrote, offering conflicting information about whether she could hear conversations taking place elsewhere at the party.

Ford's account of who was at the party had also varied. According to her therapist's notes, four boys were in the bedroom in which she was assaulted—an error, according to the *Washington Post*, as there were four boys at the party but only two in the room where the assault happened. In her letter to Senator Feinstein, Ford described the party as including "me and 4 others." Her polygraph statement said four boys and two girls were at the party. In her opening testimony, Ford said that four boys and her female friend Leland Ingham Keyser were at the party, but in response to Mitchell's questions, she said that Leland was one of the four others at the party and she remembered no others. In her statement to the polygrapher and in a text to the *Post*, she asserted that Patrick "P. J." Smyth was a "bystander," but in her testimony she said that was inaccurate.

She also had trouble remembering recent events presumably unaffected by the trauma of an assault or the vagaries of time, such as whether she had showed a reporter her therapist's notes and whether her polygraph session had been recorded. She refused to provide the therapist's notes to the committee despite relying on them for "corroboration." She said she had wanted her story to remain confidential, but the "first person other than her therapist or husband to whom she disclosed the identity of her alleged attacker" was a person operating a tip line at the *Washington Post*. The college professor said she did not know how to contact a U.S. senator, but she did know how to contact her U.S. representative.

Ford could not remember if her polygraph had been conducted the day of or the day after her grandmother's funeral, an event that should have been significant to her. Regardless, it would have been inappropriate to administer a polygraph to someone in grief.

Ford's frequent flying was at odds with the assertion that she was afraid to fly, Mitchell noted. It was also noteworthy that her attorneys had apparently not told her about offers for a private hearing in California, a breach of duty to their client that Senator Cornyn suggested warranted a referral to their local bar ethics committee.[23]

The measured report from Mitchell, based on facts, was completely different from the media coverage, which was focused on emotion. Mitchell's findings were ignored by many media outlets or seriously downplayed. The findings were buried in the final two paragraphs of a *New York Times* story about the FBI investigation.[24]

A supposed "fact check" by the *New York Times* cited no factual errors but pushed activists' assertions that Kavanaugh had been "misleading" and that his statements were "disputed" or "required context."[25] The article was self-refuting. For instance, it reported that he denied drinking to excess immediately before quoting him as saying, "Sometimes I had too many beers."

At the same time, few media outlets were investigating Kavanaugh's accusers. For example, Ford said that she had not told her husband the details of the assault until 2012. The occasion for her doing so, she said, was serious marital conflict arising out of her desire for a second front door on their $2.5 million house in Palo Alto, California—an escape hatch, as it were, for a woman traumatized by sexual assault. This odd story did not hold up under scrutiny. According to one of the only reporters to investigate, building permits for renovations on the home—which included an extra room and extra door—were completed by 2010. The door was not an escape route but an additional entrance. Ford said in her testimony she "hosted" Google interns in the additional space. And curiously, the woman who sold the house to the Fords in 2007, a marriage therapist, reportedly had continued to work out of the home, using the extra room, with its own door, for her practice.[26] A web profile says she deals with "relationship issues" and "disturbing memories from the past."[27]

The media continued to ignore community chatter, especially regarding the notable absence of Ford's family from the ranks of her public supporters. Neighbors, friends, and country club members got the distinct impression that while Ford's family supported her, they were relieved that her uncorroborated story hadn't destroyed Kavanaugh.

■   ■   ■

Things were going even worse for Julie Swetnick. NBC's Kate Snow recorded an interview with her on Sunday, to be broadcast the following day.[28] The delay was reportedly to allow the network to verify her statements and decide what to air, although NBC ultimately aired the interview despite not being able "to independently verify her claims." The network acknowledged that "there are things that she told us on camera that differ from her written statement last week," and that she was even "unclear about when she first decided to come forward." Since the publication of her sworn allegation that Kavanaugh was part of a long-running gang-rape cartel, Swetnick's credibility had been in doubt. Ex-boyfriends alerted authorities to her character problems; it was revealed that a former employer had fired her over falsified job history and her own sexual impropriety on the job; and curious ties to Debra Katz's firm began popping up.

The interview, conducted under soft lighting, began with Swetnick's describing herself as "shy" and "private," "not somebody who follows the news," "not political at all." Her allegation against Kavanaugh bore resemblances to the others. He was a mean and sloppy drunk. He tried to "shift girls' clothing," as Ford had previously alleged. Like Ford, she cited four witnesses, none of whom was able to corroborate her account.

Swetnick's story, like Ford's, had changed, although Swetnick called her own earlier sworn declaration into question. She had earlier sworn that Kavanaugh and Judge were spiking the punch, but now told Snow that they were simply handing out cups and were near the punch. She had written under oath that she saw Kavanaugh and Judge waiting in line for their turn to rape a drugged girl. She now told Snow that she could be sure only that they were standing not in lines but in groups of boys outside rooms like the one she later was raped in, adding that "it's just too coincidental." She had previously sworn that Kavanaugh and Judge were present at her rape. She now told Snow only that she had seen them earlier at the same party, and she echoed Ford's most salient memory: "I could hear them laughing and laughing." She also called into question her own timeline of the events. In her affidavit, Swetnick stated that she had attended the parties from 1981 to 1983. Yet she told Snow that she stopped attending after being raped at one of the parties at age nineteen. She turned twenty in 1982, so if her NBC interview is to be believed, her earlier date range was incorrect. Swetnick also said that Kavanaugh and his classmates wore their school uniforms to the parties because "they were very proud" of Georgetown Prep. But that school had only a dress code, not a uniform, and the boys couldn't wait to get out of their required jackets and ties.

Swetnick also gave the network the names of four people she said knew about the gang rapes. The network found that one was dead, another denied knowing a Julie Swetnick, and the other two never responded to NBC's inquiries. The next day, even Cynthia Alksne said that Swetnick was not credible and should go away.[29]

Despite Swetnick's obvious credibility problems, many in the media continued to air her accusation. Senate Democrats sent a letter to the FBI and White House stating that Swetnick's allegations should be investigated thoroughly along with Ford's and Ramirez's.[30]

As if Swetnick's interview was not damaging enough, Avenatti's other "witness" turned out to be a hoax. He had previously claimed to have additional witnesses of the conduct described by Swetnick, and tweeted a redacted affidavit from one on Tuesday, October 2, just in time to bolster Swetnick's flagging credibility.[31] In the affidavit, the witness stated that she had known Kavanaugh since 1980 and had attended at least twenty house parties with him, as well as Beach Week. She alleged that he would "'spike' the 'punch' at house parties I attended with Quaaludes and/or grain alcohol" to reduce girls' resistance to sexual advances. She also said that, while drunk, Kavanaugh would be "overly aggressive and verbally abusive toward girls." While Avenatti refused to give this witness's name to the Senate Judiciary Committee, he had passed it on to NBC two days earlier. The network interviewed the witness who, as NBC delicately put it, had "apparent inconsistencies" with her earlier sworn statement.[32] The inconsistencies in fact completely undercut the earlier statement.

As for who had spiked the punch, she said, "I didn't ever think it was Brett." When NBC inquired about whether Kavanaugh had ever acted inappropriately with women, she said, "No." While she described a heavy-drinking party scene that Kavanaugh and Judge were a part of, she also denied that Kavanaugh had been abusive toward women when she was there, adding, "I would not ever allow anyone to be abusive in my presence. Male or female." She placed much of the blame for the false statements in the declaration on Avenatti himself, saying she had only skimmed it before signing and that she had been very clear with Avenatti about facts like not having seen anyone spike the punch. She finally decided to break with Avenatti altogether, telling NBC, "I do not like that he twisted my words."

This news should have been sensational, but as other outlets ran with the story of Avenatti's apparently corroborative second affidavit, NBC stayed silent, not breaking the news of the witness's disavowal until October 25, a baffling newsroom decision that suggests the network was loath to publish more exculpatory reports for Kavanaugh. The report was ultimately released the same day the Senate Judiciary Committee referred both Swetnick and Avenatti to the Department of Justice to be investigated for making false statements to the committee in violation of federal law.[33]

■   ■   ■

The Ramirez story did not fall apart so much as it never held together to begin with. A woman, who by her own admission had been incoherently drunk during the incident she described, spent a week in September with lawyers coaching her, and the only assertions she could make were that what could have been a real penis was in her face and that Brett Kavanaugh was in the room and moved his hips. To bolster the threadbare story, the media ran stories of Kavanaugh's other college hijinks.

On the evening of October 1, the same day NBC ran the disastrous Swetnick interview, the *New York Times* ran a front-page story about a bar scuffle Kavanaugh got into while he was a college student at Yale that involved throwing ice.[34] Senator Hirono declared the episode "very relevant" and demanded that the FBI investigate.[35] Friends were aghast at the story told by Chad Ludington, saying that he was not close to Kavanaugh and that the event was overblown.

The lead author of the piece was Emily Bazelon, a former *Slate* writer who had published numerous articles deploring conservative jurisprudence and had announced her opposition to Kavanaugh's nomination earlier that summer. By normal journalistic standards, Bazelon's personal opinions about Kavanaugh at least should have been disclosed. The *Times* later admitted the error; while it still stood by the story, it stated, "[Bazelon] is not a newsroom reporter.... In retrospect, editors should have used a newsroom reporter for that assignment."[36] But it was startling that the story was published at all, let alone on the front page of a paper whose own tagline suggests that some news is in fact not fit to print.

On the same day the *Times* embarrassed itself by magnifying the trivial, NBC revealed the lengths to which the media were prepared to go to resuscitate Deborah Ramirez's discredited allegation. Heidi Przybyla and Leigh Ann Caldwell reported that Kavanaugh and his team had attempted to refute Ramirez's story before it was published.[37] If a man is asked to comment on an allegation against him of egregious sexual misconduct, it might be considered normal for him to try to clear his name before that allegation is published. In NBC's view, however, Kavanaugh's "personally talking with former classmates about Ramirez's story in advance of the *New Yorker* article that made her allegation public" was sinister. It would have been more seemly, it seems, to stand aside while a coordinated campaign was waged against him, without even calling friends to see if they would be willing to go on the record with their own testimony. (Ramirez's many calls to classmates and week of being coached by her lawyers did not raise an eyebrow.)

Przybyla and Caldwell revealed a series of private text messages between Kerry Berchem and Karen Yarasavage. Berchem, a partner at the powerful law firm Akin, Gump, Strauss, Hauer & Feld, was a year behind Kavanaugh and Yarasavage at Yale. The women were friends in college as well as friends of both Kavanaugh and Ramirez. The messages, which Berchem revealed without Yarasavage's knowledge, are a record of Berchem's increasingly heavy-handed attempts to dissuade Yarasavage from going on the record, at Kavanaugh's request, to undermine Ramirez's allegation.

Berchem thought the messages showed that Kavanaugh was trying to discredit Ramirez as early as July and that his statement in an interview with the Judiciary Committee staff on September 25 that he had no "specific recollection" of interacting with Ramirez at Yarasavage's wedding in 1997 was a lie. She summarized the messages in a memorandum, which she presented to Senator Blumenthal, who submitted it to the Senate Judiciary Committee. She also submitted the memorandum directly to the FBI. Disappointed that the FBI did not respond, she gave the messages to the press.[38]

Berchem's interpretation of the text messages as damaging to Kavanaugh is strained at best. After the announcement of Kavanaugh's nomination in July, Yarasavage shared a number of college photos with Berchem, including one from her wedding rehearsal dinner in which Ramirez and Kavanaugh appear with Berchem, Yarasavage, and three other persons. Berchem argued that the texts show that Kavanaugh "and/ or" his friends "may have initiated an anticipatory narrative" as early as July to "conceal or discredit" Ramirez. But the texts from July consist of shared photos and discussions about a get-together in August; there are no discussions of Kavanaugh.

The messages show that Yarasavage sent the wedding photo to "Brett's team" on September 22. Berchem concluded that Kavanaugh was lying three days later when he said, "I am sure I saw [Ramirez]" at the wedding but did not "have a specific recollection" of interacting with her.[39] But having seen a photo of Ramirez and himself at Yarasavage's wedding would not necessarily prompt a "specific recollection" of seeing her there.

In fact, the texts themselves are not particularly relevant to the Ramirez investigation. What they do show is Berchem furiously lobbying Yarasavage to speak out against their old friend Kavanaugh. Berchem repeatedly tried to get Yarasavage to change her statement that she did not remember Ramirez's talking about someone exposing himself to her, or at least remain silent.

Yarasavage said the allegations against Kavanaugh were laughable. She had apparently dated him briefly and described what a gentleman he had been. "Just really hard for me to reconcile any of this," she wrote. "When I say Brett was vanilla with me, I mean it. He turned his back when I changed in his room." She added that she didn't want to hurt either Kavanaugh or Ramirez, but "I know what I know about both people and I can only speak the truth." She hoped that if she told Ronan Farrow how implausible she found the story, the *New Yorker* wouldn't run it.

Yarasavage received a call on Sunday, September 23, from "Brett's guy"—one of his former clerks—apparently letting her know the *New Yorker* story was going to run after all. She told Berchem that Kavanaugh asked her to go on the record about the story, and that she was having trouble reaching anyone to speak to at the magazine. Berchem responded by suggesting that Yarasavage not go on record defending Kavanaugh. If Ramirez was telling the truth about Kavanaugh, "maybe that's why [Ramirez] has had so many issues?" Yarasavage replied that she assumed any issues Ramirez had were with her father, so Berchem tried another tack.

"You know that will kill your friendship," she wrote. Yarasavage replied, "What friendship? I haven't spoken to her in 10 years." Berchem then offered some speculative psychological explanations for why Ramirez had not stayed in touch with Yarasavage, including "your family's friendship with Brett."

After Yarasavage repeated that it was "odd that I never heard a word of this," Berchem replied, "All I am saying is we all figured out how to survive. We had different ways. [Ramirez] does not seem to have survived all that well or particularly strongly. . . . If she is making these allegations now, either she has conviction they happened or she might be crazy. But if it's the latter, and your commentary publicly makes it worse, would you really want that? . . . Bretz career is on the line. Maybe her life is on the line?" "Just be careful," she concluded. "There would be no going back."

The day after the *New Yorker* story ran, Berchem was back at it with a text reading, "I wish I had told you what to do." Yarasavage did not respond right away, and in the evening Berchem started in again. This time she speculated that Ramirez's behavior at the Yarasavage wedding was a result of the alleged exposure years earlier. "You know that at your wedding, she clung to me and [redacted]? Yeh, she was part of the group but not really. She never went near them," Berchem wrote.

By the end of the exchange, Berchem had resorted to fear. She warned that Yarasavage and her husband would be targeted for personal attacks if they publicly supported Kavanaugh—"you and [redacted] are going to get crushed"—advising her that "you guys have to get pre-pared" because "[redacted] and others have a goddamne[d]...Ven-detta." Later she added, "If he put you up to saying stuff, you should consider disclosing. Don't be the fall guys for him. Your own life/lives are being impaired."

Despite all these red flags, the NBC story relied heavily on Berchem's version of events, paying little attention to the striking differences in the women's opinions of Ramirez.

It is difficult to overstate the pressure that Yale classmates were under at this time. Yarasavage describes in the texts to Berchem the harassment she and her classmates endured from the press—in particular, her dif-ficulties interacting with Robin Pogrebin, a Yale classmate and *New York Times* reporter. According to Yarasavage, she called and spoke to her without disclosing she was speaking to her as a reporter, rather than as a friend. Yarasavage also had to consult a lawyer to respond to Pogrebin's attempts to publish Yarasavage's photo with Kavanaugh, which the reporter had obtained on Facebook.

Politics had always been the subtext among this group of friends. But when Kavanaugh was nominated to the Court, it felt like political concerns obliterated relationships that had lasted for decades. One class-mate and friend of Kavanaugh's refused to be included on an early letter of support because his jurisprudence might threaten abortion rights. After the allegations came out she went on TV to call him a liar, billing herself as a Republican and college friend of his, an identification the media accepted uncritically.

Despite the media's credulity, none of these wild allegations ever came close to being proved. But a lack of evidence never seemed to keep them from being taken seriously. A man named Tad Low, the producer of a television show called *Pants-Off Dance-Off*, alleged that he attended a particularly debauched party at the fraternity Kavanaugh had joined as an undergraduate. Kavanaugh was no longer in college when this party took place. While the accuser admitted he had no evidence Kavanaugh was anywhere near the party, much less participating in any of the objectionable activity, he thought the FBI should dig around in Kavanaugh's calendars and expressed concern that the FBI hadn't taken his statements seriously.[40]

Senator Chris Coons forwarded Mr. Low's correspondence to Senator Grassley, who wrote a blistering response: "We've reached a new level of absurdity with this allegation," which he called a "guilt-by-association tactic" that deserved "unqualified condemnation." He asked Coons to consider whether he wanted to waste committee resources with such frivolous letters in the future.[41]

Senator Lindsey Graham told a protester, "You've humiliated this guy enough and there seems to be no bottom for some of you." The protester said if Kavanaugh would take a polygraph, "This would all be over."

That was too much for Graham, who retorted, "Why don't we dunk him in water and see if he floats?"[42]

CHAPTER ELEVEN

Mrs. Collins
Goes to Washington

"Their goalposts keep shifting. But their goal hasn't moved an inch," said Mitch McConnell as he took to the Senate floor to denounce desperate attempts to sink Kavanaugh's nomination.[1] The effort to obstruct Kavanaugh's confirmation had started with preposterous demands for documentation and progressed to last-minute sexual assault allegations by accusers who supposedly couldn't fly to Washington, followed by new hearings to evaluate those allegations, which then required a supplementary FBI investigation. Then there were more increasingly outrageous allegations.

The public mood was shifting as well. Despite Kavanaugh's conviction on all charges by the media, elected officials were facing pressure to vote for confirmation, and the public was showing signs of exasperation. Republicans were livid over the delays and obstruction.

At a rally in Mississippi, President Trump did the unthinkable: he made fun of Ford's testimony, to which the media had ascribed almost biblical authority and which Kavanaugh's defenders were terrified to attack directly. "Thirty-six years ago this happened. I had one beer, right? I had one beer," the president joked. "How did you get home? I don't remember. How'd you get there? I don't remember. Where is the place? I don't remember. But I had one beer. That's the only thing I remember."[2] The press was predictably appalled at his off-teleprompter remarks,[3] as was Senator Ben Sasse, who denounced the president on the Senate floor in an eighteen-minute speech about the #MeToo movement: "His mockery of Dr. Ford last night in Mississippi was wrong— but it doesn't really surprise anyone. It's who he is." He added that he had previously urged the president to nominate someone other than Kavanaugh. "I urged the president to nominate a woman." Nevertheless, it was clear that at this point, the president's challenge to Ford's credibility resonated with many Americans.

■   ■   ■

The Republicans on the Senate Judiciary Committee had insisted that their investigators were as capable of investigating the allegations as the FBI background checkers. They had the same subpoena powers, and the penalty for lying to them was the same as the penalty for lying to the FBI. In fact, they had already referred Senator Whitehouse's constituent for investigation by the FBI for his "rape boat" allegations. Now, as the FBI investigation began to wrap up, the Democrats realized that the Bureau had simply taken statements from witnesses and compiled them in a report, much as the Senate Judiciary Committee would have done. The report was expected Wednesday night, and McConnell set up a key procedural vote for Friday.

It was time to move the goalposts again. That night, having received the hearing they asked for, as well as an FBI inquiry, Democrats attacked the breadth of the investigation. In another *New Yorker* article, Jane Mayer and Ronan Farrow complained that the FBI had not interviewed all of Kavanaugh's Yale classmates.[4]

Don McGahn, who received updates during the investigation, kept senators informed about its progress. When the investigation was completed, the report was kept in the Office of Senate Security, a secured room. The report could not be photocopied, and only senators and selected committee staff members from each party could view it.

The unusual security measures were a response to the Democrats' handling of confidential documents in the first hearings. Cory Booker's "Spartacus" incident changed the way the committee handled secure information and caused many senators and their staff to worry that they might not be given access to sensitive executive branch documents for future confirmations. Despite the high security, the FBI files were more readily available than they usually are in judicial vettings. The Office of Senate Security was open around the clock for senators, and any senator, not only Judiciary Committee members, could see the file.

Senators were guided in their review of the lengthy file by the Judiciary Committee staff. Time slots were divided between Republicans and Democrats, and many senators went through the documents with colleagues. Mike Lee, for instance, read from a single shared copy of the documents to a group of colleagues that included Jeff Flake, Susan Collins, and Ben Sasse. Flake and Collins returned many times to review the documents, each spending several hours looking at the supplemental information, including the notes from the "tip line," which anybody could call to report information about the relevant parties. They were satisfied that there was no corroborating evidence to support the allegations. In fact, there was new information that cast doubt on the original accusations.

Leland Keyser reportedly told the investigators that she had felt pressure to revise her statement about the alleged incident. After Ford testified, Keyser submitted an additional statement to the Senate Judiciary Committee indicating that although she did not remember the event that Ford described—as she had previously stated—she nevertheless believed Ford. She reportedly decided to amend her original statement after communications with persons who were friends of both Keyser and Ford. One of these persons, the *Wall Street Journal* reported, was Monica McLean, the retired FBI agent who had been identified in the letter from Ford's ex-boyfriend as the person Ford coached on passing a polygraph when McLean was applying for a position with the FBI.[5] (McLean told

ABC News that she had never received assistance of any kind in connection with a polygraph.)[6] The supplemental FBI investigation reportedly included text messages from McLean to Keyser encouraging her to amend her first statement with the statement of belief in Ford's story, a charge McLean denied.

The inclusion of Leland Keyser in the initial story caught the attention of high school friends, who remembered Keyser as a legendary and well-liked athlete. She and Ford had been good friends. If she had remembered the party, or anything approximating it, she would have said so.

Those who knew the women thought it strange that Ford had thrust Keyser into the spotlight without any warning. Keyser reportedly felt "blindsided." High school friends were particularly bothered that Ford had brought attention to Keyser's health problems—neck and back surgeries and their pain management, which had sidelined her impressive career as the Georgetown University golf coach—in front of millions watching the hearings. Family members told the *Daily Mail* that the pressure to confirm Ford's allegation and the slight in front of the Senate had upset Keyser.[7]

These reports were not entirely accurate, and what actually happened was both simpler and more complex. Keyser simply could not remember anything like what Ford described, and saying so was difficult.

Keyser, a registered Democrat, was opposed to Brett Kavanaugh's confirmation to the Supreme Court. In 2018 she was developing a liberal podcast with Bob Beckel, the Democratic political operative who was her first husband and the father of her two children. She was completely taken aback when the Senate Judiciary Committee asked her about Ford's allegation. She wished she could have corroborated the story but was unable to. She couldn't recall even meeting Kavanaugh.

Keyser and Ford, who met in seventh grade, were part of a close circle of friends at Holton-Arms who still keep in touch. In their youth, Keyser felt protective of Ford. She drove her around in a wood-paneled station wagon. Ford's other regular driver was her brother Tom Blasey, who was only a year older but in the same grade.

The summer of 1982 was one that Keyser remembered well. Her grandmother had introduced her to golf only the previous summer, and she immediately fell in love with the game and the life lessons it afforded her. She had gotten her dream job at Congressional Country Club, working for the renowned Bob Benning in the golf pro shop. The schedule was crazy—sometimes as many as sixty hours a week. Her free time was spent on the golf course, playing until dark. She loved the challenge of the sport, which would shape her life, her relationships, and even her career.

That summer, instead of hanging out with her friends, she focused on golf and playing tournaments. Athletics and Holton-Arms were central to her life then. Her immediate family didn't have much money, so her grandparents were paying for school. She appreciated the opportunity and didn't want to squander it. After Holton, she attended the University of Virginia and became the first person in her family to graduate from college.

Keyser had attended Ford's wedding, but apart from a brief exchange at a gathering of high school friends, she had had little interaction with her in the ten years prior to the allegation about Kavanaugh. The past five years in particular had been difficult. Her health challenges included daily chronic pain and addiction, and she had recently had a knee replaced. Her second marriage had ended in divorce, she had moved twice, her mother and father had passed away, and two siblings had died from addiction. Keyser herself had been in recovery for years, and her twelve-step program kept her keenly aware of her daily challenges.

On June 28, 2018, the day after Justice Kennedy announced his retirement, Ford sent Keyser a Facebook Messenger note out of the blue. It read, "Kinda freaking out that Brett K who tried to rape me in high school may be going on to the Supreme Court." It was the first time Keyser had ever heard about the alleged assault, and she found the message both surprising and alarming.

On Monday, September 17, the day after the *Washington Post* story about Ford was published, Keyser's housekeeper came up to her bedroom to tell her that a friend was waiting for her downstairs. She came down to find Emma Brown, the reporter from the *Post*, sitting at her kitchen table. Brown identified herself and began talking about the night of the alleged assault. When asked, Keyser said she believed her friend Christine. When Brown indicated that Keyser herself had supposedly been at the gathering, however, Keyser quickly texted two friends of hers and Ford's, letting them know there was a reporter in her kitchen and asking if they knew why. While the friends already knew who the reporter was, they told Keyser to speak to no reporters at all, so she asked Brown to leave.

As interest in Keyser mounted, press vehicles blocked the road to her home, and she was forced to move into a hotel. Keyser had no idea she was going to be named as a participant at the gathering in question, had never spoken to Ford about it, and had not heard from Ford or her lawyer either before or immediately after the story was published. She tried to get in touch with Ford for help understanding why she was being targeted but couldn't reach her until Wednesday, September 19, and then only briefly. Her greatest concerns were Ford's current condition and trying to understand how she herself had been involved. She was also worried that she may have ignored Ford's cries for help. Ford said she had never told her about what happened. She tried to talk some more about the alleged incident so she might recall it better. Other than suggesting Keyser was the driver that night, Ford had nothing else to offer. It later struck some friends of Keyser as strange, given the gravity of the accusation, that Ford's lawyer, Debra Katz, never contacted her before she was named as a witness.

Displaced from her home, Keyser was operating on the assumption that Ford's account was correct. She spent the time in the hotel trying to remember anything about Kavanaugh, the night in question, her involvement, and the general geography of where the party might have taken place. She looked at photos of Kavanaugh from the internet and yearbooks to try to help her remember anything, but she kept coming up dry.

The Senate Judiciary Committee, which by this point had heard that Keyser was one of Ford's named witnesses, sent her an email requesting information. A friend of hers and Ford's asked to see the email. After reading it, the friend was relieved it wasn't a subpoena and hoped Keyser would not respond to it. At this point, Keyser thought she was expected either to support the entire account or to say nothing. She was loyal to her friends; she loved Ford and wanted to support her; and she did not want Kavanaugh on the Court for the next thirty years. She also felt bound to tell the truth. After much effort Keyser knew two things: she had no recollection of the event Ford described, and she did not know Brett Kavanaugh. She felt that it was important to say this, which she did, through her attorney, in her first written statement submitted to the Senate Judiciary Committee. After the statement went public, Keyser texted Ford on September 22, "I wish I could have been more supportive and that my statement was more helpful."

Keyser was upset that Kavanaugh repeatedly referred to her statement in his testimony to "refute" Ford's account. Keyser did not recall this event and was convinced she did not know Kavanaugh. At this time, however, she did not doubt Ford's account. She informed friends and her lawyer in text messages that Kavanaugh's use of her statement angered her. She had already told a reporter that she believed Ford and felt this statement had been overlooked. While she did not want to reiterate her belief, she stood by her statement that she did not recall the event or know Kavanaugh.

Perhaps motivated by Keyser's texts, one of these friends, a woman, called Keyser's lawyer and insisted that he and Keyser had both perjured themselves. She was certain that Keyser must have known Kavanaugh. After all, she reasoned, Keyser had dated Mark Judge, and Judge was always with Kavanaugh. In fact, however, Keyser had gone on only one date with Judge, to a very large house party, and she had no recollection of Kavanaugh's being there or of ever meeting him.

Keyser's lawyer called for an immediate meeting, and he and Keyser went to the friend's home the next day, Friday, the twenty-eighth. She again insisted that Keyser must have known Kavanaugh since she went out with Mark Judge, and had therefore committed perjury in her statement. Angered that her friend was pushing her to amend her statement, Keyser emphatically maintained that it was accurate. She really did have no recollection of Kavanaugh even after a very diligent effort to try to remember him. Getting another friend on the phone, Keyser reiterated that she stood by her statement and was not going to lie to the Senate Judiciary Committee. Nonetheless, while she would not change what she had said, Keyser decided to let the committee know she still believed her friend. That same night, when the supplemental FBI investigation was announced, Keyser submitted an additional statement through her lawyer to the committee indicating her willingness to participate in the investigation. She reaffirmed that she did not know Kavanaugh and had no recollection of the gathering, but she stated that she nonetheless believed her friend.

Keyser told the FBI investigators the same thing: she didn't know Kavanaugh and didn't remember the event described by Ford. She felt relief at having followed through on her desire to cooperate with the legal process. And then she was able to do something she hadn't done since the ordeal had started—sleep, recover, and reflect.

Over the next few days, Keyser again carefully reviewed all available pictures of Kavanaugh, went through maps of the area, and retraced her steps based on Ford's statement and testimony. In addition to remembering more details of the summer of 1982, she also paid more attention to the news and the information that had been revealed about Ford's allegations. Adding up the facts, she lost confidence in Ford's account of the incident and came to the conclusion that she had to supplement her statement to the FBI. She asked her attorney to set that up.

During the second interview, Keyser described the summer with much more detail, adding that she didn't believe there was any way she was at this gathering. She expressed concern at the pressure she had felt to go along with the story or to keep quiet and told the FBI about the meeting with her friends on September 28 in which she had felt coerced to change what she said. She detailed certain parts of the story that didn't make sense to her. She also expressed her concern that her statement might be discounted because of her addiction problems throughout her adult life, but she made sure to reveal those problems so the FBI would have all the facts it needed. Saddened that her testimony might affect the lives of her dear friends, she nonetheless felt compelled to ensure that her accounting was completely accurate. Notably, she did not express any of these concerns publicly, only confidentially with the FBI.

Pressure to corroborate Ford's story also came from outside Keyser's circle of friends. Sara Corcoran, a journalist who was several years behind Ford and Keyser at Holton-Arms, published an aggressive and tasteless open letter that recounted the paralysis of Keyser's high school boyfriend, Bill, in the Columbia Country Club pool. "I still remember the chaotic scene, the paramedics, and the shock of what happened. Our parents often warned us about diving into the shallow end or at any depth." After that gruesome opening, Corcoran continued: "It was incredibly unfair to both of you that Bill broke his neck and died shortly thereafter. You were an inspiration to those of us young members at the club and students at Holton-Arms School. I am asking you [to be] an inspiration to us again by coming to the defense of Dr. Christine Blasey Ford." Playing on the trauma and guilt she had tried to stir up, Corcoran went on, "I know it seems like it is easier to turn away and revisiting the past is never easy, but your statements harmed the validity of Dr. Ford.... There was nothing you could have done to save Bill from the fate that awaited him, but you can save Christine."[8]

■   ■   ■

Ashley Kavanaugh had two major events to run as town manager. The first was on Independence Day. Her husband had missed it because of an interview with the vice president about the Supreme Court appointment. Her second event was a big neighborhood block party, scheduled for Sunday, September 30. It had already been rescheduled from the previous weekend because of rain. Even with all she was going through, and with the FBI investigation again pushing back the vote on her husband, she was determined to run the event, which had its largest turnout ever. Hoping to spare her neighbors the public scrutiny her family had been enduring, she asked the press if they'd be willing not to camp in front of their home that day, promising they wouldn't use the occasion to try to sneak out. They honored her request.

Ashley had found a psalm that gave her confidence to be in public: "Those who look to him are radiant; their faces are never covered with shame."[9] Her neighbors provided a moment of relief from the intense pressure of recent weeks. To a person, they were supportive and friendly, including those whom the Kavanaughs hardly knew and who weren't in their camp politically.

While their neighbors and the press detail showed exceptional grace and courtesy, Kavanaugh was blindsided by criticism from a surprising source. Breaking with the political reticence typical of Supreme Court justices, particularly with respect to a pending appointment, the retired justice John Paul Stevens fanned the "judicial temperament" flames by telling an audience of retirees in Florida that Kavanaugh's emotional defense of his reputation had caused him to change his view of a judge he had previously praised. The ninety-eight-year-old jurist, who had months earlier called for a repeal of the constitutional right to keep and bear arms, declared that "for the health of the court" Kavanaugh ought not to be confirmed.[10]

That evening, Kavanaugh published an op-ed in the *Wall Street Journal*, another unprecedented act for a Supreme Court nominee. As the media echoed Democratic talking points about his demeanor at the hearing, Kavanaugh sought to assure the public that his temperament was sound: "I was very emotional last Thursday, more so than I have ever been. I might have been too emotional at times. I know that my tone was sharp, and I said a few things I should not have said. I hope everyone can understand that I was there as a son, husband and dad." He further observed, "As a judge, I have always treated colleagues and litigants with the utmost respect. I have been known for my courtesy on and off the bench. I have not changed. I will continue to be the same kind of judge I have been for the last 12 years."[11]

An especially ugly confirmation of the media's irrational personal dislike of Kavanaugh came in the form of published opinions that he should no longer coach girls' basketball. Erik Brady wrote in *USA Today*, "The U.S. Senate may yet confirm Kavanaugh to the Supreme Court, but he should stay off basketball courts for now when kids are around.... The nation is deeply divided. Sometimes it feels like we don't agree on anything anymore. But credibly accused sex offenders should not coach youth basketball, girls or boys, without deeper investigation. Can't we all agree on that?"[12] Another reporter, recalling the middle school girls' basketball team Kavanaugh coached attending his hearing, had written, "The row of young girls, legs bare in their private-school skirts, looked different now."[13]

■   ■   ■

After senators had reviewed the FBI background report, McConnell announced that the cloture vote—that is, the vote to end debate so the nomination could proceed to a final vote—would take place Friday morning, October 5.

In a rare departure from his usual practice, the majority leader scheduled a vote without knowing what the result would be. All along, the Democrats had hoped that the nomination would be withdrawn, saving vulnerable Democrats from having to cast a difficult vote one way or the other. McConnell did not want to do them that favor, even if it meant losing the vote. He knew that if Manchin voted against Kavanaugh, he would be in danger of losing his seat from West Virginia.

At 10:17 on Friday morning, McConnell came to the floor of the Senate and spoke about Kavanaugh, decrying the tactics of the Democrats. At 10:30, Collins and Murkowski huddled together in their seats. They had been talking virtually every day about the nomination and had spoken early that morning when Murkowski said she was still undecided, though Collins suspected she was leaning toward voting yes. As they sat together in the noisy room, Murkowski leaned over, and Collins thought she heard her say, "I've decided that I can vote yes." Collins broke into a big smile and said that was her decision as well, and she was pleased they would be voting together. Murkowski had to let her down. Touching her arm, she clarified, "You don't understand, I'm *not* going to vote yes." Collins's face fell. She had made her own decision and was confident it was correct, but she knew it would be an even more difficult decision because she and her longtime friend would be on different sides.

The vote to advance the nomination of Kavanaugh was fifty-one in favor and forty-nine opposed. Murkowski voted no. Manchin and Collins voted yes. Manchin had not voted until after Collins and Murkowski had voted, so he was the fifty-first vote. While Kavanaugh's confirmation was still far from assured, the vote was a major step forward. Then Collins announced that she would give a speech on the Senate floor at three o'clock.

Like Kavanaugh, even after spending hours perfecting her speech, she still wanted to fine-tune it up until the last moment. She took a back elevator to the senators' dining room, hoping to avoid the press and have some time to work as she ate. But as the elevator doors opened, she saw Mitch McConnell and John Cornyn eating lunch together. They invited her to join them.

McConnell still didn't know what Collins's ultimate vote would be. Voting to end debate was not the same as voting to confirm—as Justice Alito learned when he received seventy-three votes for cloture but only fifty-eight for confirmation. If Collins voted no along with Murkowski and Manchin, it would be over. They never broached the subject, but Collins's manner suggested to McConnell that she was preparing to vote yes.

Protesters had been harassing Collins for months. Hundreds of coat hangers, the favored symbol of the abortion-rights movement, had been sent to her field offices in Maine to dramatize the threat to *Roe v. Wade* posed by Kavanaugh's appointment. In a clever gesture, she donated the hangers to a local thrift store. She also received a torrent of obscene and threatening voicemails.[14]

One rainy night, after working late, Collins was accosted outside her Capitol Hill town house by a man who shined a flashlight in her eyes and filmed her as he asked her questions, implying he was from CNN. How long he had been waiting for her in the pouring rain she didn't know, but she got past him and into her house, where she called the police. The man returned later and left a basket containing four potatoes on her doorstep, the significance of which she never determined.

As protesters besieged her Capitol Hill and Maine offices, Collins was particularly troubled by the abuse that her staff had to endure. A twenty-five-year-old in her Maine office, who helped constituents with Social Security, veterans' affairs, and immigration questions, answered a call from a man who told her that if Collins voted for Kavanaugh's confirmation then he hoped the young staffer would be raped and impregnated. The senator tried to assure her that the harassment would taper off after the vote, but she quit—a young woman driven out of public service, Collins ruefully noted, in the name of women's rights.

Protesters occupying Collins's office would take turns telling their stories of sexual harassment or assault, emphasizing that victims must be listened to. Annabelle Rutledge, a staffer for Concerned Women for America who was in the room with a group of women supportive of Kavanaugh, decided to tell her own story. Protesters rolled their eyes but listened as Annabelle spoke of having been sexually assaulted. She explained why it was unfair to blame Kavanaugh for what her assailant did: "We can't take the pain we have from each of these experiences and put it on one man. You said that a vote for Kavanaugh is a vote for everyone who has sexually assaulted us collectively, and that's just not true. You can't take the face of the people who have hurt you and have hurt other people in this room and put it on one man," she said. "I'm a woman but I'm also a sister, I'm a daughter, I am a niece. I'm a sister to four brothers. I'm an aunt to three nephews."[15]

The room erupted into angry shouts as women who insisted on "believing all women" challenged Rutledge's story. A couple of women approached Rutledge later to apologize for the rudeness of the crowd. Her powerful message was shared by many women supporting Kavanaugh.

The previous Sunday, Kellyanne Conway, the counselor to the president, had stunned Jake Tapper when, in the middle of their interview about the confirmation, she paused, cleared her throat, and revealed publicly for the first time that she had been a victim of sexual assault. "I don't expect Judge Kavanaugh, or Jake Tapper, or Jeff Flake, or anybody to be held responsible for that," she said. Conway worried that both accusers and accused were being prejudged on the basis of their sex and politics rather on the facts of each case.

Liberal activist groups tried to strong-arm Collins by raising a million dollars to confer on an opponent's campaign if she voted for Kavanaugh, a tactic that some election law experts considered dangerously close to a bribe.[16] But the senator was unmoved. "In all my years of public service, I've never seen a debate as ugly as this one," she had observed several weeks earlier. "These attempts to pressure me are not going to be a factor in my decision."[17]

Senators often address their floor speeches to an empty chamber and the C-SPAN camera, but when Senator Collins took the floor at three o'clock, at least twenty-five senators were present, including five Democrats. As she began to speak, several protesters started shouting and were removed from the room. The presence of her colleagues was touching and reassuring in light of the hecklers. She was flanked by two fellow women Republican senators, Cindy Hyde-Smith of Mississippi and Shelley Moore Capito of West Virginia. She was pleased when she realized they were behind her because so many people had attempted to say that women must uniformly oppose Kavanaugh, a position she found insulting.

It wasn't just the Senate floor that was riveted. Cable outlets broadcast the speech live. Kavanaugh's chambers, still without functional internet, relied on texts from Claire Murray at the White House about this decisive moment they had been working toward for months.

Collins began by lamenting that special interest groups and Democratic senators had announced their opposition to Kavanaugh from the moment of his nomination, one colleague even opposing the nomination before it was announced, and had misrepresented his judicial record. "Our Supreme Court confirmation process has been in steady decline for more than thirty years," she said. "One can only hope that the Kavanaugh nomination is where the process has finally hit rock bottom."[18]

Citing Alexander Hamilton, Collins stated her view that "the president has broad discretion to consider a nominee's philosophy, whereas my duty as a senator is to focus on the nominee's qualifications as long as that nominee's philosophy is within the mainstream of judicial thought."

"I have always opposed litmus tests for judicial nominees with respect to their personal views or politics, but I fully expect them to be able to put aside any and all personal preferences in deciding the cases that come before them," she said, noting her support for the five previous nominations by three presidents of different parties.

Collins then offered a review of Kavanaugh's legal reasoning on severability, executive privilege, and abortion. She highlighted his description of Justice Kennedy's *Obergefell* opinion as an "important landmark precedent," suggesting Kavanaugh would stand by the Court's redefinition of marriage to include same-sex couples. She suggested he would also honor the precedent established by the court's rulings legalizing the right to abort unborn children. Summing up his judicial career, she noted, "Judge Kavanaugh has received rave reviews for his twelve-year track record as a judge, including for his judicial temperament."

Turning to the question on which the fate of the nomination depended, Collins noted that "the Senate's advice and consent was thrown into a tailspin following the allegations of sexual assault by Professor Christine Blasey Ford. The confirmation process now involves evaluating whether or not Judge Kavanaugh committed sexual assault and lied about it to the Judiciary Committee."

"This is not a criminal trial," she noted, "and I do not believe that claims such as these need to be proved beyond a reasonable doubt." She was holding Ford's allegation to the lower standard of "more likely than not." Collins explained, "The facts presented do not mean that Professor Ford was not sexually assaulted that night or at some other time, but they do lead me to conclude that the allegations failed to meet the more-likely-than-not standard. Therefore, I do not believe that these charges can fairly prevent Judge Kavanaugh from serving on the Court."

After speaking for forty-three minutes, she finished by saying, "Mr. President, I will vote to confirm Judge Kavanaugh." With that, Kavanaugh's confirmation was virtually assured, even though the vote wouldn't take place until the next day.

Collins's courage heading into a tough election cycle was remarkable. Withstanding threats, bullying, and extreme media malpractice, she deliberated soberly and thoroughly while Republican senators facing fewer risks and under less pressure went wobbly.

Kavanaugh, working in his office, had not watched the speech live. But an emotional Ashley called him and urged him to watch it right away. Collins and Kavanaugh had developed a rapport; they respected each other's public service, preparation, and dedication. The judge knew that it would have been easier for her to give in to the tremendous pressure to vote against him, or at least to cast an affirmative vote without drawing attention to herself. Grateful for her critically important stand, expressed with strength and grace in her floor speech, he conveyed his thanks in a text message and promised that he would not disappoint her. The senator appreciated his good will, but she did not take his words as a signal that she would always agree with him, any more than she agrees with the other five justices she voted to confirm.

After her speech, Chuck Grassley approached Collins with tears in his eyes and gave her a hug. That had never happened before, and she was touched by the gesture from a senator whose composure and fairness had never failed through all the partisan hostility.

Later that afternoon, Senator Murkowski gave a rambling twenty-six-minute speech in which she praised Kavanaugh but announced that she would vote against him. It was a disappointment for the Kavanaugh team, which had bent over backwards to satisfy her requests that week. She asked for confirmation that "devil's triangle" was a drinking game. So the team scrambled to find people who confirmed it. Then she asked for clarification on "boofing."

"Literally, in the Congressional Record of the Republic of the United States of America, there is a letter describing how boofing means farting because of Lisa Murkowski and her need to feel as though this [allegation] were true," said one person working on the Kavanaugh effort. The team felt she was looking for a reason to vote no, never got it, and voted no anyway.

Murkowski did not think Kavanaugh would vote to overturn *Roe v. Wade* or undermine the constitutional status of Alaska Natives, she said, but his presence on the Court would give an unavoidable appearance of impropriety. She did not seem to believe he was the sexual predator he had been made out to be, but that apparently was not enough: "I believe that

Judge Kavanaugh is a good man. He's a good man. He's clearly a learned judge, but in my conscience, because that's how I have to vote at the end of the day, with my conscience, I could not conclude that he is the right person for the Court at this time."[19] The media's attack on Kavanaugh's temperament had hit at least one of its marks.

■   ■   ■

There was one important hurdle still to overcome. Senator Steve Daines of Montana had recently informed the leadership that he couldn't make the vote on Saturday. His daughter was getting married that day. He offered to fly back as soon as the ceremony was over. A fellow Montanan, Congressman Greg Gianforte, had offered him the use of his private plane if he needed it.

By the time Murkowski announced her decision, it was not a surprise. The conservative columnist Quin Hillyer now proposed how she could redeem her disappointing decision to vote against Kavanaugh. She should "restore a once-common Senate tradition that has fallen out of use," which would show "courtesy, decency, and mutual respect." It used to be common for a senator who could not be present for a vote to cooperate with a senator on the opposing side. That senator would "pair no" with the absent senator, who would "pair yes" (or vice versa), and neither of them would vote. To "pair no" is not the same as to vote "present," which affects the number of votes needed for a simple majority.

Hillyer wrote, "Memo to Senator Murkowski: If you won't vote for Brett Kavanaugh, at least demonstrate this collegiality so Senator Daines can act wholly as a dad on Saturday."[20] She took Hillyer's suggestion, softening the blow of her decision.

Protesters were camped out as Collins left her house to head to her office on Saturday. They started singing and chanting early that morning. As she locked up, she apologized to a neighbor for the noise. He told her the protesters' songs and chants were beautiful, but living next to a "rape apologist" was what troubled him.

On Saturday afternoon, October 6, just before four o'clock, the Senate began to vote, with Vice President Mike Pence presiding. A group from Concerned Women for America, having promised their support every step of the way, was there to pray. The vote was punctuated by the screams of protestors removed for violating the rule against "expressions of approval or disapproval." Months of emotional outbursts like this had backfired, pushing some undecided votes away. The behavior of the conservatives who worked hard and kept their heads down—sometimes quite literally, as when they prayed—was a stark and appreciated contrast for these senators.

Brett Kavanaugh was confirmed as an associate justice of the Supreme Court by a margin of fifty to forty-eight. When the vote was over, many senators headed for the hills. Lee and Flake shared a car to the airport. It was unusual for a vote to take place on Saturday, and Senator Daines was not the only one with other plans.

"Whatever happens, I'm just glad we ruined Brett Kavanaugh's life," the comedy writer Ariel Dumas tweeted. She later apologized for her "tone-deaf attempt at sarcasm." The tweet was at least an acknowledgment that the left had engaged in the politics of personal destruction.

■　■　■

All week long, Grassley's staff had encouraged him to go on the Sunday-morning news shows to discuss his successful handling of the Kavanaugh nomination. While Grassley had overseen some of the Senate's most contentious hearings and safely delivered Kavanaugh out of his committee against seemingly insurmountable odds, a lot of credit had gone to others. He said he would think about it. But on Saturday, he stood up and voted, walked out of the Senate chamber, and was on his way to the airport before the final vote was counted. "I don't need to crow about it," he told his staff. He later reflected, "Who wants to do that when I can be in Iowa? I go to my home church in Iowa. I eat with a couple of my kids after church. That's the only time I get any peace and quiet and see the real world and contemplate things that ought to be contemplated every day." "I always thought landslides were kind of boring anyway," McConnell joked afterwards at a press conference, predicting that the anger in the Senate would blow over.

■   ■   ■

When a justice is confirmed by the Senate, he is sworn in as soon as possible by the chief justice, and Chief Justice Roberts did the honors in the conference room behind the courtroom a few hours later, with Justices Ginsburg, Kagan, Thomas, and Alito attending. Gorsuch, Sotomayor, and Breyer were unable to be there. The show of support was notable, since some justices have taken their oath with no colleagues present. Roberts had let the other justices know their presence was welcomed.

While the Kavanaugh family took part in the ceremony and a small reception inside the Supreme Court building, the chaos continued outside. Marshals had grown accustomed to the protesters trailing Kavanaugh throughout the confirmation process, but the Supreme Court police were caught off guard when hundreds of raucous protesters rushed the steps of the building, apparently trying to open the thirteen-ton bronze doors. Instead of trying to disperse them, the police monitored the mix of protesters and onlookers milling about, including one topless woman with a Hitler mustache who stood in front of the doors and another woman who climbed up into the lap of the giant statue of a woman representing the Contemplation of Justice.

When Justices Ginsburg and Kagan left the building, their car was surrounded by protesters throwing tomatoes and water bottles. So when the Kavanaughs and their guests were ready to leave, the Supreme Court police assembled a caravan, which exited through the south gate, sirens blaring, before the protesters realized what was happening. The Kavanaugh girls, thrilled by the sirens and police escort, assumed this was how they would travel from now on. Their parents hoped they were wrong.

On Monday, all the justices assembled in the East Room of the White House for Kavanaugh's ceremonial swearing-in, some of them having sought assurance from the White House that the event would not be too political. Justice Kennedy arrived with his robe, unsure if he should wear it for the swearing-in. He had worn it when he administered the oath of office to Neil Gorsuch in a Rose Garden ceremony the year before. For Kavanaugh, he decided against it.

After introducing the justices and thanking Don McGahn, President Trump introduced Justice Kennedy and praised his lifetime of service. After the past few brutal weeks, everyone in the room was ebullient and ready to cheer. Senator McConnell received applause as well.

Trump said he would like to do something important: "On behalf of our nation, I want to apologize to Brett and the entire Kavanaugh family for the terrible pain and suffering you have been forced to endure. Those who step forward to serve our country deserve a fair and dignified evaluation, not a campaign of political and personal destruction based on lies and deception. What happened to the Kavanaugh family violates every notion of fairness, decency, and due process."

"In our country, a man or woman must always be presumed innocent unless and until proven guilty," the president said. Turning to Kavanaugh's young children, he continued, "Margaret and Liza, your father is a great man. He is a man of decency, character, kindness, and courage who has devoted his life to serving his fellow citizens. And now, from the bench of our nation's highest court, your father will defend the eternal rights and freedoms of all Americans. You know that." As a former justice prepared to administer the oath to his successor and former clerk, Trump commented that it was "a beautiful moment which reminds us that freedom is a tradition passed down from generation to generation."[21]

Justice Thomas, the only man in the room who fully understood what Kavanaugh had endured, clapped loudly.

Kavanaugh was glad his children could hear the kind remarks. When it was his turn to speak, he carefully avoided any hint of partisanship, reassuring the American people that he would be the same judge as always and would carry no bitterness with him. Some had questioned whether the man who testified in the second round of hearings could be impartial. He had been a judge for twelve years and was known for his equanimity after the partisan attacks occasioned by his appointment to the court of appeals. He had given a spirited defense of himself and his reputation at his Senate hearing, but that was an entirely different forum from the courtroom. He wanted to make sure that his new colleagues knew that.

Kavanaugh moved into chambers overlooking the Library of Congress, toward the back of the Supreme Court building. Alito had occupied those chambers for the previous nine years, and Scalia for eighteen years before that. For the thirty years before that, they belonged to Justice William Brennan. His office includes a working fireplace prepared each morning to be lit. During the winter months, Kavanaugh was grateful for its comfort and warmth.

The other justices made him feel welcome, each paying a visit to show his or her support. Justice Sotomayor told him that what matters is what he does on the Court and reminded him that "we're family here." While Justice Thomas had endured a uniquely brutal confirmation process, all the justices remembered it's taking a heavier toll on them than they had expected.

As overwhelming an ordeal as Kavanaugh had just endured, he couldn't afford even a day's rest; oral arguments would take place on Tuesday, October 9. He had browsed a brief before his confirmation vote, but wasn't able to focus until Sunday, the day after his confirmation. Other justices offered help by sharing bench memos.

On Kavanaugh's first day on the bench, October 9, Justice Kagan made a point of talking to him during the bar admission ceremony before oral arguments, demonstrating to the public that Kavanaugh's "team of nine" analogy was not far wrong. At the end of arguments she publicly shook his hand when they got up. The gracious act was reassuring, as protesters were still gathered outside. The culture of the Court is more like a family. Even the spouses of retired and deceased justices, such as Mary Kennedy and Maureen Scalia, return for events.

While Kavanaugh began to participate in deliberations immediately, his formal investiture did not take place until November 8. In attendance were family and friends, his former colleagues on the court of appeals, and Senators Mitch McConnell and Lindsey Graham. Don McGahn almost didn't make it inside. Having left his job as White House counsel, he no longer had a security detail. He had parked a few blocks away, and when he arrived at the Supreme Court, the police were shutting off access. By the time he got through security and into the Court, he was told that he was a moment too late, so he sent Kavanaugh a text message that they had turned him away and left the building. Outside, someone flagged him down and brought him back in. The White House staff secretary, Derek Lyons, had taken his seat, so he sat in the next row back, beside Justice Kennedy.

Kavanaugh was seated in Chief Justice John Marshall's chair, which has been used for the investiture of every member of the Court since Lewis F. Powell Jr. in 1972. He lowered himself into it carefully, so as not to damage the historical artifact. President and Mrs. Trump were the last ones seated, entering the room just after McGahn.

The ceremony lasted only a few minutes. Kavanaugh's commission was presented by Matthew Whitaker, who had been named the acting attorney general only the day before. A large man, Whitaker had scrambled to find a formal morning coat that he could fit into.

The interval of a few weeks before the investiture allowed Ashley to order a dress for the occasion. The White House ceremony in October took place immediately after confirmation, so she had to select from something in her closet. She was conscious that she couldn't have too much fun with fashion or accessories without photos looking dated in the future. The confirmation battle had been brutal, but she and her husband believed it had happened for a reason. Refined by fire, they had emerged stronger.

Traditionally, a newly invested justice, accompanied by the chief justice, descended the long set of steps from the Court to the plaza, where his family awaited him. Assuming that the traditional walk would be an invitation to protesters, Kavanaugh decided to pose for pictures with the chief justice in the conference room instead. Other members of the court regretted the passing of the tradition, but Kavanaugh preferred a celebratory message of unity.

Justice Ginsburg did not attend the investiture ceremony. She had broken three ribs in a fall two days earlier.

CHAPTER TWELVE

Legitimacy

The election night of November 6, 2018, was filled with uncertainty. Republicans had enjoyed massive gains in the House of Representatives during the Obama years—the 2010 midterm elections saw them pick up sixty-three seats, the biggest electoral gain for a major party since 1948. But now that a Republican was president, history and the polls suggested that this would be a good night for the Democrats. And it was. They gained thirty-nine seats, reclaiming a majority in the House for the first time in eight years.

The Senate was a different story. Despite political headwinds, Republicans benefited from a favorable electoral map—far fewer GOP incumbents were up for reelection than Democrats. Ten of the twenty-five Democratic senators running for reelection were in states that Trump had carried, and six of those seats were considered vulnerable: North Dakota, Florida, West Virginia, Indiana, Missouri, and Montana. Republicans were expected to expand their slim majority in the upper chamber, but the forecast was clouded by the "X-factor": the Kavanaugh confirmation.

When Christine Blasey Ford's allegation turned an already contentious confirmation process into a political conflagration, Democrats began to hope that the controversy might change their fortunes in the Senate. In a *New York Times* piece titled "Kavanaugh Was Supposed to Be a Midterm Boon for G.O.P. Not Anymore," Jonathan Martin reported that "in Missouri and other politically competitive battleground states, leaders in both parties are increasingly doubtful that [Republican senatorial candidate Josh] Hawley and other Republicans can wield the Kavanaugh nomination as a cudgel without risking unpredictable repercussions in the midterm elections."[1]

As allegations piled up and the confirmation seemed in doubt, Democrats were openly whispering that taking down Kavanaugh was part of a comprehensive electoral strategy. If Kavanaugh's confirmation failed, "Dems believe they can juice turnout—already hitting record levels—by playing off the huge public attention to the court, and *Roe v. Wade* in particular," reported Axios's Mike Allen. Further, "They envision President Obama and Michelle Obama locking arms with the Clintons, the Bidens, and Democratic congressional leaders to crank up a presidential-election-sized campaign. They feel confident every rich liberal in America would help fund this effort."[2]

By the final week of Kavanaugh's confirmation process, however, it was becoming clear that the circus atmosphere and the torrent of absurd allegations were instead firing up Republicans. An NPR–PBS News-Hour–Marist poll released on October 3 found that the so-called "enthusiasm gap" had evaporated. "In July, there was a 10-point gap between the number of Democrats and Republicans saying the November elections were 'very important,'" noted the pollsters. Now the enthusiasm of Republicans and Democrats was even.[3]

And the timing and a plethora of anecdotes from Republican officials strongly suggest that Kavanaugh was the cause of the GOP boost. "It's got to be Kavanaugh," the Republican pollster Robert Blizzard told the McClatchy news service. Another Republican pollster, Whit Ayres, also confirmed to McClatchy that the Kavanaugh fight was motivating voters: "It's the difference between victory and defeat in a close race. They're pretty upset about how Kavanaugh has been treated." Other Republican pollsters and strategists confirmed there had been a polling bump in individual Senate races, as well as gains in support from Republican women, in response to Kavanaugh.[4] The connection seemed obvious enough to Senate Majority Leader Mitch McConnell. "The ironies of ironies, this has actually produced an incredible surge of interest among these Republican voters going into the fall election," he told *USA Today* the day Kavanaugh was confirmed to the Supreme Court. "We've all been perplexed about how to get our people as interested as we know the other side is, well this has done it."[5]

After Kavanaugh was confirmed, it was hard to spin what had happened as anything other than a defeat for Democrats, who had given their all—including a portion of their decency—to stop the nomination. Nonetheless, as soon as congressional Democrats saw that defeat was imminent, they signaled their plans to keep the issue alive through the election. The day before Kavanaugh was confirmed, five members of the House Judiciary Committee, including the ranking member, Jerry Nadler of New York, promised further investigations of the sexual assault allegations and of charges that Kavanaugh had perjured himself in explaining his past drinking and the embarrassing contents of his yearbook. Still, Kavanaugh and the Supreme Court did not dominate Democratic messaging heading into November, as Democrats stuck to tried-and-true themes such as health care and opposition to Trump.

The president, on the other hand, had come to power by deftly capitalizing on grassroots Republican concerns about respect for law, and he trumpeted his success in putting two new justices on the high court. "This will be an election of Kavanaugh, the caravan [of illegal migrants], law and order, and common sense," he said at a campaign rally in Montana on October 18.[6] At a Trump rally with the GOP senate candidate Josh Hawley on November 3, the crowd spontaneously chanted "Kavanaugh! Kavanaugh!" after Hawley lauded the president for putting "pro-Constitution judges on the bench."[7]

Of course, the cliché in politics is that election day is the only poll that matters, and for good reason. The Democrats' thirty-nine-seat gain in the House reflected an 8.6 percent margin in the popular vote, which might have affected the Senate races more than it did. Going into the election, Republican hopes for expanding on their Senate majority were muted. Of the six most vulnerable Democratic incumbents in the Senate, the polling website FiveThirtyEight had Republicans favored to win only in North Dakota. Republicans beat expectations, winning four of those races. The two they lost were West Virginia and Montana. The victor in West Virginia, Joe Manchin, was the only Democratic senator to vote for Kavanaugh, and that vote was widely recognized as important to his victory. Indeed, his opponent, Patrick Morrisey, used Manchin's late vote to confirm Kavanaugh—after it was already clear he would be confirmed—as a talking point.[8]

The Democrat in Montana, Jon Tester, won his race after voting against Kavanaugh, but of the Democrats whose seats were vulnerable, Tester had the strongest polling numbers after Manchin. The four races Republicans won were all upsets, and their candidate in Florida, Rick Scott, won by a razor-thin margin of ten thousand votes out of more than eight million cast.

The Democrats had hoped to take a seat from the Republicans in the deep-red state of Tennessee, which Trump had carried by twenty-six points. The popular former governor Phil Bredesen was running for the open Senate seat against the Republican congresswoman Marsha Blackburn. Bredesen led early in the race, and as late as mid-September he was up by five points in a CNN poll. The race wasn't polled again until the weekend heading into the final week of testimony in the Kavanaugh confirmation, when Fox News showed Blackburn up by five. Bredesen never recovered his lead.[9]

This definitive shift in the Tennessee race did not appear to be coincidental. The no-holds-barred attacks on Kavanaugh were hurting Bredesen's campaign. After months of dodging questions about the judge, Bredesen announced his support of Kavanaugh's confirmation on October 5, just one day before the confirmation vote.[10] The last-minute and seemingly calculated show of support didn't help. Blackburn won the race by more than ten points.

The press could no longer deny that the brutal campaign against Kavanaugh had backfired against Democrats. "Democratic Senators Lost in Battleground States after Voting against Kavanaugh" was the headline in *USA Today* the morning after the election. Exit polling by ABC News in the Senate battlegrounds of North Dakota, Indiana, Florida, and Missouri showed that voters for whom the Kavanaugh confirmation was an important factor in their vote consistently broke for Republicans by large margins.[11]

Democrats had poured effort and money into an issue that motivated Republicans more than their own base. By angering the GOP base, they may have sealed their own defeat in a number of close races—not only for the Senate, but extremely tight governor's races in Florida and Georgia as well.

Congressional Democrats, supposedly convinced of Kavanaugh's guilt, have hesitated to expend more political capital pursuing him since taking control of the House. To date, there has been no further investigation of the allegations against him or the charge that he perjured himself. Jerry Nadler, now chairman of the House Judiciary Committee, has acknowledged that all the talk at the beginning of October 2018 about impeachment was merely a tactic to shift the balance of the Court.[12]

Part of the reason Democrats changed the subject is that the confirmation battle helped Republicans as much as or more than it did Democrats. While polls showed the vocal Kavanaugh opponents Hirono, Leahy, and Klobuchar among the ten most popular senators in their home states, Republicans who supported him received a tremendous bump as well. January 2019 polls showed increased Republican support for Senators Collins, Graham, and McConnell. The latter, usually the least popular senator, saw his net approval jump by ten points from the previous quarter. Lindsey Graham's approval rose fifteen points, the second-highest increase in the country, after his spirited defense of Kavanaugh. On the other hand, Senator Murkowski's net approval fell by ten points, eighteen points among Republicans, and Senator Flake ended his time in office as the least popular senator.[13]

■   ■   ■

Overcoming vicious political attacks, Brett Kavanaugh had been duly confirmed by the Senate and taken his seat on the U.S. Supreme Court, but the effort from some quarters to persecute him persisted. After undergraduates at George Mason University discovered that he was to teach a course at Mason's Antonin Scalia Law School, they began protesting. Demand Justice began running Facebook ads promoting a petition that he be fired.[14] New York witches placed multiple hexes on "Brett Kavanaugh and upon all rapists and the patriarchy which emboldens, rewards and protects them."[15] The new justice had to contend with eighty-three ethics complaints stemming from his confirmation hearing, including allegations of perjury, as well as supposedly unbecoming conduct when he defended himself against gang rape accusations.[16] A federal court dismissed all the complaints in December 2018.[17]

The left-wing magazine *The Nation* took it from there, calling on the Democrat-controlled House to impeach Kavanaugh. Even if impeachment were constitutionally possible for pre-confirmation actions, Republican control of the Senate would make it a pointless but potentially disastrous gesture.[18] But the author of the article, Elie Mystal, was undeterred: "I know some Democrats will say that bringing charges against Brett Kavanaugh—impeaching him—is pointless. Some Democrats insist on living in a country where nothing is 'worth it' unless Republicans are likely to agree. I refuse to live in that world. If I waited for Republican approval before I tried something, I'd be shining shoes at Grand Central, as would befit my station."[19]

Mystal may have landed on the central question to come out of the Kavanaugh nomination. Were the deplorable attacks, which inflicted so much damage on numerous lives and on the political process, worth it?

Many journalists and activists were so enthralled with a portrait of Brett Kavanaugh that had been cultivated by a coordinated and politicized gang of lawyers, public relations specialists, and distant acquaintances of the nominee that they were blind to the very different portrait painted by those who knew him longest and best.

Kavanaugh was a good friend, a kind and thoughtful man, a hard worker with high standards who nonetheless was committed to living on the "sunrise side of the mountain." He liked beer and had fun with the rest of the crowd but had a steady, even-keeled personality. He was never the one to make lewd comments about women or brag about sexual conquests. He was always one of the smartest kids in his class but also one of the hardest workers, always ready to help a friend with his homework. It is not his standout personality but his steadiness and loyalty that people remember. It was surely much more interesting and politically useful to paint him as a sloppy drunk groping women at every turn, who somehow ruthlessly climbed to the pinnacle of his profession, willing to steamroll any woman, senator, or ethical norm that stood in his way.

High school, college, and law school friends exchanged stories about the reporters who called looking for dirt. When they replied that the drunken assailant was not the man they had known, in some cases for decades, their accounts were ignored.

"Many recent media articles feature quotes from people who appear to know Kavanaugh barely, if at all," wrote Mark Perry, a co-clerk and longtime friend, on the day of the confirmation vote. "I've known him for almost 30 years, and I've spoken on the record to loads of reporters about him, yet I have never been quoted in any story. Is this because I have nothing salacious to say? Whatever the reason, the result is a one-sided and inaccurate depiction."[20]

It brings to mind the famous line from *The Man Who Shot Liberty Valance*: "This is the West, sir. When the legend becomes fact, print the legend."[21] Time and again, when a reporter was faced with firsthand evidence that Judge Kavanaugh's reputation as a man of outstanding character was true, he declined to print the story.

■   ■   ■

Being ignored was perhaps the best that Kavanaugh supporters could hope for. Professor Akhil Amar of Yale Law School provoked the fury of the left by arguing that Kavanaugh was the best possible nominee from the Trump administration.[22] The scholar's arguments were derided in the mainstream press as "crap" and "horses--t" and dismissed as self-serving elitist back-scratching.[23] Amar backtracked somewhat on his support after the allegations broke, calling for some investigation of Ford's claims while noting that his opinion about Kavanaugh's legal abilities remained unchanged.[24]

After the confirmation, Senator Susan Collins continued to receive hate mail and threats, including to her family. On October 15, as she was traveling home from Washington, her husband texted her a photo of himself in full hazmat gear. An envelope addressed to him had contained a letter that purported to be infused with ricin. By the time Collins finished her stressful two-hour drive from Portland, her street was blocked off with yellow crime scene tape and her home taken over by the local police and fire department, the FBI, and the army's weapons of mass destruction unit. The house was quarantined, including their black lab puppy. Their neighbors rushed to their aid, and a local Chinese restaurant and a Wendy's tried to figure out how to break the blockade and get their favorite meals to them. Collins saw a silver lining: it had provided an excellent drill for the first responders and nobody got hurt. A few days later another envelope was sent to her home labeled "anthrax."[25] Postal inspectors intercepted it and, after determining it contained cornstarch, were able to trace it to the sender, who was charged with sending threatening communications.

Women who attested to Kavanaugh's character in high school lost friends. Many had to drop off of social media during the confirmation process. All lost a degree of privacy and peace when their names were made public, and reporters hounded them for information about the judge.

Joel Kaplan, a vice president of global public policy for Facebook in Washington, D.C., faced a revolt in his workplace over his desire to support his longtime friend. Kaplan and Kavanaugh and their future wives had worked together in the Bush administration, and the families had remained close—so much so that they would even spend Christmas together. The Kaplans decided to attend the September 27 hearing as a gesture of solidarity. Laura Cox Kaplan held Ashley's hand. Joel sat behind the judge. He took the day off work and didn't think to run it by his supervisors because he was there in a personal capacity, standing by a friend during one of his most difficult moments.

When employees at Facebook identified Kaplan in the broadcasts of the hearings, they were outraged. Company message boards were swamped by hundreds of comments, many interpreting his presence at the hearings, implausibly enough, as an implicit endorsement of Kavanaugh by the entire company.

The political atmosphere at Facebook, of course, is monolithically liberal. Just weeks before Kavanaugh's first hearing, a senior engineer had started the group FB'ers for Political Diversity in protest of the left-wing intolerance that makes Facebook employees "afraid to say anything when they disagree with what's around them politically."[26] The company had come under scrutiny for such intolerance, and Kaplan was hired as a gesture of political open-mindedness.

Whatever the corporate leadership's intentions were, Facebook employees did not get the message. They saw Kaplan's attendance at the hearing as a thumb in the eye of the liberal culture at Facebook. A program manager angrily concluded, "His seat choice was intentional, knowing full well that journalists would identify every public figure appearing behind Kavanaugh. He knew that this would cause outrage internally, but he knew that he couldn't get fired for it. This was a protest against our culture, and a slap in the face to his fellow employees."[27] Those who sat behind Ford were not subject to such scrutiny, much less attacks.

Other employees interpreted Kaplan's support for his friend, and even Mark Zuckerberg's defense of that friendship, as a source of "stress and trauma."[28] A statement by Facebook's high-profile chief operating officer, Sheryl Sandberg, echoed what seemed to be the universal sentiment at the company: "As a woman and someone who cares so deeply about how women are treated, the Kavanaugh issue is deeply upsetting to me—as I know it is to many women and men in our company and around the world." This implied that the accusations themselves settled the question; the judge's personal innocence was irrelevant.[29] Kaplan's own apology stopped short of repudiating his friendship but called the episode "deeply painful, both internally and externally." It was more than many thought he should have to say, but it seemed necessary for a company with the bulk of its workforce in revolt.

Outside the Silicon Valley bubble, many were shocked by the reaction at Facebook, as if Kaplan's attendance at the hearing was tantamount to the corporation's endorsement of Kavanaugh. In any case, believing that he was innocent of the accusations was hardly the equivalent of dismissing all complaints about sexual assault. Some Facebook employees and even executives were dismayed by the inability of many of their colleagues—mostly of the "millennial" generation—to deal with a diversity of political opinion. But having learned from Kaplan's experience with the liberal mobs, they kept their expressions of support private.

Laura Cox Kaplan also drew fire for supporting her friend in the form of nasty messages from strangers, but the response within her professional network was markedly different from her husband's Silicon Valley experience. She had been more vocal in Kavanaugh's defense than her husband, having participated in the September press conference of longtime women friends supporting Kavanaugh. Before that press conference, she had notified the many organizations on whose boards she served, aware that her stance could provoke controversy and offering to step down if that happened. She needn't have bothered—the press conference was ignored by the media. But her colleagues, perhaps because they were from a generation more accustomed to embracing friendships across the aisle, were universally supportive.

Kaplan co-chairs Running Start, a nonprofit organization that trains women from both parties to run for office. Her co-chairman, Tasha Cole, a Democrat and the vice president of the Congressional Black Caucus Foundation, went out of her way to support Kaplan's stand. "Watching her support a dear friend in this political climate with conviction, class, grace and perseverance turns a new page in our friendship," Cole wrote in a Facebook post.[30] The two have used the experience as a teaching moment for the young women they mentor through

Running Start, encouraging them to use their voices, even when that may be unpopular.

That model of friendship despite political differences was embraced by Lisa Blatt, the Washington "super lawyer" who introduced Kavanaugh at his first hearing. The self-described liberal feminist holds the title for the most Supreme Court arguments by any woman—thirty-seven—and has won an astonishing thirty-four of those.[31] She said Kavanaugh was "unquestionably well-qualified, brilliant, has integrity and is within the mainstream of legal thought."[32]

In response, Brian Fallon, Hillary Clinton's former press spokesman, called Blatt's endorsement of Kavanaugh a "transactional ploy" and criticized her for "selling out progressive causes in order to advance her corporate clients' interests."[33] Slate asked, "Why Is Lisa Blatt Endorsing Brett Kavanaugh?" and then answered its own question: "Because rich clients trump justice."[34]

Blatt took Slate's criticism in stride, considering it understandable but inaccurate. Lawyers on both sides of the aisle face those charges when they endorse someone they are likely to appear before as litigants. What she found patronizing and insulting was the assertion of people like Brian Fallon—even before the Ford allegations—that because she believed Brett Kavanaugh was a good person, she wasn't a real liberal or was a patsy for the Republicans. Even worse was the hate mail she received, including people expressing hope that her daughter would be assaulted.

Most of Blatt's friends who shared her politics distanced themselves from her. She offered them a choice: be her friend and agree to disagree about Kavanaugh or live in their political bubble without her. Most chose politics. Only two friends decided they could stand by her. They helped her pick out a dress to wear to the hearings and were able to appreciate how exciting it was for her to be invited to testify before the Senate. Many of Blatt's colleagues were no more supportive than her friends, suggesting that her stand for Kavanaugh was hurting hiring at the firm. Others were patronizing or condescending, offering to help her back away from her support of Kavanaugh toward the end of the process. They didn't realize she still wanted him confirmed. She switched jobs and has now found a group of partners who can get along even while embracing a wide range of political viewpoints. It's a model that is all too rare in today's world.

Blatt is sanguine about her experience. "Far from feeling like a victim, I am proud to have stood by him and would do the same thing all over again," she says. If she has lost friends, she views it as their loss. In fact, she describes it as "the best thing that ever happened to me." And, of course, she has the luxury of having great options and another firm that welcomed her. Her bluntness is refreshing in a world of snowflakes, forced apologies, and social ostracism. She called their bluff, and by walking away from their demands for conformity, she robbed them of their power. Imagine a world where fewer people were scared to stand up for what they believed. It could start a virtuous circle, in which every person who bucked the popular views would drive down the cost of standing up.

Many things went horribly wrong on Brett Kavanaugh's road to the Supreme Court. But more importantly, many things went right. It was no accident that, when confronted with the most aggressive, coordinated, and well-funded attack on a judicial nominee in this nation's history, the effort to confirm Kavanaugh was successful. There were at least five reasons for this success.

First, the nation had a president who supported the conservative judicial movement. His campaign had assembled a coalition that included that movement, and he embraced the cause of nominating principled originalist judges.

Winning an election, however, is not enough. The appointment of a Supreme Court justice is the work of key members of the president's senior staff, who must make the nomination and confirmation a priority. Once in office, President Trump put in place a highly qualified team, headed by Don McGahn, who enabled him to fulfill his campaign promise of putting reliable originalists on the Court. And Trump stood by the project when it became politically imperiled.

Second, Republicans controlled the Senate. In today's polarized environment, the likelihood of a Democrat's voting for any Republican nominee, however qualified, is miniscule (although there are still plenty of Republicans who will compliantly vote for a Democratic nominee).

Controlling the Senate is therefore essential for appointing a conservative to the Court.

Third, an array of organizations made the confirmation of originalist judges a priority. That infrastructure made the Gorsuch and Kavanaugh victories possible. And that infrastructure was the product of thirty-five years of work by the conservative legal movement to establish itself as a potent and well-organized force for changing the judiciary and the legal culture. It nurtured the lawyers who would staff the White House and the Department of Justice, who would be elected to the Senate and become key aides, and who would become judges themselves. And it carried out the slow but crucial task of educating the public on the importance of constitutional principles and the judiciary's role in upholding them. This relentless work eventually produced the public demand for a president who would make the judiciary a priority.

Fourth, new media outlets emerged to challenge the liberalism that had reigned in the press for decades. These publications, web magazines, and podcasts refused to let liberal media control the narrative. They confidently reported the facts and showed courage in the face of overwhelming pressure.

Finally, none of these achievements would have been possible without conservative Americans themselves. They rallied behind candidates, provided their needed campaign funds, and organized and funded advocacy groups. Americans' instinctual understanding of the value of the rule of law played an important role.

■   ■   ■

Despite the personal fallout for Kavanaugh and those involved in the confirmation battle, it was obvious from the beginning that the frenzy surrounding his confirmation was not about his qualification for the job. Instead it was about control of the Supreme Court, an institution that plays an increasingly large—and increasingly questionable—role in America's social, economic, and political life.

The growth of the Court's influence has coincided with that of the federal government itself. As the ambition of federal legislation increased from the New Deal onward, the possibilities for running afoul of the law increased dramatically. At the same time, the growth of the administrative state introduced the proliferating regulations of a multitude of federal agencies, administrations, and commissions, which have the force of law. Members of Congress found it simpler to "do something" about major problems by writing vague legislation and leaving the details to be worked out by "experts" in administrative agencies. They could pass laws that aspired to solving great problems without having to reach the compromises required to gain the necessary votes or being accountable for making the hard choices that governing demands.

All too often, the unelected experts charged with making those hard calls were not the non-political technocrats they were billed as but were pursuing a partisan end. Even an administrative state staffed by a mythical breed of pure-minded, disinterested bureaucrats would be subject to an almost irresistible tendency to metastasize. Regulation by agencies is relatively simple to promulgate—it merely takes the time and patience necessary to announce a rule, take comments, and show that the comments were in some way taken into consideration. Navigating bureaucratic procedure and red tape is easy compared with cobbling together a majority (or supermajority) of both houses of Congress and winning the president's support. So with the growth of the administrative state, the volume and scope of federal law also grew. Issues that once were left to the states or the people were now literally made into federal cases.

As Congress's ability to legislate has declined, the temptation to turn to simpler ways of governing has grown. Unable to work with Congress, President Obama famously turned to his "pen and phone," that is, to executive orders and administrative agency action. Another alternative to dealing with a gridlocked Congress has been the courts, which themselves have abdicated some of their own authority.

In the 1980s, the Supreme Court began attempting to extract itself from an ever more complicated regulatory state by deferring to agencies when they interpreted statutes and, eventually, their own regulations. It may have saved the courts from making hard legal calls, but it put those decisions in the hands of the regulators—a heavy thumb on the scale for the bureaucrats whenever they were in a lawsuit. In the resulting system, in which all ties were decided in favor of government regulators, it was difficult for courts to be impartial interpreters of the law.

While abandoning some of their proper role, courts have also usurped the powers normally reserved to Congress. The legislative process is notoriously messy, and nobody thinks the sausage factory produces a perfect product every time. So when a judge is faced with a law that seems to function poorly, there is a temptation to step in. The legislators appear sloppy or foolish or, if it is an old law, blinded by the prejudices of their time. A nip here, a tuck there, and the law will function so much better. But the Constitution doesn't establish the judiciary as the copy editors of the legislature. They are supposed to apply the law, not improve it.

There is a saying among lawyers that "hard cases make bad law." It arises from the natural instinct of the judge or jury to bend the law to reach the result that their heart tells them is right. But in the bending, the law is deformed, and ever more pronounced departures from the original language follow.

Much of the temptation for courts to correct, rewrite, update, or amend statutes, and even the Constitution, arises from the perception that change through the proper channels is not feasible. Many legislators are content for the courts and the agencies to do their hard work for them. But some legislators also welcome judicial editing of the law to implement policies that do not have the broad support necessary to make it through the legislative process. When Senator Klobuchar questioned Judge Neil Gorsuch during his confirmation hearings about his ruling that the Religious Freedom Restoration Act (RFRA) covers corporations, he carefully explained the federal Dictionary Act, which defines "person" as it is used in federal legislation, and pointed out to the senator that if she thought the statute's coverage of corporations was a bad idea, it was her job as a legislator to remedy that: "Senator, if in RFRA again, if this body wishes to say only natural persons enjoy RFRA rights, that is fine, and I will abide that direction. I am not here to make policy; I am here to follow it."[35]

In fact, the Democrats did try to amend RFRA, but the effort went nowhere. To some, that is precisely the kind of situation in which the courts should intervene to implement the "correct" or "just" policy that politics failed to achieve. But however frustrated a minority of the Congress and the country may be with RFRA, those frustrated persons are still just that—a minority. If the majority of the country doesn't want to change a valid law, the Constitution does not give the courts authority to second-guess it.

Sometimes Congress has exercised its authority to change a law after the Supreme Court has recognized that judicial fiat is not the constitutional means to do so. When Lilly Ledbetter, shortly before her retirement, sued her employer for paying her less than it paid her male counterparts, her action was found to be barred by the statute of limitations. When the Supreme Court held that the statute required her case to be dismissed, the political reaction was immediate and hysterical.[36] The majority was excoriated for not fudging the statutory deadline in Ledbetter's favor. In this case, however, the desired change had the support needed for legislative action. Congress passed the Lilly Ledbetter Fair Pay Act of 2009, which starts the limitation period over with each new paycheck. That's exactly the type of response our system is designed to produce. Congress wrote a law. When the Court applied it as written, a new Congress wanted a different result and amended the law.

The same solution is available for constitutional disputes. Unhappy with what the Constitution says about speech, guns, abortion, or the scope of federal power? There's an amendment process for that—intentionally difficult, but not insurmountable. The Constitution has been amended more than two dozen times, and it could be amended again if an issue were sufficiently important to the American people. It is no answer to say that causes that cannot garner the support of a broad majority of Americans should instead be enacted by a bare majority of unelected judges.

The notion that judges are competent to make even small improvements in the law leads almost imperceptibly to a much more expansive agenda. Once the judge is unshackled from the text set down by the people's elected representatives (or their unelected regulators), he will wander wherever his own judgment leads him to implement the stated or even unstated intent of the law.

This flexible legal approach, applied to the Constitution, has resulted in the creation of broad new rights uncontemplated by those who framed and ratified the original document and its amendments. These new rights, in turn, have increased the range of activity governed by federal law. The influence of federal law, and of the courts that interpret that law, is therefore greater than it ever has been in history.

As the unelected bureaucrats of the burgeoning administrative state exercise de facto legislative power, the only remaining constraint on them is constitutionalists in the judiciary. At the same time, activists on the left cajole the judiciary to impose their favored policies—including revolutionary social changes—by an "exercise of raw judicial power," as Justice Byron White described it, and since the Warren Court era, liberal judges have been happy to oblige.[37]

Is it any wonder, then, that the stakes in judicial appointments, especially to the Supreme Court, have become so high? Rather than being "the least dangerous branch," as Alexander Hamilton predicted, the judiciary has become the forum where philosopher kings impose the final decision in our most divisive political and social disputes.[38]

Justice Scalia, observing the ever-intensifying confirmation process for Supreme Court justices in 2012, explained that the process has become more political because judges have become more political:

> [A]s much as I dislike the spectacle of—of confirmation hearings now, I prefer them to the alternative. As long as the court is revising the Constitution, by God, the people ought to have some say and they ought to be able to ask the nominee, you know, what kind of a Constitution are you going to give us? That's the most important question. Why shouldn't they be able to ask that? So you know, I don't like it, I would like to go back to the old system, but not if the Supreme Court is rewriting the document.[39]

Among the many issues on the liberal wish list that cannot be achieved through democratic means, one in particular motivated the opposition to Kavanaugh: abortion. It loomed over the entire confirmation process—from the nationwide speaking tour "Rise up for Roe" to the laser-like focus on the two Republican senators who support abortion rights, Collins and Murkowski. Planned Parenthood and NARAL were there every step of the way, financing protesters, TV ads, and celebrity appearances.

The nation's abortion regime is dependent on the Supreme Court's decision creating a federal constitutional right to abortion. Without that intervention, it is almost certain that a nationalized abortion law would never have been achieved through the democratic process, whether through a constitutional amendment, legislation in each of the fifty states, or a federal law mandating abortion on demand. Accordingly, a vocal, lavishly funded segment of the left has staked everything on upholding *Roe v. Wade*. It is a cause of such overriding importance that no means of sustaining it, not even the idea of tearing down an honorable man with scurrilous and unverified stories, can be ruled out.

Ironically, *Roe* stands as a key example of the serious damage done to the country when courts stray from the rights actually protected in the Constitution. Justice Ginsburg, herself an avid defender of the right to abortion, was nonetheless critical of *Roe* not because it amounted to legislating from the bench, which she acknowledged, but because it moved too quickly. From her perspective, the decision to "ste[p] boldly in front of the political process" was wrong not in itself but as a prudential matter because it "halted a political process that was moving in a reform direction and thereby, I believe, prolonged divisiveness and deferred stable settlement of the issue."[40]

It may be that slow-motion legislation from the bench would have provoked less opposition than the one-fell-swoop decision of *Roe v. Wade* did. But people's bristling at having major issues removed from public debate by unelected judges is evidence of an instinctive American recognition that such activism runs counter to the rule of law. After all, if the people have no recourse from judicial alteration of our laws and Constitution, what remains of our representative system of government?

Another problem with constitutionalizing important issues is that it undermines the federalist structure of the Constitution and the American nation. The framers established a federal government with limited powers on the foundation of preexisting sovereign states. While the Constitution does federalize certain rights, expanding their number and scope without popular consent turns our federal structure into an all-or-nothing system, which raises the stakes for every decision. If abortion were still governed by the states, there would likely be a range of laws throughout the country. There would be room for the experimentation and balancing that the Supreme Court foreclosed. People could vote with their feet. Each legislative or legal battle over abortion would be geographically limited. While such a system slows down change in either direction, it also puts it much closer to the people themselves and the fundamentally American ideal of self-governance.

■   ■   ■

Whatever happens to *Roe*, there is good reason to believe that a conservative majority on the high court would roll back at least some of the liberal excesses of the past few decades and, at the very least, prevent an activist federal judiciary from imposing new liberal policies on America by fiat. After Kavanaugh, the brightest lights in the Democratic Party are not hiding their desire to regain control of the Supreme Court by any means necessary, and "packing" the Court has become a serious topic of discussion on the left.

Attempts at court-packing are simply history repeating itself. While the number of justices on the Supreme Court varied in the early years of the republic, it has been fixed at nine since the Judiciary Act of 1869. "Court-packing" entered the political lexicon in 1937 when President Franklin Roosevelt, frustrated by a Supreme Court that had declared key components of his New Deal unconstitutional, proposed the Judicial Procedures Reform Bill, which would have allowed him to appoint as many as six additional justices. Even a president as popular as FDR could not get away with such a naked power grab, and he failed to get the bill through a Congress controlled by his own party.

The historical consensus is that Roosevelt's court-packing plan ultimately gave him the Court he wanted, albeit indirectly. Congress passed a watered-down version of Roosevelt's bill, which left the Court at nine seats but allowed justices who retired to receive full, rather than one-half, pensions.[41] Four justices stepped down within the next four years, and two more died in the same period, giving FDR his opportunity to remake the Court.

But the most memorable development on the Court was the sudden change in Justice Owen Roberts's voting. Roberts underwent a conversion of sorts in his constitutional views and began voting to uphold Roosevelt's agenda in what has been dubbed the famous "switch in time that saved nine," on the assumption that his vote changes were made because he was attempting to head off the president's changes to the composition of the court. (Although that conventional wisdom has since been called into question.)[42]

A justice who allows the president's political maneuverings to change his vote does not show his independence. He shows that justices can be manipulated. Democrats who are agitating for a change on the Court now may be making the same calculation, hoping that some justices may still be susceptible to outside pressure. It seems clear that increasing the size of the Court would not only shift it dramatically and immediately to the left but would trigger retaliation that would make the Court more a political football than it already is. By holding the Court hostage, left-wing activists hope to convince at least one justice to move to the left, obviating the need for drastic action.

Unfortunately, this tactic has worked at least once before with this Court. In 2012, when a constitutional challenge to the Affordable Care Act, President Obama's signature legislative accomplishment, was before the Court, the initial vote of the justices was to strike down the entire law because its requirement that all Americans purchase health insurance, on penalty of a fine—the so-called "individual mandate"—violated the Commerce Clause. But Chief Justice Roberts was uneasy with the prospect of the Court's making such a major change to the health care law and feared it would be blamed for the likely fallout in the insurance markets. The media, senators, and even the president were also previewing arguments they would use if he voted to overturn the law, calling it partisan and activist and a blow to the Court as an institution.

Behind the scenes, the chief justice negotiated a deal with Justices Kagan and Breyer. They would vote to overturn the law's expansion of Medicaid, contrary to their own reading of the statute, in exchange for his upholding the individual mandate as a tax.[43] Both inside and outside the Court, the assumption was that he had buckled under the pressure.

Whatever Chief Justice Roberts's reasons, the result was not an improvement in the Court's reputation. Pew reported that after the decision the Court remained at its all-time-low 52 percent approval rating. The accepted narrative, even among those who welcomed the chief's decision, was that he changed his legal position not on principle but in response to public pressure. The right lost respect for him, and the decision won him no friends on the left, which still portrays him as unforgivably conservative and a craven political operative.[44] It was a regrettable outcome for anyone concerned about the legitimacy of the Court. Some of the people responsible for putting Kavanaugh on the Court hoped that if he were tempted to modify his position in hope of adulation, he would know it leads to scorn.

The media tend to confuse the legitimacy of the Court with respect for the Court, but there is a difference between the two. Acting according to law is the essence of legitimacy in a legal sense, while "respect" is a sign only of social legitimacy in the eyes of the public. The problem with attempting to build social legitimacy is that it can easily devolve into a popularity contest.

The media regularly and shamelessly suggest that Supreme Court cases decided along partisan lines will undermine the legitimacy of the Court—or at least that's the suggestion when the arguments of conservative justices prevail. But the media's repeated attacks on the legitimacy of a court controlled by constitutionalists has almost become a self-fulfilling prophesy. If they continue to criticize the court, should anyone be surprised that the public's faith in the Court's legitimacy is waning?

But legitimacy is not the same thing as popularity. The framers knew that good judges would not always—or even often—be popular. That's why they gave them life tenure. They knew that the Court's true legitimacy derives from its freedom to make decisions in accordance with law, not in its reaching decisions that will win favor.

■   ■   ■

Make no mistake, the smear campaigns against judicial nominees are themselves an attack on the Court's legitimacy. Even if they don't prevent a justice's appointment, they are a tool to delegitimize him after he is on the Court. A case in point is Justice Clarence Thomas. At the time of his confirmation, polling showed a substantial majority of Americans—black and white, male and female—believed him over Anita Hill. But the campaign against Justice Thomas never stopped. For a quarter-century, the refrain in the media and in legal academia has been that Clarence Thomas's guilt is simply a fact of history.

A similar campaign is already underway against Kavanaugh. The impeachment talk will continue, although it will likely never amount to much because the underlying claims are so baseless. Glowing stories are being written about Christine Blasey Ford. She was listed as one of *Time*'s "100 Most Influential People" of 2019, along with politicians, athletes, and movie stars. She introduced Rachael Denhollander, the gymnast who brought the USA Gymnastics sexual abuse scandal to light, as *Sports Illustrated*'s "Inspiration of the Year." The publicity stunt disgusted politicians as temperamentally divergent as President Trump and Senator Collins. The man who abused Denhollander and hundreds of other girls pleaded guilty and is in prison for the rest of his life. It is unconscionable to compare the two stories, as if Ford's accusations were similarly credible.

And for all the hysteria, there is still no indication that anyone on the left is walking away from the Kavanaugh confirmation chastened by the electoral consequences or determined to prevent more damage to the credibility of the judiciary. Although Justice Kavanaugh's investiture was a celebratory moment, there was an ominous note. When the justices took their seats behind the bench, one was missing. Ruth Bader Ginsburg, at eighty-six the Court's oldest member, was in the hospital. She had fallen the day before, breaking three ribs. Her doctors then discovered a cancerous mass in her lung, her third bout with cancer.[45] She has beaten cancer twice, and doctors say the latest treatment was a success. She has no intention of stepping down. But sooner or later there will be another vacancy on the Court, whether it is her seat or another justice's.

It's hard to imagine how a confirmation battle could compete with Kavanaugh's for ugliness. But if the next appointment portends a major ideological shift, it could be worse. When President Reagan had a chance to replace Louis Powell, a swing vote, with Bork, Democrats went to the mat to oppose him. When Thurgood Marshall, one of the Court's most liberal members, stood to be replaced by Clarence Thomas, the battle got even uglier. And trading the swing vote Sandra Day O'Connor for Alito triggered an attempted filibuster.

As ugly as Kavanaugh's confirmation battle became, he is unlikely to shift the Court dramatically. Except on abortion and homosexuality, Justice Kennedy usually voted with the conservatives. If Justice Ginsburg were to retire while Trump was in the White House, the resulting appointment would probably be like the Thomas-for-Marshall trade. Compared with what might follow, the Kavanaugh confirmation might look like the good old days of civility.

Vicious confirmation battles will unfortunately dissuade the best Americans from being considered for the nation's judiciary. Some good people will undoubtedly still serve out of a sense of civic duty. One of Kavanaugh's colleagues says the process is so tough that it isn't worth it as a career move, but only out of a sense of duty or vocation. "Personally I don't wish that on anybody. But when you're called—think of the men whom we send into harm's way. Think of the Marines storming the beaches in World War II. If you think you're being asked to give more than them, don't do it."

Unfortunately, the only reason many other good people will continue to sign up for the job is the naïve belief that it won't happen to them precisely *because* they are good people. But it can happen, it does happen, and it just happened. The big unknown is whether America will let it happen again.

Note to readers

This book is based on interviews of more than one hundred people, including the president of the United States, several Supreme Court justices, high-ranking White House and Department of Justice officials, and dozens of senators. The authors also spoke with leaders of advocacy groups and legal experts, with family, friends, and former law clerks of Justice Kavanaugh, and with many others involved in the effort to confirm a successor to Justice Anthony Kennedy.

These people graciously gave of their time and knowledge, many sitting for multiple interviews, some for as many as ten hours total. The vast majority of the interviews were conducted "on background," which means that the information could be used, but the source asked not to be identified. Most anecdotes have multiple sources. Characterizations of how someone felt come from either the source or someone the source spoke to. In addition to interviews, sources generously shared historical documents, contemporaneous notes, and memos.

This account draws heavily from contemporaneous news reports, the scholarship of Supreme Court historians, and the exhaustive archives of C-SPAN.

The book also relies on the personal knowledge of the authors, acquired through their work during the Kavanaugh confirmation process and with the conservative legal movement. Carrie Severino, the leader of the Judicial Crisis Network, was deeply involved with the promotion of Judge Kavanaugh's confirmation from the time of his nomination. She is a Harvard Law School graduate who clerked at the Supreme Court. Mollie Hemingway is a senior editor of *The Federalist*, a web magazine that covers politics, policy, and culture, and a contributor to Fox News. Through their work, they became closely acquainted with key players and their views as well as with important themes and events that have not been previously reported.

The book arose out of a desire by participants in these extraordinary events to tell their stories to writers who had not joined in the media's public opposition to Justice Kavanaugh's appointment. While both authors admit to a right-of-center perspective, they have endeavored to produce an objective account that reflects a respect for the rule of law and the presumption of innocence.

Acknowledgments

This book would not have been possible without the help and support of many people. We apologize in advance for any we have unintentionally omitted.

Tom Spence has been a major blessing on this project. He has performed the literary equivalent of making a house into a home. He wove our 110,000-word manuscript into a cohesive story. And he did so under the tightest of deadlines and with constant "breaking news" being added to the manuscript even in the final hours of editing.

We are grateful that Marji Ross and Regnery Publishing were willing to take on this whirlwind of a project. Nobody else could have taken us from a signed contract in January to a finished product in July, and we are indebted to them for their trust in us and this project.

Our interns were another major stroke of providence. Hillsdale College's Kirby Center provided us five thorough, enterprising, and reliable assistants at various points in the writing. Kristyna Skurk and Solomon Chen put in long hours checking and correcting our endnotes and researching the more obscure corners of Supreme Court history. The budding journalist Alexis Nester was intrepid in tracking down and interviewing sources. And Hanna Thullen and Jackson Frerichs assisted in straightening out our timeline of events.

Thank you to our many sources for their generosity with their time and stories, for their patience in explaining to us everything from the intricacies of Senate rules to the conventions of suburban Maryland high school culture. We are grateful to President Trump for the time he afforded us to discuss judicial selection. Thank you to Senate Majority Leader Mitch McConnell and Judiciary Committee Chairman Chuck Grassley for their generosity with their time. We would also like to thank John Abegg, Randy Barnett, Shari Berger, Robert Bork Jr., Jonathan Bunch, Justin Clark, Marjorie Dannenfelser, Mike Davis, Doreen Denny, Julie DeVol, Mario Diaz, Annie Donaldson, Antonia Ferrier, Sara Field, Taylor Foy, George Hartmann, Laura Kaplan, Kerri Kupec, Leonard Leo, Ted Lehman, John Malcolm, Jenny Beth Martin, Gary Marx, Attorney General Ed Meese, Rachel Mitchell, Patricia Miles, Penny Nance, Vice President Mike Pence, Sarah Pitlyk, Mallory Quigley, Ralph Reed, Annabelle Rutledge, Raj Shah, Janae Stracke, Brett Talley, Garrett Ventry, and Helgi Walker.

Carrie Severino

I never planned to write a book. When people close to the Kavanaugh confirmation shared with me their concerns that the books being written on the topic would be biased, I hoped that a respected and principled journalist like Mollie would agree to write the true story. But when Mollie called me, saying she would do it only if I agreed to be a co-author, her partnership gave me the confidence to take on a project that felt totally beyond me. In truth, it still does. Looking back on how many persons we were able to interview and how much information we were able to amass in a mere four months, I'm still not sure how we managed it.

To write a book is one thing, but to co-author a book as involved as this one was daunting in a different way. Would we hate each other by the time the manuscript was finished? How could we split up the work so that neither of us, with her many other obligations, felt unfairly over-burdened? It is amazing that we have emerged from that pressure-cooker not only without mutual animosity but as stronger friends and partners. After spending nearly a decade on the other side of the microphone, I have received an intensive apprenticeship in journalism with Mollie that is without parallel. She has taught me to have a healthy skepticism of persons and motives, how to protect my sources, and how to interview for both accuracy and color to give life to the narrative. The icing on the cake is that Mollie came equipped with a husband as astute and articulate as she.

I am profoundly grateful for my colleagues at the Judicial Crisis Network. They shared generously of their expertise on decades of confirmations, identified all the best books on the confirmation process and loaned them out indefinitely, helped dig through facts and remember events, and allowed me the flexibility to take unofficial leave to write. I couldn't ask for a better group of friends to work with or a better cause to work for.

One of my major inspirations for writing this book has been Justice Clarence Thomas. I spent one year in his chambers, but his commitment to his clerks is lifelong. He has maintained his fidelity to the Constitution and to the oath he took before God despite the scorn of our society's opinion-makers. But he taught me that such scorn is its own kind of blessing. Knowing that he would never have the applause of the elites freed him from one of the many temptations of a judge. I have seen first-hand the unrelenting ad hominem attacks of the hostile media and legal academy. If, through my work, I can do something to help prevent that from happening to another person, I owe it to the justice to try.

In his memoirs, Justice Thomas recalls the moment when he realized that his confirmation had been transformed from a political battle to a spiritual one. I felt the same during the Kavanaugh confirmation when, on the feast of St. Michael the Archangel (September 29), I began a nine-day prayer novena to Our Lady of Victory, asking for the truth, whatever it was, to be revealed. After a decisive speech at three o'clock on the afternoon of the first Friday in October, Justice Kavanaugh was confirmed on the final day of that novena. There were so many moments of providential grace throughout the writing of this book, I feel my guardian angel deserves co-author credit.

Justice Thomas, reminiscing about his relationship with Justice Scalia, remarked that they connected almost immediately despite their different backgrounds and upbringings. They could anticipate each other's moves like great dance partners. I am thankful for my great dance partner and husband, Roger, without whose love and support this book would not have been possible. This project—and the confirmation itself—came along when his own job was incredibly demanding, but he never wavered in his encouragement of my work. He adjusted his schedule to be home in time to shuttle children to and from events and to get them ready for school in the morning and for bed at night. He is my advocate when I sell myself short. And he is definitely my better half when it comes to editing. He has the best words.

My six children have amazed me with their patience and fortitude through this whole process. When Justice Kennedy retired in 2018, I warned them it would be a busy summer, but that things would slow down after the hearings in September. In fact, they only sped up. Over and over I told them, "One more week!" And then when it ended, with a brief breather, it started up again with a book which has had its own series of supposedly final deadlines!

I've seen them all grow in maturity throughout this process. The eldest three—aged thirteen, ten, and eight—have stepped up to take care of their younger siblings and to make dinner and to clean up, even hosting a cooking competition for us in the midst of the craziness with two delicious three-course meals to show for it. My six-year-old is learning to step up with loving acts of service, and the four- and one-year-old are a constant source of amusement and joy. It's like having a pair of comic sidekicks around 24-7. I know I have failed at times to strike the elusive balance between work and family, but I hope they, along with me, have learned how to let go of the small things, while focusing on making time for each other when it seems that there is no time to be had.

I never could have managed that balance without the unflappable, loving, and superlatively efficient assistance of Andra Sanchez, our nanny. She has kept the ship of our household running for the past three years with patience, love, and humor.

I also must thank my parents, Mark and Martha Campbell, and my in-laws, Leonardo and Leticia Severino. All have given generously of their time to support our family, even traveling across the country to help out. I am who I am because of my parents' love and encouragement, their support of me in all my endeavors, and the sharing of their passions, from baking and music to reading and theology. Becoming a parent myself has made me appreciate even more deeply their love and wisdom.

In the final push before the confirmation, I tried to explain to my children that they were the reason I was doing this. I want them to grow up in a country devoted to the rule of law and in which ideas are debated vigorously, but civilly. They will be the ones living in the America governed by this Supreme Court, and it will be their justices'—or their own—confirmations that we hope will be run in a more humane way in the future.

Mollie Hemingway

My contribution to this book would not have been possible without the support of my colleagues, family, and friends. Thank you.

This book's achievements are the result of the work of Carrie Severino, a shockingly good journalist, in addition to being a spectacular attorney. Her precision for details and word choice, brilliant legal mind, and tenacious pursuit of information were a thrill to observe. That she worked around the clock while caring for her six beautiful children, including a baby babbling on her lap, made it only more impressive. She could not have done her remarkable work without her husband Roger's support. His input from the beginning helped focus and clarify the project as well. I went into the project admiring both of them and came out of it absolutely loving them. For several months, I spoke more each day to Carrie than to everyone else in my life combined.

My colleagues at *The Federalist* enthusiastically and graciously supported my work. Thank you to Ben Domenech for his vision and for seeing my potential when so few others did. Sean Davis, who has become a professional partner in multiple ways, helped me think through interviews, research, and storylines. His edits, suggestions, and counsel kept me on course throughout. David Harsanyi, whom it is my joy and privilege to work with, freely gave advice based on his experience of writing many books. I am beyond grateful to, and humbled by, Joy Pullmann for not just working around the clock, but for picking up extra work while I was unavailable. Madeline Osburn has made *The Federalist* better each day with her infectiously cheerful attitude and work ethic and helped us immeasurably when we dealt with the death of our dear friend and colleague Bre Payton in December 2018. Bre's joyful spirit, abiding faith, and love for life were a constant source of comfort for me in the dark months following her death.

Thank you to my Fox News colleagues, who have taught me so much about journalism and broadcasting. Brit Hume saw potential in me and gave me confidence to try out a new medium. Charles Krauthammer encouraged me to find my voice and hold strong to it. Bret Baier and Howard Kurtz brought me on board and allowed me to participate in their excellent programs. Thank you also to Shannon Bream, Tucker Carlson, Laura Ingraham, Ashley Moir, and Mary Pat Dennert. A particular thank you to everyone in the hair and makeup room for transforming me night after night for readiness on the television, a task made more difficult the less sleep I got. They were some of my chief champions and encouragers when I grew weary.

My colleagues at Hillsdale College, Matthew Spalding and John Miller, provided ready counsel, supportive words, and excellent advice.

Thank you to my readers at *The Federalist* and viewers at Fox News. Their feedback and support gave me the courage to speak out in a city where conformity is demanded. While this book focuses on the key players in Washington, D.C., Carrie and I tried not to lose sight of the American people and their frustration with beltway politics.

Immanuel Lutheran Church, my spiritual home, continued its decades of support. Thank you to Pastor Christopher Esget for spiritual care. My friend Dolores Hardtke's regular encouragement over the years has been life-changing. Thank you to Kara Lloyd for the help and friendship. Many friends emotionally supported me in this process, none as much as Matthew Braun and Julia Habrecht. Thank you for listening to my stories and for unending hospitality. I thank God he brought them into my life. Thank you to Mary Diamond Stirewalt for pushing me to do broadcast work, teaching me how to do it, and for doing so much with so little credit and to Liz Sheld for a little bit of everything.

Thank you also to my parents, Larry and Carolyn Ziegler, and my siblings, Kirsten Pratt and Erich Ziegler, for putting up with me throughout my challenging adolescence, and inculcating in me a love of the Constitution. I will never forget watching the Thomas hearings with my mother while traveling through California that fall. My parents' conversations and debates stayed with me, as did their gracious giving of time to discuss politics, economics, and, most importantly, our Christian faith. Thank you also to my aunts and uncles, cousins, and in-laws, particularly Bill and Kathy Hemingway, for their unflinching support. A special word of thanks for my friends Erica Beeney Wyatt and Patrice Wittrig Stilley, whose intelligence inspired me and challenged me to reach new heights.

Because of an implausibly short timeline, my husband and children spent months without my full participation in home life. My children took to sleeping in my office to spend time with me, which simultaneously wracked me with guilt and gave me such comfort on long nights. Mark, as he has for nearly thirteen years, kept us all healthy and happy. He has always been my biggest supporter, and I am thankful God blessed me with such an amazing head to our household. The love in my heart for him is inexpressible. When Carrie and I began this project, Mark helped us envision what it could be, encouraged us to emphasize storytelling, and pushed us over the finish line.

Notes

Chapter One: The Primary

1. Adam Liptak and Maggie Haberman, "Inside the White House's Quiet Campaign to Create a Supreme Court Opening," *New York Times*, June 29, 2018, A1.
2. *Obergefell v. Hodges*, 576 U.S. ___ (2015).
3. *Roe v. Wade*, 410 U.S. 113 (1973).
4. Jeffrey Toobin (@JeffreyToobin), "Anthony Kennedy is retiring. Abortion will be illegal in twenty states in 18 months. #SCOTUS," Twitter, June 27, 2018, 11:06 a.m., https://twitter.com/jeffreytoobin/status/1012034512312832001.
5. Adam Liptak and Maggie Haberman, "Inside the White House's Quiet Campaign to Create a Supreme Court Opening," *New York Times*, June 29, 2018, A1.
6. Neera Tanden (@neeratanden), "Just to state this: Justice Kennedy's son gave a billion dollar loan to Trump when no one would give him a dime, and Justice Kennedy has been ruling in favor of the Trump Administration position for 2 years as the Court decides 5-4 case after 5-4 case," Twitter, June 29, 2018, 4:54 a.m., https://twitter.com/neeratanden/status/1012665534297624577.
7. Salvador Rizzo, "The thinly sourced theories about Trump's loans and Justice Kennedy's son," *Washington Post*, July 12, 2018, https://www.washingtonpost.com/news/fact-checker/wp/2018/07/12/untangling-the-links-between-trump-deutsche-bank-and-justice-kennedys-son/; Katie Akin, "Did Justice Kennedy quit due to family ties to Trump and Russia?" Politifact, July 10, 2018, https://www.politifact.com/truth-o-meter/statements/2018/jul/10/blog-posting/did-justice-kennedy-quit-due-family-ties-trump-and/.
8. Ian Millhiser, "Justice Kennedy deserves this nasty, unflinching sendoff," ThinkProgress, https://thinkprogress.org/kennedy-was-a-bad-justice-76e464024d78/.
9. Chris Matthews, "Justice Kennedy Announces Retirement From Supreme Court," *MSNBC Live with Katy Tur*, MSNBC, June 27, 2018, https://archive.org/details/MSNBCW_20180627_180000_MSNBC_Live_With_Katy_Tur/start/2106/end/2166.
10. Mitch McConnell, "Senator McConnell on Justice Kennedy Retirement and Replacement," C-SPAN, video file, June 28, 2018, https://www.c-span.org/video/?447582-3/senator-mcconnell-justice-kennedy-retirement-replacement.
11. "SCOTUS Agrees with Kavanaugh," Senate RPC, July 24, 2018, https://www.rpc.senate.gov/policy-papers/scotus-agrees-with-kavanaugh.
12. Jan Crawford Greenburg, *Supreme Conflict: The Inside Story of the Struggle for Control of the United States Supreme Court* (New York: Penguin, 2007), 61.

13. Jeffrey Toobin, "Holding Court," *New Yorker*, March 19, 2012, https://www.newyorker.com/magazine/2012/03/26/holding-court.

14. Dan Burns, "Online bettors see Kavanaugh as likely U.S. Supreme Court nominee," Reuters, June 27, 2018, https://www.reuters.com/article/us-usa-court-kennedy-bets/online-bettors-see-kavanaugh-as-likely-u-s-supreme-court-nominee-idUSKBN1JN350.

15. Michael D. Shear and Maggie Haberman, "Trump Interviews 4 Supreme Court Prospects in Rush to Name Replacement," *New York Times*, July 2, 2018, https://www.nytimes.com/2018/07/02/us/politics/trump-supreme-court-nomination.html.

16. Michael D. Shear and Thomas Kaplan, "Court Vacancy in Election Year Jolts the Parties," *New York Times*, June 29, 2018.

17. Ruth Graham, "Amy Coney Barrett Is Allegedly a Member of a Religious Group That's Been Called a 'Cult,'" *Slate*, July 3, 2018, https://slate.com/human-interest/2018/07/amy-coney-barretts-alleged-religious-group-people-of-praise-what-is-it.html.

18. JCN, "Judicial Crisis Network Launches #AnotherGreatJustice, a Seven-Figure Ad-Buy on Supreme Court Vacancy," Judicial Crisis Network, June 27, 2018, https://judicialnetwork.com/in-the-news/judicial-crisis-network-launches-anothergreatjustice-a-seven-figure-ad-buy-on-supreme-court-vacancy/.

19. Edith Roberts, "Potential nominee profile: Brett Kavanaugh," SCOTUSblog, June 28, 2018, https://www.scotusblog.com/2018/06/potential-nominee-profile-brett-kavanaugh/.

20. Christopher Jacobs, "How Potential SCOTUS Pick Brett Kavanaugh Wrote a Roadmap For Saving Obamacare," *The Federalist*, July 2, 2018, http://thefederalist.com/2018/07/02/potential-scotus-pick-brett-kavanaugh-wrote-roadmap-saving-obamacare/.

21. David French, "Brett Kavanaugh Is an Excellent Judge, but Is He the Best Choice?," *National Review*, July 5, 2018, https://www.nationalreview.com/2018/07/brett-kavanaugh-supreme-court-potential-pick/.

22. Sarah E. Pitlyk, "Judge Brett Kavanaugh's Impeccable Record of Constitutional Conservatism," *National Review*, July 3, 2018, https://www.nationalreview.com/2018/07/judge-brett-kavanaughs-impeccable-record-of-constitutional-conservatism/.

23. Ed Whelan, "Contra Ben Shapiro on Judge Kavanaugh," *National Review*, June 28, 2018, https://www.nationalreview.com/bench-memos/contra-ben-shapiro-on-judge-kavanaugh/.

24. Ben Shapiro, "THE RUN-DOWN: Here's What You Need To Know About Trump's Top 5 Possible Nominees," The Daily Wire, June 27, 2018, https://www.dailywire.com/news/32411/run-down-heres-what-you-need-know-about-trumps-top-ben-shapiro.

25. Richard Wolf, "Basketball, Popeyes, 2 Live Crew: The year Neil Gorsuch and Brett Kavanaugh clerked for Anthony Kennedy," *USA Today*, August 30, 2018,

https://www.usatoday.com/story/news/politics/2018/08/30/brett-kavanaugh-neil-gorsuch-learned-supreme-court-ropes-together/1050836002/.

26. Benny Johnson, "Movement Conservatives Fume at Trump SCOTUS Favorite: 'This is the Low-Energy Jeb Bush Pick,'" *Daily Caller,* July 3, 2018, https://dailycaller.com/2018/07/03/conservatives-trump-supreme-court-brett-kavanaugh/.

27. Such requests for feedback have a lengthy history. George Washington reportedly kept correspondence from people proposing themselves or others to the Supreme Court in a drawer in his New York office. When visitors would arrive, he'd spread out the letters on the top of his desk and solicit their thoughts. John Anthony Maltese, *The Selling of Supreme Court Nominees* (Baltimore, Maryland: Johns Hopkins University Press, 1995), 24.

28. Maggie Haberman and Jonathan Martin, "McConnell Prods Trump On Nominee To the Court," *New York Times,* July 8, 2018, A16.

29. Mark Landler and Maggie Haberman, "President Has the Perfect Template for His Second Nominee: His First. Order Reprints," *New York Times,* July 6, 2018, A15.

30. Philip Elliott, "Inside Donald Trump's Supreme Court Deliberations," *Time,* July 8, 2018, http://time.com/5332628/inside-donald-trumps-supreme-court-deliberations/.

31. 2 Corinthians 12:7–10, New American Bible (Revised Edition).

Chapter Two: The List

1.   His speech took place four months, nine days before the November 3, 1992, election and six months, twenty-six days before Bush left office. "Biden in 1992: President Should Not Name Supreme Court Nominee Until After The November Election," RealClearPolitics, February 22, 2016, https://www.realclearpolitics.com/video/2016/02/22/biden_in_1992_bush_should_not_name_a_nominee_until_after_the_november_election.html.

2.   "Private: Text of Senator Schumer's Speech," American Constitution Society, ACSblog, July 27, 2007, https://www.acslaw.org/acsblog/text-of-senator-schumers-speech/.

3.   Burgess Everett and Glenn Thrush, "McConnell throws down the gauntlet: No Scalia replacement under Obama," *Politico,* February 13, 2016, https://www.politico.com/story/2016/02/mitch-mcconnell-antonin-scalia-supreme-court-nomination-219248.

4.   Ted Barrett, Manu Raju, and Laurie Ure, "Kirk blasts GOP leaders for inaction on Supreme Court nominee," CNN, March 29, 2016, https://www.cnn.com/2016/03/29/politics/merrick-garland-supreme-court-republican-meeting/index.html.

5.   Manu Raju, "In reversal, GOP senator says he does not favor hearings for Garland," CNN, April 1, 2016, https://www.cnn.com/2016/04/01/politics/jerry-moran-merrick-garland-supreme-court-obama/index.html.

6. Mike DeBonis, "GOP senator 'more convinced than ever' that Garland should get hearing," *Washington Post*, April 5, 2016, https://www.washingtonpost.com/news/powerpost/wp/2016/04/05/gop-senator-more-convinced-than-ever-that-garland-should-get-hearing/.

7. Burgess Everett, "Flake says it might be Garland time," *Politico*, October 20, 2016, https://www.politico.com/story/2016/10/jeff-flake-merrick-garland-vote-supreme-court-230109.

8. "Grassley Statement on Justice Scalia," Chuck Grassley Senate website, News Releases, February 13, 2016, https://www.grassley.senate.gov/news/news-releases/grassley-statement-justice-scalia.

9. Jennifer Steinhauer and David M. Herszenhorn, "Charles Grassley Faces Formidable Challenger in Iowa Senate Race," *New York Times*, March 3, 2016, https://www.nytimes.com/2016/03/04/us/politics/charles-grassley-patty-judge-iowa-senate-race.html.

10. Julie Hirschfeld Davis and David M. Herszenhorn, "White House Is Said to Be Vetting Iowa Judge for Supreme Court Seat," *New York Times*, March 2, 2016, https://www.nytimes.com/2016/03/03/us/politics/white-house-vetting-jane-kelly-judge-supreme-court.html.

11. Federal judges hold their seats for life but become eligible for "senior" status after age sixty-five based on a formula combining their age and years on the bench. Senior judges officially vacate their seat and no longer take part in circuit-wide "en banc" hearings or interim motions. They often remain relatively engaged in the business of judging, however, opting to carry up to a full load of regular cases or traveling to sit on cases in other circuits. A major incentive to take senior status is the generous pension: full salary at the time of retirement, plus cost-of-living increases; "Pro-life Women Sound the Alarm: Donald Trump is Unacceptable," Susan B. Anthony List, January 26, 2016, https://www.sba-list.org/home/pro-life-women-sound-the-alarmdonald-trump-is-unacceptable.

12. Paige Winfield Cunningham, "How the November election could alter the future of abortion," *Washington Examiner*, January 31, 2016, https://www.washingtonexaminer.com/how-the-november-election-could-alter-the-future-of-abortion.

13. "Donald Trump: The Full 'With All Due Respect' Interview," interview by Mark Halperin and John Heilemann, Bloomberg, August 26, 2015, https://www.bloomberg.com/news/videos/2015-08-26/donald-trump-the-full-with-all-due-respect-interview.

14. Paige Winfield Cunningham, "How the November election could alter the future of abortion," *Washington Examiner*, January 31, 2016, https://www.washingtonexaminer.com/how-the-november-election-could-alter-the-future-of-abortion.

15. Mark Hemingway, "Cruz Control," *National Review*, April 16, 2009, https://www.nationalreview.com/magazine/2009/05/04/cruz-control/.

16. *Washington Post* Staff, "Wednesday's GOP Debate Transcript, annotated," Washington *Post*, September 16, 2015, https://www.washingtonpost.com/news/the-fix/wp/2015/09/16/annotated-transcript-september-16-gop-debate/.

17. Sahil Kapur, "Ted Cruz Vows to Put Hard-Core Conservatives on Supreme Court," Bloomberg, December 2, 2015, https://www.bloomberg.com/news/articles/2015-12-02/ted-cruz-vows-to-put-hard-core-conservatives-on-the-supreme-court.

18. While federal judges are generally nominated by the president and must be confirmed by the Senate before taking office, the Constitution provides for unilateral appointments by the president for vacancies that occur "during the recess of the Senate." U.S. Constitution, Article II, section 2. Judges so appointed must be confirmed by the Senate before the next session of Congress ends or their appointment expires. Both Warren and Brennan were ultimately confirmed by the Senate.

19. Eisenhower did carry the historically Catholic and Democrat strongholds of New Jersey, Rhode Island, Massachusetts, and New York in the 1956 election, just one month after Brennan was confirmed. It is not clear how much Brennan's appointment contributed to this victory, however, as he had won those same states in 1952 as well. See Stephan J. Wermiel, "The Nomination of Justice Brennan: Eisenhower's Mistake? A Look at the Historical Record," *Constitutional Commentary* 11 (1995): 533.

20. Patricia Brennan, "Seven Justices, On Camera," *Washington Post*, October 6, 1996, Y06.

21. *Brown v. Board of Education of Topeka*, 347 U.S. 483 (1954).

22. *Engel v. Vitale*, 370 U.S. 421 (1962); *School District of Abington Township v. Schempp*, 374 U.S. 203 (1963).

23. See, e.g., *Mapp v. Ohio*, 367 U.S. 643 (1961); *Miranda v. Arizona*, 384 U.S. 436 (1966); *Katz v. United States*, 389 U.S. 347 (1967).

24. *Griswold v. Connecticut*, 381 U.S. 479 (1965).

25. Ibid., 484–85.

26. Ibid., 507 (Black, J., dissenting), 527 (Stewart, J., dissenting).

27. Ibid., 521 (Black, J., dissenting).

28. *Roe v. Wade*, 410 U.S. 113, 152 (1973).

29. No less an originalist scholar than Robert Bork called *Brown* "a great and correct decision," but added that it "was supported by a very weak opinion." While making his own originalist case for why the Fourteenth Amendment's Equal Protection Clause did require overturning Jim Crow laws, he worried that the decision appeared to legitimize a type of judging that put results before reasoning. Judging by the *Brown* decision, the Court clearly didn't think the "obvious moral rightness" of the result was supported by the history and text of the Constitution itself. So it viewed itself as "depart[ing] from the original understanding in order to do the socially desirable thing." The irony, from Bork's perspective, is that the original understanding in fact compelled that very result. See Robert H. Bork, *The Tempting of America* (New York: The Free Press, 1990), 75–76. Other originalists, like Michael McConnell, have presented persuasive evidence that the generation that ratified the Fourteenth Amendment believed it required the desegregation of schools and other public facilities. See

Michael W. McConnell, "The Originalist Case for *Brown v. Board of Education*," *Harvard Journal of Law and Public Policy* 19 (1995): 457.

30. Learned Hand, *The Bill of Rights: The Oliver Wendell Holmes Lectures* (New York: Atheneum, 1986), 54–55.

31. Benjamin Eric Sasse, "The Anti-Madalyn Majority: Secular Left, Religious Right, and the Rise of Reagan's America," Dissertation for the Graduate School of Yale University, May 2004, https://blurblawg.typepad.com/files/sasse-dissertaiton.pdf.

32. *Reynolds v. Sims*, 377 U.S. 533 (1964).

33. William G. Ross, "The Role of Judicial Issues in Presidential Campaigns," *Santa Clara Law Review* 42 (2002): 429–30.

34. The *Miranda* dissenters were eloquent in their criticism of the Court's creation of new law in that case. Justice Harlan wrote, "Nothing in the letter or the spirit of the Constitution or in the precedents squares with the heavy-handed and one-sided action that is so precipitously taken by the Court in the name of fulfilling its constitutional responsibilities. The foray which the Court makes today brings to mind the wise and farsighted words of Mr. Justice Jackson in *Douglas v. Jeannette*…'This Court is forever adding new stories to the temples of constitutional law, and the temples have a way of collapsing when one story too many is added.'" *Miranda*, 384 U.S. at 525–26 (Harlan, J., dissenting). Justice White added, "The proposition that the privilege against self-incrimination forbids in-custody interrogation without the warnings specified in the majority opinion and without a clear waiver of counsel has no significant support in the history of the privilege or in the language of the Fifth Amendment." Ibid., 526 (White, J., dissenting). White also lambasted the majority for not even examining the facts of the cases they decided to determine whether coercion was present. Neither law nor fact mattered where there was a convenient opportunity to change the Constitution in a direction for which they had five votes.

35. Ross, "The Role of Judicial Issues in Presidential Campaigns," 436.

36. In a 1969 memo favorably received by President Nixon, aide Tom Charles Huston said judicial nominations were the "least considered aspect of Presidential power," and urged the president to establish "*his* criteria" and "*his* machinery for insuring that the criteria are met." When done, the "appointments will be *his*, in fact, as in theory." Nixon responded, "Have this analysis in mind when making judicial nominations." John Anthony Maltese, *The Selling of Supreme Court Nominees*, (Baltimore: Johns Hopkins University Press, 1995), 2–4.

37. George F. Will, "George Will: Unleash the high court," *Washington Post*, June 15, 2012, http://www.washingtonpost.com/opinions/george-will-unleash-the-high-court/2012/06/15/gJQAMwvpfV_story.html.

38. Ford specifically endorsed Stevens's views on "the secular character of the Establishment Clause and the Free Exercise Clause, on securing procedural safeguards in criminal case and on the constitution's broad grant of regulatory authority to Congress." He also praised the justice's wit and sense of humor. Letter from Gerald R. Ford to William Michael Treanor (September 21, 2005),

reproduced in William Michael Treanor, "Introduction: The Jurisprudence of Justice Stevens Symposium," *Fordham Law Review* 74 (2006): 1559.

39. *Chevron v. National Resources Defense Council*, 467 U.S. 837 (1984).
40. *District of Columbia v. Heller*, 554 US 570 (2008).
41. "Republican Party Platform of 1980," The American Presidency Project, July 15, 1980, https://www.presidency.ucsb.edu/node/273420.
42. Elizabeth Olson, "Justice Potter Stewart, who has served on the Supreme. . .," UPI, June 18, 1981, https://www.upi.com/Archives/1981/06/18/ Justice-Potter-Stewart-who-has-served-on-the-Supreme/7197361684800/.
43. "Transcript of Ronald Reagan's Remarks at News Conference in Los Angeles," *New York Times*, October 15, 1980, A24.
44. Jan Crawford Greenburg, *Supreme Conflict: The Inside Story of the Struggle for Control of the United States Supreme Court* (New York: Penguin, 2007), 13.
45. Senator Howell Heflin joked about the Italian American lovefest during Scalia's hearing, trying to find his own excuse to praise Scalia's heritage. "I would be remiss if I did not mention the fact that my great-great-grandfather married a widow who was married first to an Italian American." Joan Biskupic, *American Original: The Life and Constitution of Supreme Court Justice Antonin Scalia* (New York: Sarah Crichton Books, 2009), 110.
46. Ibid., 110, 121.
47. "Senator Kennedy Opposes Bork Nomination," C-SPAN, July 1, 1987, https:// www.c-span.org/video/?c4594844/senator-kennedy-opposes-bork-nomination.
48. 432 U.S. 43 (1977).
49. Jeffrey Toobin, "Jeffrey Toobin: Kennedy and the Court," *New Yorker*, August 26, 2009, https://www.newyorker.com/news/news-desk/ jeffrey-toobin-kennedy-and-the-court.
50. PFAWdotorg, "1987 Robert Bork TV ad, narrated by Gregory Peck," YouTube video, July 16, 2008, https://www.youtube.com/watch?v=NpFe10lkF3Y.
51. Maltese, *The Selling of Supreme Court Nominees*, 88.
52. Ibid., 133.
53. Statement of Honorable Edward M. Kennedy, "Nomination of Justice William Hubbs Rehnquist," United States Senate Committee on the Judiciary, 99th Congress, 2nd Session. (Washington, D.C.: U.S. Government Printing Office, 1987), 14.
54. Office of Legal Policy, Department of Justice, *By and With the Advice and Consent of the Senate: The Bork and Kennedy Confirmation Hearings and the Implications for Judicial Independence* (Washington: American Conservative Union, January 31, 1989), 6.
55. "bork," *Merriam-Webster's Collegiate Dictionary*, 11th ed. (Springfield, MA: Merriam-Webster, 2003), https://www.merriam-webster.com/dictionary/bork.
56. "Robert Bork Discusses on the Committee Report of His Nomination," C-SPAN, October 9, 1987, https://www.c-span.org/video/?825-1/robert-bork-discusses-committee-report-nomination&start=36.
57. Jan Crawford Greenburg, *Supreme Conflict*, 53.

58. Linda Greenhouse and Special to the New York Times, "Reagan Nominates Anthony Kennedy to Supreme Court," *New York Times*, November 12, 1987, A1.
59. Associated Press, "Reagan, on 3rd Try, Picks Californian for High Court: 'Bit Wiser' After Two Defeats," *Los Angeles Times*, November 11, 1987, http://articles.latimes.com/1987-11-11/news/mn-13624_1_supreme-court.
60. Linda Greenhouse, "While Examining Kennedy, Senators Look Back at Bork," *New York Times*, December 20, 1987, section 4, page 1.
61. Linda Greenhouse and Special to the New York Times, "The Year the Court Turned to the Right," *New York Times*, July 7, 1989, A1.
62. "Chief Justice Souter?" *Wall Street Journal*, February 29, 2000, https://www.wsj.com/articles/SB951789438683921325.
63. Jeremy Rabkin, "The Sorry Tale of David Souter, Stealth Justice," *Weekly Standard*, November 6, 1995.
64. John Fund, "The Borking Begins," *Wall Street Journal*, January 8, 2001.
65. Senator Warren Rudman, a Republican who endorsed Souter, later said he would have voted against Thomas if he had been the decisive vote and declared that confirming Thomas was "a vote I'm not proud of." "Interview with Warren Rudman," interview by Janet E. Heininger and Stephen Knott, Edward M. Kennedy Oral History Project, May 16, 2006; Kevin Merida and Michael Fletcher, *Supreme Discomfort: The Divided Soul of Clarence Thomas* (New York: Doubleday, 2007), 203.
66. Ross, "The Role of Judicial Issues in Presidential Campaigns," 461.
67. Ibid.
68. *National Federation of Independent Business v. Sebelius*, 567 U.S. 519 (2012); *King v. Burwell*, 576 U.S. ___ (2015).
69. Joan Biskupic, *The Chief* (New York: Basic Books, 2019): 234–48.
70. Colin Campbell, "Donald Trump dials up his attacks: 'Ted Cruz gave us Obamacare,'" Business Insider, February 4, 2016, https://www.businessinsider.com/donald-trump-ted-cruz-obamacare-2016-2.
71. Fred Barnes, "Bush Scalia," *Weekly Standard*, July 5, 1999, https://www.weeklystandard.com/fred-barnes/bush-scalia.
72. "October 8, 2004 Debate Transcript," Commission on Presidential Debates, October 8, 2004, https://www.debates.org/voter-education/debate-transcripts/october-8-2004-debate-transcript/.
73. Robert Barnes, "How the Bush-nominated Chief Justice Roberts became target in GOP debates," *Washington Post*, September 17, 2015, https://www.washingtonpost.com/politics/chief-justice-roberts-is-target-of-conservative-fire-in-gop-debates/2015/09/17/c66c62ba-5d43-11e5-8e9e-dce8a2a2a679_story.html?utm_term=.2dc37c186d9c.
74. Jessica Hopper, "Ted Cruz Plans to Filibuster Any Supreme Court Nominee Made by President Obama," ABC News, February 14, 2016, https://abcnews.go.com/Politics/ted-cruz-plans-filibuster-supreme-court-nominee-made/story?id=36922959.

75. Jon Prior, "GOP Candidates spar over Chief Justice Roberts," *Politico*, February 14, 2016, https://www.politico.com/story/2016/02/scalia-roberts-supreme-court-justices-219284.

76. Melinda Henneberger, "In Death, Scalia may Succeed in Blocking Trump," *Roll Call,* February 15, 2016, https://www.rollcall.com/news/in-death-scalia-may-succeed-in-blocking-trump.

77. Textualism is what Justice Scalia referred to as the "commonsensical interpretive principle" that judges should interpret the words of a statute according to their meanings as reasonably understood in context when they were enacted. Antonin Scalia and Bryan A. Garner, *Reading Law: The Interpretation of Legal Texts* (St. Paul: Thomson/West: 2012), 15.

78. "Donald Trump News Conference," C-SPAN, March 21, 2016, https://www.c-span.org/video/?407049-1/donald-trump-news-conference-washington-dc& start=2330.

79. Malcolm explains that he considered putting together a longer list of judges and would have included Judges Neil Gorsuch and Ray Kethledge, who ultimately made it onto the Trump list. But given the time crunch and his inability to vet so many people quickly, he settled on a shorter but safer list with the qualification that he didn't view it as exclusive.

80. It was a good call. Judge Rogers Brown retired just eight months into Trump's presidency and would be replaced by McGahn's own deputy, Greg Katsas.

81. Don Willett (@JusticeWillett), "Donald Trump haiku—Who would the Donald Name to #SCOTUS? The mind reels. *weeps—can't finish tweet*," Twitter, June 16, 2015, 10:09 a.m., https://twitter.com/JusticeWillett/status/6108567912 91916290.

82. Lawrence Hurley, "Trump's Supreme Court list: all conservative, some provocative," Reuters, May 19, 2016, https://www.reuters.com/article/us-usa-election-trump-court-list/trumps-supreme-court-list-all-conservative-some-provocative-idUSKCN0YA2XV; Stephanie Mencimer, "Trump's Supreme Court Short List is Really, Really Anti-Contraception," *Mother Jones*, May 18, 2016, https://www.motherjones.com/politics/2016/05/trumps-supreme-court-nominees-nod-towards-evangelicals/; Nina Totenberg, "Trump's Supreme Court List Might Reassure Conservatives, But Leaves Out Big Names," NPR, May 18, 2016, https://www.npr.org/2016/05/18/478609623/trumps-supreme-court-list-might-reassure-conservatives-but-leaves-off-big-names.

83. Adam Liptak, "Trump's Supreme Court List: Ivy League is Out, the Heartland is In," *New York Times*, November 15, 2016, A21.

84. Ted Cruz, Facebook, September 23, 2016, https://www.facebook.com/tedcruzpage/posts/10154476728267464.

85. While the Garland nomination threatened to be big news earlier in the campaign, it became such a non-issue that the Obama nominee's name wasn't even mentioned during the Democratic National Committee convention in Philadelphia. Concern for the courts simply did not motivate Democratic voters the way that it was energizing Republicans.

86. Mark Tushnet, "Abandoning Defensive Crouch Liberal Constitutionalism," Balkinization, May 6, 2016, https://balkin.blogspot.com/2016/05/abandoning-defensive-crouch-liberal.html.

87. *Citizens United v. Federal Election Commission*, 558 U.S. 310 (2010).

88. Philip Bump, "A quarter of Republicans voted for Trump to get Supreme Court picks – and it paid off," *Washington Post,* June 26, 2018, https://www. washingtonpost.com/news/politics/wp/2018/06/26/a-quarter-of-republicans-voted-for-trump-to-get-supreme-court-picks-and-it-paid-off/.

89. Philip Rucker and Seung Min Kim, "'We have to pick a great one': Inside Trump's plan for a new Supreme Court justice," *Washington Post*, June 30, 2018, https://www.washingtonpost.com/politics/we-have-to-pick-a-great-one-inside-trumps-plan-for-a-new-supreme-court-justice/2018/06/30/610dcd4e-7bb0-11e8-80be-6d32e182a3bc_story.html.

90. Mollie Hemingway, "Fact, not opinion," Getreligion, October 9, 2006, https:// www.getreligion.org/getreligion/2006/10/fact-not-opinion.

Chapter Three: Complicit in Evil

1. Robin Givhan, "Back to the '50s/Roberts family image was a little too perfect," SFGate, July 31, 2005, https://www.sfgate.com/living/article/BACK-TO-THE-50S-Roberts-family-image-was-a-2651504.php.

2. "Transcript of President Bush's Nomination of Miers to the Supreme Court," National Public Radio, October 3, 2005, https://www.npr.org/templates/story/story.php?storyId=4933801.

3. "Remarks by President Trump Announcing Judge Brett M. Kavanaugh as the Nominee for Associate Justice of the Supreme Court of the United States," White House website, July 9, 2018, https://www.whitehouse.gov/briefings-statements/remarks-president-trump-announcing-judge-brett-m-kavanaugh-nominee-associate-justice-supreme-court-united-states/.

4. "The Confirmation Hearings of Judge David Souter: The Legal and Political Context," NARAL, https://www.govinfo.gov/content/pkg/GPO-CHRG-SOUTER/pdf/GPO-CHRG-SOUTER-5-48-1.pdf, 371.

5. "Trump Announces Brett Kavanaugh as Supreme Court Nominee: Full Video and Transcript," *New York Times,* July 9, 2018, https://www.nytimes.com/2018/07/09/us/politics/trump-supreme-court-announcement-transcript.html.

6. Elena Kagan, "Speech on Being Nominated to Serve as U.S. Supreme Court Justice," American Rhetoric website, May 10, 2010, https://www.americanrhetoric.com/speeches/elenakaganusscnomination.htm.

7. Sonia Sotomayor, "Full Text: Judge Sonia Sotomayor's Speech," *Time,* May 26, 2009, http://content.time.com/time/politics/article/0,8599,1900940,00.html.

8. "WTAS: Continued Support for Judge Brett Kavanaugh's Nomination to the Supreme Court," White House website, July 10, 2018, https://www.whitehouse.gov/briefings-statements/wtas-continued-support-judge-brett-kavanaughs-nomination-supreme-court/.

9. Aaron Blake, "Brett Kavanaugh's remarkably political intro speech," *Washington Post*, July 10, 2018, https://www.washingtonpost.com/news/the-fix/wp/2018/07/10/brett-kavanaughs-remarkably-political-intro-speech/.

10. "Colbert Has A Lot To Say About Trump's Supreme Court Pick Brett Kavanaugh, 'Cover Model for Generic Dad's Monthly,'" Digg, http://digg.com/video/brett-kavanaugh-colbert.

11. NARAL (@NARAL), "We'll be DAMNED if we're going to let five men— including some frat boy named Brett—strip us of our hard-won bodily autonomy and reproductive rights. #StopKavanaugh #SaveRoe," Twitter, July 10, 2018, 5:04 p.m., https://twitter.com/NARAL/status/1016835475494064128.

12. Aaron Blake, "Brett Kavanaugh's first claim as a Supreme Court nominee was bizarre," *Washington Post*, July 10, 2018, https://www.washingtonpost.com/news/the-fix/wp/2018/07/10/brett-kavanaughs-first-claim-as-a-supreme-court-nominee-was-bizarre/.

13. "Trump Announces Brett Kavanaugh as Supreme Court Nominee: Full Video and Transcript," *New York Times*, July 9, 2018, https://www.nytimes.com/2018/07/09/us/politics/trump-supreme-court-announcement-transcript.html.

14. Bob Casey (@SenBobCasey), "I will oppose the nomination the President will make tonight because it represents a corrupt bargain with the far Right, big corporations, and Washington special interests," Twitter, July 9, 2018, 8:50 a.m., https://twitter.com/senbobcasey/status/1016348863328931840?lang=en.

15. The Editorial Board, "Democrats: Do Not Surrender the Judiciary," *New York Times*, July 6, 2018, https://www.nytimes.com/2018/07/06/opinion/democrats-fight-trump-supreme-court.html.

16. "Schumer Statement on Nomination of Judge Brett Kavanaugh to the Supreme Court," Senate Democrats website, July 9, 2018, https://www.democrats.senate.gov/schumer-statement-on-nomination-of-judge-brett-kavanaugh-to-the-supreme-court.

17. William Cummings, "Women's March slammed for goof in statement on Kavanaugh Supreme Court nomination," *USA Today*, July 10, 2018, https://www.usatoday.com/story/news/politics/onpolitics/2018/07/10/womens-march-gaffe-kavanaugh-statement-derided-and-mocked/773650002/.

18. Jim Geraghty (@jimgeraghty), "Somebody rushed this out!" Twitter, July 9, 2018, 6:12 p.m., https://twitter.com/jimgeraghty/status/1016490300364206080?ref_src=twsrc%5Etfw%7Ctwcamp%5Etweetembed%7Ctwterm%5E1016490300364206080&ref_url=https%3A%2F%2Fwww.washingtontimes.com%2Fnews%2F2018%2Fjul%2F9%2Fwomens-march-mocked-press-release-opposing-supreme%2F.

19. Ben Sasse (@BenSasse), "Went to the Supreme Court to talk to the protestors. But it turns out to be a Mad-Lib protest. #Fill-In-The-Blank," Twitter, January 31, 2017, 7:01 p.m., https://twitter.com/BenSasse/status/826626482642489345.

20. Davis Richardson, "Liberal Activist Groups Prepared to Protest All of Trump's SCOTUS Picks," Observer, July 10, 2018, https://observer.com/2018/07/liberal-activist-groups-protest-trump-scotus-pick/.

21. "Center for American Progress Rally at Supreme Court," C-SPAN, July 9, 2018, https://www.c-span.org/video/?448152-1/lawmakers-activists-protest-judge-brett-kavanaugh-nomination-supreme-court.

22. After working on President Bill Clinton's 1996 campaign, she worked as an aide in his White House. She also worked for Hillary Clinton on her senate campaign, in her senate office, and on her 2008 and 2016 campaigns. She was then one of the four leaders of Hillary Clinton's 2016 transition team, during which time her emails to John Podesta were exposed on WikiLeaks. She was so close to the Clinton family that then-First Lady Hillary Clinton threw her a baby shower at the White House. See "Neera Tanden," Influence Watch, https://www.influencewatch.org/person/neera-tanden/; "Center for American Progress Rally at Supreme Court," C-SPAN, July 9, 2018, https://www.c-span.org/video/?448152-1/lawmakers-activists-protest-judge-brett-kavanaugh-nomination-supreme-court.

23. Shannon Bream (@ShannonBream), "Very few times I've felt threatened while out in the field. The mood here tonight is very volatile. Law enforcement appears to be closing down 1st Street in front of SCOTUS," Twitter, July 9, 2018, 6:31 p.m., https://twitter.com/shannonbream/status/1016495007249911809.

24. Tony Perkins, "On Trump's pick of Kavanaugh, conservatives should trust but verify," Washington Examiner, July 11, 2018, https://www.washingtonexaminer.com/opinion/on-trumps-pick-of-kavanaugh-conservatives-should-trust-but-verify.

25. Alyssa Milano (@Alyssa_Milano), "TRUMP SHOULD NOT BE ABLE TO CHOOSE A LIFETIME APPOINTEE WHILE HE IS UNDER FEDERAL INVESTIGATION. FULL STOP," Twitter, Jun 27, 2018, 10:20 p.m., https://twitter.com/Alyssa_Milano/status/1012204061817491456.

26. Paul Schiff Berman, "A Better Reason to Delay Kennedy's Replacement," New York Times, June 29, 2018, https://www.nytimes.com/2018/06/29/opinion/a-better-reason-to-delay-kennedys-replacement.html.

27. Adam J. White, "Rage at the End of Justice Kennedy's Camelot," Weekly Standard, June 30, 2018, https://www.weeklystandard.com/adam-j-white/liberal-law-professors-want-to-pack-the-supreme-court-after-trump-replaces-kennedy.

28. "Democrats Agree: Don't Delay SCOTUS Nominee," John Cornyn Senate website, June 28, 2018, https://www.cornyn.senate.gov/content/news/democrats-agree-don%E2%80%99t-delay-scotus-nominee.

29. Mark Walsh, "A 'view' from the East Room: The Brett Kavanaugh story," SCOTUSblog, July 10, 2018, https://www.scotusblog.com/2018/07/a-view-from-the-east-room-the-brett-kavanaugh-story/.

30. The organization's name changed in 2010 as it expanded its reach into more areas than simply confirmations. Although the group was active in the Sotomayor and Kagan confirmations during the Obama administration, as well

as in the fights over the use of the filibuster, there was a limit to how much could be done with a hostile administration. The group took the opportunity to expand its work into state judicial selection as well as commentary on major Supreme Court cases from a perspective of the same textualist and originalist philosophy it promoted in judicial nominees.

31. Patrick B. McGuigan and Dawn M. Weyrich, *Ninth Justice: The Fight for Bork* (Lanham, MD: University Press of America, 1990), 252–53.

32. R. H. Bork Jr., "The Media, Special Interests, and the Bork Nomination," in McGuigan and Weyrich, *Ninth Justice: The Fight for Bork* (Lanham, MD: University Press of America, 1990), 252.

33. Patrick B. McGuigan and Dawn M. Weyrich, *Ninth Justice: The Fight for Bork* (Washington D.C.: Free Congress Research and Education Foundation, 1990), 252 (media essay by Robert Bork Jr.).

34. The group had previously budgeted $7 million in support of Senator McConnell's efforts to keep the Scalia vacancy open to "let the people decide" on who would pick the next Supreme Court justice. When that effort was successful, they launched a $10 million campaign to confirm Gorsuch.

35. Amy Brittain, "Supreme Court nominee Brett Kavanaugh piled up credit card debt by purchasing Nationals tickets, White House says," *Washington Post*, July 11, 2018, https://www.washingtonpost.com/investigations/supreme-court-nominee-brett-kavanaugh-piled-up-credit-card-debt-by-purchasing-nationals-tickets-white-house-says/2018/07/11/8e3ad7d6-8460-11e8-9e80-403a221946a7_story.html.

36. Ariana Tobin and Justin Elliott, "Did You Go to a Washington Nationals Game With Supreme Court Nominee Brett Kavanaugh?" ProPublica, August 13, 2018, https://www.propublica.org/getinvolved/brett-kavanaugh-nationals-baseball-supreme-court.

37. Hailey Fuchs and Adelaide Feibel, "A sports junkie who are pasta with ketchup: Law school friends reflect on Kavanaugh's time at YLS," *Yale Daily News*, July 12, 2018, https://yaledailynews.com/blog/2018/07/12/a-sports-junkie-who-ate-pasta-with-ketchup-law-school-friends-reflect-on-kavanaughs-time-at-yls/.

38. "Kavanaugh Nomination Falters After Washington Post Publishes Shocking Editorial Claiming He Forgot Daughter's Piano Recital," The Onion, July 13, 2018, https://politics.theonion.com/kavanaugh-nomination-falters-after-washington-post-publ-1827581330.

39. *Emily's List v. Federal Election Commission*, 581 F.3d 1 (2009).

40. Neera Tanden (@neeratanden), "Just to state this: Justice Kennedy's son gave a billion dollar loan to Trump when no one would give him a dime, and Justice Kennedy has been ruling in favor of the Trump Administration position for 2 years as the Court decide 5-4 case after 5-4 case," Twitter, June 29, 2018, 4:54 a.m., https://twitter.com/neeratanden/status/1012665534297624577; "Can you imagine if this happened in the Obama Administration? If this were Justice Kagan and Obama? Both would be impeached immediately," Twitter June 29, 2018, 4:54 a.m., https://twitter.com/neeratanden/status/1012665696516562945.

The *Washington Post* fact-checker gave her statements four pinnochios. See Salvador Rizzo, "The thinly sourced theories about Trump's loans and Justice Kennedy's son," *Washington Post*, July 12, 2018, https://www.washingtonpost.com/news/fact-checker/wp/2018/07/12/untangling-the-links-between-trump-deutsche-bank-and-justice-kennedys-son/?utm_term=.2c940c9721d4.

41. Brett M. Kavanaugh, "Separation of Powers During the Forty-Fourth Presidency and Beyond," *Minnesota Law Review* 103, http://www.minnesotalawreview.org/wp-content/uploads/2012/01/Kavanaugh_MLR.pdf.

42. Ryan J. Foley and Curt Anderson, "Kavanaugh's ties to disgraced mentor loom over confirmation," August 29, 2018, Associated Press News, https://www.apnews.com/e37ba9bc11014b72a5db6f926f80eb42.

43. "Report on the Record of Supreme Court Nominee Brett M. Kavanaugh," Demos, https://www.demos.org/sites/default/files/publications/Record%20of%20Supreme%20Court%20Nominee%20Brett%20M%20Kavanaugh.pdf.

44. "Demand Justice," Facebook, August 18, 2018, https://www.facebook.com/wedemandjusticenow/videos/272437933362642/.

45. Thomas Jipping, "Opposing Kavanaugh by 'Whatever Means Necessary,'" *National Review*, September 24, 2018, https://www.nationalreview.com/bench-memos/opposing-kavanaugh-by-whatever-means-necessary/.

46. Karen Hosler, "Ashcroft confirmed amid fierce criticism," *Baltimore Sun*, February 2, 2001, https://www.baltimoresun.com/news/bs-xpm-2001-02-02-0102020249-story.html.

47. Neil A. Lewis, "Mixed Results for Bush in Battles Over Judges," *New York Times*, October 22, 2004, https://www.nytimes.com/2004/10/22/politics/campaign/mixed-results-for-bush-in-battles-over-judges.html; "Washington Talk; Democrats Readying for Judicial Fight," *New York Times*, May 1, 2001, https://www.nytimes.com/2001/05/01/us/washington-talk-democrats-readying-for-judicial-fight.html.

48. "'He Is Latino,'" *Wall Street Journal*, November 14, 2003, https://www.wsj.com/articles/SB106877910996248300.

49. The number was important since seven Democrats were enough to determine whether Democrats could filibuster and seven Republicans were enough to determine whether Republicans could invoke the "nuclear option" that got rid of the 60-vote cloture.

50. Several other Republican nominees were ultimately blocked by the filibuster: Miguel Estrada, Charles Pickering, Carolyn Kuhl, William Myers, and Henry Saad. All ultimately withdrew after having their votes blocked.

51. Michael Steele, "The SCOTUS nomination clearly demonstrates that elections have consequences," July 11, 2018, *The Hill*, https://thehill.com/opinion/judiciary/396476-the-scotus-nomination-clearly-demonstrates-elections-have-consequences.

52. Bill Scher, "Democrats Should Not Fear the Nuclear Option," *Politico Magazine*, February 2, 2017, https://www.politico.com/magazine/story/2017/02/democrats-should-not-fear-the-nuclear-option-214730.

Chapter Four: Mootings, Meetings, and Mobs

1. *United States v. Jones*, 565 U.S. 400 (2012).
2. *Brown v. Board of Education of Topeka*, 347 U.S. 483 (1954).
3. *Lawrence v. Texas*, 539 U.S. 558 (2003).
4. *Citizens United v. FEC*, 558 U.S. 310 (2010).
5. *Janus v. AFSCME*, No. 16-1466, 585 U.S. ___ (2018).
6. Justin Wm. Moyer, "74 arrested protesting Brett Kavanaugh's Supreme Court nomination on Capitol Hill," *Washington Post*, August 2, 2018, B03.
7. "Missouri: Trump vs. Clinton," RealClearPolitics, https://www.realclearpolitics.com/epolls/2016/president/mo/missouri_trump_vs_clinton-5609.html.
8. *Emily's List* v. *Federal Election Commission*, 581 F.3d 1 (D.C. Cir. 2009).
9. "Sen. Claire McCaskill–Missouri Contributors 2005–2018," OpenSecrets.org, https://www.opensecrets.org/members-of-congress/contributors?cid=N00027694&cycle=CAREER&type=I.
10. "Booker: Senators Who Support Trump's SCOTUS Pick are 'Complicit in Evil,'" Fox News Insider, July 25, 2018, https://insider.foxnews.com/2018/07/25/cory-booker-dems-who-support-trumps-scotus-pick-complicit-evil.
11. Patrick Leahy, "Kavanaugh's Long, Long Record," *New York Times*, July 24, 2018, A21.
12. Stephen Bates, "Brett Kavanaugh and the Starr Report: How Our Office Drafted the Impeachment Referral," LawFare, July 13, 2018, https://www.lawfareblog.com/brett-kavanaugh-and-starr-report-how-our-office-drafted-impeachment-referral.
13. Yuval Levin, "The Kavanaugh Paper Flow," *National Review*, July 11, 2018, https://eppc.org/publications/the-kavanaugh-paper-flow/.
14. "Questionnaire For Nominee to the Supreme Court," United States Senate Committee on the Judiciary, https://www.judiciary.senate.gov/imo/media/doc/Brett%20M.%20Kavanaugh%20SJQ%20(PUBLIC).pdf, 63.
15. "Judge Roberts' Judiciary Committee Questionnaire," United States Senate Committee on the Jusiciary, 54–59, on CFIF.org, https://www.cfif.org/htdocs/legislative_issues/federal_issues/hot_issues_in_congress/supreme_court_watch/roberts-judiciary-questionnaire.htm.
16. "Questionnaire For Nominee to the Supreme Court," United States Senate Committee on the Judiciary, https://www.judiciary.senate.gov/imo/media/doc/Neil%20M.%20Gorsuch%20SJQ%20(Public).pdf.
17. "Grassley: Kavanaugh Review Will Be Thorough and Fair, but No Taxpayer-Funded Fishing Expedition," Committee on the Judiciary website, July 18, 2018, https://www.judiciary.senate.gov/press/rep/releases/grassley-kavanaugh-review-will-be-thorough-and-fair-but-no-taxpayer-funded-fishing-expedition.
18. "Democratic Leaders on Judge Kavanaugh," C-SPAN via archive.org, July 31, 2018, https://archive.org/details/CSPAN_20180731_232900_Democratic_Leaders_on_Judge_Kavanaugh/start/120/end/180.
19. Thomas McKinless, "Senate GOP Stacks 167 Boxes to Illustrate Amount of Kavanaugh Papers Getting Released," *Roll Call*, August 2, 2018, https://www.

rollcall.com/video/senate_gop_stacks_167_boxes_to_illustrate_amount_of_
kavanaugh_papers_getting_released.

20. Jordain Carney, "Schumer: Share 'confidential' Kavanaugh documents with
    entire Senate," *The Hill*, August 20, 2018, https://thehill.com/blogs/floor-
    action/senate/402771-schumer-share-confidential-kavanaugh-documents-
    with-entire-senate.

21. Chuck Grassley (@ChuckGrassley), "SenSchumer, as chair I welcome any
    senator 2 stop by judic cmte any day (& nite) incl wknds 2 review cmte conf docs
    A desk is waiting +there r the hundreds of thousands docs already avail w/ more
    all the time Is nom now under consideration or is vote still pre-determined NO?"
    Twitter, August 20, 2018, 2:38 p.m., https://twitter.com/ChuckGrassley/
    status/1031656659167404032.

22. Burgess Everett and Elana Schor, "Schumer, Democrats wrestled over staging
    mass Kavanaugh walkout," *Politico*, September 4, 2018, https://www.politico.
    com/story/2018/09/04/kavanaugh-democrats-supreme-court-hearing-806567.

23. The transcript of the hearings will be quoted throughout this chapter. "Senate
    Judiciary Committee Hearing on the Nomination of Brett Kavanaugh to be an
    Associate Justice of the Supreme Court," CQ Transcriptions, September 4, 2018.

24. Frank Thorp (@frankthorp), "Sources tell @Kasie and me that this is a coordinated
    effort by Senate Dems on the Judiciary Committee, and that it was discussed during
    the holiday weekend on a call organized by Schumer," Twitter, September 4, 2018,
    7:01 a.m., https://twitter.com/frankthorp/status/1036977514281934853.

25. Everett and Schor, "Schumer, Democrats wrestled."

26. CNN Politics (@CNN Politics), "GOP Sen. John Cornyn says this is the first
    Supreme Court confirmation hearing that he's seen being carried out 'according
    to mob rule,' adding that it's 'hard to take seriously' when Democrats have
    'already made up their mind before the hearing,'" Twitter, September 4, 2018,
    7:44 a.m., https://twitter.com/CNNPolitics/status/1036988415844208640.

27. *Marbury v. Madison*, 5 U.S. (1 Cranch) 137 (1803).

28. Virginia Kruta, "Kavanaugh's Hearing by the Numbers, Straight from Deputy
    Press Secretary Raj Shah," *Daily Caller*, September 4, 2018, https://dailycaller.
    com/2018/09/04/kavanaughs-hearing-numbers-raj-shah/.

29. Elizabeth Landers, "Meet the protestors interrupting Brett Kavanaugh's
    confirmation hearing," CNN, September 5, 2018, https://www.cnn.
    com/2018/09/05/politics/kavanaugh-hearing-protests/index.html.

30. Eugene Gu (@eugenegu), "Kavanaugh's former law clerk Zina Bash is flashing a
    white power sign behind him during his Senate confirmation hearing. They
    literally want to bring white supremacy to the Supreme Court. What a national
    outrage and a disgrace to the rule of law," Twitter, September 4, 2018, 12:44
    p.m., https://twitter.com/eugenegu/status/1037063912896643072.

31. Dylan Matthews, "No, a former Kavanaugh clerk didn't flash a 'white power
    sign.' Here's what really happened," Vox, September 5, 2018, https://www.vox.
    com/2018/9/5/17821946/white-power-hand-signal-brett-kavanaugh-confirmation-
    hearing-zina-bash-4chan.

32. Eli Rosenberg and Abby Ohlheiser, "Zina Bash Moved her Hand—and the
    #Resistance saw a white power symbol. Then she did it again," *Washington*

Post, September 8, 2018, https://www.washingtonpost.com/news/the-intersect/wp/2018/09/04/that-was-no-white-power-hand-signal-at-the-kavanaugh-hearing-zina-bashs-husband-says/?utm_term=.c29628288213; Mahita Gajanan, "A Kavanaugh Supporter Was Accused of Making a White Power Symbol. She's a Descendant of Holocaust Survivors," *Time Magazine*, September 5, 2018, http://time.com/5386860/zina-gelman-bash-white-power-symbol/.

33. Ed Whelan, "Refuting Anti-Kavanaugh Smears—Manny Miranda Controversy," *National Review*, September 10, 2018, https://www.nationalreview.com/bench-memos/refuting-anti-kavanaugh-smears-manny-miranda-controversy/.

34. Seung Min Kim (@seungminkim), "Re: Kamala and her Qs re whether Kavanaugh discussed Mueller probe with anyone at Kasowitz – Dem aide tells me they have reason to believe that a conversation happened and are continuing to pursue it," Twitter, September 5, 2018, 6:42 p.m., https://twitter.com/seungminkim/status/1037516325437022208.

35. Elana Schor, "Kavanaugh stumbles when grilled on whether he discussed Mueller probe," *Politico*, September 5, 2018, https://www.politico.com/story/2018/09/05/kavanaugh-mueller-probe-hearings-809115.

36. John T. Bennett, "Harris Lands First Blow on Kavanaugh—But It Only Grazes Him" *Roll Call*, September 6, 2018, https://www.rollcall.com/news/politics/harris-lands-first-blow-on-kavanaugh-but-it-only-grazes-him.

37. Jennifer Rubin, "The second-most-intense guessing game in D.C.," *Washington Post*, September 6, 2018, https://www.washingtonpost.com/news/opinions/wp/2018/09/06/the-second-most-intense-guessing-game-in-d-c/.

38. Senator Whitehouse is known for his liberal use of visual aids during hearings. During his opening statement his aide held up ten different signs with photos of the justices, charts, and tables. One intended to show why, contrary to all Supreme Court precedents, Kavanaugh should recuse himself from cases dealing with the president who appointed him, arguing that Trump had "a significant and dispropotiate [sic] influnce [sic] in placing the judge on the case." See Mike Brest, "Dem Uses Poster With Spelling Mistakes to Suggest Kavanaugh Is Obligated to Recuse Himself If Hearing a Case About Trump," *Daily Caller*, September 6, 2018, https://dailycaller.com/2018/09/06/dem-spelling-kavanaugh-trump/.

39. Cortney O'Brien, "Sen. Whitehouse Condemns Federalist Society…There Are Just a Few Problems," *Townhall*, September 5, 2018, https://townhall.com/tipsheet/cortneyobrien/2018/09/05/sen-whitehouse-condemns-federalist-societytheres-just-one-problem-n2516136.

40. Since 2013 alone the League of Conservation Voters has given Senator Whitehouse nearly two hundred thousand dollars. See "Sen. Sheldon Whitehouse–Rhode Island," https://www.opensecrets.org/members-of-congress/contributors?cid=N00027533&cycle=2018&type=C; Michael Beckel, "League of Conservation Voters Becoming 'Dark Money' Heavyweight," The

Center for Public Integrity, May 12, 2014, https://publicintegrity.org/federal-politics/league-of-conservation-voters-becoming-dark-money-heavyweight/.

41. Evan Mandery, "Why There's No Liberal Federalist Society," *Politico*, January 23, 2019, https://www.politico.com/magazine/story/2019/01/23/why-theres-no-liberal-federalist-society-224033.

42. And that doesn't even include the powerful forces of legal academia and the professional establishment of the American Bar Association and state bar associations—hardly less liberal than the explicitly ideological groups. While there is a controversy over whether the ABA can be properly be called neutral in its judicial evaluations (discussed elsewhere in this book), the policy positions it takes as an organization are undeniably liberal. Eighty-two percent of law school professors in the 2010s were Democrats, and the figure was even higher at elite schools. Kate Hardiman, "Law schools dominated by Democrat professors, research finds," The College Fix, August 31, 2015, https://www.thecollegefix.com/law-schools-dominated-by-democrat-professors-research-finds/; James Lindgren, "Measuring Diversity: Law Faculties in 1997 and 2013," *Harvard Journal of Law and Public Policy* 39, (January 2016): 89. Ninety-eight percent of donations from Harvard Law School professors went to Democrats. Daniel Halper, "98% of Harvard Law Faculty Political Donations Go to Democrats," *Weekly Standard*, May 1, 2015, https://www.weeklystandard.com/daniel-halper/98-of-harvard-law-faculty-political-donations-go-to-democrats.

43. Kevin Drum, "No Liberal Equivalent of the Federalist Society? Please.," *Mother Jones*, January 24, 2019, https://www.motherjones.com/kevin-drum/2019/01/no-liberal-equivalent-of-the-federalist-society-please/.

44. Anna Massoglia and Geoff West, "Kennedy's resignation sparks millions in conservative, liberal ad campaigns," Center for Responsive Politics, June 28, 2018, https://www.opensecrets.org/news/2018/06/kennedys-resignation-sparks-seven-figure-ad-campaigns-from-conservative-liberal-groups/.

45. "Sixteen Thirty Fund," Influence Watch, https://www.influencewatch.org/non-profit/sixteen-thirty-fund/; "Sixteen Thirty Fund Form 990," Influence Watch, https://www.influencewatch.org/app/uploads/2019/03/Sixteen-Thirty-Fund-Form-990-2017.pdf.

46. Peter Olsen-Phillips, "Democrats Increasingly Rely on Dark Money," U.S. News & World Report, April 30, 2019, https://www.usnews.com/news/politics/articles/2019-04-30/democrats-increasingly-rely-on-dark-money.

47. Eric Kessler is the founder and principal at Arabella Advisors and also serves on the board of the New Venture Fund and the Sixteen Thirty Fund.

48. One singularly ironic group, Every Voice, purports to be attempting to remove the influence of money in politics and supporting "small donor election programs," while feeding at the trough of big donors including not only Sixteen Thirty Fund but Jonathan Soros, the Soros-funded Open Society Policy Center, and the Tides Foundation. "Every Voice," Influence Watch, https://www.influencewatch.org/non-profit/every-voice/.

49. "New Venture Fund 990," Influence Watch, https://www.influencewatch.org/app/uploads/2019/03/New-Venture-Fund-2017-Form-990-reduced.pdf.

50. Whitehouse also took aim at the Pacific Legal Foundation, criticizing it for engaging in impact litigation by finding sympathetic clients to bring cases it hoped would shift the law in the direction they favored. That technique was pioneered by the ACLU and NAACP and included such famous cases as Rosa Parks and *Brown v. Board of Education*. Whitehouse treated it as a devious and underhanded ploy, although Judge Kavanaugh attempted to explain that it is a common tool of legal groups across the political spectrum.

51. Senator Cory Booker, "Booker Confidential–Kavanaugh Hearing," Scribd, September 5, 2018, https://www.scribd.com/document/387988906/Booker-Confidential-Kavanaugh-Hearing.

52. Hans A. von Spakovsky," Kavanaugh hearing day four: Democrats still land no punches," Fox News, September 7, 2018, https://www.foxnews.com/opinion/kavanaugh-hearing-day-four-democrats-still-land-no-punches.

53. Kevin Breuninger and Tucker Higgins, "Democrats defy GOP warnings about Senate rules, release Kavanaugh documents," CNBC, September 6, 2018, https://www.cnbc.com/2018/09/06/democratic-senators-say-they-will-risk-expulsion-fight-to-release-kavanaugh-documents.html.

54. Associated Press, "Sen. Cory Booker releases 28 new documents related to Kavanaugh," NBC News, September 12, 2018, https://www.nbcnews.com/politics/supreme-court/sen-cory-booker-releases-28-new-documents-related-kavanaugh-n909101.

55. David Sherfinski, Alex Swoyer, and Stephen Dinan, "Accusations fly against Kavanaugh in craziest Supreme Court confirmation hearings in decades," *Washington Times*, September 6, 2018, https://www.washingtontimes.com/news/2018/sep/6/brett-kavanaugh-confirmation-hearings-feature-wild/.

56. Henry Rodgers, "Liz Warren Supports Protesters Who Interrupted Kavanaugh Hearing, Wants Them to Stay," *Daily Caller*, September 4, 2018, https://dailycaller.com/2018/09/04/elizabeth-warren-protesters-kavanaugh/.

57. Jessica Chasmar, "Ruth Bader Ginsberg blasts Brett Kavanaugh hearings as 'highly partisan show,'" *Washington Times*, September 13, 2018, https://www.washingtontimes.com/news/2018/sep/13/ruth-bader-ginsburg-blasts-brett-kavanaugh-hearing/.

58. Richard Wolf, "Brett Kavanaugh coasts toward Supreme Court confirmation despite document dispute, public protest," *USA Today*, September 6, 2018, https://www.usatoday.com/story/news/politics/2018/09/06/brett-kavanaugh-faces-third-day-supreme-court-confirmation-hearings/1205309002/.

Chapter Five: All Hell Breaks Loose

1. Kavanaugh's responses to the questions for the record are quoted throughout this section. Judge Brett Kavanaugh, "Senator Chuck Grassley Questions for the Record," Senate Judiciary Committee, September 12, 2018, https://www.

judiciary.senate.gov/imo/media/doc/Kavanaugh%20Responses%20to%20
Questions%20for%20the%20Record.pdf.

2.   *Rice v. Cayetano*, 528 U.S. 495 (2000).

3.   *Hamdan v. Rumsfeld*, 548 U.S. 557 (2006).

4.   Ryan Grim, "Dianne Feinstein Withholding Brett Kavanaugh Document From
      Fellow Judiciary Committee Democrats," *The Intercept*, September 12, 2018,
      https://theintercept.com/2018/09/12/brett-kavanaugh-confirmation-dianne-
      feinstein/.

5.   "Executive Business Meeting," Committee on the Judiciary website, September
      13, 2018, https://www.judiciary.senate.gov/meetings/09/13/2018/executive-business-
      meeting.

6.   Lissandra Villa and Paul McLeod, "Senate Democrats Have Referred A Secret
      Letter About Brett Kavanaugh To The FBI," *Buzzfeed News*, September 13,
      2018, https://www.buzzfeednews.com/article/lissandravilla/senate-democrats-
      have-sent-a-secret-letter-about-brett; Lisa Mascaro, "Inside Democrats' struggle
      with the Kavanaugh accusation," AP News, September 24, 2018, https://
      apnews.com/af6b15bd2abb490b858098ee889b57bd.

7.   "Sexual Harrasment in the Workplace," C-SPAN, September 12, 2018, https://
      www.c-span.org/video/?451364-1/bipartisan-womens-caucus-examines-
      sexual-harassment-workplace.

8.   "Feinstein Statement on Kavanaugh," Committee on the Judiciary website,
      September 13, 2018, https://www.judiciary.senate.gov/press/dem/releases/
      feinstein-statement-on-kavanaugh.

9.   Mascaro, "Inside Democrats' struggle."

10.   Stephanie Kirchgaessner and Jessica Glenza, "Dianne Feinstein alerts authorities
      to secret Brett Kavanaugh letter," *The Guardian*, September 13, 2018, https://
      amp.theguardian.com/us-news/2018/sep/13/
      brett-kavanaugh-dianne-feinstein-confidential-letter.

11.   Brett T, "SERIOUSLY? So THIS is what Sen. Dianne Feinstein's secret Brett
      Kavanaugh letter was about?" Twitchy, September 13, 2018, https://twitchy.
      com/brettt-3136/2018/09/13/seriously-so-this-is-what-sen-dianne-feinsteins-
      secret-brett-kavanaugh-letter-was-about/.

12.   Jennifer Slye Aniskovich et al., Letter to Charles Grassley and Dianne Feinstein,
      https://www.judiciary.senate.gov/imo/media/doc/2018-09-14%2065%20
      Women%20who%20know%20Kavanaugh%20from%20High%20School%20
      -%20Kavanaugh%20Nomination.pdf.

13.   Jane Mayer and Ronan Farrow, "Four Women Accuse New York's Attorney
      General Of Physical Abuse," *New Yorker*, May 7, 2018, https://www.
      newyorker.com/news/news-desk/four-women-accuse-new-yorks-attorney-
      general-of-physical-abuse; Ronan Farrow, "From Aggressive Overtures to
      Sexual Assault: Harvey Weinstein's Accusers Tell Their Stories," *New Yorker*,
      October 10, 2017, https://www.newyorker.com/news/news-desk/from-
      aggressive-overtures-to-sexual-assault-harvey-weinsteins-accusers-tell-their-
      stories; Ronan Farrow, "Les Moonves and CBS Face Allegations of Sexual

Misconduct," *New Yorker*, July 27, 2018, https://www.newyorker.com/magazine/2018/08/06/les-moonves-and-cbs-face-allegations-of-sexual-misconduct.

14. Ronan Farrow and Jane Mayer, "A Sexual-Misconduct Allegation Against the Supreme Court Nominee Brett Kavanaugh Stirs Tension Among Democrats in Congress," *New Yorker*, September 14, 2018, https://www.newyorker.com/news/news-desk/a-sexual-misconduct-allegation-against-the-supreme-court-nominee-brett-kavanaugh-stirs-tension-among-democrats-in-congress.

15. John Bresnahan (@BresPolitico), ".@ChuckGrassley releases a letter from 65 women who knew Kavanaugh in high school (showing Rs knew about this high-school rape allegation.) These women say Kavanaugh 'behaved honorably and treated women with respect.'" Twitter, September 14, 2018, 8:02 a.m., https://twitter.com/BresPolitico/status/1040616745499848704; "/ 2 ADD – Judiciary Cmte Republicans object to my tweet. GOP aides say they didn't know the substance of the Feinstein letter or the nature of the allegations. GOP aide also says Judiciary Cmte Rs received updated FBI file on Kavanaugh yesterday after Feinstein letter," September 14, 2018, 8:32 a.m., https://twitter.com/BresPolitico/status/1040624414814072837; "/3 But clearly it took some effort to fund 65 women who attended high school at same time as Kavanaugh 30-odd years ago. This took some time to round up signatures," September 14, 2018, 8:35 a.m., https://twitter.com/BresPolitico/status/1040625006449971200.

16. Elana Schor, "Anita Hill: Kavanaugh Accuser deserves 'fair and neutral' process," *Politico*, September 14, 2018, https://www.politico.com/story/2018/09/14/anita-hill-kavanaugh-accuser-deserves-fair-and-neutral-process-825111.

17. The leak from the FBI background file, a serious breach of Senate procedure, triggered a special counsel investigation into its source. The counsel was never able to identify the source, but made the unremarkable conclusion that it was unlikely to have been leaked by Republican staffers; Neil A. Lewis, "Inquiry Fails to Find Source of Leak at Thomas Hearing," *New York Times*, May 6, 1992, A00018. Feinstein's staffers probably knew this history, which may have influenced how they handled the letter from Kavanaugh's accuser.

18. When Thomas took the stand on Friday evening, October 11, his testimony received higher ratings than a baseball playoff game the same night. The ratings continued to be high throughout the weekend. By contrast, the Bork hearings weren't even televised after the first day. John Anthony Maltese, *The Selling of Supreme Court Nominees*, (Baltimore: Johns Hopkins University Press, 1995), 92–93.

19. Emma Brown interview on *Morning Joe*, MSNBC, September 17, 2008, https://archive.org/details/MSNBCW_20180917_100000_Morning_Joe/start/1860/end/1920.

20. The *Washington Post* story about Ford's allegations will be quoted throughout this chapter. Emma Brown, "California professor, writer of confidential Brett

Kavanaugh letter speaks out about her allegation of sexual assault," *Washington Post*, September 16, 2018, A1.

Chapter Six: Delay, Delay, Delay

1. Kasie DC (@Kasie DC), "BREAKING: Sen. Bob Corker says he believes a vote on Kavanaugh should not be held until his accuser speaks to the Senate Judiciary Committee. If she wishes to do so, he says, 'she should do it promptly.'" Twitter, September 16, 2018, 6:03 p.m., https://twitter.com/KasieDC/status/1041492710526525440.
2. Elana Schor, "Flake's revenge? Trump antagonist holds power over Supreme Court pick," *Politico*, September 16, 2018, https://www.politico.com/story/2018/09/16/flake-kavanaugh-trump-revenge-826067.
3. Jenny Hollander, "Why 'Believe Women' Means Believing Women Without Exception," Bustle, November 21, 2017, https://www.bustle.com/p/why-believe-women-means-believing-women-without-exception-5532903.
4. Elizabeth Landers (@ElizLanders), ".@gregclarycnn asked Sen Susan Collins if she believed the accuser, Christine Blasey Ford. Collins said: 'I don't know enough to create the judgment at this point.'" Twitter, September 16, 2018, 3:20 p.m., https://twitter.com/ElizLanders/status/1041451852032819201.
5. Caitlin Flanagan, "I Believe Her," *The Atlantic*, September 17, 2018, https://www.theatlantic.com/ideas/archive/2018/09/me-too/570520/.
6. John T. Bennett, "Three Ways Kavanaugh Nomination Could Play Out After Accuser Speaks," *Roll Call*, September 16, 2018, https://www.rollcall.com/news/politics/kavanaugh-3-ways-nomination.
7. Alanna Vagianos, Amanda Terkel, and Jenna Amatulli, "Brett Kavanaugh's Supporters Now Far More Reluctant To Speak Up Publicly," *HuffPost*, September 18, 2018, https://www.huffingtonpost.com/entry/brett-kavanaugh-supporters_us_5ba12864e4b04d32ebfd446d.
8. Kalhan Rosenblatt and Rebecca Shabad, "Senators seek delay of Kavanaugh vote after Christine Blasey Ford reveals sexual assault allegation," NBC News, September 17, 2018, https://www.nbcnews.com/politics/supreme-court/senators-call-delay-kavanaugh-confirmation-vote-after-woman-reveals-sexual-n910026.
9. Benjamin Wittes, "Kavanaugh Bears the Burden of Proof," *The Atlantic*, September 21, 2018, https://www.theatlantic.com/ideas/archive/2018/09/kavanaugh-confirmation/571021/.
10. Eli Rosenberg, "Totally misreading court records and other ways people are trying to undermine Kavanaugh's accuser," *Washington Post*, September 18, 2018, https://www.washingtonpost.com/politics/2018/09/18/how-conservative-media-reacted-christine-ford-accusation-against-brett-kavanaugh/.
11. "Kellyanne Conway on Christine Blasey Ford," C-SPAN via YouTube, September 17, 2018, https://www.youtube.com/watch?v=DpxSChWOMBk.

12. Debra Katz interview, "Kavanaugh Confirmation Controversy," NBC News via archive.com, September 17, 2018, https://archive.org/details/KNTV_20180917_140000_Today/start/900/end/960.

13. Debra Katz interview by Alisyn Camerota, "Confirmation Battle: Kavanaugh Accuser Comes Forward, Details Alleged Attack," *New Day With Alisyn Camerota and John Berman*, CNN via archive.org, https://archive.org/details/CNNW_20180917_110000_New_Day_With_Alisyn_Camerota_and_John_Berman/start/1740/end/1800.

14. Debra Katz interview, "Kavanaugh Assault Allegation," *CBS This Morning*, CBS via archive.org, https://archive.org/details/KPIX_20180917_140000_CBS_This_Morning/start/720/end/780.

15. Seung Min Kim and Josh Dawsey, "'Incredibly frustrated': Inside the GOP effort to save Kavanaugh amid assault allegations," *Washington Post*, September 22, 2018, https://www.washingtonpost.com/politics/incredibly-frustrated-inside-the-gop-effort-to-save-kavanaugh-amid-assault-allegation/2018/09/22/6808baf6-bde0-11e8-b7d2-0773aa1e33da_story.html.

16. Office of the Chairman, Senator Chuck Grassley, "Memorandum Re: Senate Judiciary Committee Investigation of Numerous Allegations Against Justice Brett Kavanaugh During the Senate Confirmation Proceedings," November 2, 2018, 38.

17. "Read: Christine Blasey Ford's attorneys' letter requesting FBI Investigation," CNN, September 19, 2018, https://www.cnn.com/2018/09/18/politics/ford-attorneys-letter-grassley/index.html.

18. Daniel Chaitin, "DOJ: Allegation against Brett Kavanaugh 'does not involve any potential federal crime,'" *Washington Examiner*, https://www.washingtonexaminer.com/news/doj-allegation-against-brett-kavanaugh-does-not-involve-any-potential-federal-crime. The Department of Justice would later confirm that "the FBI does not make any judgment about the credibility or significance of any allegation," and that, in the absence of a federal crime, their role is simply "to provide information for the use of the decision makers." Matt Shuham, "DOJ Issues Statement on Kavanaugh Background Check," Talking Points Memo, September 19, 2018, https://talkingpointsmemo.com/news/doj-issues-statement-on-kavanaugh-background-check.

19. Katey Rich, "Julia Louis-Dreyfus Signed an Open Letter Defending Brett Kavanaugh's Accuser," *Vanity Fair*, September 17, 2018, https://www.vanityfair.com/style/2018/09/julia-louis-dreyfus-christine-blasey-ford-letter; Kyle Swenson, "As conservatives attack, hundreds sign setters Supporting Kavanaugh accuser Christine Blasey Ford," *Washington Post*, September 18, 2018, https://www.washingtonpost.com/news/morning-mix/wp/2018/09/18/as-conservatives-attack-hundreds-sign-letters-supporting-kavanaugh-accuser-christine-blasey-ford/.

20. Amanda Terkel and Arthur Delaney, "Alumnae of Christine Blasy Ford's High School Circulate Letter of Support," *HuffPost*, September 17, 2018, https://www.huffingtonpost.com/entry/christine-blasey-ford-holton-arms-brett-kavanaugh_us_5b9fb3c2e4b04d32ebfabbc6.

21. John Bowden, "Kavanaugh accuser forced out of her home over threats, lawyers say," *The Hill*, September 18, 2019, https://thehill.com/blogs/blog-briefing-room/news/407336-lawyer-kavanaugh-accuser-has-received-death-threats-and.

22. Kelsey Snell and Scott Detrow, "Republicans Reject Kavanaugh Accuser's Request to Delay Hearing For FBI Investigation," NPR, https://www.npr.org/2018/09/18/649209595/hearing-with-kavanaugh-and-accuser-alleging-sexual-assault-in-turmoil.

23. Burgess Everett, Elana Schor, Eliana Johnson, and Brent D. Griffiths, "Kavanaugh accuser: FBI should investigate claims of sexual assault," *Politico*, September 18, 2018.

24. Michael Dresser, "Gov. Hogan rules out state police investigation of Kavanaugh allegations; Montgomery County police not investigating," *Capital Gazette*, September 25, 2018, https://www.capitalgazette.com/news/government/bs-md-hogan-kavanagh-20180921-story.html.

25. Jim Joyner, "Montgomery officials 'prepared to investigate' Kavanaugh allegations—if an alleged victim comes forward," *Baltimore Sun*, September 28, 2018, https://www.baltimoresun.com/news/maryland/bs-md-montgomery-police-kavanaugh-response-20180928-story.html.

26. "Ford 'Wasn't Clear' Committee Offered California Interview in lieu of Public Washington Hearing," Committee on the Judiciary website, October 2, 2018, https://www.judiciary.senate.gov/press/rep/releases/ford-wasnt-clear-committee-offered-california-interview-in-lieu-of-public-washington-hearing.

27. John Bowden, "Dem: 'Bulls—-' to say GOP doing everything to contact Kavanaugh accuser," *The Hill*, September 19, 2018, https://thehill.com/homenews/senate/407527-dem-bulls-to-say-gop-doing-everything-to-contact-kavanaugh-accuser.

28. Cheyenne Haslett, "Sen. Mazie Hirono's message to American men: 'Just shut up and step up,'" ABC News, September 18, 2018, https://abcnews.go.com/Politics/sen-mazie-hironos-message-american-men-shut-step/story?id=57920219.

29. *National Review* Editors, "If Kavanaugh's Accuser Won't Testify, the Senate Should Vote," *National Review*, September 20, 2018, https://www.nationalreview.com/2018/09/brett-kavanaugh-allegations-christine-blasey-ford-invitation-to-testify/; Andrew C. McCarthy, "It's a Set-up," *National Review*, September 19, 2018, https://www.nationalreview.com/2018/09/brett-kavanaugh-accuser-must-testify/.

30. Cheyenne Haslett, "Sen. Mazie Hirono's message to American men."

31. Mike Allen and Jim VandeHei, "Dems plot massive campaign if Kavanaugh falls," Axios, September 20, 2018, https://www.axios.com/brett-kavanaugh-confirmation-democrats-2018-midterm-elections-3ce55ebf-dc62-46b9-8ffa-bb1a7fe7cb18.html.

32. Ariel Edwards-Levy, "Brett Kavanaugh Is Accused Of Sexual Assault. That Hasn't Changed Public Opinion At All.," *HuffPost*, September 19, 2018, https://

www.huffingtonpost.com/entry/brett-kavanugh-sexual-assault-allegation-public-opinion_us_5ba23ce2e4b013b09780d1b3.

33. David Byler, "What Do the Polls Say About Brett Kavanaugh?" *Weekly Standard*, September 20, 2018, https://www.weeklystandard.com/david-byler/have-christine-blasey-fords-allegations-against-brett-kavanaugh-affected-his-polling.

34. Gabriel Sherman, "'Cut Bait': As The Kavanaugh Nightmare Escalates, Trump Is Gripped With Uncertainty As Ivanka Suggests Cutting The Judge Loose," *Vanity Fair*, September 18, 2018, https://www.vanityfair.com/news/2018/09/kavanaugh-allegations-trump-ivanka.

35. Julie Pace, "Bredesen backs Senate vote if Kavanaugh accuser won't appear," AP News, September 19, 2018, https://apnews.com/f316ae20e8a340f584cb53a8866171d0.

36. Mollie Hemingway, "The Kavanaugh Allegation Process Is A Miscarriage Of Justice For Everyone," *The Federalist*, September 19, 2018, http://thefederalist.com/2018/09/19/the-kavanaugh-allegation-process-is-a-miscarriage-of-justice-for-everyone/.

37. Chris Cillizza (@CillizzaCNN), "Walking a VERY dangerous line here. . . . ." Twitter, September 18, 2018, 8:21 a.m., https://twitter.com/cillizzacnn/status/1042071101105467393.

38. Moriah Balingit, "'What happens at Georgetown Prep stays at Georgetown Prep': Kavanaugh remarks in 2015 speech get renewed scrutiny," *Washington Post*, September 19, 2018, https://www.washingtonpost.com/education/2018/09/19/what-happens-georgetown-prep-stays-georgetown-prep-kavanaugh-remarks-speech-get-renewed-scrutiny/.

39. Naomi Lim, "Elizabeth Warren attacks Brett Kavanaugh for once saying, 'What happens at Georgetown Prep, stays at Georgetown Prep,'" *Washington Examiner*, September 18, 2018, https://www.washingtonexaminer.com/news/elizabeth-warren-attacks-brett-kavanaugh-for-once-saying-what-happens-at-georgetown-prep-stays-at-georgetown-prep.

40. "CNN Airs Edited Kavanaugh Clips, Says It Shows 'There Are Portions of His Childhood He'd Rather Not Come to Light,'" Grabien, https://grabien.com/story.php?id=194065.

41. Rebecca Morin, "Kavanaugh in 2015: 'What happens at Georgetown Prep, stays at Georgetown Prep,'" *Politico*, September 18, 2018, https://www.politico.com/story/2018/09/18/kavanaugh-what-happens-geogetown-prep-828420; *Washington Post* (@washingtonpost), 'What happens at Georgetown Prep say at Georgetown Prep': Kavanaugh remarks in 2015 speech get renewed scrutiny," Twitter, September 19, 2018, 8:18 p.m., https://twitter.com/washingtonpost/status/1042613840335265792.

42. Jack Crowe, "Classmate of Kavanaugh Accuser Backtracks after Guilty Claim Goes Viral," *National Review*, September 19, 2018, https://www.nationalreview.com/news/brett-kavanaugh-accusers-classmate-backtracks-after-guilty-claim-goes-viral/.

43. Domenico Montanaro, "Kavanaugh Accuser's Classmate: 'That It Happened Or Not, I Have No Idea,'" NPR, September 20, 2018, https://www.npr.

org/2018/09/20/649787076/
kavanaugh-accuser-classmate-that-it-happened-or-not-i-have-no-idea.

44. Jack Crowe, "Classmate of Kavanaugh Accuser Backtracks."

45. Ken Dilanian, Brandy Zadrozny, and Ben Popken, "Accuser's schoolmate says she recalls hearing of alleged Kavanaugh incident," NBC News, September 19, 2018, https://www.nbcnews.com/politics/supreme-court/accuser-s-schoolmate-says-she-recalls-hearing-alleged-kavanaugh-incident-n911111.

46. Emily Peck, "Brett Kavanaugh Liked Female Clerks Who Looked A 'Certain Way,' Yale Student Was Told," *HuffPost*, September 19, 2018, https://www.huffpost.com/entry/yale-student-brett-kavanaugh-clerkship-look_n_5ba2f051e4b0181540d9e2bb.

47. Stephanie Kirchgaessner and Jessica Glenza, "'No accident' Brett Kavanaugh's female law clerks 'looked like models,' Yale professor told students, " *The Guardian*, September 20, 2018, https://www.theguardian.com/us-news/2018/sep/20/brett-kavanaugh-supreme-court-yale-amy-chua.

48. Adam Edelman and Kasie Hunt, "Yale Law dean: Reports that professor groomed female clerks for Kavanaugh 'of enormous concern,' NBC News, September 20, 2018, https://www.nbcnews.com/politics/supreme-court/yale-law-dean-reports-professor-groomed-female-clerks-kavanaugh-enormous-n911571.

49. Abigail Shrier (@AbigailShrier), "I was a student of @amychua's a YLS. She has a very quick wit and an off-beat sense of humor. If she said this, it was part of her sparkling repartee, often tongue-in-cheek. What McCarthyist hell are we living?" Twitter, September 20, 2018, 8:24 p.m., https://twitter.com/AbigailShrier/status/1042977834082295813.

50. Amy Chua (@amychua), "As some of you many know, there have been stories about me in the recent news cycle. All the claims are outrageous and 100% false. Here is a statement I released to the Yale Law School community:" Twitter, September 22, 2018, 4:21 p.m., https://twitter.com/amychua/status/1043641537102532608.

51. Farnoush Amiri, "Yale law professor denies reports she groomed Kavanaugh's Prospective Clerks," NBC News, September 22, 2018, https://www.nbcnews.com/politics/politics-news/yale-law-professor-denies-reports-she-groomed-kavanaugh-s-prospective-n912226.

52. Kaitlan Collins, "Former Classmate of Kavanaugh's denies being at party in sexual assault allegation," CNN, September 19, 2018, https://www.cnn.com/2018/09/18/politics/pj-smyth-brett-kavanaugh/index.html.

53. Susan Heavey and Tim Ahmann, "Grassley sets Friday deadline for Trump top court pick Kavanaugh's accuser," Reuters, https://www.reuters.com/article/us-usa-court-kavanaugh-testimony-grassle/grassley-sets-friday-deadline-for-trump-top-court-pick-kavanaughs-accuser-idUSKCN1LZ2GJ.

54. Ed Whelan (@EdWhelanEPPC), Twitter, "I made an appalling mistake of judgment in posting the tweet thread in a way that identified Kavanaugh's Georgetown Prep classmate. I take full responsibility for that mistake, and I

deeply apologize for it. I realize that does not undo the mistake," Twitter, September 21, 2018, 5:38 a.m., https://twitter.com/edwhelaneppc/status/ 1043117304152817664.

55. Elana Schor and Burgess Everett, "Grassley extends deadline on Kavanaugh accuser's decision to testify," *Politico*, September 21, 2018, https://www.politico. com/story/2018/09/21/trump-kavanaugh-christine-blasey-ford-charges-834664.

56. Annie Karni, "Kavanaugh accuser leans on Democratic operative for advice," *Politico*, September 20, 2018, https://www.politico.com/story/2018/09/20/ kavanaugh-accuser-democratic-operative-advice-833013.

57. Ari Redbord, "Rock the Leftist Vote," *Weekly Standard*, July 28, 1996, https:// www.weeklystandard.com/ari-redbord/rock-the-leftist-vote.

58. Frieda Powers, "Advisor to Kavanaugh's accuser was caught on audio in July predicting a coming plot to destroy nomination," BizPac Review website, September 22, 2018, https://www.bizpacreview.com/2018/09/22/ advisor-to-kavanaughs-accuser-was-caught-on-audio-in-july-predicting-a- coming-plot-to-destroy-nomination-676531.

59. Donald J. Trump (@realDonaldTrump), "I have no doubt that, if the attack on Dr. Ford was as bad as she says, charges would have been immediately filed with local Law Enforcement Authorities by either her or her loving parents. I ask that she bring those filings forward so that we can learn date, time, and place!" Twitter, September 21, 2018, 6:14 a.m., https://twitter.com/realdonaldtrump/ status/1043126336473055235.

60. Laurie Kellman, "How it looks: Optics key in fight over Kavanaugh hearing," AP News, September 21, 2018, https://www.apnews.com/76086187160044e99 b7e026ca64722fc.

61. Jonathan V. Last, "It's Time for Some Brett Kavanaugh Game Theory," *Weekly Standard*, September 21, 2018, https://www.weeklystandard.com/jonathan-v- last/brett-kavanaugh-what-happens-if-trump-withdraws- the-nomination-over-the-christine-ford-allegations.

62. Paul McLeod, "Mitch McConnell Told Supporters Senate Republicans Will 'Plow Right Through' To Confirm Kavanaugh," *BuzzFeed News*, September 21, 2018, https://www.buzzfeednews.com/article/paulmcleod/mcconnell- kavanaugh-supreme-court-vote.

63. Robert Bork, Jr. (@Robert_Bork_Jr), "Yes. Yes, I can," Twitter, October 6, 2018, 9:57 a.m., https://twitter.com/Robert_Bork_Jr/status/1048618238790254592.

64. Alex Pappas, "Grassley sets Friday deadline for Kavanaugh accuser to say if she will testify," Fox News, September 20, 2018, https://www.foxnews.com/ politics/grassley-sets-friday-deadline-for-kavanaugh-accuser-to-say-if-she- will-testify.

65. Schor and Everett, "Grassley extends deadline."

66. Chuck Grassley (@ChuckGrassley), "With all the extensions we give Dr Ford to decide if she still wants to testify to the Senate I feel like I'm playing 2nd trombone in the judiciary orchestra and Schumer is the conductor," Twitter,

September 21, 2018, 8:55pm, https://twitter.com/chuckgrassley/status/104334
8132657025025.

67. "Final Agreement document," from Mollie Ziegler Hemingway email,
September 23, 2018.

68. Kevin Breuninger and Javier E. David, "Senate Judiciary Committee threatens
to vote on Kavanaugh nomination if Ford doesn't accept proposal to testify,"
CNBC, September 21, 2018, https://www.cnbc.com/2018/09/21/gop-counter-
offer-to-brett-kavanaugh-accuser-proposes-wednesday-hearing.html.

69. Chuck Grassley (@ChuckGrassley), "Five times now we hv granted extension for
Dr Ford to decide if she wants to proceed w her desire stated one wk ago that she
wants to tell senate her story Dr Ford if u changed ur mind say so so we can
move on I want to hear ur testimony. Come to us or we to u," Twitter,
September 21, 2018, 8:27 p.m., https://twitter.com/chuckgrassley/status/
1043341000989712384.

70. Chuck Grassley (@ChuckGrassley), "Judge Kavanaugh I just granted another
extension to Dr Ford to decide if she wants to proceed w the statement she made
last week to testify to the senate She shld decide so we can move on I want to
hear her. I hope u understand. It's not my normal approach to b indecisive,"
Twitter, September 21, 2018, 8:42 p.m., https://twitter.com/chuckgrassley/
status/1043344767684366336.

71. MJ Lee, "Ford told friends she is uncomfortable in enclosed spaces, airplanes,"
CNN, September 23, 2018, https://www.cnn.com/2018/09/20/politics/ford-
uncomfortable-in-enclosed-spaces-airplanes/index.html.

72. Jennifer Rubin (@JRubinBlogger), "So far today, Trump attacked Ford,
unleashing a storm of MeToo accounts and aggravating Collins. They tell a
woman who needs to drive cross country she can't have one extra day. None of
these people should be in office," Twitter, September 21, 2018, 12:43 p.m.,
https://twitter.com/jrubinblogger/status/1043224319407652867.

73. Heidi Przybyla, "Spokesman for GOP on Kavanaugh nomination resigns; has
been accused of harassment in the past," NBC News, September 22, 2018,
https://www.nbcnews.com/politics/supreme-court/spokesman-gop-kavanaugh-
nomination-resigns-has-been-accused-harassment-past-n912156.

74. Seung Min Kim, Sean Sullivan, and Emma Brown, "Christine Blasey Ford
moves closer to deal with Senate Republicans to testify against Kavanaugh,"
Washington Post, September 23, 2018, https://www.washingtonpost.com/
politics/lawyers-for-christine-blasey-ford-say-she-has-accepted-senate-judiciary-
committees-request-to-testify-against-kavanaugh/2018/09/22/e8199c6a-be8f-
11e8-8792-78719177250f_story.html.

75. Marcia Coyle and Tony Mauro, "Veteran Prosecutor Michael Bromwich Joins
Kavanaugh Accuser's Legal Team," National Law Journal, September 25, 2018,
https://www.law.com/nationallawjournal/2018/09/22/
veteran-prosecutor-michael-bromwich-joins-kavanagh-accusers-legal-team/.

76. Ariane de Vogue, "Committee contacts Ford's friend about party; 'she has no
recollection' of it, lawyer says," CNN, September 22, 2018, https://amp.cnn.
com/cnn/2018/09/22/politics/kavanaugh-ford-accuser-nomination/index.html.

77. Emma Brown, "California professor, writer of confidential Brett Kavanaugh letter, speaks out about her allegations of sexual assault," *Washington Post*, September 16, 2018, https://www.washingtonpost.com/investigations/california-professor-writer-of-confidential-brett-kavanaugh-letter-speaks-out-about-her-allegation-of-sexual-assault/2018/09/16/46982194-b846-11e-8-94eb-3bd52dfe917b_story.html.

78. Kim, Sullivan, Brown, "Christine Blasey Ford moves closer."

79. Kimberley Strassel (@KimStrassel), "11) Wow. 'Before her name became public, Ford told…' That is WaPo admitting that it had the name, and had Ford's response to what would clearly be a Keyser denial, but NEVER PUT IT OUT THERE. Again, why? A lot of people have a lot questions to answer," Twitter, September 22, 2018, 8:47 p.m., https://twitter.com/KimStrassel/status/1043 708375299584000.

80. Ariane de Vogue, "Committee contacts Ford's friend."

81. Sarah Young, *Jesus Calling*: *Enjoying Peace in His Presence* (Nashville: Thomas Nelson, 2004), 272.

Chapter Seven: Too Big To Fail

1. "Another Woman?" Drudge Report Archive, September 23, 2018, http://www.drudgereportarchives.com/data/2018/09/23/index.htm?s=flag.

2. This *New Yorker* story about the Ramirez allegations will be quoted throughout this chapter. Ronan Farrow and Jane Mayer, "Senate Democrats Investigate A New Allegation of Sexual Misconduct, From Brett Kavanaugh's College Years," *New Yorker*, September 23, 2018, https://www.newyorker.com/news/news-desk/senate-democrats-investigate-a-new-allegation-of-sexual-misconduct-from-the-supreme-court-nominee-brett-kavanaughs-college-years-deborah-ramirez.

3. Madison Feller, "*The New Yorker*'s Jane Mayer Is Holding the World's Most Powerful Men Accountable," *Elle*, October 8, 2018, https://www.elle.com/culture/career-politics/a23626662/new-yorker-jane-mayer-brett-kavanaugh-ronan-farrow/?platform=hootsuite.

4. John McCormack, "Kavanaugh Classmate Named in Letter Strongly Denies Allegations of Misconduct," *Weekly Standard*, September 14, 2018, https://www.weeklystandard.com/john-mccormack/kavanaugh-classmate-named-in-letter-strongly-denies-allegations-of-misconduct.

5. Michael Avenatti (@MichaelAvenatti), Twitter, September 23, 2018, 4:33 p.m., https://twitter.com/MichaelAvenatti/status/1044006928416825344.

6. Michael Avenatti (@MichaelAvenatti), Twitter, September 23, 2018, 6:16 p.m., https://twitter.com/michaelavenatti/status/1044032678951960576.

7. It was a sentiment echoed by previous Supreme Court nominees, such as Nixon's defeated nominee Clement Haynsworth. He was nominated in 1969 for the vacancy left by the resignation of Abe Fortas, whose elevation to chief justice had been blocked in 1968 amid criticism of his political activity as a justice. Fortas resigned after the revelation of further conflicts of interest and ethical concerns. Haynsworth was a respected Fourth Circuit judge but also a Republican and a

Southerner replacing one of the Court's strong liberals, whose defeat was still a sore spot. While his life's work showed him to be relatively moderate, the NAACP and AFL-CIO charged that he supported segregation and corporate interests, citing the outcomes of certain opinions rather than the legal reasoning buttressing them. They were soon joined by other groups raising concerns. A concerted campaign against Haynsworth gained steam because it tapped into the same ethical concerns that had derailed the Fortas nomination. Haynsworth was accused of an incredibly complex conflict of interest. He had ruled in favor of a firm that had a relationship with a vending machine firm he'd once served on the board of. He held stock in the vending firm, yet didn't recuse, because he did not know the two businesses were related. Although legal analysts ultimately concluded no real conflict had been present, the media coverage was brutal, with one newspaper saying he "appeared edgy and stuttering." He had a slight speech impediment, but the description left the impression he was hiding something. And the politics were horrible, as the very Republicans he needed for confirmation had led the charge opposing Fortas for superficially similar reasons. The White House hung back from the fight until he was on the Senate floor, then engaged in a heavy-handed campaign that may have cost Haynsworth even more votes. Two weeks after his nomination failed, he met with Nixon in the White House. Even so soon after the defeat, he seemed to have recovered enough to joke that, after reading the *New York Times* during his nomination, he had become convinced that anyone as bad as he was didn't deserve to be in the Supreme Court.

8. "What You Need to Know About Allegations Made in The New Yorker Article on Judge Brett Kavanaugh," Fact Sheets, White House website, September 23, 2018, https://www.whitehouse.gov/briefings-statements/need-know-allegations-made-new-yorker-article-judge-brett-kavanaugh/.

9. *Coffin v. United States*, 156 U.S. 432, 454–55 (1895).

10. *See, e.g.*, David Lisa, Lori Gardinier, Sarah C. Nicksa, and Ashley M. Cote, "False Allegations of Sexual Assault: An Analysis of Ten Years of Reported Cases," *Violence Against Women* 16, no. 12 (2010): 1318–1334; Liz Kelly, Jo Lovett and Linda Regan, "A gap or a chasm? Attrition in reported rape cases," *Home Office Research Study 293*, (London: Home Office Research, Development and Statistics Directorate, 2005).

11. CNN Politics (@CNNPolitics), "CNN's Jake Tapper: 'Doesn't Kavanaugh have the same presumption of innocence as anyone else in America?' Sen. Mazie Hirono: 'I put his denial in the context of everything that I know about him in terms of how he approaches his cases' #CNNSOTU," Twitter, September 23, 2018, 6:40 a.m., https://twitter.com/CNNPolitics/status/1043857714860834821.

12. David Rutz, "Coons: Kavanaugh 'Bears the Burden of Disproving These Allegations," Free Beacon, September 24, 2018, https://freebeacon.com/politics/coons-kavanaugh-bears-the-burden-of-disproving-these-allegations/.

13. Benny Johnson (@bennyjohnson), "Chuck Schumer, in his own words, Brett Kavanaugh has 'No presumption of innocence.' This explains much of the

Democrats approach to these accusations," Twitter, September 25, 2018, 1:19 p.m., https://twitter.com/bennyjohnsozn/status/1044682895682662400.

14. U.S. Congress, Senate Judiciary Committee, *Nomination of Judge Clarence Thomas to be Associate Justice of the Supreme Court of the United States*, 102nd Cong., Pt.4, (Washington, D.C.: G.P.O., 1993), 268, https://www.congress.gov/supreme-court/GPO-CHRG-THOMAS-4.pdf.

15. Philip Rucker, "Joe Biden: When a woman alleges sexual assault, presume she is telling the truth," *Washington Post*, September 17, 2018, https://www.washingtonpost.com/politics/joe-biden-when-a-woman-alleges-sexual-assault-presume-she-is-telling-the-truth/2018/09/17/7718c532-badd-11e8-a8aa-860695e7f3fc_story.html; Remarks of Mitch McConnell, September 26, 2018, 9:30 a.m.

16. Matt Naham, "Faculty at Brett Kavanaugh's Alma Mater Are Demanding Screeching Halt to His Confirmation," Law & Crime website, September 21, 2018, https://lawandcrime.com/high-profile/faculty-at-brett-kavanaughs-alma-mater-are-demanding-screeching-halt-to-his-confirmation/.

17. Matt Naham, "Yale Law Students Refuse to Go to Class, Stage 'Sit-in' Over Brett Kavanaugh Assault Claims," Law & Crime website, September 24, 2018, https://lawandcrime.com/high-profile/yale-law-students-refuse-to-go-to-class-stage-sit-in-over-brett-kavanaugh-assault-claims/.

18. Diane Herbst, "Over 1000 Female Yale Grads Sign Letter Supporting Brett Kavanaugh Accusers: 'We Have Their Backs,'" *People*, September 24, 2018, https://people.com/politics/female-yale-grads-letter-support-brett-kavanaugh-accusers/.

19. Charles C. W. Cooke, "On *The New Yorker*'s Grossly Irresponsible Story," *National Review*, September 24, 2018, https://www.nationalreview.com/corner/on-the-new-yorkers-grossly-irresponsible-story/.

20. Sheryl Gay Stolberg and Nicholas Fandos, "Christine Blasey Ford Reaches Deal to Testify at Kavanaugh Hearing," *New York Times*, September 23, 2018, https://www.nytimes.com/2018/09/23/us/politics/brett-kavanaugh-christine-blasey-ford-testify.html.

21. New Day (@NewDay), "This is a fairly high level of evidence for this kind of a case…This exceeds the evidentiary basis we've used in the past in several cases that were found to be very credible," says @RonanFarrow of his reporting on the new allegations against Brett Kavanaugh," Twitter, September 24, 2018, 4:39 a.m., https://twitter.com/NewDay/status/1044189464602370048.

22. David Marcus, "Ronan Farrow Hurts The Me Too Movement With His Anti-Kavanaugh Hatchet Job," *The Federalist*, September 24, 2018, http://thefederalist.com/2018/09/24/ronan-farrow-hurts-me-too-movement-with-his-anti-kavanaugh-smear/.

23. "Ronan Misfires?" Drudge Report Archives: 19:30:07, September 24, 2018, 7:30 p.m., https://www.drudgereportarchives.com/data/2018/09/25/20180925_004008.htm.

24. Elizabeth Dias, "A Mormon Women's Group Seeks a Break in the Process," *New York Times*, September 27, 2018, A20.

25. Jessica Contrera, Ian Shapira, Emma Brown, and Steve Hendrix, "Kavanaugh accuser Christine Blasey Ford moved 3,000 miles to reinvent her life. It wasn't far enough," *Washington Post*, September 27, 2018, https://www.washingtonpost.com/local/christine-blasey-ford-wanted-to-flee-the-us-to-avoid-brett-kavanaugh-now-she-may-testify-against-him/2018/09/22/db942340-bdb1-11e8-8792-78719177250f_story.html.

26. Aaron Blake, "Mark Judge's conspicuous absence from Thursday's hearing," *Washington Post*, September 26, 2018, https://www.washingtonpost.com/politics/2018/09/25/how-world-is-mark-judge-not-testifying/.

27. Elizabeth Bruenig, "What Do We Owe Her Now?" *Washington Post*, September 23, 2018, AA04.

28. Senate Judiciary Committee, *Nomination of Judge Clarence Thomas*, 252.

29. John Anthony Maltese, *The Selling of Supreme Court Nominees* (Baltimore, Maryland: Johns Hopkins University Press, 1995), 97.

30. Margaret Sullivan (@Sulliview), "Female interviewer, check. Fox News, check. Bill Shine approved, check. When an "exclusive interview" promises to be a challenge-free infomercial," Twitter, September 24, 2018, 12:50 p.m., https://twitter.com/Sulliview/status/1044313198399238146.

31. Margaret Sullivan (@Sulliview), "Wife at your side, check," Twitter, September 24, 2018, 12:53 p.m., https://twitter.com/Sulliview/status/104431 3932419268608.

32. Margaret Sullivan (@Sulliview), "Unquestioning adoration would probably be the right look," Twitter, September 24, 2018, 12:57 p.m. https://twitter.com/Sulliview/status/1044314975152549889.

33. Brett Kavanaugh interviewed by Martha MacCullum, "Brett Kavanaugh: Full transcript of Fox Interview," *USA Today*, September 24, 2018, https://www.usatoday.com/story/news/nation/2018/09/24/brett-kavanaugh-transcript-interview-fox-news-martha-maccullum/1415548002/.

34. Emily Heil, "Kavanaugh's alma mater Georgetown Prep is hiring a director of alumni relations," *Washington Post*, October 18, 2018, https://www.washingtonpost.com/arts-entertainment/2018/10/18/kavanaughs-alma-mater-georgetown-prep-is-hiring-director-alumni-relations/.

35. Mark Landler and Peter Baker, "Trump accuses Democrats of running 'con game' against Kavanaugh," *Post-Gazette*, September 25, 2018, https://www.post-gazette.com/news/politics-nation/2018/09/25/Donald-Trump-Accuses-Democrats-Running-Con-Game-Against-Brett-Kavanaugh/stories/2018 09250128.

36. Jennifer Rubin (@JRubinBlogger), "this makes sense since the alleged behavior was disgusted, juvenile, emotionally stunted," Twitter, September 24, 2018, 3:23 p.m., https://twitter.com/JRubinBlogger/status/1044351579162378240.

37. Bre Payton, "Gropemaster Jimmy Kimmel: Let's Cut Off Brett Kavanaughs 'Pesky' Genitals," *The Federalist*, September 26, 2018, http://thefederalist.com/2018/09/26/gropemaster-jimmy-kimmel-lets-cut-off-brett-kavanaughs-pesky-genitals/.

38. Eugene Scott, "The virginity defense is a reminder of our ignorance about sexual violence," *Washington Post*, September 25, 2018, https://www.washingtonpost.com/politics/2018/09/25/virginity-defense-is-reminder-our-ignorance-about-sexual-violence/.

39. Aaron C. Davis, Emma Brown, and Joe Heim, "Kavanaugh's 'choir boy' image on Fox interview rankles former Yale classmates," *Washington Post*, September 25, 2018, https://www.washingtonpost.com/investigations/2018/09/25/ea5e50d4-c0eb-11e8-9005-5104e9616c21_story.html.

40. Andrew Cohen, "Brett Kavanaugh Has Already Disqualified Himself," *New Republic*, September 24, 2018, https://newrepublic.com/article/151359/brett-kavanaugh-already-disqualified.

41. TicToc by Bloomberg (@tictoc), "Michael Avenatti says his yet-unnamed client 'with credible information regarding Judge Kavanaugh' has been fully vetted, and that he's spoken to multiple other witnesses bloom.bg/2O65Xwq," Twitter, September 24, 2018, 4:10 p.m., https://twitter.com/tictoc/status/1044363400808026112.

42. Tom Elliott (@tomselliott), "Avenatti: Kavanaugh saying he was a virgin in HS 'shows he's lying.' 'Does that mean he performed oral sex or had oral sex performed on him? … Does he want America to believe that the only thing he did until well into his college years was effectively kiss or French kiss?'" Twitter, September 24, 2018, 6:38 p.m., https://twitter.com/tomselliott/status/1044400627667881984.

43. Natasha Korecki, "Avenatti stars in 'avenging angel' role," *Politico*, September 24, 2018, https://www.politico.com/story/2018/09/24/michael-avenatti-kavanaugh-2020-trump-838149.

44. Chris Woodyard and Jorge L. Oritz, "Third Kavanaugh accuser, a former US Mint employee, '100 percent credible,' Avenatti says," *USA Today*, September 24, 2018, https://www.usatoday.com/story/news/politics/2018/09/24/brett-kavanaugh-avenatti-third-accuser-emerge-48-hours/1416699002/.

45. Ben Domenech, "This is Just a Smear Campaign Now," The Transom, September 24, 2018.

46. "Quotation of the Day: Court Vacancy in Election Year Jolts the Parties," *New York Times*, June 28, 2018, https://www.nytimes.com/2018/06/28/todayspaper/quotation-of-the-day-court-vacancy-in-election-year-jolts-the-parties.html.

47. Kate Kelly and David Enrich, "Yearbook '83: Football, Kegs and Innuendo," *New York Times*, September 25, 2018, A1, https://www.nytimes.com/2018/09/24/business/brett-kavanaugh-yearbook-renate.html.

48. Mollie Hemingway, "New York Times Hid Multiple Key Facts in Kavanaugh Yearbook Hit," *The Federalist*, September 25, 2018, https://thefederalist.com/2018/09/25/new-york-times-hid-multiple-key-facts-in-kavanaugh-yearbook-hit/.

49. Mark Gauvreau Judge, *Wasted: Tales of a Gen X Drunk* (Center City, Minn.: Hazelden, 1997).

50. Mark Gavreau Judge, *If It Ain't Got That Swing: The Rebirth of Grown-Up Culture* (Dallas: Spence Publishing, 2000).

51. Gabriel Pogrund, Carol D. Leonnig, and Aaron C. Davis, "'How'd you find me?': Mark Judge has been holed up in a beach house in Delaware amid a media firestorm," *Washington Post*, September 24, 2018, https://www. washingtonpost.com/investigations/howd-you-find-me-mark-judge-has-been-holed-up-in-a-beach-house-in-delaware-amid-a-media-firestorm/2018/09/24/9d4829aa-c041-11e8-be77-516336a26305_story.html.

52. Rachel Kurzius, "Protesters Confront Sen. Ted Cruz at Fiola, Changing, 'We Believe Survivors,'" DCist, September 24, 2018, https://dcist.com/ story/18/09/24/protesters-confront-sen-ted-cruz-fiola/.

53. Peter Doocy (@pdoocy), "NEW: Sen. Feinstein, D-Ca, just told me 'I have no way of knowing' if Dr. Ford is actually going to show up to Kavanaugh hearing Thursday – if outside counsel is asking the questions," Twitter, September 25, 2018, 12:05 p.m., https://twitter.com/pdoocy/status/1044664321815515137.

54. James Hohmann (@jameshohmann), "Republican leadership planning to keep the Senate in session all weekend to confirm Kavanaugh as quickly as possible," Twitter, September 25, 2018, 12:49 p.m., https://twitter.com/jameshohmann/ status/1044675292999094272.

55. Bre Payton, "Watch Joe Biden Call FBI Investigation Into Sexual Harassment Worthless," *The Federalist*, September 26, 2018, http://thefederalist.com/ 2018/09/26/watch-joe-biden-call-fbi-investigations-sexual-harrasment-worthless/.

56. "Grassley: Committee Can and Should Investigate Ford Allegations," Chuck Grassley Senate website, September 19, 2018, https://www.grassley.senate.gov/ news/news-releases/grassley-committee-can-and-should-investigate-ford-allegations; Matt Shuham, "DOJ Issues Statement On Kavanaugh Background Check," Talking Points Memo, September 19, 2018, https://talkingpointsmemo. com/news/doj-issues-statement-on-kavanaugh-background-check.

57. The Declaration of Julie Swetnick will be quoted throughout this chapter. Office of the Chairman, Senator Chuck Grassley, "Senate Judiciary Committee Investigation of Numerous Allegations Against Justice Brett Kavanaugh During the Senate Confirmation Proceedings," United States Senate, November 2, 2018, exhibit 33, https://www.judiciary.senate.gov/imo/media/doc/2018-11-02%20 Kavanaugh%20Report.pdf.

58. Michael Avenatti (@MichaelAvenatti), Twitter, September 26, 2018, https:// twitter.com/MichaelAvenatti/status/1044960428730843136.

59. Byron York, "Finally, a day of reckoning for Michael Avenatti?" *Washington Examiner*, October 29, 2018, https://www.washingtonexaminer.com/opinion/ columnists/byron-york-finally-a-day-of-reckoning-for-michael-avenatti.

60. "Schumer Floor Remarks On The Need to Reopen Judge Kavanaugh's FBI Background Investigation," Senate Democrats website, September 26, 2018, https://www.democrats.senate.gov/schumer-floor-remarks-on-the-need-to-reopen-judge-kavanaughs-fbi-background-investigation.

61. Michael E. Miller, Steve Hendrix, Jessica Contrera, and Ian Shapira, "Who is Julie Swetnick, the third Kavanaugh accuser?" *Washington Post*, October 1, 2019, https://www.washingtonpost.com/local/who-is-julie-swetnick-the-

third-kavanaugh-accuser/2018/09/26/91e16ed8-c1bc-11e8-97a5-ab1e46bb3bc7_
story.html.

62. Phil Mattingly and Manu Raju, "Collins privately raises concerns about new
allegations, lack of subpoena for Kavanaugh friend," CNN, https://www.cnn.
com/2018/09/26/politics/susan-collins-brett-kavanaugh/index.html.

63. Christina Wilkie, "Kavanaugh denies latest accusation: 'This is ridiculous and
from the Twilight Zone,'" CNBC, September 26, 2018, https://www.cnbc.
com/2018/09/26/kavanaugh-denies-allegation-this-is-ridiculous.html.

64. Jonathan Chait, "Julie Swetnick's Allegations Likely to Finish Off Brett
Kavanaugh," *Intelligencer*, September 26, 2018, http://nymag.com/
intelligencer/2018/09/julie-swetnicks-allegations-brett-kavanaugh-withdraw.
html?gtm=bottom&gtm=bottom.

65. Marc Caputo and Natasha Korecki, "Ex-boyfriend filed restraining order
against third Kavanaugh accuser," *Politico*, September 26, 2018, https://www.
politico.com/story/2018/09/26/
ex-boyfriend-filed-restraining-order-against-kavanaugh-accuser-845348.

66. The Declaration of Julie Swetnick will be quoted throughout this chapter. Office
of the Chairman, Senator Chuck Grassley, "Senate Judiciary Committee
Investigation of Numerous Allegations Against Justice Brett Kavanaugh During
the Senate Confirmation Proceedings," United States Senate, November 2, 2018,
exhibit 42, https://www.judiciary.senate.gov/imo/media/doc/2018-11-02%20
Kavanaugh%20Report.pdf.

67. Ibid., 3.

68. Kate Sullivan, "Kavanaugh accuser's attorney says GOP staff blew off scheduled
call," CNN Politics, September 25, 2018, https://www.cnn.com/2018/09/25/
politics/deborah-ramirez-attorney-kavanaugh-cnntv/index.html.

69. John McCormack, "The Lasting Damage of the Kavanaugh Confirmation
Battle, *Weekly Standard*, October 12, 2018, https://www.weeklystandard.com/
john-mccormack/how-the-kavanaugh-battle-damaged-the-court-congress-the-media-
and-the-country.

70. Christopher Wray, Letter to Jeff Sessions, Committee on the Judiciary,
September 29, 2018, https://www.judiciary.senate.gov/imo/media/doc/2018-
09-29%20Grassley%20to%20DOJ,%20FBI%20-%20Referral%20for%20
Criminal%20Investigation.pdf.

71. Kasie Hunt, Leigh Ann Caldwell, Heidi Przybyla, and Frank Thorp V, "Senate
probed new allegation of misconduct against Kavanaugh," NBC News,
September 26, 2018, https://www.nbcnews.com/politics/supreme-court/
senate-probing-new-allegation-misconduct-against-kavanaugh-n913581.

72. Joe Tacopino, "Man apologizes for making false allegation against Kavanaugh,"
New York Post, September 26, 2018, https://nypost.com/2018/09/26/
man-apologizes-for-making-false-allegation-against-kavanaugh/.

73. Ellis Kim, "Federal Judge Who Dated Kavanaugh Defends Character, Dismisses
Anonymous Tip," *National Law Journal*, September 27, 2018, https://www.
law.com/nationallawjournal/2018/09/27/d-c-federal-judge-denies-anonymous-
tip-alleging-kavanaugh-abuse/.

74. Matt Naham, "'I was Angry': Woman Referred to DOJ and FBI for Alleged False Rape Claim Against Kavanaugh," Law and Crime website, November 2, 2018, https://lawandcrime.com/high-profile/i-was-angry-woman-referred-to-doj-and-fbi-for-making-false-rape-allegation-against-kavanaugh/.

75. Jenna Johnson and Robert Costa, "'It's the culture war on steroids.' Kavanaugh fight takes on symbolism in divided era," *Washington Post*, September 24, 2019, https://www.washingtonpost.com/politics/its-the-culture-war-on-steroids-kavanaugh-fight-takes-on-symbolism-in-divided-era/2018/09/24/15ccc792-c028-11e8-be77-516336a26305_story.html.

Chapter Eight: Fear of Flying

1. Lara Bazelon, "A Sexist, Cowardly Ploy," *New York Times*, September 25, 2018, A27.

2. Niels Lesniewski, "Outside Counsels Never Steal the Spotlight From Senators, Except When They Do," *Roll Call*, September 27, 2018, https://www.rollcall.com/news/politics/outside-counsels-never-steal-spotlight-senators-except.

3. The transcript of the hearing will be cited throughout this chapter. "Senate Judiciary Committee Hearing on the Nomination of Brett M. Kavanaugh to be an Associate Justice of the Supreme Court, Day 5, Focusing on Allegations of Sexual Assault, Part 1," CQ Transcriptions, September 27, 2018.

4. Sam Reed, "Is There a Symbolic Meaning Behind Dr. Blasey Ford's Blue Suit?" *InStyle*, September 28, 2018, https://www.instyle.com/news/christine-blasey-ford-anita-hill-blue-suits.

5. The term "victim" is a legal term of art that does not presume guilt on the part of the accused, but is used in sex crimes units for anyone alleged to have been assaulted.

6. Yvonne Wingett Sanchez, Michael Kiefer, and Ronald J. Hansen, "Who is Rachel Mitchell? A prosecutor who 'comes from the point of view where you believe victims,'" AzCentral website, September 26, 2018, https://www.azcentral.com/story/news/politics/arizona/2018/09/26/rachel-mitchell-arizona-prosecutor-who-question-christine-blasey-ford-brett-kavanaugh-supreme-court/1432244002/.

7. *MSNBC Live with Velshi and Ruhle*, MSNBC via archive.org, September 27, 2018, https://archive.org/details/MSNBCW_20180927_150000_MSNBC_Live_With_Velshi_and_Ruhle/start/2025/end/2085.

8. Dan Merica, "Democrat apologizes for fundraising off Kavanaugh allegations," CNN, September 27, 2018, https://www.cnn.com/2018/09/27/politics/mazie-hirono-brett-kavanaugh-fundraising/index.html.

9. Julie Bykowicz, "Sen. Kamala Harris Blankets Facebook With Anti-Kavanaugh Ads," *Wall Street Journal*, September 26, 2018, https://www.wsj.com/livecoverage/campaign-wire-2018-midterms/card/1537991168.

10. Cokie Roberts, "Kavanaugh Confirmation Hearing," *Good Morning America*, ABC via archive.org, September 27, 2018, https://archive.org/details/ KGO_20180927_140000_Good_Morning_America.

11. Until 2007 the home belonged to Sylvia Randall, who listed it as her office address for her psychotherapy practice, including couples therapy. Her name is still listed in many directories for the property. Presumably Ford's hosting of interns is done free of charge, given the local restrictions on subleasing. The minimum lot size for an attached second dwelling unit is at 9,450 square feet. The Fords' lot is 7,000 square feet. 18.12.070(b)(2).

12. "Live ABC News Kavanaugh Confirmation Hearing," *Good Morning America*, ABC via archive.org, September 27, 2018, https://archive.org/details/ KGO_20180927_140000_Good_Morning_America/start/ 5400/end/5460.

13. "Questioning of Christine Blasey-Ford to Resume Shortly," *Today*, NBC via archive.org, September 27, 2018, https://archive.org/details/ KNTV_20180927_140000_Today/start/5820/end/5880.

14. Office of the Chairman, Senator Chuck Grassley, "Memorandum Re: Senate Judiciary Committee Investigation of Numerous Allegations Against Justice Brett Kavanaugh During the Senate Confirmation Proceedings," November 2, 2018 (Exhibit 2, Resume of Dr. Christine Blasey).

15. Jeffrey Toobin, *Inside Politics*, CNN via archive.org, September 27, 2018, https://archive.org/details/CNNW_20180927_160000_Inside_Politics/ start/2760/end/2820.

16. "Brett Kavanaugh, Christine Blasey Ford Testify At Senate Hearing," NBC News, September 27, 2018, http://mms.tveyes.com/transcript.asp?PlayClip=FAL SE&DTSearch=TRUE&DateTime=09%2F27%2F2018+12%3A43%3A00&m arket=m100&StationID=165.

17. Kyle Drennen, "Kelly Tells NBC Panel: 'The Media is Not Exactly in Kavanaugh's Corner,'" MRC NewsBusters, September 27, 2018, https://www. newsbusters.org/blogs/nb/kyle-drennen/2018/09/27/kelly-tells-nbc-panel-media-not-exactly-kavanaughs-corner.

18. James Poniewozik, "Two Voices with a Noticeable Contrast in Volume," *New York Times*, September 28, 2018, A16.

19. Steve Schmidt (@SteveSchmidtSES), "Every GOP campaign strategist and Hill staffer wishes they had the button to open the trap door under Rachel Mitchell's chair. What a total and complete Political disaster for Republicans," Twitter, September 27, 2018, 9:16 a.m., https://twitter.com/steveschmidtses/status/104 5346483564949506.

20. Mimi Rocah, *Andrea Mitchell Reports*, MSNBC, September 27, 2018, https:// archive.org/details/MSNBCW_20180927_160000_Andrea_Mitchell_Reports/ start/3000/end/3060.

21. Joyce Vance, *MSNBC Live with Craig Melvin*, MSNBC, September 27, 2018, https://archive.org/details/MSNBCW_20180927_170000_MSNBC_Live_ With_Craig_Melvin/start/60/end/120.

22. Steve Schmidt (SteveSchmidtSES), "The GOP members are putting on a clinic for political cowardice. Will not one of them, while watching a hectoring and

minimally prepared Rachel Mitchell, harass Dr. Ford, step up and take back their time and denounce this kangaroo court?" Twitter, September 27, 2018, 9:54 a.m., https://twitter.com/steveschmidtses/status/1045355909428531201.

23. Saturday Night Live, "Kavanaugh Hearing Cold Open – SNL," YouTube, September 29, 2018, https://www.youtube.com/watch?v=VRJecfRxbr8.

24. Katz was an active Democrat. She and her law partner were slated to host a "Cocktails and Conversation" fundraiser October 1 for Senator Tammy Baldwin, with tickets going for up to $1,000, but she had to take her name off the invitations after the Blasey Ford story broke to avoid the suggestion of partisanship.

25. Fred Lucas, "The Political Pasts of the Lawyers Representing Kavanaugh Accusers," *Daily Signal*, October 3, 2018, https://www.dailysignal.com/2018/10/03/the-political-pasts-of-the-lawyers-representing-kavanaugh-accusers/.

26. Laura Collins, "Exclusive: 'Christine Ford threw her under the bus.' Strained 'sex assault' witness Leland Keyser is seen for the first time as close family member confirms she did NOT corroborate school friend Ford's story to FBI," *Daily Mail*, October 4, 2018, https://www.dailymail.co.uk/news/article-6235463/Christine-Fords-high-school-friend-blindsided-named-corroborating-witness.html.

27. R. Edward Geiselman and Ronald P. Fisher, "Interviewing Witnesses and Victims," UCLA Psychology, https://www.psych.ucla.edu/sites/default/files/documents/other/Current_CI_Research.docx.

28. Cynthia Alskne, *MSNBC Live with Katy Tur*, MSNBC, September 27, 2018, https://archive.org/details/MSNBCW_20180927_180000_MSNBC_Live_With_Katy_Tur/start/960/end/1080.

29. Ashley Parker and Brian Williams, *MSNBC Live with Katy Tur*, MSNBC, September 27, 2018, https://archive.org/details/MSNBCW_20180927_180000_MSNBC_Live_With_Katy_Tur/start/2040/end/2100.

30. Loftus is not only the author of a leading treatise on memory, she is frequently consulted as a legal expert on the malleability of memory. High-profile cases in which she consulted include the cases of Rodney King, O. J. Simpson, and Ted Bundy.

31. American Psychological Association, "Gold Medal Award for Life Achievement in the Science of Psychology," *American Psychologist* 68, no. 5 (2013): 331–33, https://pdfs.semanticscholar.org/4415/13f11e489b1478a326debb7720b74322c7fa.pdf; Steven J. Haggbloom et al., "The 100 Most Eminent Psychologists of the 20th Century," *Review of General Psychology* 6, no. 2 (2002): 139–52.

32. Lawrence Patihis et al., "Are the 'Memory Wars' Over? A Scientist-Practitioner Gap in Beliefs About Repressed Memory," *Psychological Science* 25, no. 2 (February 2014): 519–30, https://journals.sagepub.com/doi/abs/10.1177/0956797613510718.

33. Lisa D. Butler et al., "Meditation with yoga, groups therapy with hypnosis, and psychoeducation of long-term depressed mood: a randomized pilot trial," *Journal of Clinical Psychology* 64, no. 7 (2008): 808.

34. John T. Wixted et al., "Initial Eyewitness Confidence Reliably Predicts Eyewitness Identification Accuracy," *American Psychologist* 70, no. 6 (2015): 515–26, http://wixtedlab.ucsd.edu/publications/wixted2015/American_Psychologist_in_press.pdf.

35. Studies have shown that inaccurate but highly confident eyewitness identification is a serious problem in the criminal justice field, accounting for 70 percent of the more than three hundred exonerations of men and women based on DNA evidence. This has led some researchers to argue against the use of eyewitness information at trial altogether.

36. Others suggested that it is possible to "beat the test" if you are a psychopath or a highly skilled liar.

37. Jessica Contrera and Ian Shapira, "Christine Blasey Ford's family has been nearly silent amid outpouring of support," *Washington Post*, September 27, 2018, https://www.washingtonpost.com/local/christine-blasey-fords-own-family-has-been-nearly-silent-amid-outpouring-of-support/2018/09/26/49a3f4a6-c0d6-11e8-be77-516336a26305_story.html.

38. David Catron, "Did Christine Blasey Ford Use Anonymity to 'Get' Kavanaugh?" The American Spectator, September 17, 2018, https://spectator.org/did-christine-blasey-ford-use-anonymity-to-get-kavanaugh/.

39. Jessica Contrera, Ian Shapira, Emma Brown, and Steve Hendrix, "Kavanaugh accuser Christine Blasey Ford moved 3,000 Miles to reinvent her life. It wasn't far enough," *Washington Post*, September 27, 2018, https://www.washingtonpost.com/local/christine-blasey-ford-wanted-to-flee-the-us-to-avoid-brett-kavanaugh-now-she-may-testify-against-him/2018/09/22/db942340-bdb1-11e8-8792-78719177250f_story.html.

Chapter Nine: Miracle

1. "Prepared Written Testimony of Judge Brett M. Kavanaugh," Nomination Hearing to Serve as an Associate Justice of the Supreme Court, September 27, 2018, https://www.judiciary.senate.gov/imo/media/doc/BK%20Written%20Testimony%20-%20Submitted%20Sept%2026.pdf.

2. For a vivid description of Thomas's hearings, see Clarence Thomas, *My Grandfather's Son, a Memoir*, (New York: Harper Collins, 2007).

3. 2 Corinthians 12:10.

4. Matthew 26: 39.

5. Thomas, *My Grandfather's Son*, 257.

6. Senate Judiciary Committee, *Nomination of Judge Clarence Thomas to be Associate Justice of the Supreme Court of the United States*, Pt. 4. (Washington: U.S. G.P.O., 1993), 8.

7. Ibid., 157.

8. Ibid., 158.

9. Thomas, *My Grandfather's Son*, 271.

10. Megan Brenan, "Gallup Vault: Anita Hill's Charges Against Clarence Thomas," Gallup News, September 21, 2018, https://news.gallup.com/vault/242417/gallup-vault-anita-hill-charges-against-clarence-thomas.aspx.

11. Video and transcript available at "American Rhetoric: Movie Speech 'Miracle' (2004)," https://www.americanrhetoric.com/MovieSpeeches/moviespeechmiracle2.html.

12. The transcript of the hearing will be cited throughout this chapter. "Senate Judiciary Committee Hearing on the Nomination of Brett M. Kavanaugh to be an Associate Justice of the Supreme Court, Day 5, Focusing on Allegations of Sexual Assault, Part 2," CQ Transcriptions, September 27, 2018.

13. Lester Holt, *News4 at 4*, NBC News via archive.org, September 27, 2018, https://archive.org/details/WRC_20180927_200000_News4_at_4/start/660/end/720.

14. Andrea Mitchell and Chuck Todd, *News4 at 4*, NBC News via archive.org, September 27, 2018, https://archive.org/details/WRC_20180927_200000_News4_at_4/.

15. Chris Spargo, "Brett Kavanaugh testimony divides pundits, with some calling his remarks 'gut-wrenching' and others declaring the Supreme Court nominee a 'liar' and 'unhinged,'" *Daily Mail*, September 27, 2018, https://www.dailymail.co.uk/news/article-6216707/Brett-Kavanaugh-testimony-divides-pundits-calling-remarks-gut-wrenching-lies.html.

16. Jeffrey Toobin, *The Lead With Jake Tapper*, CNN via archive.org, September 27, 2018, https://archive.org/details/CNNW_20180927_200000_The_Lead_With_Jake_Tapper/start/1103/end/1163.

17. Brian Fallon (@brianefallon), "If Senate GOP ignores Dr. Blasey Ford and tries to muscle an attempted rapist onto the Supreme Court: 1. They will pay dearly this November. 2. Senators up in 2020 (Collins, Gardner et al) will feel intense heat for next two years. 3. Kavanaugh will not serve for life." Twitter, September 27, 2018, 4:16 p.m., https://twitter.com/brianefallon/status/1045452225454239744.

18. The plan had always been for senators to take over when Mitchell was done. Her role was not to help Kavanaugh to defend himself through her questioning, nor was it to cross-examine him. It was impossible to continue questioning the nominee for the remainder of the hearing about an incident he said had not taken place and for which there was no evidence apart from Ford's bald assertion. But Mitchell was unaware of the procedure to cede control of the questioning back to the senators, and worried that if she asked only her remaining short questions at the outset of a five-minute block that she might forfeit the remainder of that time. So she signaled she was done just before Senator Graham's segment began.

19. Samuel Chamberlain, "Kavanaugh's prep school friends say 'Devil's Triangle' was a drinking game," Fox News, October 4, 2018, https://www.foxnews.com/politics/kavanaughs-prep-school-friends-say-devils-triangle-was-a-drinking-game.

20. "Feinstein: I Didn't Ask My Staff But I Know They Didn't Leak Ford's Allegation," Grabien, https://grabien.com/story.php?id=196259.

Chapter Ten: The Anteroom Where It Happened

1. Lauren Gambino (@laurenegambino), "Flake will vote to confirm Kavanaugh," Twitter, September 28, 2018, 6:27 a.m., https://twitter.com/laurenegambino/status/1045666220077445121/.

2. Manu Raju (@mkraju), "Flake is torn: 'They both did well and he offered a defense like you would expect from someone who felt that they were wrongly accused. And she offered compelling testimony as well. But I have to go with what is the standard here. Where is the burden. It's tough' @TheOtherKeppler," Twitter, September 27, 2018, 6:06 pm, https://twitter.com/mkraju/status/104547 9744987435008; Jennifer Jacobs (@JenniferJJacobs), "Jeff Flake was one senator Bush talked with—and the former president urged a 'yes' vote, I'm told," Twitter, September 27, 2018, 8:03 p.m., https://twitter.com/JenniferJJacobs/status/1045509283020976128.

3. Elizabeth Landers (@ElizLanders), ".@JeffFlake is a YES on Kavanaugh. @SunlenSerfaty broke that news to Sen. Coons in the hallway as he walked into the hearing. Coons said, 'Oh f—k,' then choked up, 'We each make choices for our own reason. I'm struggling, sorry.'" Twitter, September 28, 2018, 6:35 a.m., https://twitter.com/ElizLanders/status/1045668429364187136.

4. Open Society Foundations, "Citizen Engagement Laboratory," https://www.opensocietyfoundations.org/about/programs/us-programs/grantees/citizen-engagement-laboratory-1. UltraViolet claims to have trained three hundred of the protesters who confronted senators in the hallways during the Kavanaugh fight. Their financial structure is similar to Demand Justice—they were "incubated" by a parallel donor stream, the Soros-funded Citizen Engagement Laboratory.

5. CNN, "Tearful woman confronts Senator Flake on elevator," CNN via YouTube, September 28, 2018, https://www.youtube.com/watch?v=bshg OZ8QQxU.

6. Suzanne Malveaux, "The elevator moment: when to speak up, when to stay quiet, and the power of both," CNN, September 30, 2018, https://www.cnn.com/2018/09/30/politics/suzanne-malveaux-reporters-notebook-jeff-flake-elevator/index.html.

7. CNN, "Tearful woman confronts Senator Flake."

8. Brett Samuels, "FBI concludes interview of Mark Judge," *The Hill*, October 2, 2018, https://thehill.com/regulation/court-battles/409437-fbi-concludes-interview-of-mark-judge.

9. Jack Crowe, "American Bar Association Backs Kavanaugh Despite Previous Letter to the Contrary," *National Review*, October 1, 2018, https://www.nationalreview.com/news/american-bar-association-backs-kavanaugh-despite-previous-letter-to-the-contrary/.

10. Manu Raju, "American Bar Association: Delay Kavanaugh until FBI investigates assault allegations," CNN, October 2, 2018, https://www.cnn.com/2018/09/27/politics/kavanaugh-american-bar-association/index.html.

11. Meg Wagner, Brian Ries, Paul P. Murphy, Sophie Tatum and Jessie Yeung, "Brett Kavanaugh nomination faces delay," CNN, September 28, 2018, https://

www.cnn.com/politics/live-news/kavanaugh-senate-committee-vote/h_81a14e4
8dc39350455a028858cba4065.

12. "Senate Judiciary Meeting On Brett Kavanaugh Nomination," *Supreme Court Confirmation*, C-SPAN, September 28, 2018, https://www.c-span.org/video/ ?452084-1/senator-flake-calls-delaying-kavanaugh-vote-fbi-background-check-reopen.

13. Sue Reisinger, "Institute for Legal Reform Adds Beltway Insider John Abegg to Help Lead Legal Team," Association of Corporate Counsel, May 2, 2019, https://www.law.com/corpcounsel/2019/05/02/institute-for-legal-reform-adds-beltway-insider-john-abegg-to-help-lead-legal-team/; "Harold Kim Promoted to Chief Operating Officer," U.S. Chamber Institute for Legal Reform, May 1, 2019, https://www.instituteforlegalreform.com/resource/us-chamber-institute-for-legal-reform-welcomes-former-chief-counsel-for-sen-majority-leader-mitch-mcconnell.

14. "Senate Judiciary Meeting On Brett Kavanaugh Nomination," *Supreme Court Confirmation*, C-SPAN.

15. "Statement from the Senate Judiciary Committee," Committee on the Judiciary website, September 28, 2018, https://www.judiciary.senate.gov/press/rep/ releases/statement-from-the-senate-judiciary-committee.

16. Eugene Robinson, "Senators to Begin Vote on Kavanaugh Tomorrow Morning," *Deadline Whitehouse*, MSNBC via archive.org, October 4, 2018, https://archive.org/details/MSNBCW_20181004_200000_Deadline_White_ House/start/1560/end/1620.

17. Ken Dilanian, Geoff Bennett, and Kristen Welker, "Limits to FBI's Kavanaugh investigation have not changed, despite Trump's comments," NBC News, September 29, 2018, https://www.nbcnews.com/politics/politics-news/ white-house-limits-scope-fbi-s-investigation-allegations-against-brett-n915061.

18. Brooke Singman, "Grassley taunts Bernie Sanders in salty response to Kavanaugh probe letter," Fox News, October 1, 2018, https://www. foxnews.com/politics/grassley-taunts-bernie-sanders-in-salty-response-to-kavanaugh-probe-letter.

19. Grace Segers, "Nancy Pelosi calls Brett Kavanaugh 'hysterical,' says he is unfit to serve on the Supreme Court," CBS News, September 29, 2018, https://www. cbsnews.com/news/nancy-pelosi-calls-brett-kavanaugh-hysterical-says-he-is-unfit-to-serve-on-the-supreme-court/.

20. Mark Sherman and Jessica Gresko, "Nominee's attack on Democrats poses risk to Supreme Court," Associated Press News, September 29, 2018, https://apnews. com/29557f45334f470fb55bce5dacba591a.

21. Nicholas Fandos (@npfandos), "Rachel Mitchell, Republican's outside questioner, privately told GOP senators tonight that based on the evidence she heard at the hearing, she would not have prosecuted or even been able to obtain a search warrant, according to three Republicans," Twitter, September 27, 2018, 7:25 p.m., https://twitter.com/npfandos/status/1045499632657354752.

22. The Mitchell memorandum will be cited throughout this section. Rachel Mitchell, Nominations Investigative Counsel, "Memorandum re: Analysis of Dr. Christine Blasey Ford's Allegations," September 30, 2018, https://assets. documentcloud.org/documents/4952137/Rachel-Mitchell-s-analysis.pdf.

23. John Cornyn interview, "Sen. Cornyn Joins the Five," *The Five*, FOX News, October 4, 2018, https://archive.org/details/FOXNEWSW_20181004_210000_ The_Five/start/2460/end/2520.

24. Peter Baker and Michael S. Schmidt, "Trump Allows Wider Review of Kavanaugh," *New York Times*, October 2, 2018, A1.

25. Mike McIntire, Linda Qiu, Steve Eder and Kate Kelly, "Defense From Judge Misleads And Veers Off Course at Times," *New York Times*, September 29, 2018, A1.

26. Thomas Lipscomb, "Records Raise Questions About Ford's Double-Door Story," RealClearPolitics, October 2, 2018, https://www.realclearpolitics.com/ articles/2018/10/02/records_raise_questions_about_fords_double-door_ story__138225.html.

27. "Sylvia Adkins Randall," *Psychology Today*, October 3, 2018, https://www. psychologytoday.com/us/therapists/sylvia-adkins-randall-west-linn-or/7021.

28. The Swetnick interview will be quoted throughout this section. "Julie Swetnick speaks about alleged behavior by Judge Kavanaugh," Interview by Kate Snow, MSNBC, October 1, 2018, https://www.msnbc.com/msnbc/watch/julie-swetnick-speaks-about-alleged-behavior-by-judge-kavanaugh-1334265923929. Transcript available at "FBI expanding probe into Kavanaugh. TRANSCRIPT: 10/1/2018, The Best w Ari Melber," MSNBC, October 1, 2018, http://www. msnbc.com/transcripts/msnbc-live-with-ari-melber/2018-10-01.

29. Aryssa Damron, "MSNBC Legal Analyst: Swetnick's Allegation Against Kavanaugh Is 'Not Credible' and 'Should Go Away,'" The Washington Free Beacon, October 2, 2018, https://freebeacon.com/politics/ msnbc-legal-analyst-swetnicks-allegation-kavanaugh-not-credible-go-away/.

30. Richard Blumenthal et al., Letter to Don McGahn and Christopher Wray, October 1, 2018, https://www.feinstein.senate.gov/public/_cache/ files/9/2/92e7876b-670e-48c7-9b55-b66b09c7ad4e/ D70322512DA91E37F4B966721A744469.fbi-and-whi-re-fbi-investigation-klobuchar-witnesses.pdf.

31. Michael Avenatti (@MichaelAvenatti), Twitter, October 2, 2018, https://twitter. com/MichaelAvenatti/status/1047226356831059970.

32. Kate Snow and Anna Schecter, "New Questions raised about Avenatti claim regarding Kavanaugh," NBC News, October 25, 2018, https://www.nbcnews. com/politics/justice-department/new-questions-raised-about-avenatti-claims-regarding-kavanaugh-n924596.

33. Office of the Chairman, Senator Chuck Grassley, "Senate Judiciary Committee Investigation of Numerous Allegations Against Justice Brett Kavanaugh During the Senate Confirmation Proceedings," Exhibit 51.

34. Elizabeth Bazelon and Ben Protess, "At Beery Yale, Curses, Fists, Glass, Blood And a Student," *New York Times*, October 2, 2018, A13.

35. Andrew Kugle, "Hirono: Kavanaugh Throwing Ice at Someone in College is 'Very Relevant,' Reason FBI Must Investigate," The Washington Free Beacon, October 2, 2018, https://freebeacon.com/politics/ hirono-kavanaugh-throwing-ice-college-relevant-reason-fbi-investigate/.

36. David Bauder, "Times says it was wrong to have writer on Kavanaugh story," AP News, October 2, 2018, https://apnews.com/9de214e064cd4f58b328b 63d645d41d3.

37. Heidi Przybyla and Leigh Ann Caldwell, "Text messages suggest Kavanaugh wanted to refute accuser's claim before it became public," NBC News, October 1, 2018, https://www.nbcnews.com/politics/supreme-court/ mutual-friend-ramirez-kavanaugh-anxious-come-forward-evidence-n915566.

38. The Judiciary Committee included the text exchange as an exhibit in its November 2 memorandum regarding the Kavanaugh confirmation. They also indicated that committee investigators discussed the texts by phone with her on October 3, although Berchem still continued to falsely claim she had not been contacted by the committee. The Yarasavage-Berchem texts are quoted throughout this section. Office of the Chairman, Senator Chuck Grassley, "Senate Judiciary Committee Investigation of Numerous Allegations Against Justice Brett Kavanaugh During the Senate Confirmation Proceedings," Exhibit 31, https://www.judiciary.senate. gov/imo/media/doc/2018-11-02%20Kavanaugh%20Report.pdf.

39. Ibid., Exhibit 50, Transcript of Kavanaugh Phone Interview, 17.

40. Nancy Dillon, "Letter reveals what Yale alum saw at Brett Kavanaugh's frat house that 'shocked' him," *Daily News*, October 2, 2018, https://www. nydailynews.com/news/ny-news-tad-low-report-kavanaugh-frat-20181002- story.html.

41. Jack Crowe, "Grassley Smacks Down Latest Kavanaugh Allegation," *National Review*, October 2, 2018, https://www.nationalreview.com/news/ chuck-grassley-smacks-down-latest-brett-kavanaugh-allegation/.

42. BlazeTV (@BlazeTV), "PROTESTOR: "If he would [take] a polygraph, this would be all over, Senator Graham." GRAHAM: "Why don't we dunk him in water and see if he floats." Who is this new @LindseyGrahamSC!?!?!" Twitter, October 4, 2018, 8:53 a.m., https://twitter.com/BlazeTV/ status/1047877264434589698.

Chapter Eleven: Mrs. Collins Goes to Washington

1. Jeffrey Cimmino, "McConnell Hammers Dems on Kavanaugh Nomination: 'Their Goalposts Keep Shifting, but Their Goal Hasn't Moved an Inch,'" The Washington Free Beacon, October 1, 2018, https://freebeacon.com/politics/ mcconnell-hammers-dems-moving-goalposts-kavanaugh-nomination/.

2. Nikki Schwab, "Trump mocks Christine Blasey Ford's Senate testimony," *New York Post*, October 2, 2018, https://nypost.com/2018/10/02/trump-mocks-christine- blasey-fords-senate-testimony/.

3. E.J. Dionne Jr., "Trump's lying, mocking, despicable verbal mugging of Christine Blasey Ford," *Washington Post*, October 3, 2018, https://www.washingtonpost.com/opinions/trumps-lying-mocking-despicable-verbal-mugging-of-christine-blasey-ford/2018/10/03/7906e5a4-c73a-11e8-9b1c-a90f1daae309_story.html.

4. Jane Mayer and Ronan Farrow, "The F.B.I Probe Ignored Testimonies From Former Classmates of Kavanaugh," *New Yorker*, October 3, 2018, https://www.newyorker.com/news/news-desk/will-the-fbi-ignore-testimonies-from-kavanaughs-former-classmates.

5. Natalie Andrews, Rebecca Ballhaus, and Sadie Gurman, "Friend of Dr. Ford Felt Pressure to Revisit Statement," *Wall Street Journal*, October 5, 2018, https://www.wsj.com/articles/friend-of-dr-ford-felt-pressure-to-revisit-statement-1538715152.

6. Terry Moran (@TerryMoran), "WRONG. Monica Mclean, retired FBI SSA and friend of Ford, gave @ABC this statement: "I have NEVER had Christine Blasey Ford, or anybody else, prepare me, or provide any other type of assistance whatsoever in connection with any polygraph exam I have taken at anytime." Twitter, October 3, 2018, 7:13 a.m., https://twitter.com/terrymoran/status/1047489913720115202.

7. Laura Collins, "Leland Keyser told the FBI she felt pressured by friends of Christine Ford to revise her statement saying she didn't remember the party where Kavanaugh allegedly assaulted Ford—not that it had never happened," *Daily Mail*, October 5, 2018, https://www.dailymail.co.uk/news/article-6244715/Leland-Keyser-told-FBI-felt-pressured-friends-Christine-Ford-revise-statement.html.

8. Sara Corcoran, "Opinion: An Open Letter to Leland Ingham Keyser," *Daily Caller*, October 1, 2018, https://dailycaller.com/2018/10/01/letter-leland-ingham-keyser/.

9. Psalm 34:5.

10. John Paul Stevens, "Former Justice John Paul Stevens on the Supreme Court," C-SPAN, October 4, 2018, https://www.c-span.org/video/?451375-1/retired-justice-stevens-judge-kavanaughs-hearing-performance-disqualifying.

11. Brett Kavanaugh, "I Am an Independent, Impartial Judge," *Wall Street Journal*, October 4, 2018, https://www.wsj.com/articles/i-am-an-independent-impartial-judge-1538695822.

12. Erik Brady, "Opinion: Is Brett Kavanaugh right that he can no longer coach girls basketball?" *USA Today*, September 28, 2018, https://www.usatoday.com/story/sports/columnist/erik-brady/2018/09/28/brett-kavanaugh-right-he-can-no-longer-coach-girls-basketball/1459496002/; Erik Wemple, "USA Today essentially retracts Kavanaugh-shouldn't-coach piece," *Washington Post*, October 1, 2018, https://www.washingtonpost.com/blogs/erik-wemple/wp/2018/10/01/usa-today-essentially-retracts-kavanaugh-shouldnt-coach-opinion-piece/?utm_term=.60cfacb0ff42.

13. Molly Ball, "Brett Kavanaugh's Supreme Court Confirmation is Now the Ultimate Test of Political Power in 2018," *Time*, September 20, 2018, http://time.com/5401624/brett-kavanaugh-confirmation/.

14. Judson Berger, "Susan Collins reveals vulgar, threatening voicemails left during Kavanaugh confirmation," Fox News, December 19, 2018, https://www.foxnews.com/politics/susan-collins-reveals-profane-threatening-voicemails-left-during-kavanaugh-confirmation.

15. Ian Mason, "Leftists Confront Sex Assault Survivor Who Supports Kavanaugh," Breitbart, October 5, 2018, https://www.breitbart.com/clips/2018/10/05/leftists-confront-sex-assault-survivor-who-supports-kavanaugh/.

16. Eli Rosenberg, "Activists Raised $1 Million to Defeat Susan Collins if She Votes for Kavanaugh. She Says It's Bribery," *Washington Post*, September 12, 2018, https://www.washingtonpost.com/politics/2018/09/12/activists-raised-million-defeat-susan-collins-if-she-votes-kavanaugh-she-says-its-bribery/. While the crowd-funders maintained that their donation would not officially qualify as a bribe, Collins disagreed, supported by a prominent election lawyer. David A. Patten, "Group Threatens Sen. Collins with $1.3 Million Donation Over Kavanaugh Vote," Newsmax, September 10, 2018, https://www.newsmax.com/newsfront/susan-collins-brett-kavanaugh-supreme-court/2018/09/10/id/881082/.

17. James Pindell, "With Brett Kavanaugh vote, Susan Collins is in middle of a firestorm," *Boston Globe*, September 18, 2018, https://www.bostonglobe.com/news/nation/2018/09/18/angry-calls-threats-thousands-hangers-susan-collins-middle-political-firestorm/EO1XqIK0cUCyYV8jbxhf5J/story.html.

18. Collins's floor speech will be quoted throughout this section. Susan Collins, "Senate Floor Speech in Support of Brett Kavanaugh," C-SPAN via American Rhetoric website, October 5, 2018, https://www.americanrhetoric.com/speeches/susancollinssenatefloorbrettkavanaugh.htm.

19. "Sen. Lisa Murkowski's Senate speech on why she opposed Kavanaugh," *Anchorage Daily News*, October 8, 2018, https://www.adn.com/politics/2018/10/05/sen-lisa-murkowskis-full-senate-speech-on-why-shes-not-supporting-kavanaugh/.

20. Quin Hillyer, "Lisa Murkowski Should 'Pair No' with Steve Daines's 'Paired Yes,'" *National Review*, October 5, 2018, https://www.nationalreview.com/corner/lisa-murkowski-steve-dainess-brett-kavanaugh-vote/.

21. "Remarks by President Trump at Swearing-in Ceremony of the Honorable Brett M. Kavanaugh as Associate Justice of the Supreme Court of the United States," White House website, October 8, 2018, https://www.whitehouse.gov/briefings-statements/remarks-president-trump-swearing-ceremony-honorable-brett-m-kavanaugh-associate-justice-supreme-court-united-states/.

Chapter Twelve: Legitimacy

1. Jonathan Martin, "Kavanaugh Was Supposed to Be a Midterm Boon for G.O.P. Not Anymore," *New York Times*, September 23, 2018, https://www.nytimes.com/2018/09/23/us/politics/kavanaugh-senate-republicans-elections.html.

2. Mike Allen and Jim VandeHei, "Dems plot massive campaign if Kavanaugh falls," Axios, September 20, 2018, https://www.axios.com/brett-kavanaugh-confirmation-democrats-2018-midterm-elections-3ce55ebf-dc62-46b9-8ffa-bb1a7fe7cb18.html.

3. Domenico Montanaro, "Poll: Amid Kavanaugh Confirmation Battle, Democratic Enthusiasm Edge Evaporates," NPR, October 3, 2018, https://www.npr.org/2018/10/03/654015874/poll-amid-kavanaugh-confirmation-battle-democratic-enthusiasm-edge-evaporates.

4. Katie Glueck and Adam Wollner, "Republican enthusiasm surges amid Supreme Court battle," McClatchy DC Bureau, October 4, 2018, https://www.mcclatchydc.com/news/politics-government/election/midterms/article219488090.html.

5. Eliza Collins, "McConnell predicts Republican 'surge' from Kavanaugh confirmation heading into midterms," *USA Today*, October 6, 2018, https://www.usatoday.com/story/news/politics/elections/2018/10/06/brett-kavanaugh-mcconnell-confirmation-gop-surge/1549762002/.

6. Tal Axelrod, "Trump says midterms about 'Kavanaugh, the caravan, law and order and common sense,'" *The Hill*, October 18, 2018, https://thehill.com/homenews/administration/412172-trump-midterms-a-referendum-on-kavanaugh-the-caravan-law-and-order.

7. Will Schmitt, "President Trump joins Josh Hawley to urge Missouri Republicans to get out and vote," *Springfield News-Leader*, September 21, 2018, https://www.news-leader.com/story/news/politics/2018/09/21/trump-rally-springfield-missouri-hawley-defends-kavanaugh/1346171002/.

8. On October 6 Morrisey tweeted, "Thanks to @realDonaldTrump & Republicans in the Senate who confirmed Kavanaugh. Remember, Manchin refused to commit to Kavanaugh until AFTER the Senate had the votes. Manchin piled on—he had no courage and empowered the Schumer circus. #wvsen #wvpol." AG Patrick Morrisey (@MorriseyWV), Twitter, October 6, 2018, 1:36 p.m., https://twitter.com/MorriseyWV/status/1048673350220963841. It took PolitiFact over a month to fact-check this claim, releasing its assessment of "True" a week after the election, too late to be helpful to West Virginia voters. Kristen Mohammadi, "How late did Joe Manchin decide on Kavanaugh vote?" PolitiFact, November 15, 2018, https://www.politifact.com/west-virginia/statements/2018/nov/15/patrick-morrisey/how-late-did-joe-manchin-decide-kavanaugh-vote/.

9. "Tennessee Senate–Blackburn vs. Bredesen," RealClearPolitics, https://www.realclearpolitics.com/epolls/2018/senate/tn/tennessee_senate_blackburn_vs_bredesen-6308.html#polls.

10. Joel Ebert, "Brett Kavanaugh vote: Phil Bredesen says he supports Supreme Court nominee," *Tennessean*, October 5, 2018, https://www.tennessean.com/story/news/politics/tn-elections/2018/10/05/key-kavanaugh-vote-u-s-senate-begins-bredesen-says-he-supports-nominee/1524565002/.

11. Manchin was an exception, as he voted in favor of Kavanaugh. But 40 percent of West Virginia voters called the Kavanaugh vote a key issue, and those broke for Manchin, although Morrissey would also have voted to confirm Kavanaugh. Gary Langer and Benjamin Siu, "Election 2018 exit poll analysis: Voter turnout soars, Democrats take back the House, ABC News projects," ABC News, November 7, 2018, https://abcnews.go.com/Politics/election-2018-exit-poll-analysis-56-percent-country/story?id=59006586.

12. Mollie Hemmingway, "Incoming Democrat Chairman: Dems Will Go 'All-In' On Russia, Impeach Kavanaugh For 'Perjury,'" *The Federalist*, November 7, 2018, https://thefederalist.com/2018/11/07/incoming-democrat-chairman-dems-will-go-all-in-on-russia-impeach-kavanaugh-for-perjury/.

13. Eli Yokley, "America's Most and Least Popular Senators," Morning Consult, January 10, 2019, https://morningconsult.com/2019/01/10/americas-most-and-least-popular-senators-q4-2018/.

14. Jennifer Bendery, "Group to Run Ads Urging University to Cancel Brett Kavanaugh's Teaching Gig," *HuffPost*, April 12, 2019, https://www.huffpost.com/entry/george-mason-university-brett-kavanaugh_n_5cae552ee4b0308735d48efd.

15. Cady Lang, "Here's Why This Witch Is Preparing for Midterm Election by Hosting a Hex on Brett Kavanaugh," *Time*, November 2, 2018, http://time.com/5442528/brett-kavanaugh-hex/.

16. Anne E. Marimow and Robert Barnes, "Judiciary dismisses 'serious' misconduct complaints against Brett M. Kavanaugh," *Washington Post*, December 18, 2019, https://www.washingtonpost.com/local/legal-issues/judiciary-dismisses-serious-misconduct-complaints-against-brett-m-kavanaugh/2018/12/18/f55416b0-0301-11e9-b6a9-0aa5c2fcc9e4_story.html.

17. Marcia Coyle, "New Dismissal of Kavanaugh Ethics Claims Divides 10th Circuit Panel," March 15, 2019, https://www.law.com/2019/03/15/new-dismissal-of-kavanaugh-ethics-claims-divides-10th-circuit-panel/.

18. Legal scholars differ on whether impeachment is available for pre-confirmation actions. See, e.g., Elizabeth B. Bazan, "Impeachment: An Overview of Constitutional Provisions, Procedures, and Practice," Congressional Research Service, December 9, 2010, https://fas.org/sgp/crs/misc/98-186.pdf. David Rivkin and Lee Casey argue that it is not available in Kavanaugh's case. David B. Rivkin Jr. and Lee A. Casey, "Democrats Abandon the Constitution," *Wall Street Journal*, October 15, 2018, https://www.wsj.com/articles/democrats-abandon-the-constitution-1539645364.

19. Elie Mystal, "The Time Has Come for Democrats to Impeach Brett Kavanaugh," *The Nation*, March 20, 2019, https://www.thenation.com/article/impeach-brett-kavanaugh-supreme-court/.

20. Mark A. Perry, "The Brett Kavanaugh I know," *Spokesman Review*, October 6, 2018, http://www.spokesman.com/stories/2018/oct/06/mark-a-perry-the-brett-kavanaugh-i-know/.

21. *The Man Who Shot Liberty Valance*, directed by John Ford (1962; Thousand Oaks, CA, Paramount Studios).

22. Akhil Reed Amar, "A Liberal's Case for Brett Kavanaugh," *New York Times*, July 9, 2018, https://www.nytimes.com/2018/07/09/opinion/brett-kavanaugh-supreme-court-trump.html; "Testimony of Akhil Reed Amar," United States Senate Committee on the Judiciary, September 7, 2018, https://www.judiciary.senate.gov/download/amar-testimony.

23. Jordan Weissmann, "The Liberal Case for Kavanaugh Is Complete Crap," *Slate*, July 10, 2018, https://slate.com/news-and-politics/2018/07/the-liberal-case-for-brett-kavanaugh-is-complete-garbage.html; Jay Willis, "The 'Liberal Case' for Brett Kavanaugh is a Bunch of Horseshit," *GQ*, July 10, 2018, https://www.gq.com/story/liberal-case-for-brett-kavanaugh-lol; Eleanor Marie Lawrence Brown, "Elite law professors are brushing politics aside to support fellow elite Brett Kavanaugh. That's inexcusable in the Trump era," Vox, July 25, 2018, https://www.vox.com/the-big-idea/2018/7/25/17609844/brett-kavanaugh-confirmation-yale-law-school-elites-supreme-court-amar.

24. Akhil Amar, "AMAR: Second thoughts on Kavanaugh," *Yale News*, September 24, 2018, https://yaledailynews.com/blog/2018/09/24/amar-second-thoughts-on-kavanaugh/; Akhil Amar, "AMAR: Third Thoughts on Kavanaugh," *Yale News*, October 10, 2018, https://yaledailynews.com/blog/2018/10/10/amar-third-thoughts-on-kavanaugh/.

25. Matt Byrne, "Maine woman charged with mailing threat, powder to Sen. Collins," *Press Herald*, April 8, 2018, https://www.pressherald.com/2019/04/08/burlington-woman-charged-with-mailing-threat-powder-to-susan-collins/.

26. Kate Conger and Sheera Frenkel, "At Facebook, Workers Cite Intolerance By Liberals," *New York Times*, August 28, 2018, B1.

27. Mike Isaac, "Rifts Break Open at Facebook Over Kavanaugh Hearing," *New York Times*, October 4, 2018, A19.

28. Ibid.

29. Donie O'Sullivan, 'Emotional' Facebook staff meeting addresses exec who supported Kavanaugh," CNN Business, October 5, 2018, https://www.cnn.com/2018/10/05/tech/facebook-joel-kaplan-backlash/index.html.

30. Tasha Cole, Facebook, September 25, 2018, https://www.facebook.com/TashaCole17/posts/1985438491479549.

31. At the time of publication she had only lost two cases; one was still pending.

32. Lisa Blatt, "I'm a Liberal Feminist Lawyer. Here's Why Democrats Should Support Judge Kavanaugh," *Politico*, August 2, 2018, https://www.politico.com/magazine/story/2018/08/02/im-a-liberal-feminist-heres-why-i-support-judge-kavanaugh-219081.

33. Amanda Terkel, "'Liberal Feminist Lawyer' Stands to Gain From Her Public Advocacy For Brett Kavanaugh," *HuffPost*, August 31, 2018, https://www.huffingtonpost.com/entry/lisa-blatt-brett-kavanvaugh_us_5b885424e4b0511db3d64064.

34. Mark Joseph Stern, "Why Is Lisa Blatt Endorsing Brett Kavanaugh?" *Slate*, September 4, 2018, https://slate.com/news-and-politics/2018/09/why-is-lisa-blatt-endorsing-brett-kavanaugh.html.

35. "Confirmation Hearing On The Nomination of Hon. Neil M. Gorsuch To Be An Associate Justice Of The Supreme Court Of The United States," Committee on the Judiciary United States Senate, (U.S GPO: Washington D.C., 2018), https://www.govinfo.gov/content/pkg/CHRG-115shrg28638/pdf/CHRG-115shrg28638.pdf, 153.

36. *Ledbetter v. Goodyear Tire & Rubber Co.*, 550 U.S. 618 (2007).

37. *Doe v. Bolton*, 410 U.S. 179, 222 (1973) (White, J., dissenting).

38. Alexander Hamilton, "Federalist 78–The Judiciary Department," in *The Federalist* (University Park, IL: Liberty Fund, 2010).

39. PoliticallyBlazed, "Gun Control – Supreme Court Justice Scalia," *Fox News Sunday* via YouTube, January 6, 2013, https://www.youtube.com/watch?v=BOmM6qBnbrI.

40. Ruth Bader Ginsburg, "Speaking in a Judicial Voice," *New York University Law Review* 67, no. 6 (1992): 1206, 1208.

41. See Jamie L. Carson, "A Switch in Time Saves Nine: Institutions, Strategic Actors, and FDR's Court Packing Plan," Public Choice 113: 301–324 (2002). David Stras makes a compelling argument that increasing judicial pensions generally played a more important role in encouraging retirements than had been previously recognized. David R. Stras and Ryan W. Scott, "Retaining Life Tenure: The Case for a 'Golden Parachute,'" Washington University Law Quarterly, 83 (2005): 1397.

42. Internal Court voting records reveal that Roberts's vote in *West Coast Hotel v. Parrish*, 300 U.S. 379 (1937), typically cited as the decisive shift in his approach, actually was cast months before Roosevelt's plan was announced, although it was published much later. Randy E. Barnett and Josh Blackman, *An Introduction to Constitutional Law: 100 Supreme Court Cases Everyone Should Know*, (2019), 167–69.

43. For a detailed description of Chief Justice Roberts's change in the case, see chapter nine of Joan Biskupic's book, The Chief: The Life and Turbulent Times of Chief Justice John Roberts, (New York: Basic Books, 2019).

44. See, e.g., Adam Cohen, "The 'Enigma' Who Is the Chief Justice of the United States," *New York Times*, March 24, 2019, BR1 (describing Roberts as having, "with few exceptions, been the sort of hard-line ideological chief justice his conservative backers hoped he would be," characterizing him as "particularly meanspirited in gay rights cases," and lamenting his "deep-seated bias against the weak").

45. She had been treated for colon cancer in 1999 and pancreatic cancer in 2009.

Index

About the Authors

MOLLIE ZIEGLER HEMINGWAY is a senior editor at *The Federalist* and a contributor to Fox News, where she regularly appears on *Special Report* with Bret Baier. Her work has appeared in the *Wall Street Journal, USA Today*, the *Los Angeles Times*, the *Guardian*, the *Washington Post*, CNN, *Claremont Review of Books, National Review, Christianity Today*, Federal Times, *Radio & Records*, and many other publications. Mollie was a Phillips Foundation Journalism Fellow in 2004, a Lincoln Fellow of the Claremont Institute in 2014, and the Eugene C. Pulliam Distinguished Fellow in Journalism at Hillsdale College in 2016. She earned a bachelor's degree in economics from the University of Colorado and serves on the board of the News Literacy Project and the Fund for American Studies' Institute on Political Journalism.

CARRIE SEVERINO is chief counsel and policy director of the Judicial Crisis Network, the most important outside group advancing the Kavanaugh nomination. An expert on the confirmation process, Mrs. Severino has been extensively quoted in the media and regularly appears on television, including MSNBC, FOX, CNN, C-SPAN, and ABC's *This Week*. Carrie has written and spoken on a wide range of judicial issues, particularly the constitutional limits on government, the federal nomination process, and state judicial selection. She has testified before Congress on constitutional issues and briefed senators on judicial nominations, and she regularly files briefs in high-profile Supreme Court cases. Before joining JCN, she was an Olin-Searle Fellow and a Dean's Visiting Scholar at Georgetown University Law Center. She was previously a law clerk to Justice Clarence Thomas of the U.S. Supreme Court and to Judge David B. Sentelle of the U.S. Court of Appeals for the D.C. Circuit. She received her bachelor's degree from Duke University, her master's degree in linguistics from Michigan State University, and her law degree, cum laude, from Harvard University.